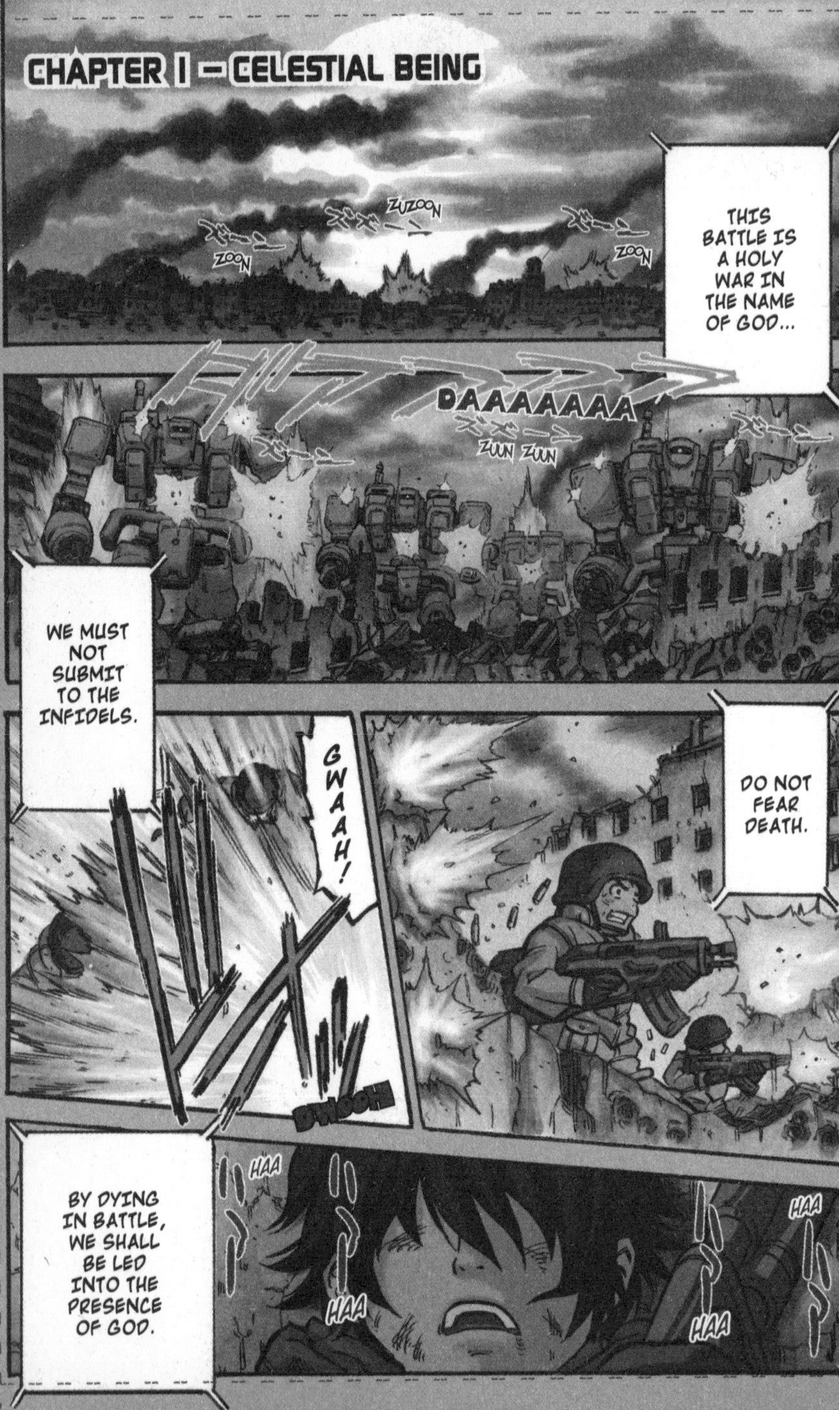
CHAPTER 1 – CELESTIAL BEING
THIS BATTLE IS A HOLY WAR IN THE NAME OF GOD...
ZOON
ZUZOON
ZOON
DAAAAAAA
ZUUN ZUUN
WE MUST NOT SUBMIT TO THE INFIDELS.
DO NOT FEAR DEATH.
GWAAAH!
HAA
HAA
HAA
HAA
BY DYING IN BATTLE, WE SHALL BE LED INTO THE PRESENCE OF GOD.

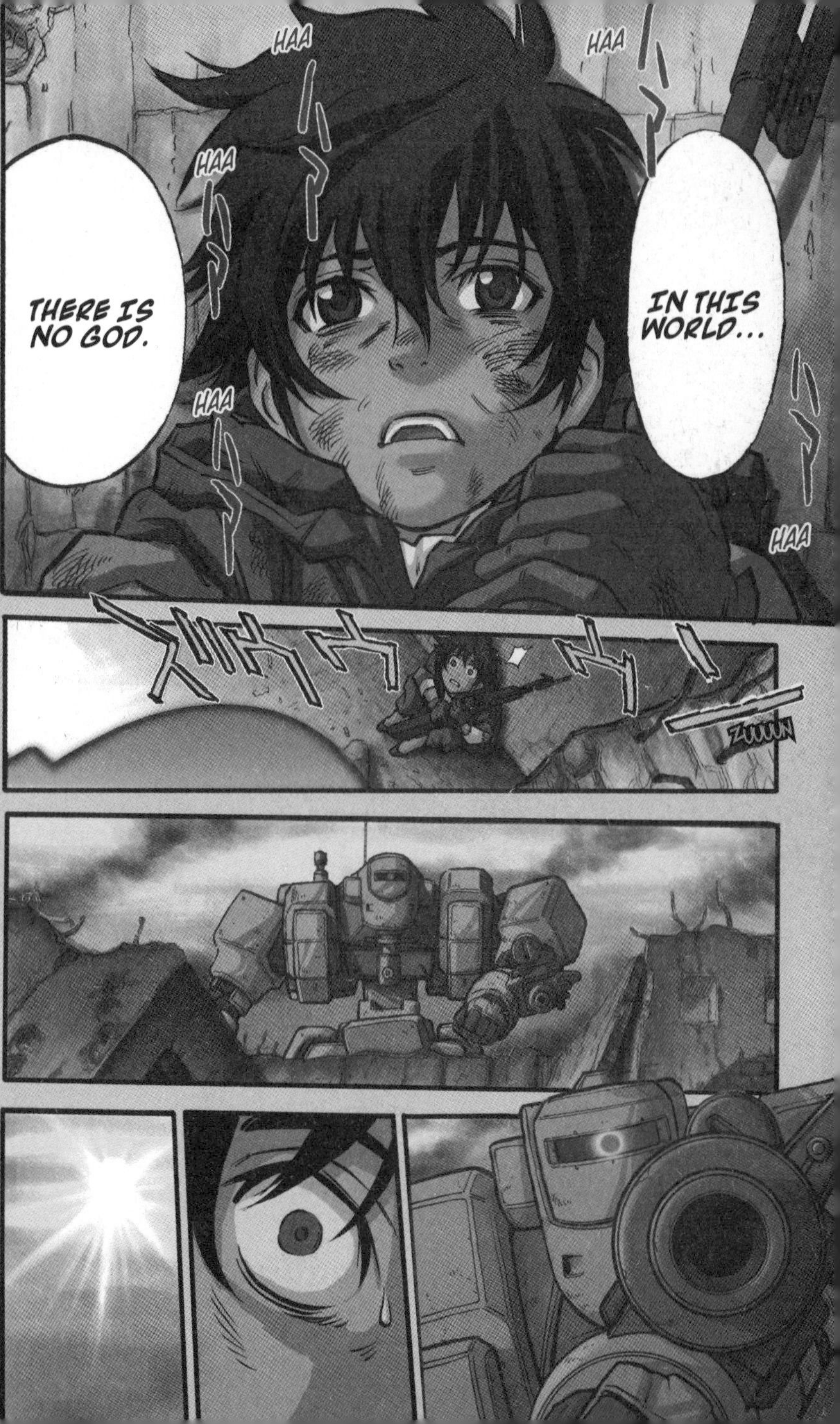
HAA
HAA
IN THIS WORLD...
HAA
THERE IS NO GOD.
HAA
HAA
ZUUUUN

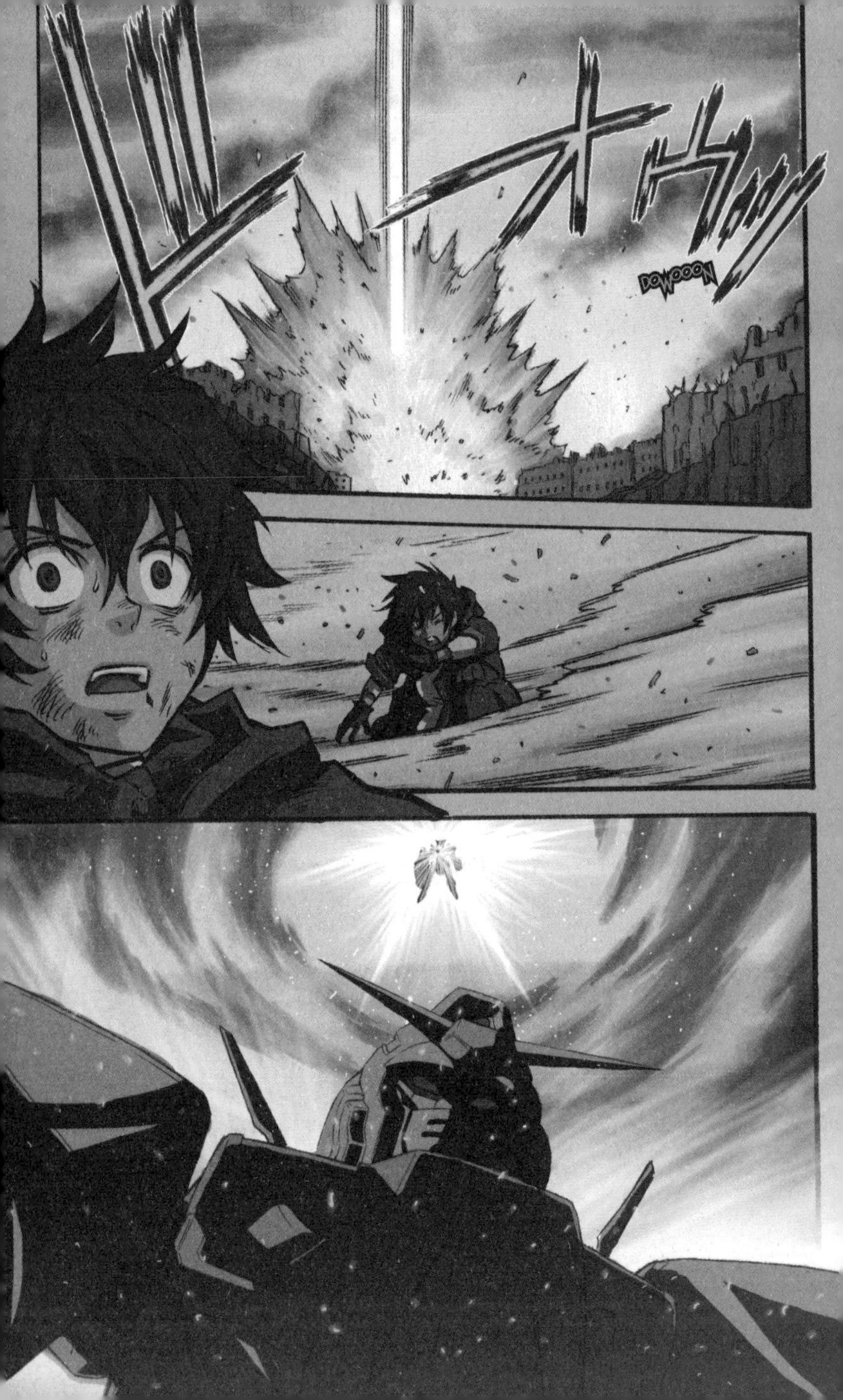
DOWOOON

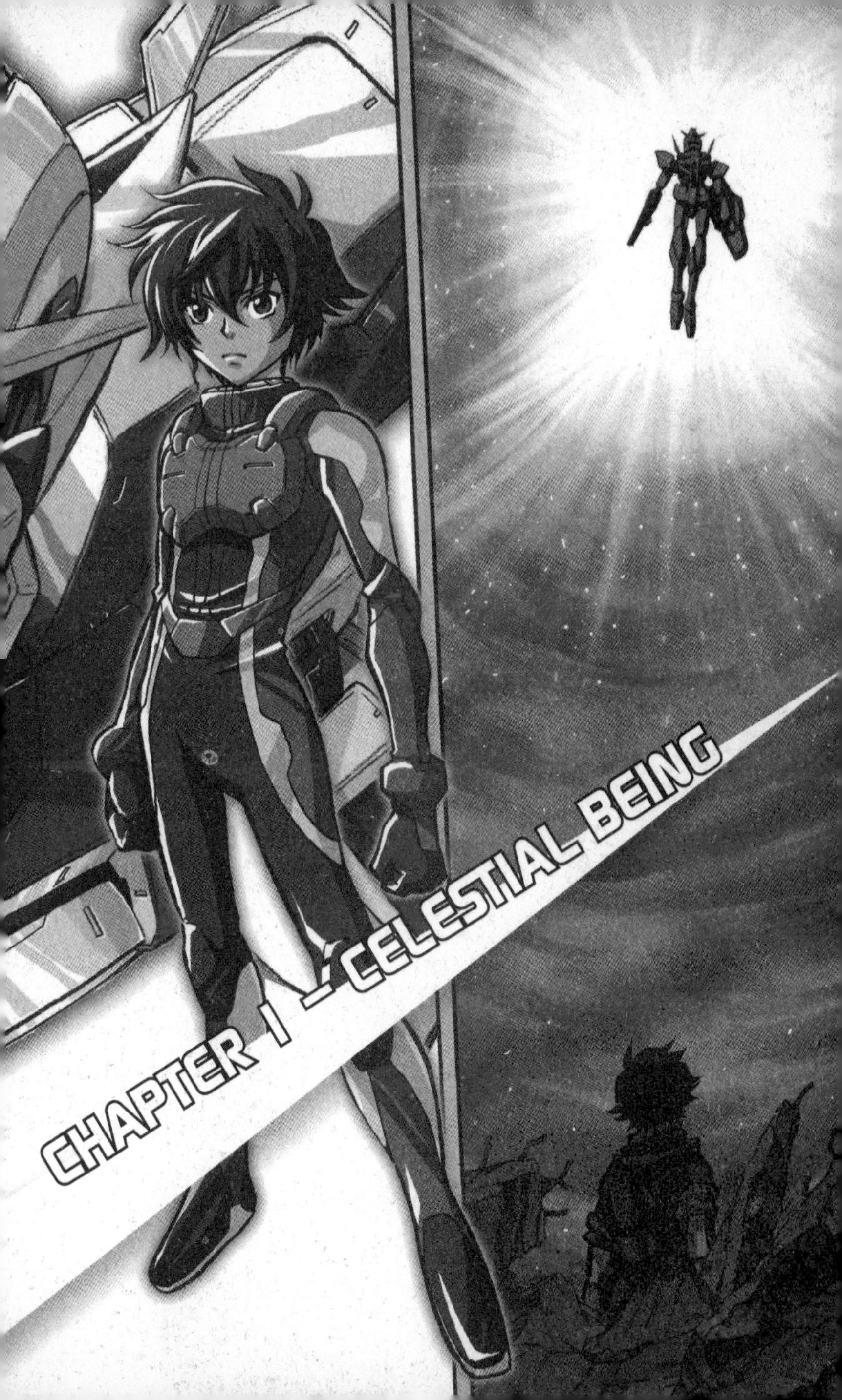
CHAPTER 1 – CELESTIAL BEING

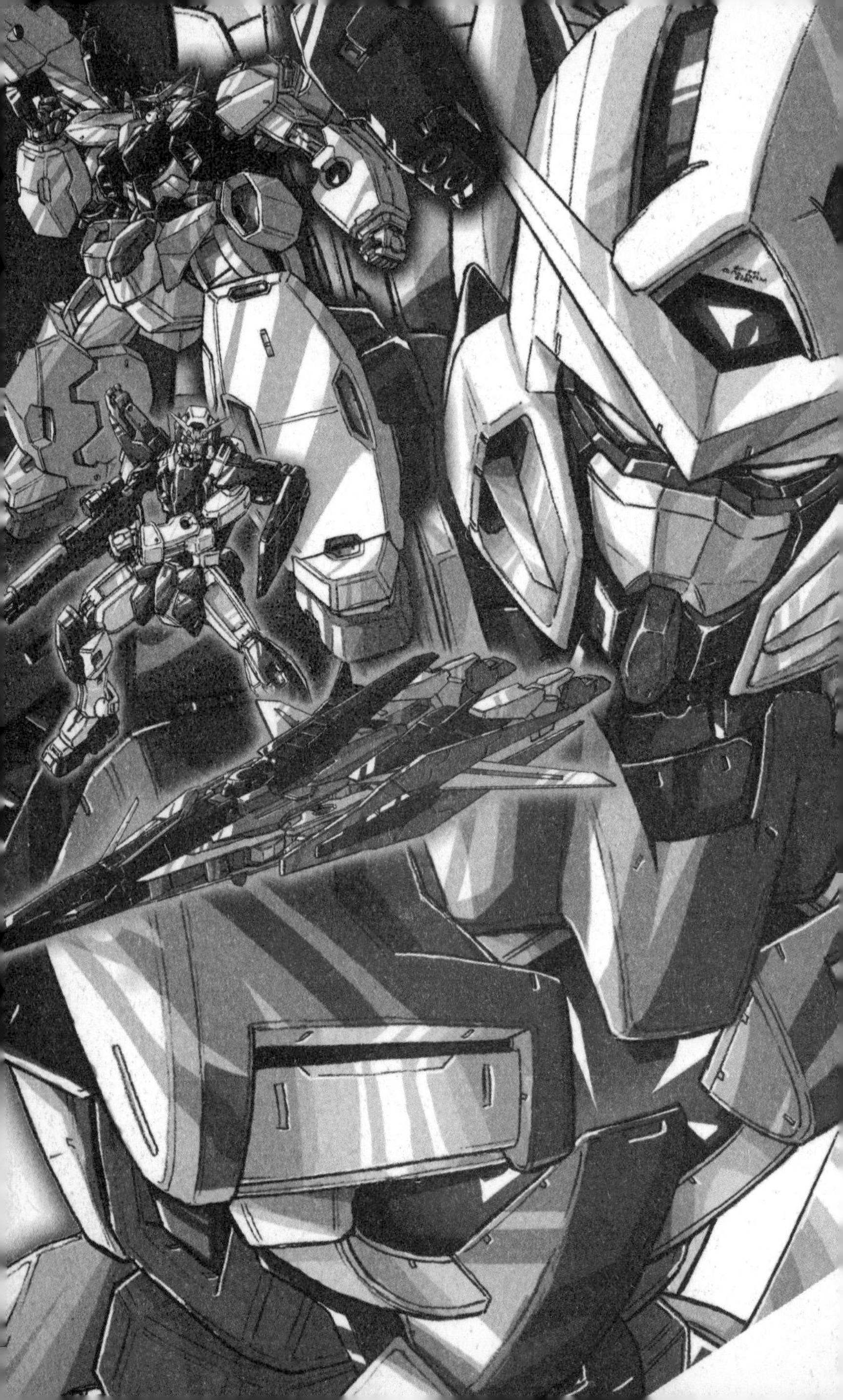

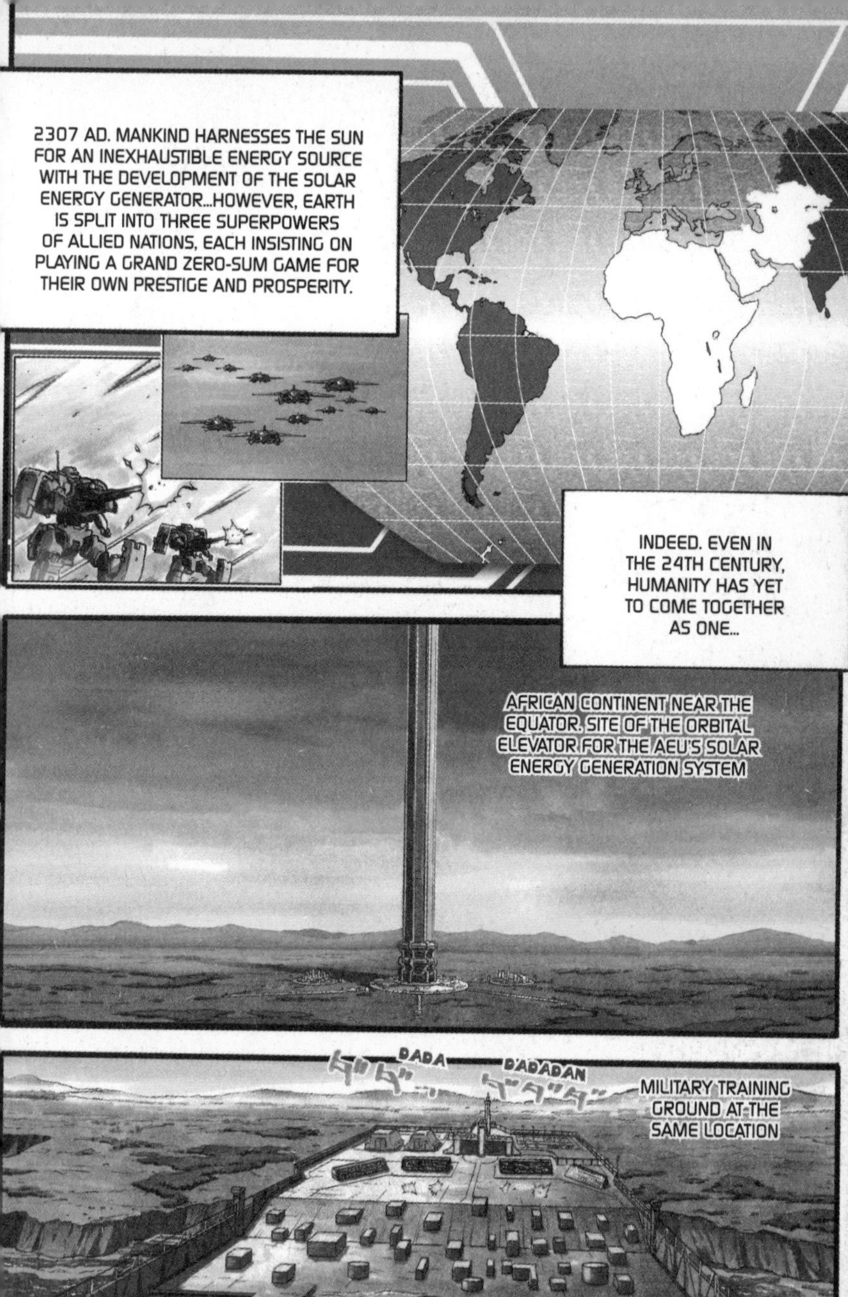
2307 AD. MANKIND HARNESSES THE SUN FOR AN INEXHAUSTIBLE ENERGY SOURCE WITH THE DEVELOPMENT OF THE SOLAR ENERGY GENERATOR...HOWEVER, EARTH IS SPLIT INTO THREE SUPERPOWERS OF ALLIED NATIONS, EACH INSISTING ON PLAYING A GRAND ZERO-SUM GAME FOR THEIR OWN PRESTIGE AND PROSPERITY.
INDEED. EVEN IN THE 24TH CENTURY, HUMANITY HAS YET TO COME TOGETHER AS ONE...
AFRICAN CONTINENT NEAR THE EQUATOR. SITE OF THE ORBITAL ELEVATOR FOR THE AEU'S SOLAR ENERGY GENERATION SYSTEM
MILITARY TRAINING GROUND AT THE SAME LOCATION
D'ADADAN
DADA

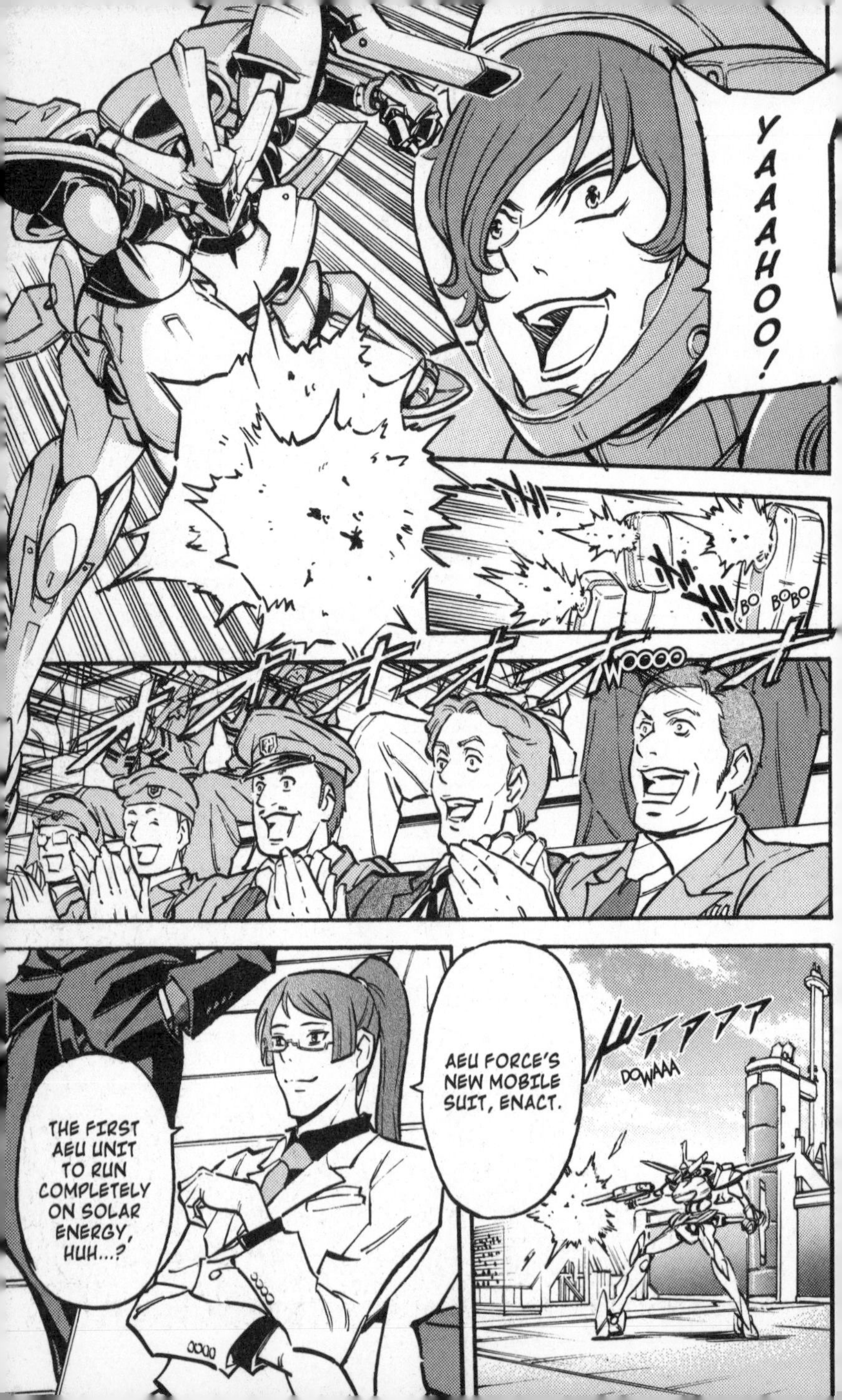
YAAAHOO!
BO BOBO
WOOOO
DOWAAA
AEU FORCE'S NEW MOBILE SUIT, ENACT.
THE FIRST AEU UNIT TO RUN COMPLETELY ON SOLAR ENERGY, HUH...?

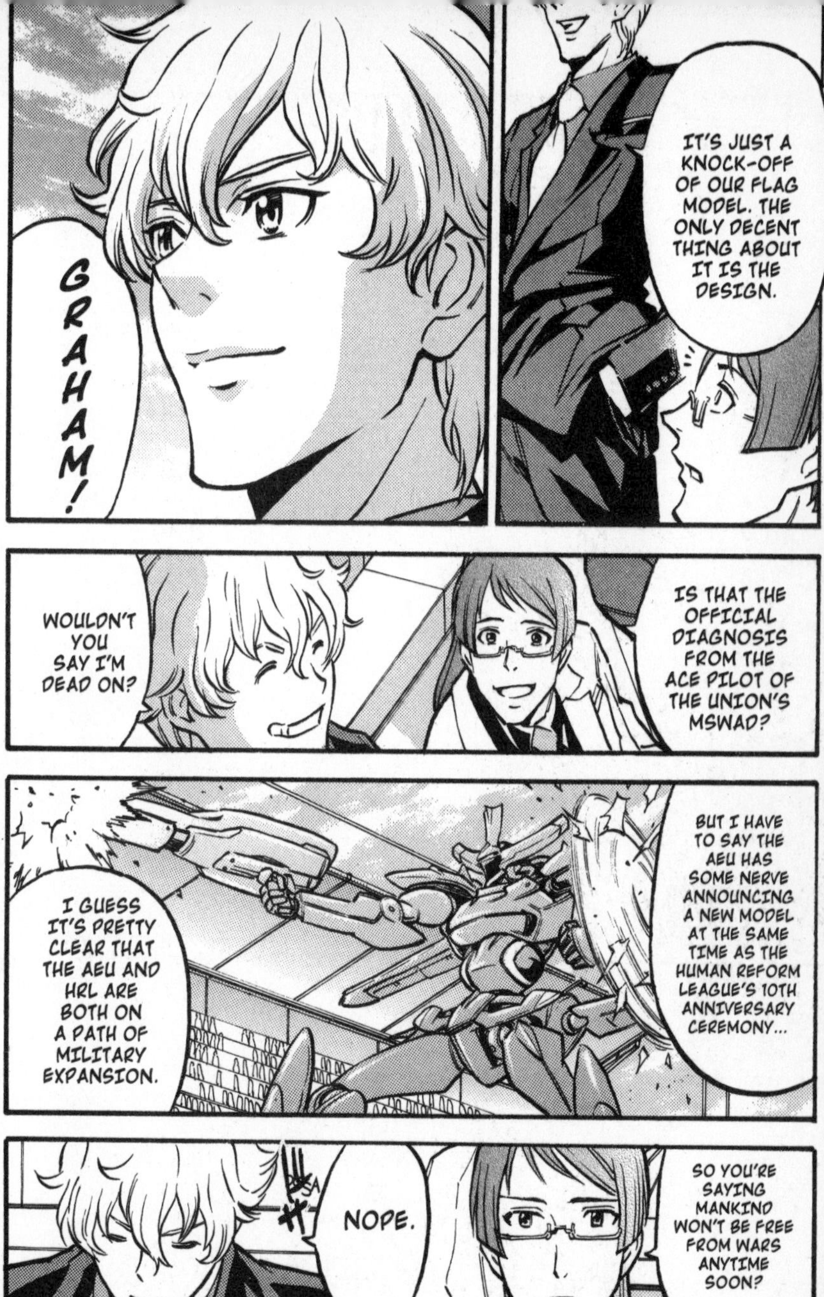
IT'S JUST A KNOCK-OFF OF OUR FLAG MODEL. THE ONLY DECENT THING ABOUT IT IS THE DESIGN.
GRAHAM!
IS THAT THE OFFICIAL DIAGNOSIS FROM THE ACE PILOT OF THE UNION'S MSWAD?
WOULDN'T YOU SAY I'M DEAD ON?
BUT I HAVE TO SAY THE AEU HAS SOME NERVE ANNOUNCING A NEW MODEL AT THE SAME TIME AS THE HUMAN REFORM LEAGUE'S 10TH ANNIVERSARY CEREMONY...
I GUESS IT'S PRETTY CLEAR THAT THE AEU AND HRL ARE BOTH ON A PATH OF MILITARY EXPANSION.
SO YOU'RE SAYING MANKIND WON'T BE FREE FROM WARS ANYTIME SOON?
NOPE.

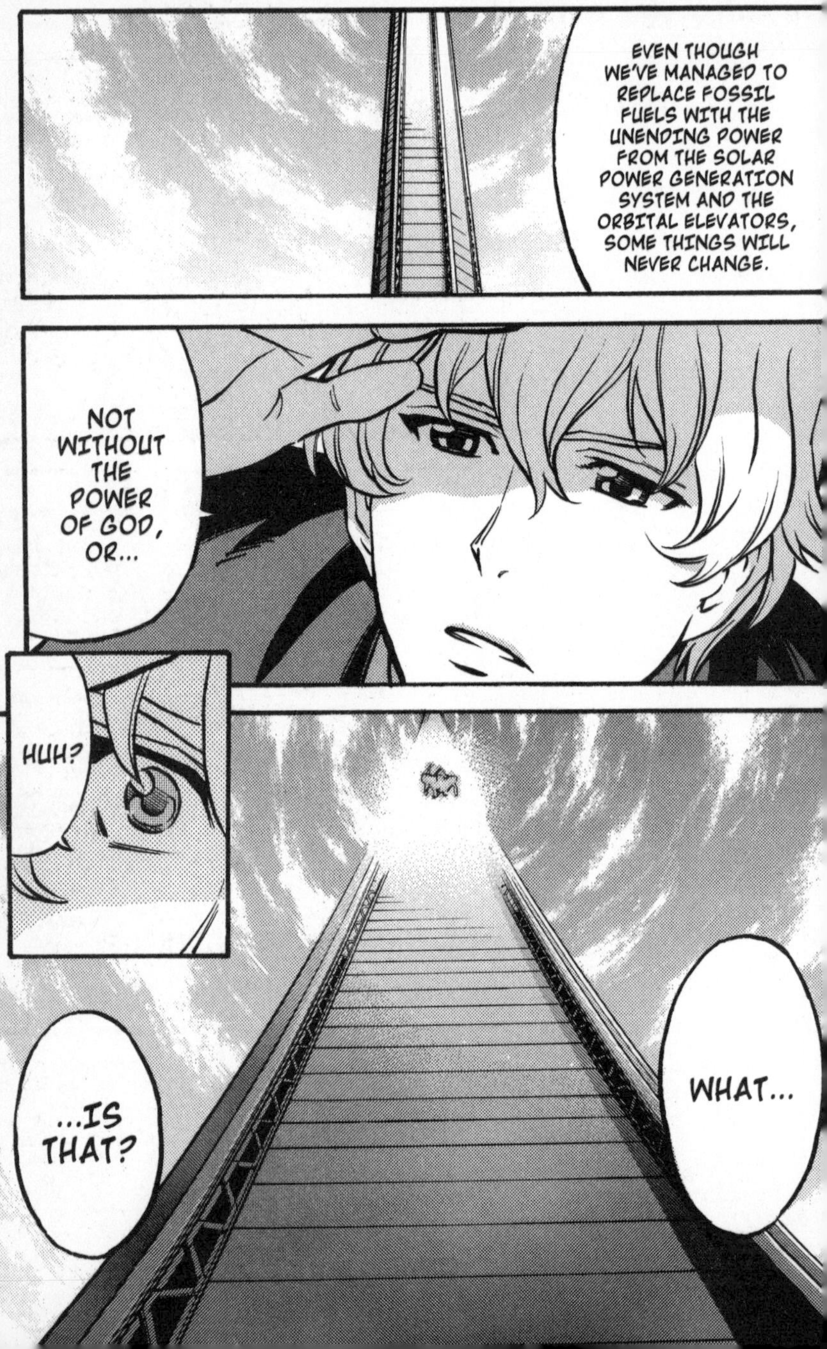
EVEN THOUGH WE'VE MANAGED TO REPLACE FOSSIL FUELS WITH THE UNENDING POWER FROM THE SOLAR POWER GENERATION SYSTEM AND THE ORBITAL ELEVATORS, SOME THINGS WILL NEVER CHANGE.
NOT WITHOUT THE POWER OF GOD, OR...
HUH?
WHAT...
...IS THAT?

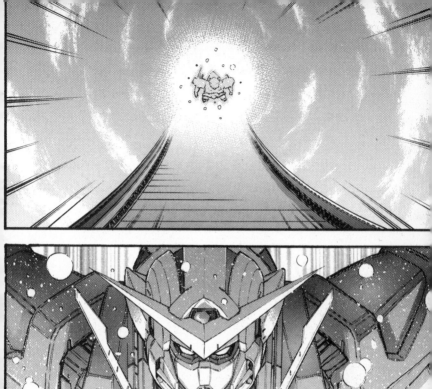

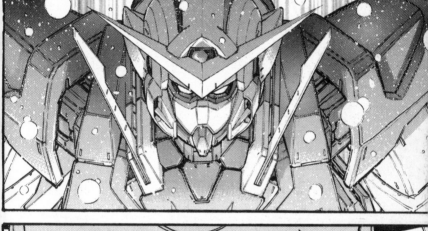

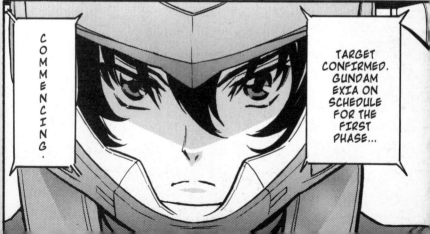

COMMENCING.

TARGET CONFIRMED. GUNDAM EXIA ON SCHEDULE FOR THE FIRST PHASE...

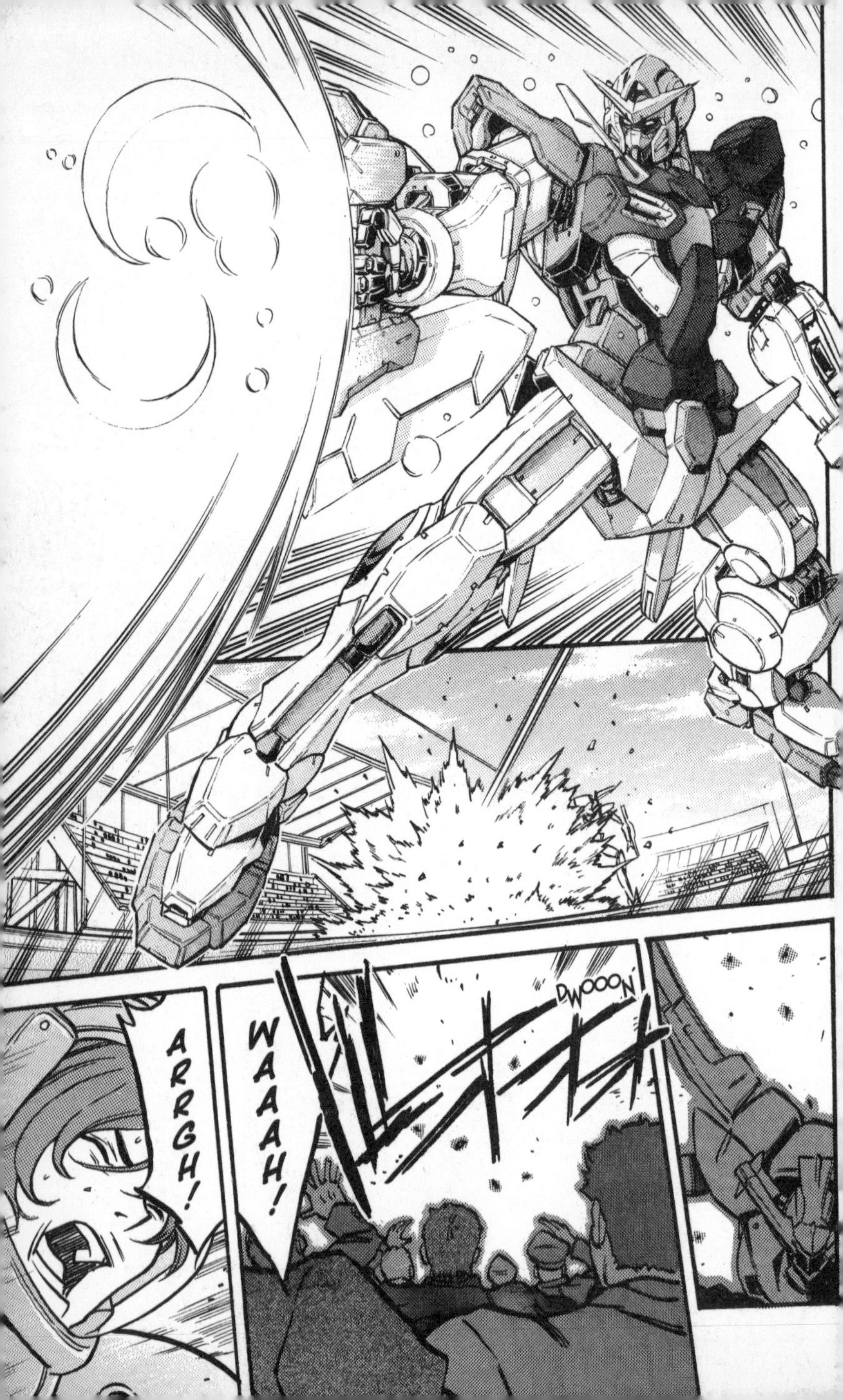
DWOOON
WAAAAH!
ARRGH!

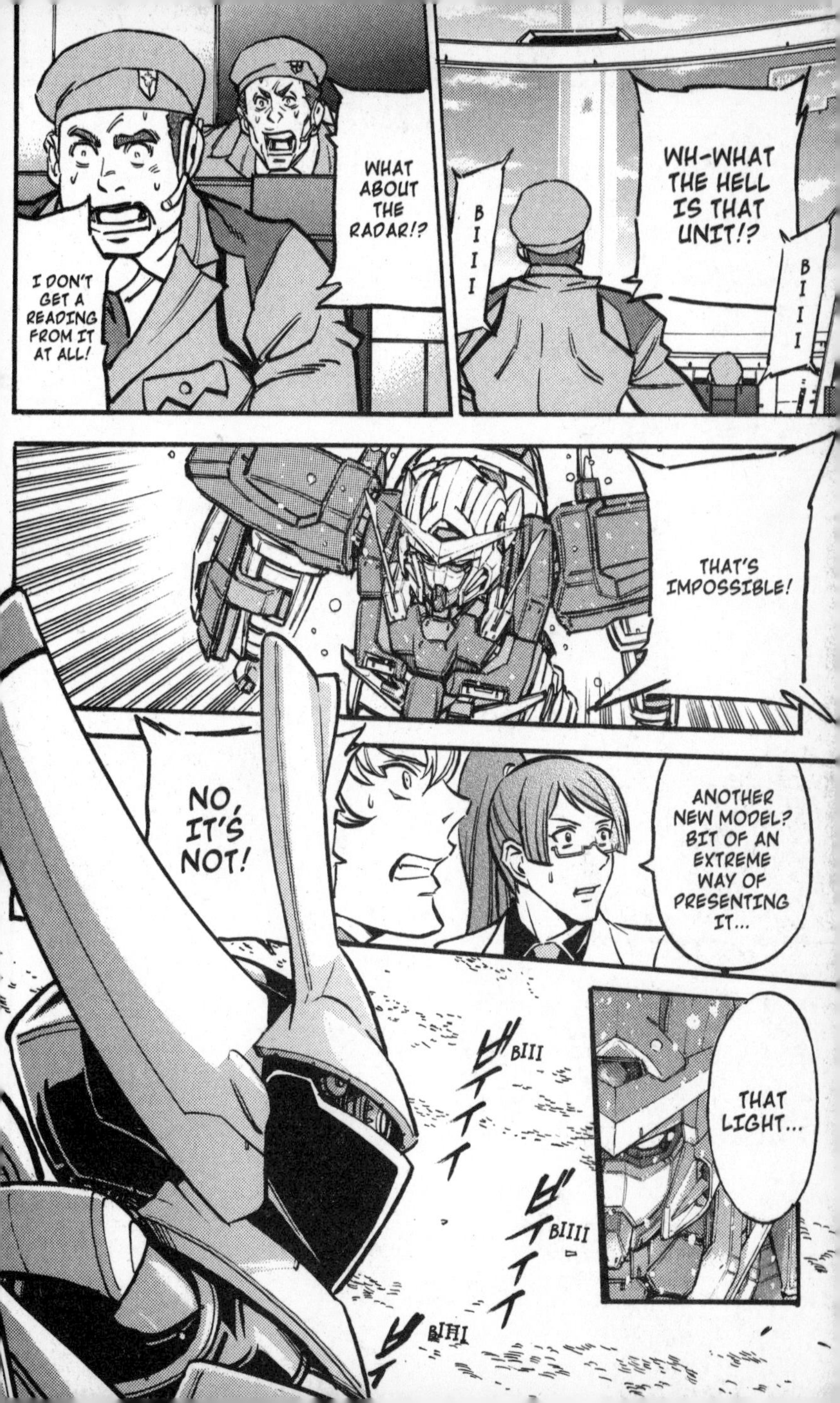
WH-WHAT THE HELL IS THAT UNIT!?
BIII
BIII
WHAT ABOUT THE RADAR!?
I DON'T GET A READING FROM IT AT ALL!
THAT'S IMPOSSIBLE!
ANOTHER NEW MODEL? BIT OF AN EXTREME WAY OF PRESENTING IT...
NO, IT'S NOT!
THAT LIGHT...
BIII
BIIII
BIII

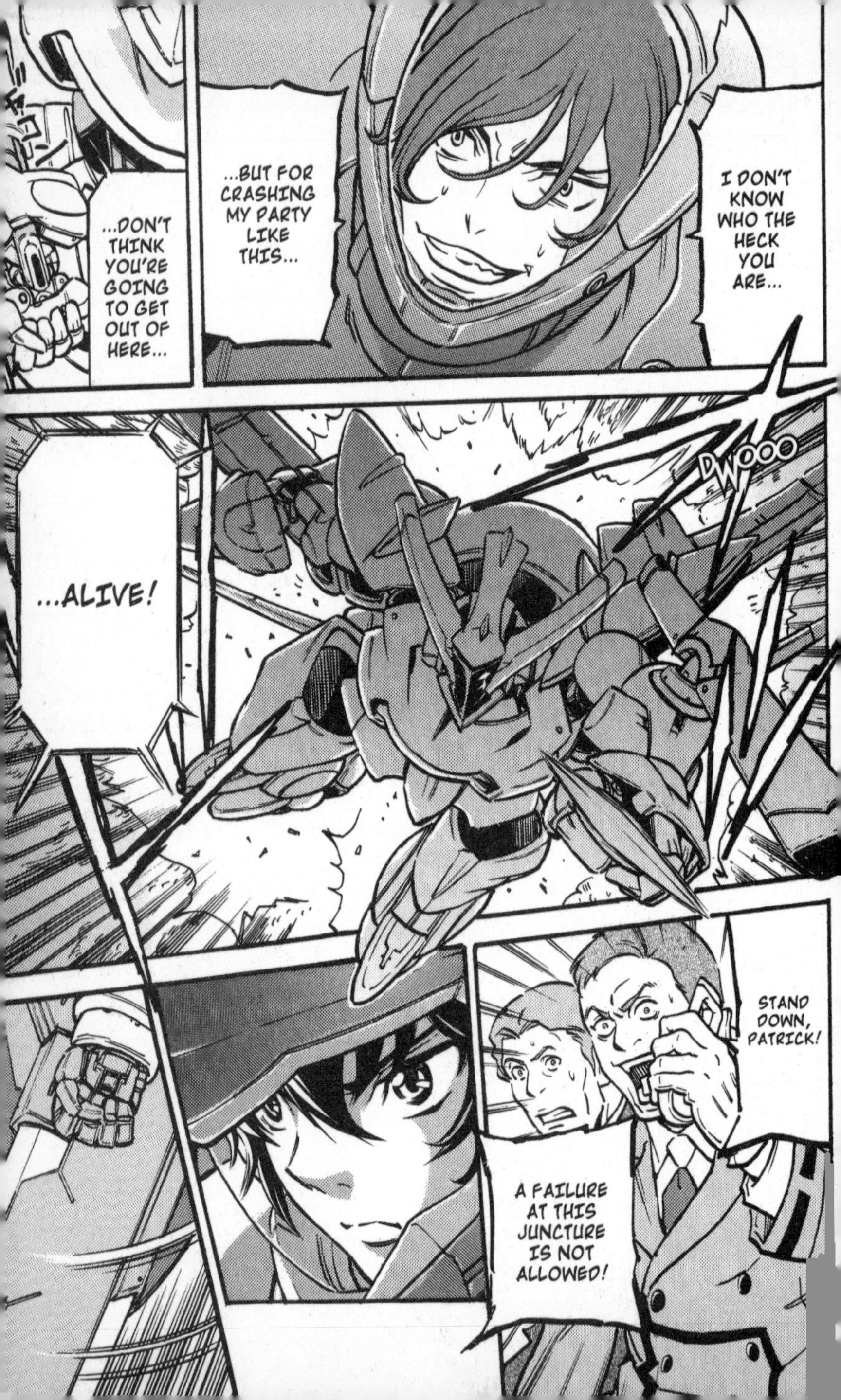
I DON'T KNOW WHO THE HECK YOU ARE...
...BUT FOR CRASHING MY PARTY LIKE THIS...
...DON'T THINK YOU'RE GOING TO GET OUT OF HERE...
DWOOO
...ALIVE!
STAND DOWN, PATRICK!
A FAILURE AT THIS JUNCTURE IS NOT ALLOWED!

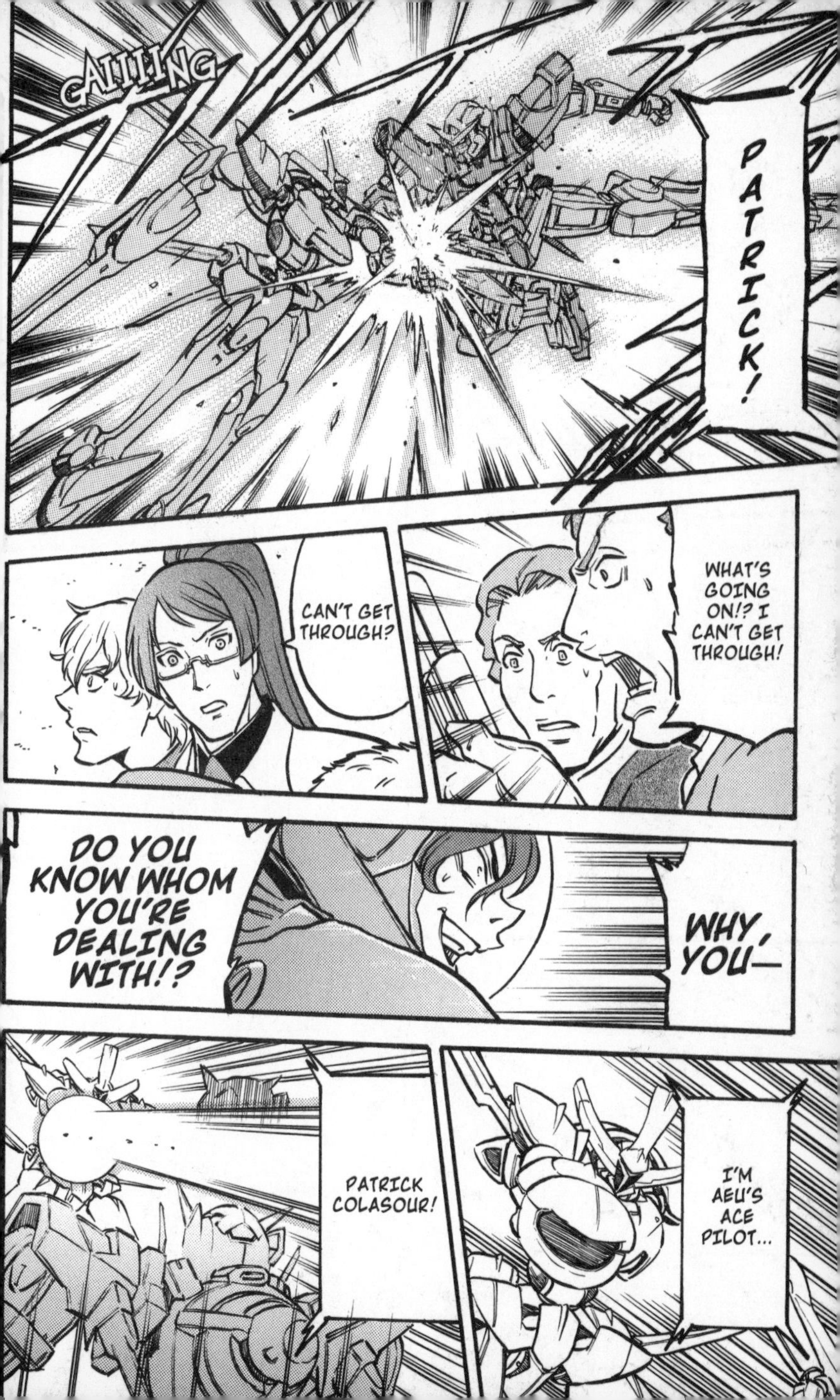
CAIIIING
PATRICK!
WHAT'S GOING ON!? I CAN'T GET THROUGH!
CAN'T GET THROUGH?
WHY, YOU—
DO YOU KNOW WHOM YOU'RE DEALING WITH!?
I'M AEU'S ACE PILOT...
PATRICK COLASOUR!

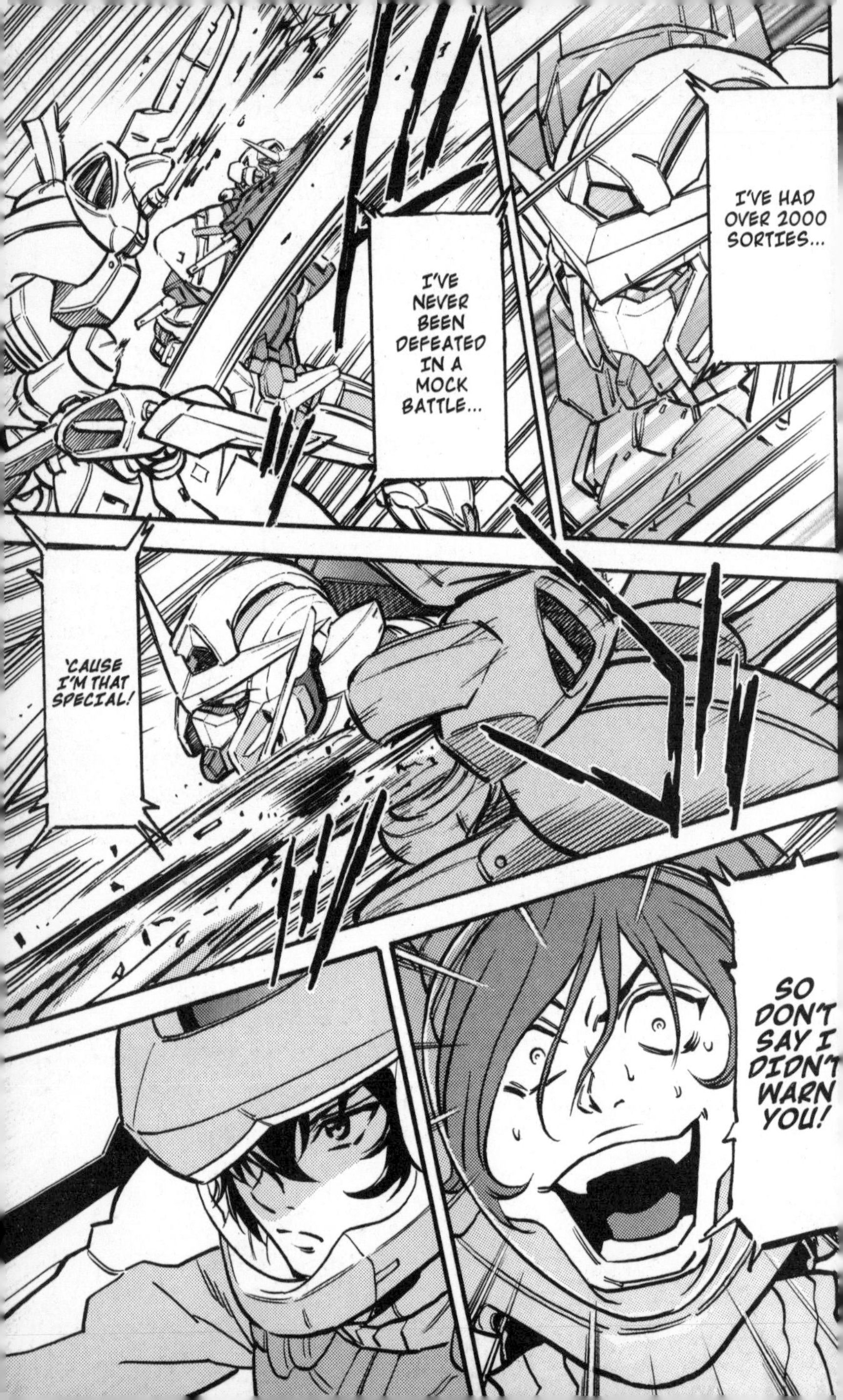
I'VE HAD OVER 2000 SORTIES...
I'VE NEVER BEEN DEFEATED IN A MOCK BATTLE...
'CAUSE I'M THAT SPECIAL!
SO DON'T SAY I DIDN'T WARN YOU!

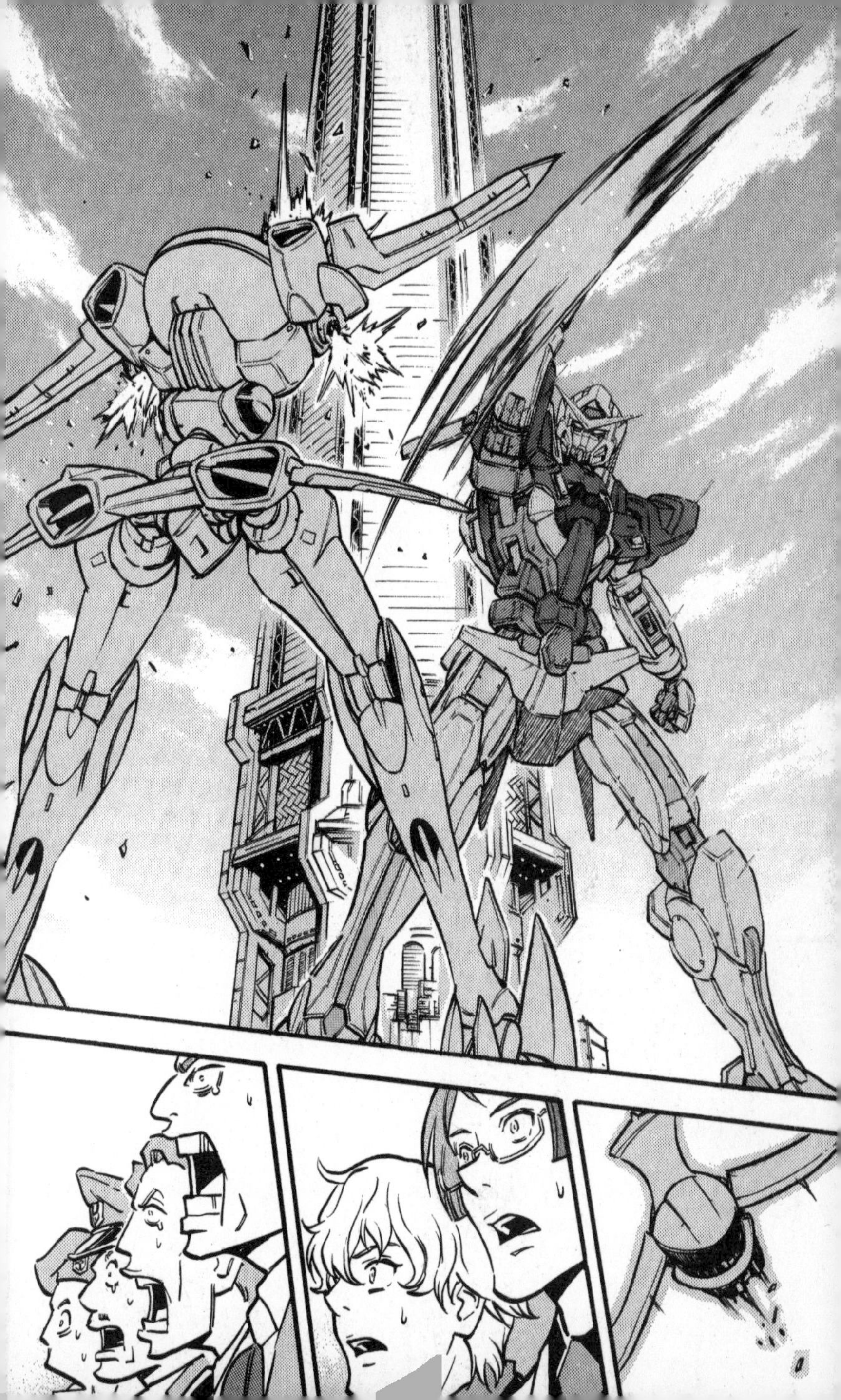

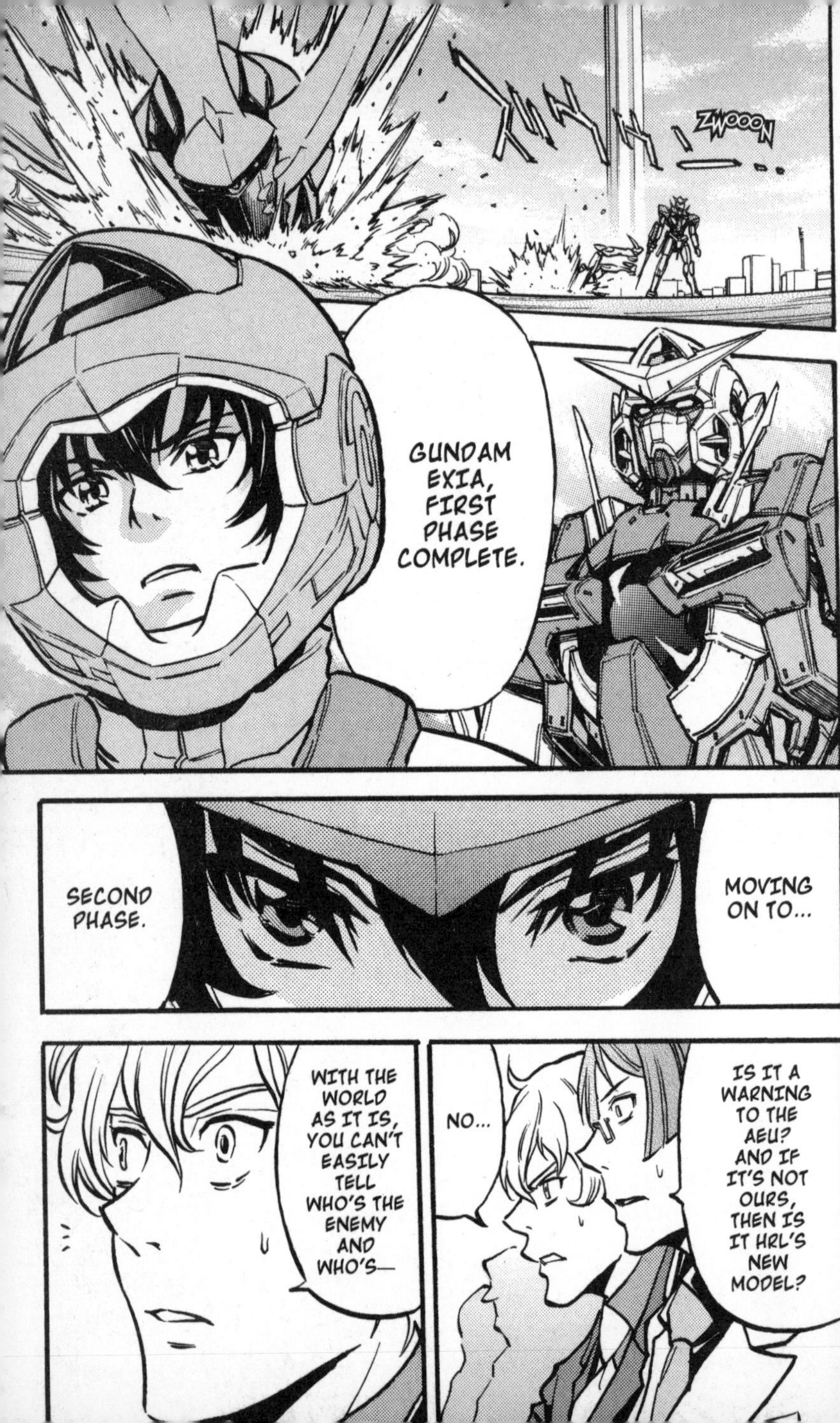
ZWOOON
GUNDAM EXIA, FIRST PHASE COMPLETE.
MOVING ON TO...
SECOND PHASE.
IS IT A WARNING TO THE AEU? AND IF IT'S NOT OURS, THEN IS IT HRL'S NEW MODEL?
NO...
WITH THE WORLD AS IT IS, YOU CAN'T EASILY TELL WHO'S THE ENEMY AND WHO'S—

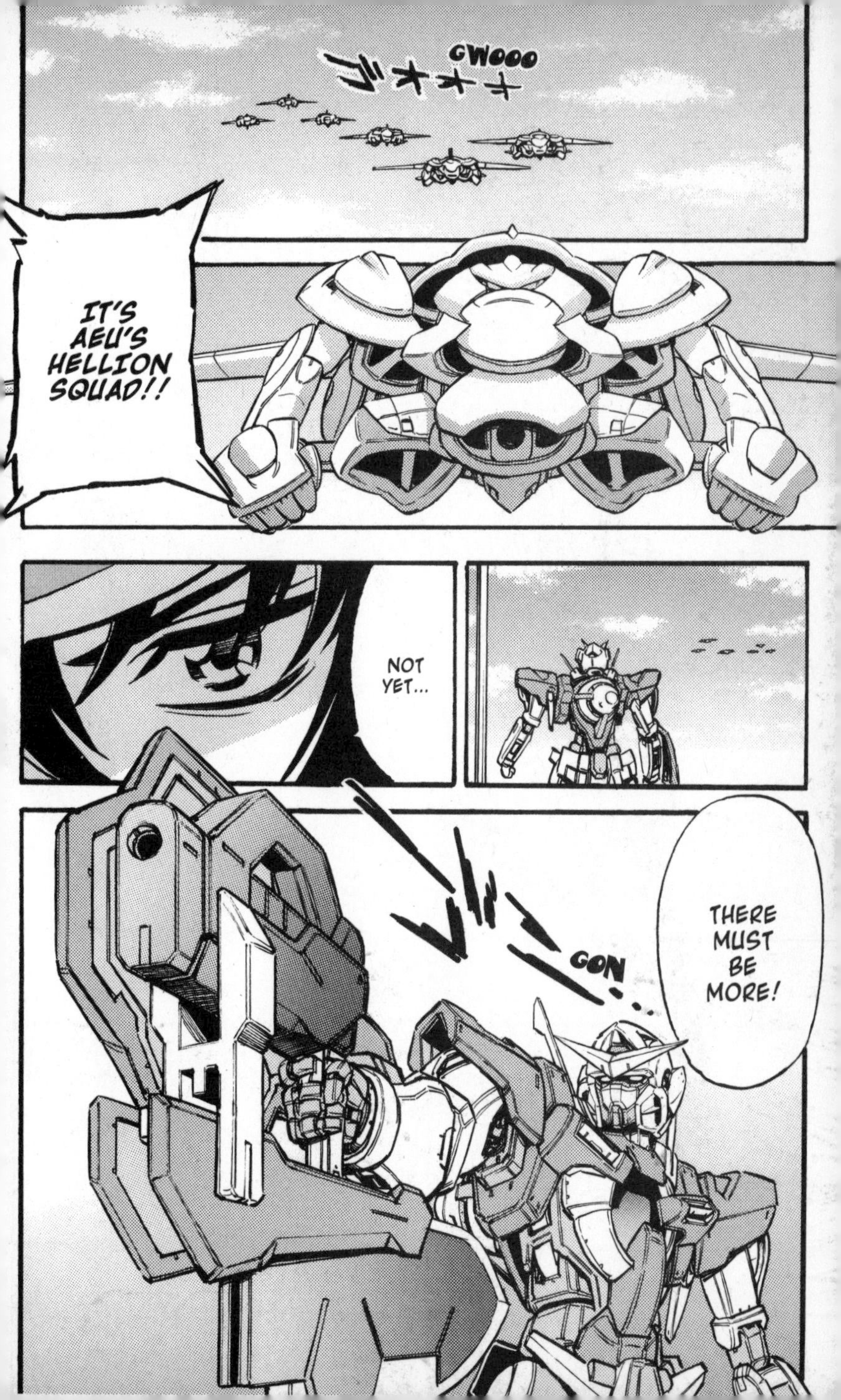
GWOOO
IT'S AEU'S HELLION SQUAD!!
NOT YET...
GON
THERE MUST BE MORE!

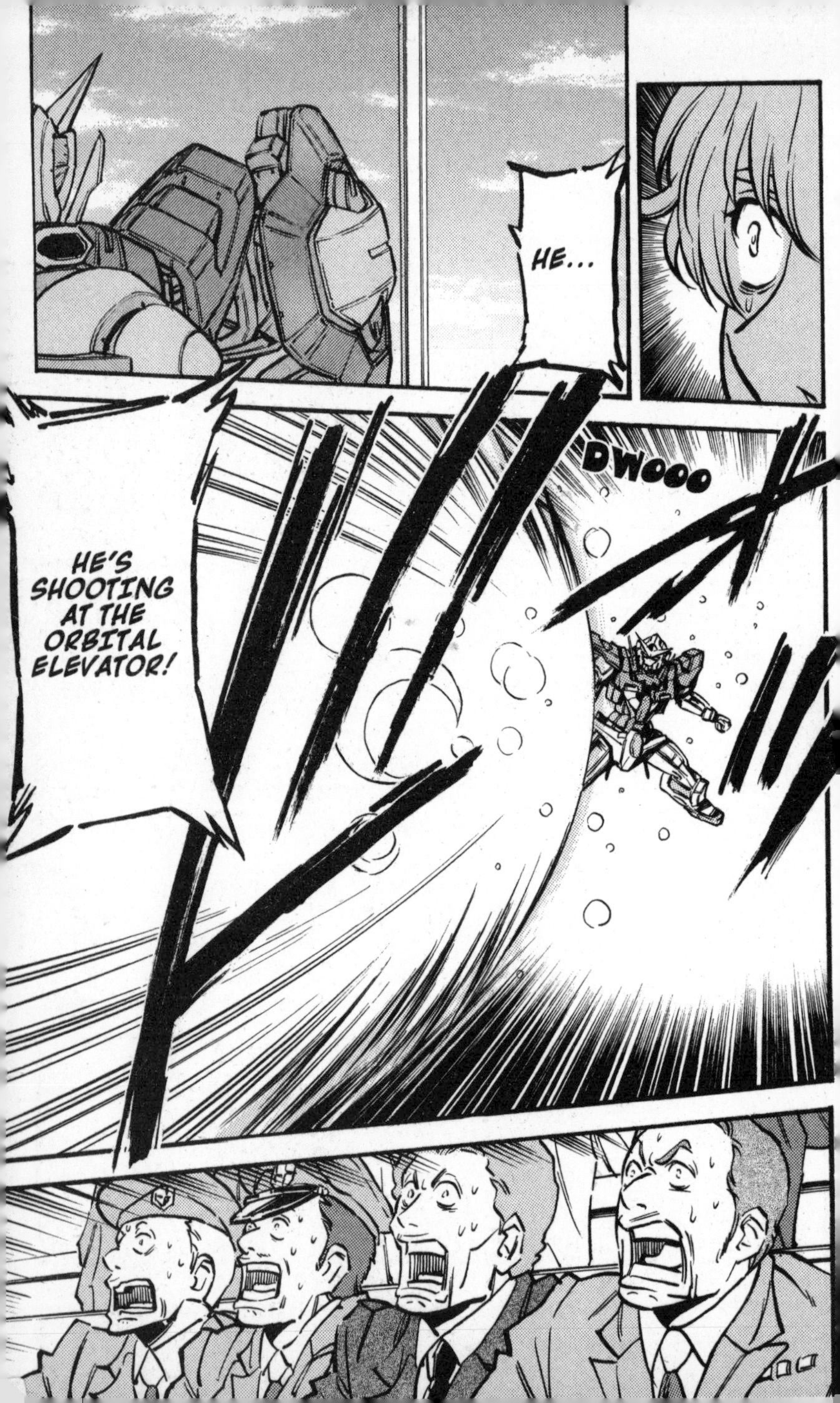
HE...
DWOOO
HE'S SHOOTING AT THE ORBITAL ELEVATOR!

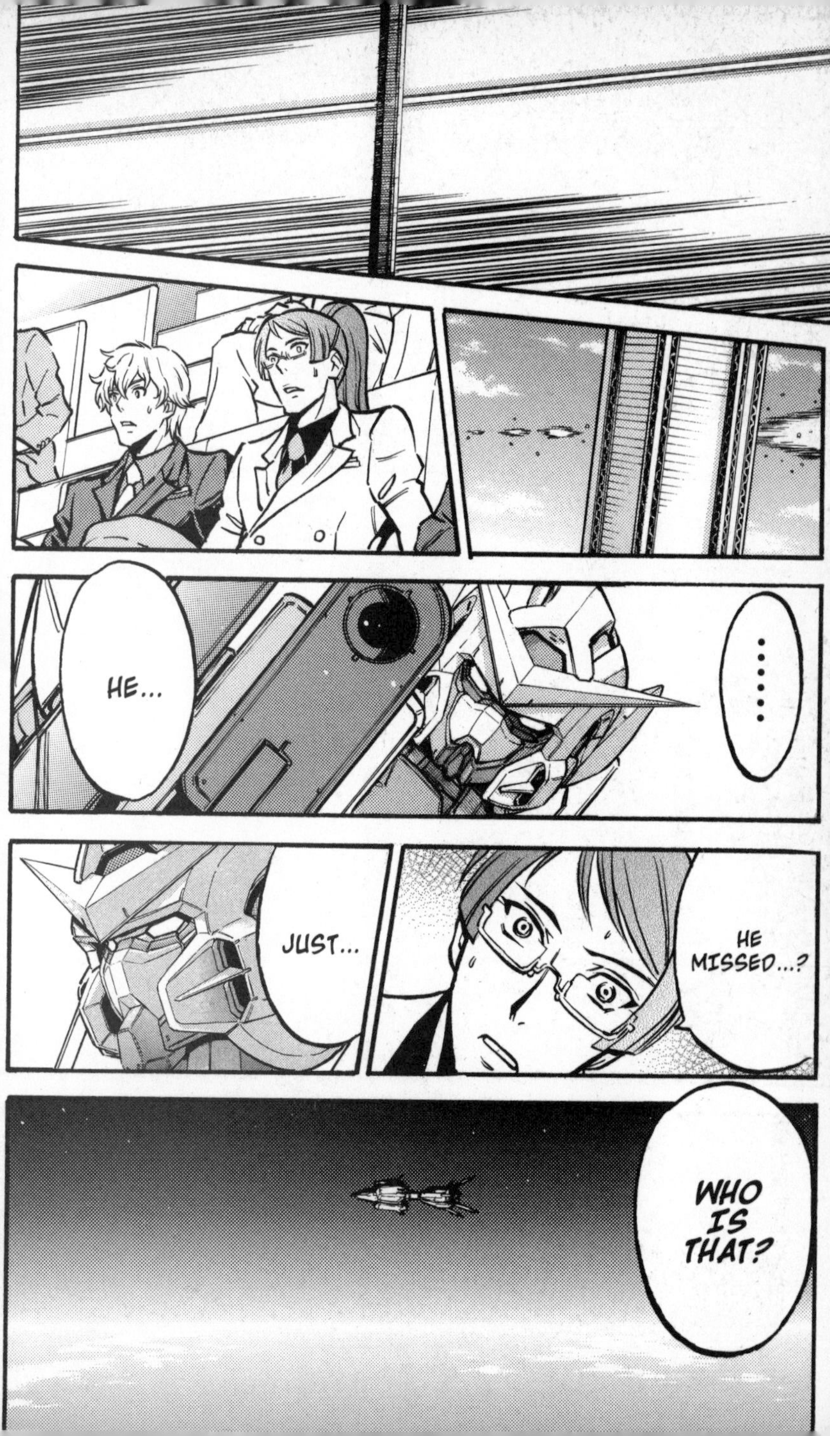
......
HE...
HE MISSED...?
JUST...
WHO IS THAT?

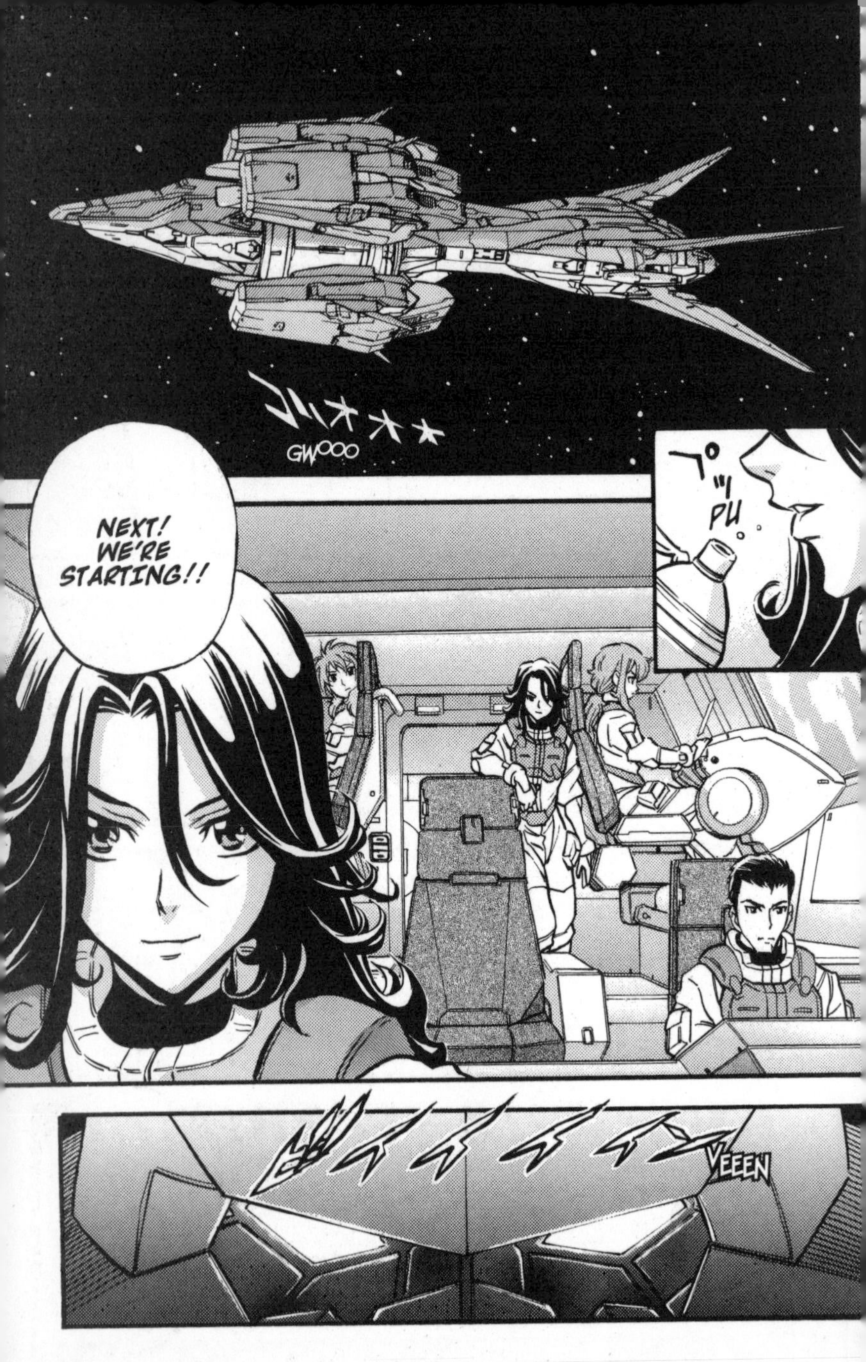
GWOOO
PU
NEXT! WE'RE STARTING!!
VEEEN

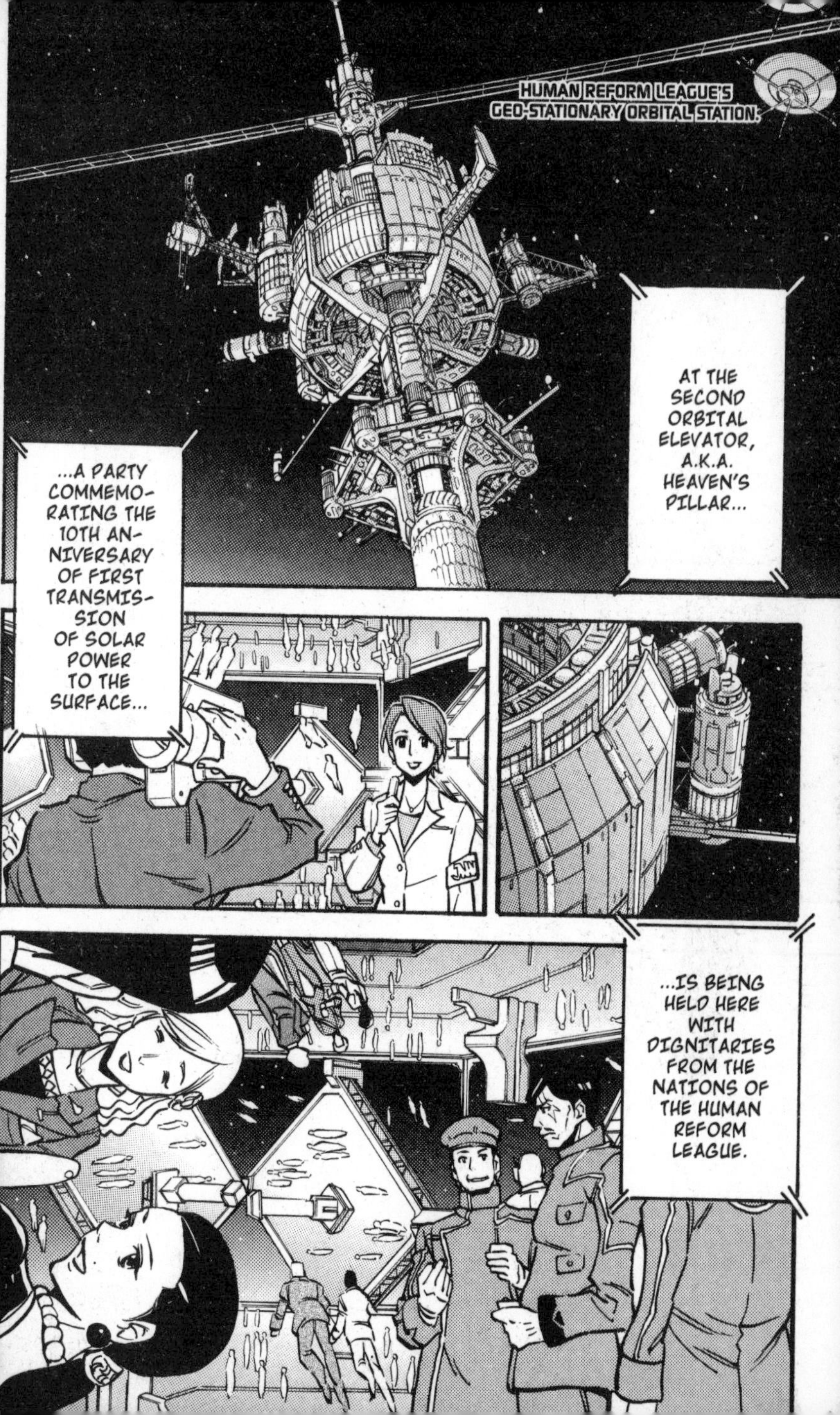
HUMAN REFORM LEAGUE'S GEO-STATIONARY ORBITAL STATION.
AT THE SECOND ORBITAL ELEVATOR, A.K.A. HEAVEN'S PILLAR...
...A PARTY COMMEMORATING THE 10TH ANNIVERSARY OF FIRST TRANSMISSION OF SOLAR POWER TO THE SURFACE...
...IS BEING HELD HERE WITH DIGNITARIES FROM THE NATIONS OF THE HUMAN REFORM LEAGUE.

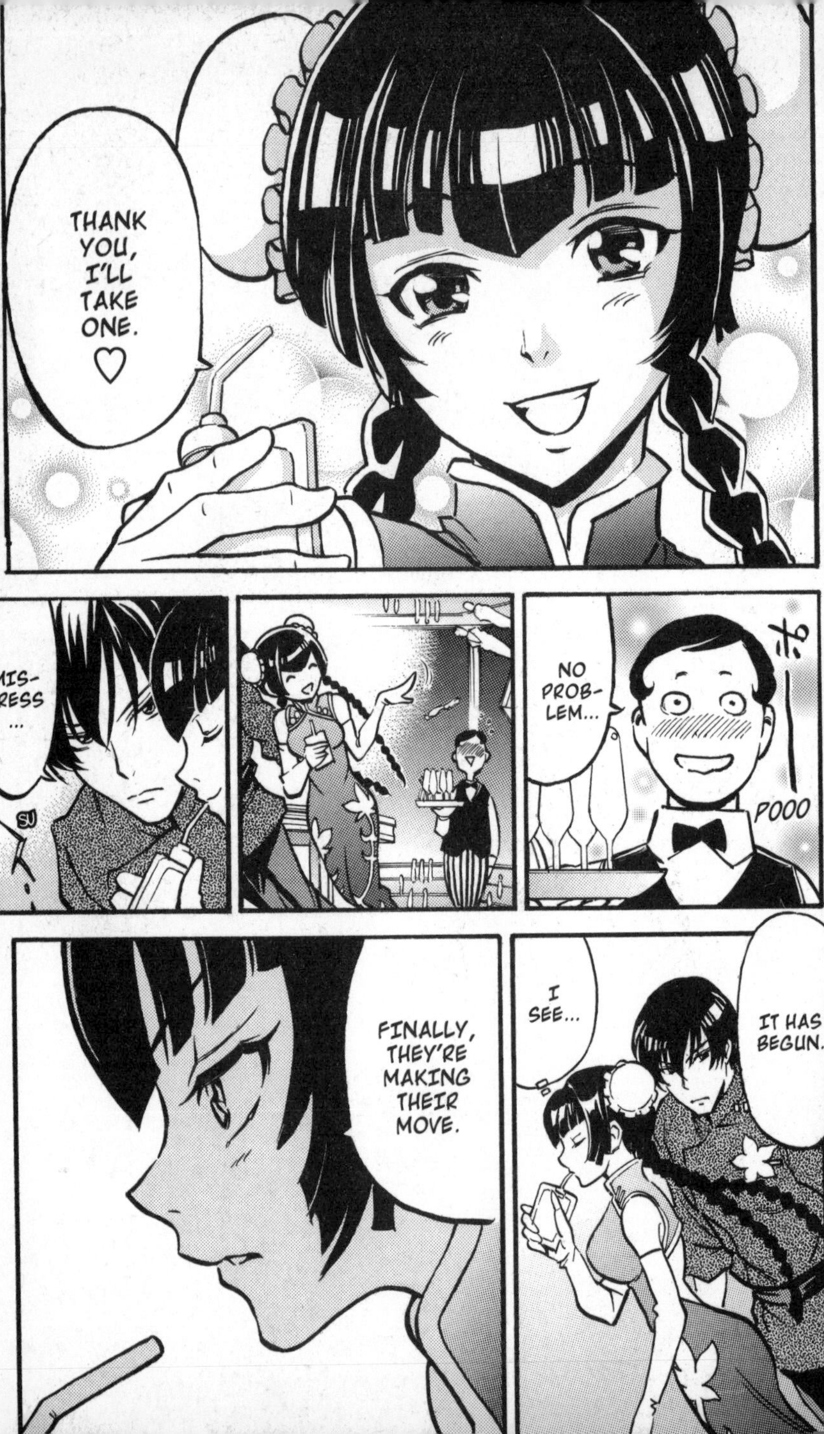
THANK YOU, I'LL TAKE ONE. ♡
NO PROB-LEM...
POOO
MIS-TRESS...
SU
IT HAS BEGUN.
I SEE...
FINALLY, THEY'RE MAKING THEIR MOVE.

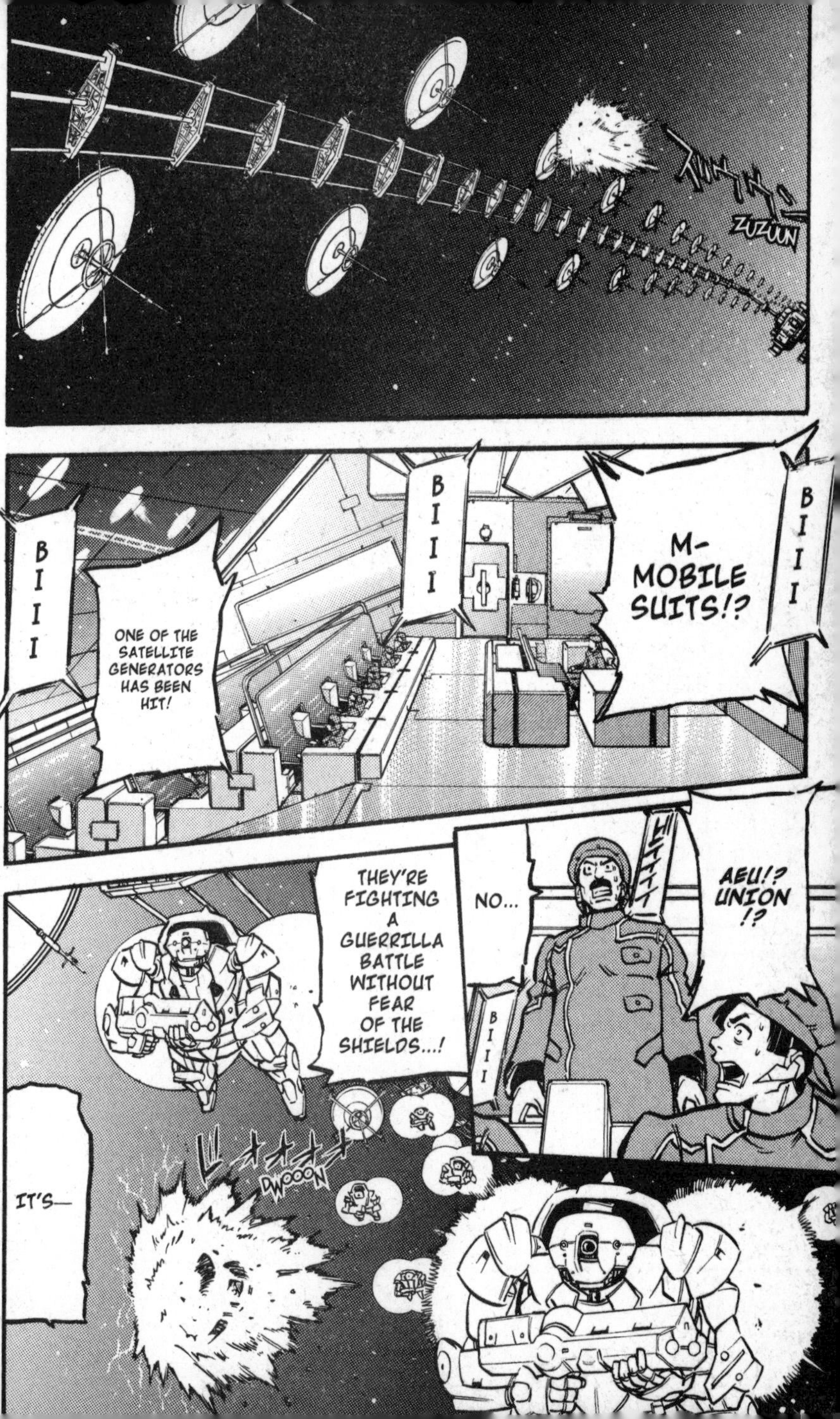
ZUZUUN
BIII
M-MOBILE SUITS!?
BIII
ONE OF THE SATELLITE GENERATORS HAS BEEN HIT!
BIII
AEU!? UNION!?
NO...
BIII
THEY'RE FIGHTING A GUERRILLA BATTLE WITHOUT FEAR OF THE SHIELDS...!
DWOOON
IT'S—

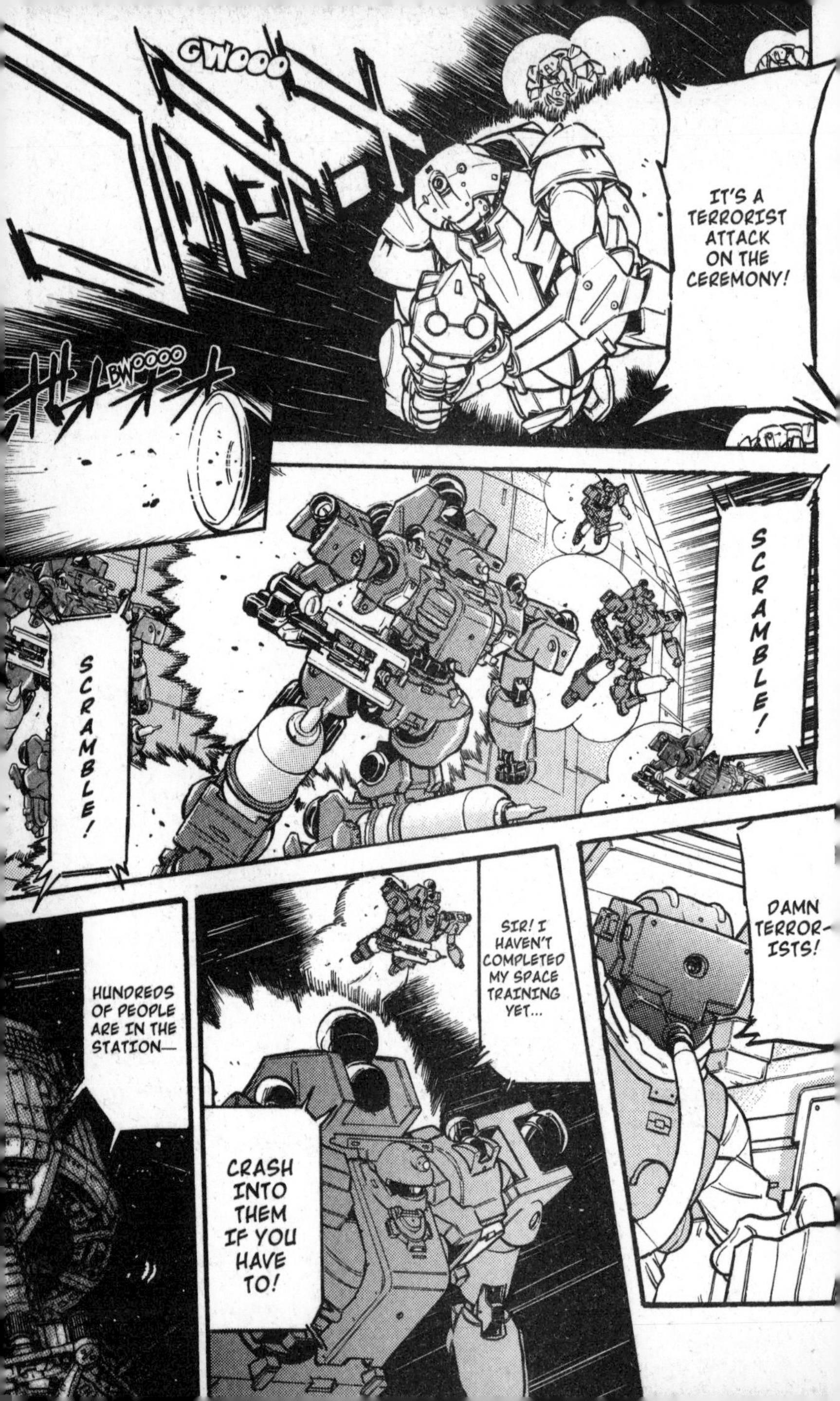
GWOOO
IT'S A TERRORIST ATTACK ON THE CEREMONY!
BWOOOO
SCRAMBLE!
SCRAMBLE!
DAMN TERRORISTS!
SIR! I HAVEN'T COMPLETED MY SPACE TRAINING YET...
CRASH INTO THEM IF YOU HAVE TO!
HUNDREDS OF PEOPLE ARE IN THE STATION—

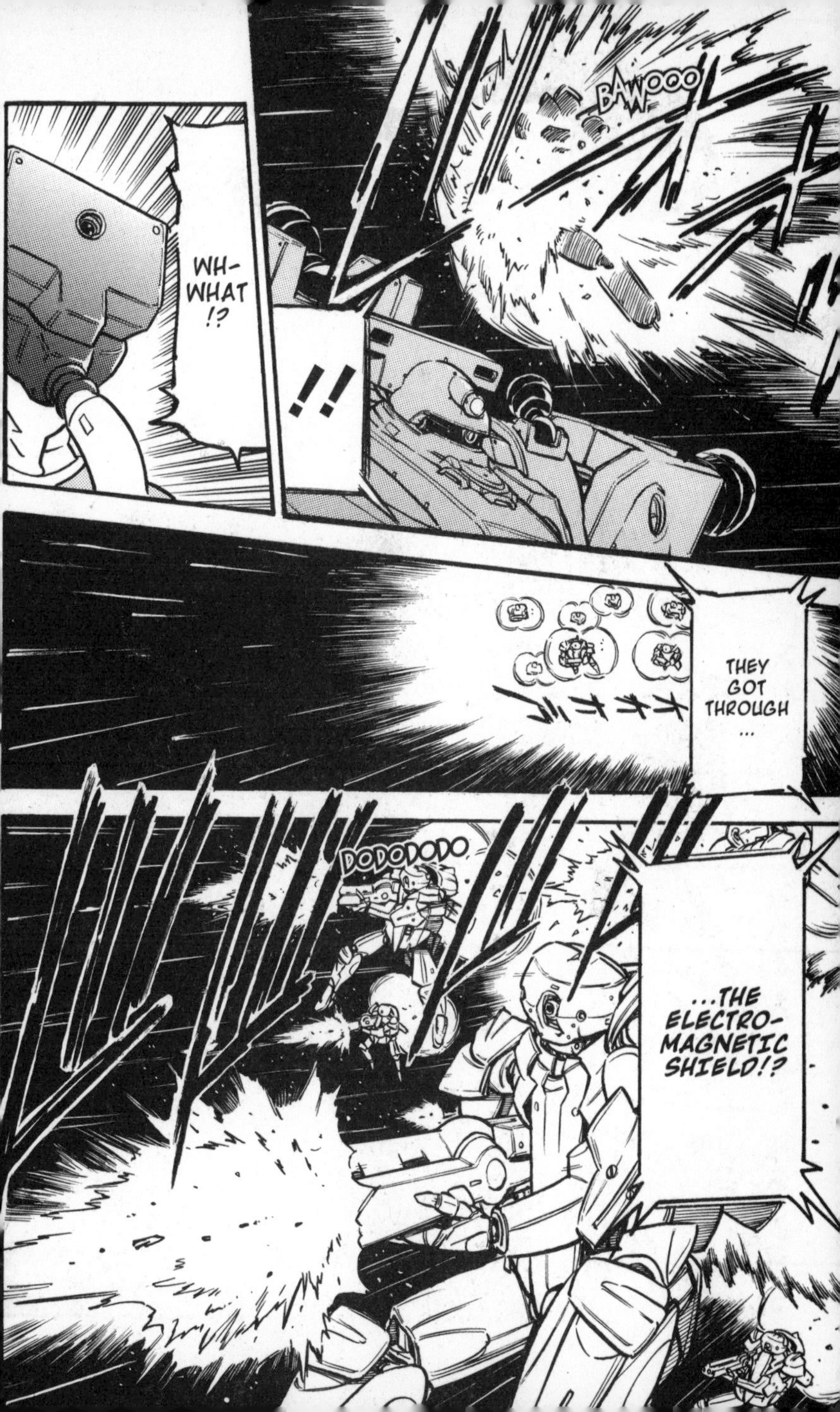
BAWOOO
!!
WH-WHAT!?
THEY GOT THROUGH...
DODODODO
...THE ELECTRO-MAGNETIC SHIELD!?

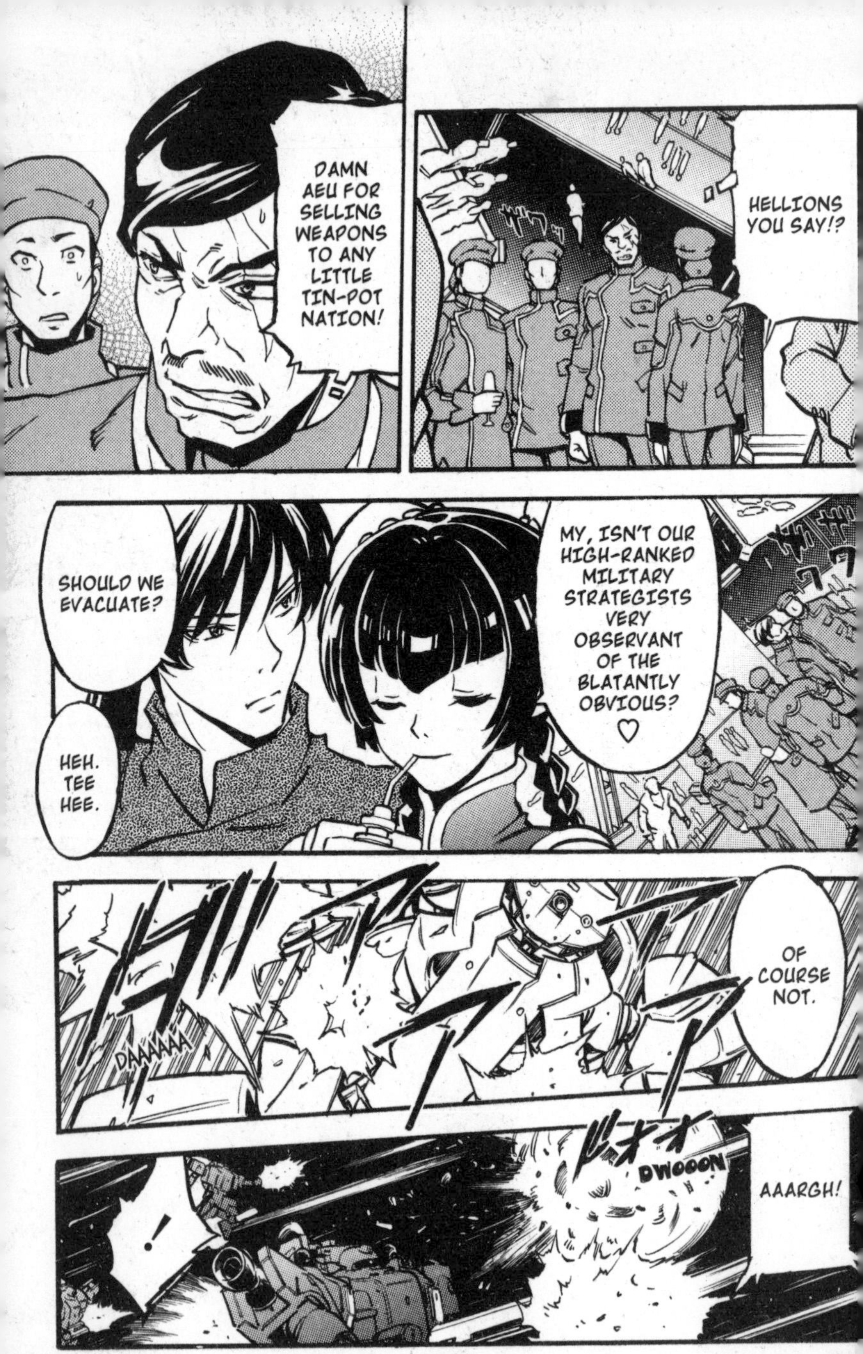
HELLIONS YOU SAY!?
DAMN AEU FOR SELLING WEAPONS TO ANY LITTLE TIN-POT NATION!
MY, ISN'T OUR HIGH-RANKED MILITARY STRATEGISTS VERY OBSERVANT OF THE BLATANTLY OBVIOUS? ♡
SHOULD WE EVACUATE?
HEH. TEE HEE.
OF COURSE NOT.
DAAAAAA
AAARGH!
DWOOON
!

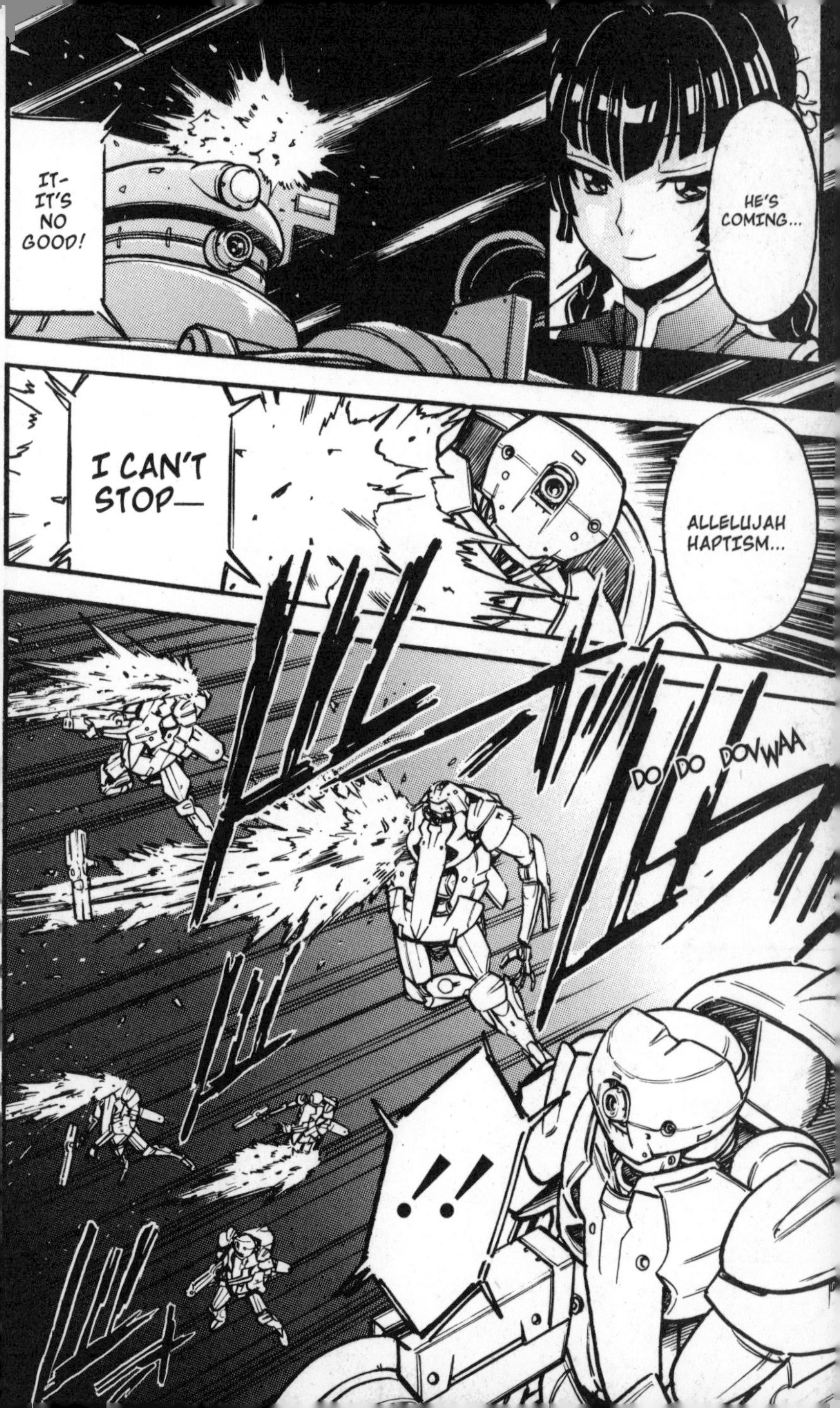
HE'S COMING...
IT-IT'S NO GOOD!
ALLELUJAH HAPTISM...
I CAN'T STOP—
DO DO DOVWAA
!!

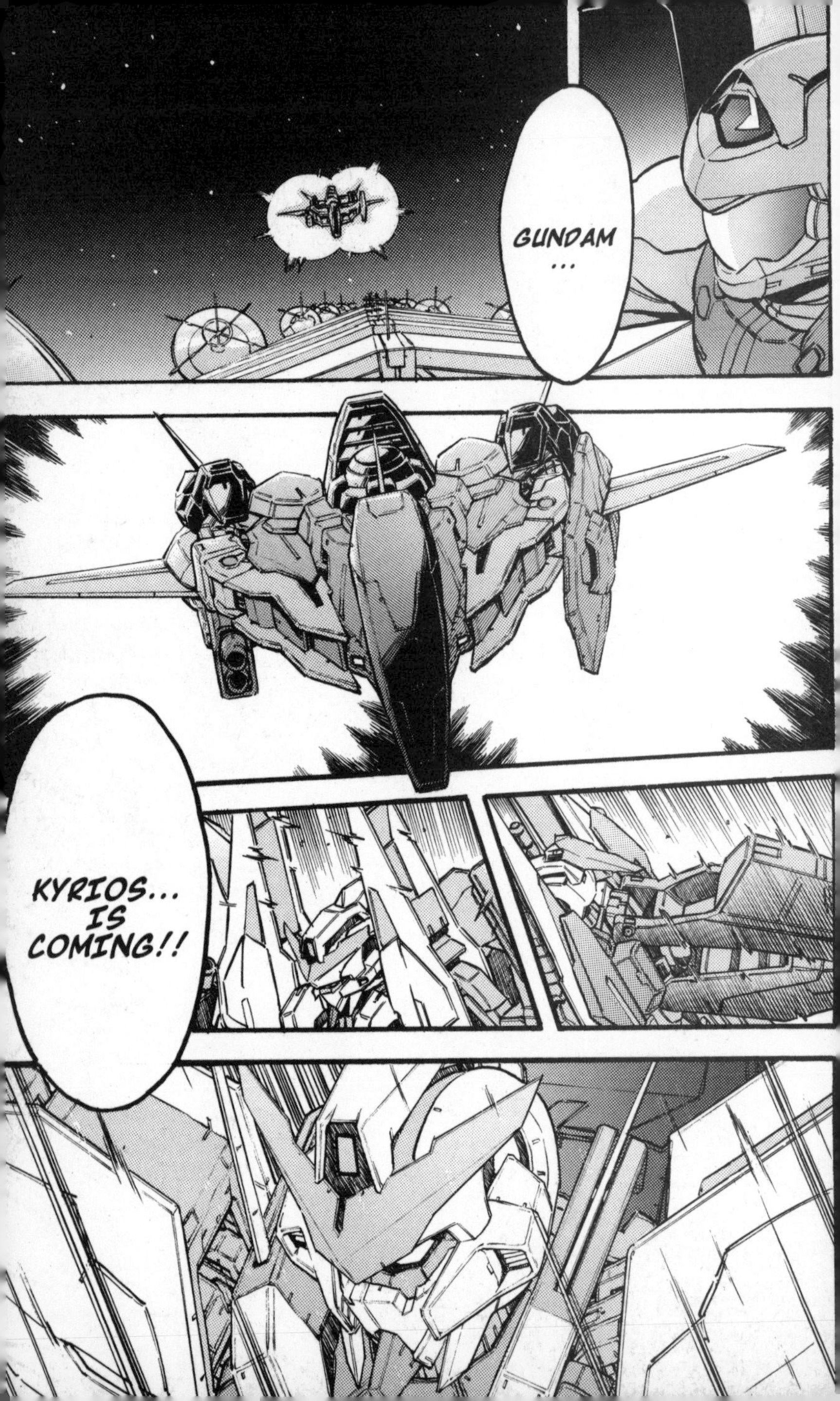
GUNDAM ...
KYRIOS... IS COMING!!

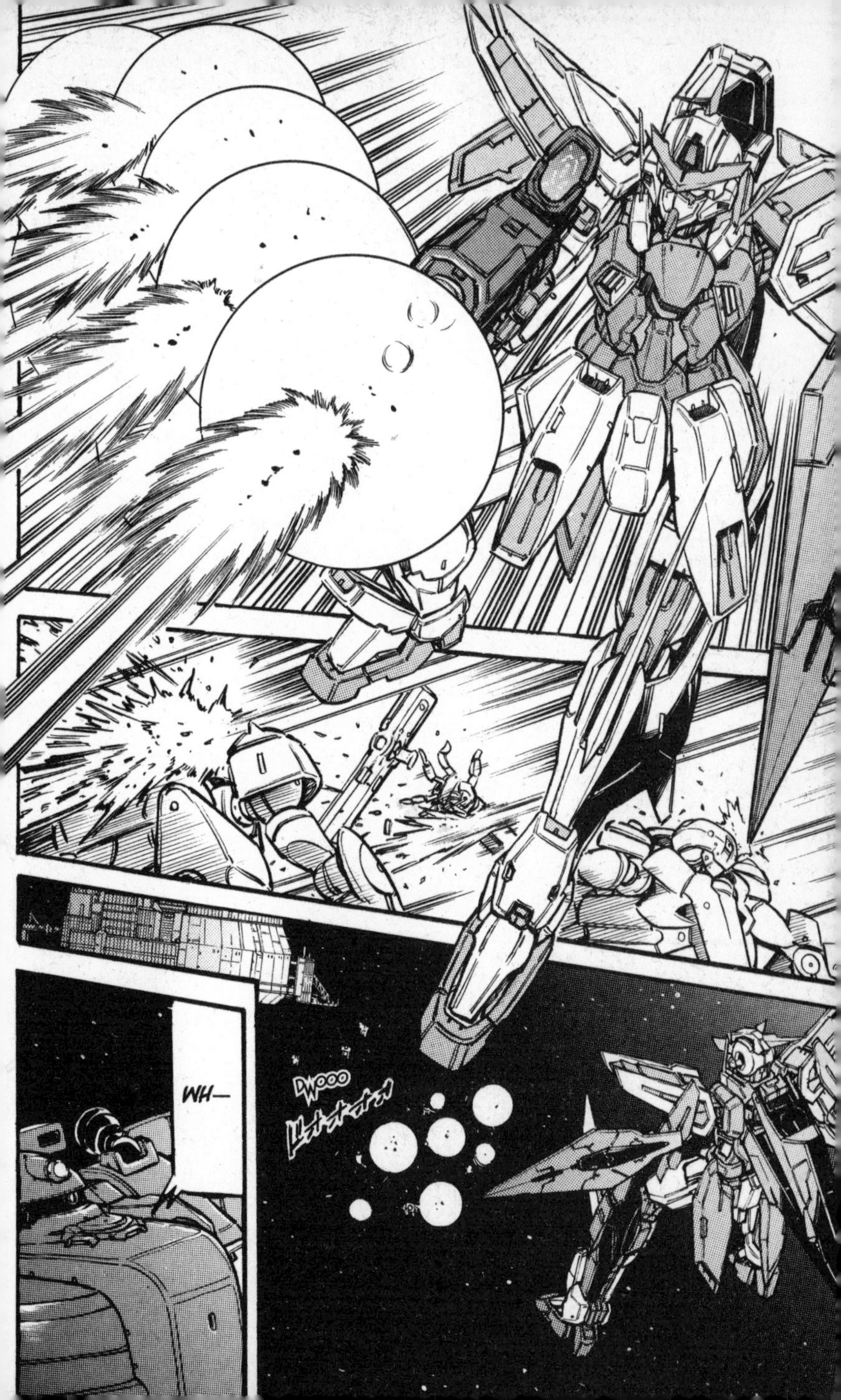
DWOOO
WH—

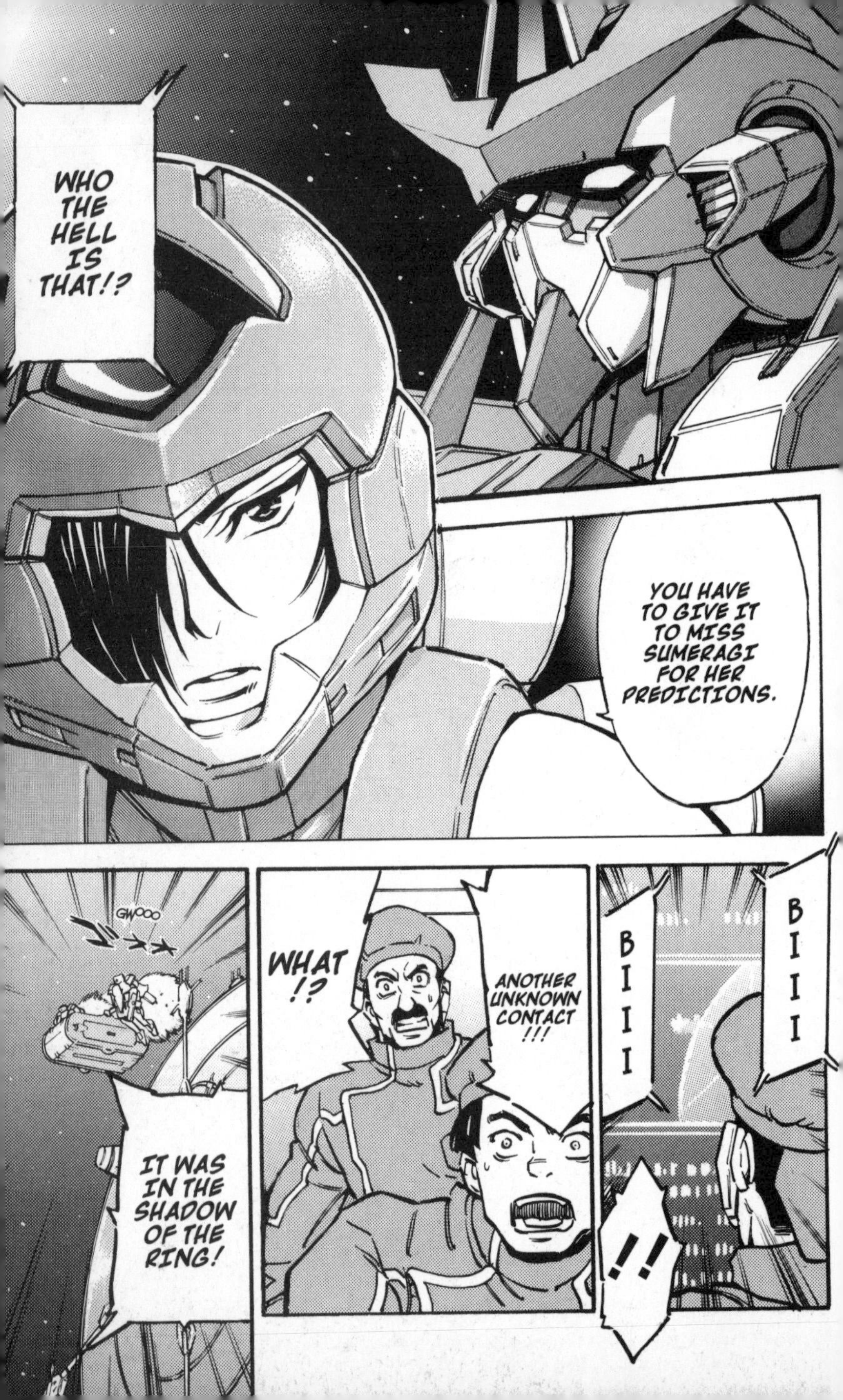

WHO THE HELL IS THAT!?
YOU HAVE TO GIVE IT TO MISS SUMERAGI FOR HER PREDICTIONS.
BIII
BIII
!!
ANOTHER UNKNOWN CONTACT!!!
WHAT!?
GWOOO
IT WAS IN THE SHADOW OF THE RING!

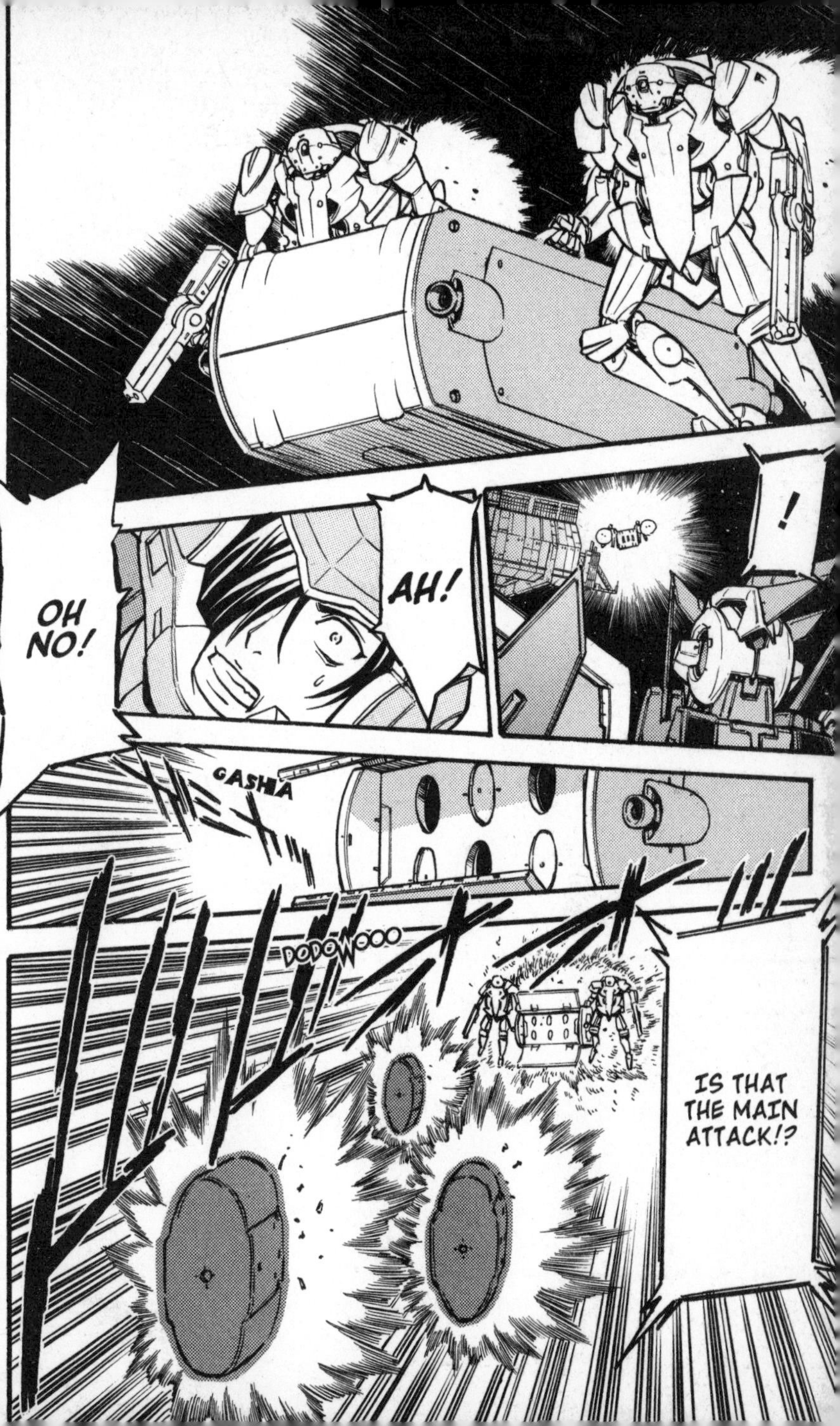
!
AH!
OH NO!
GASHA
DODOWOOO
IS THAT THE MAIN ATTACK!?

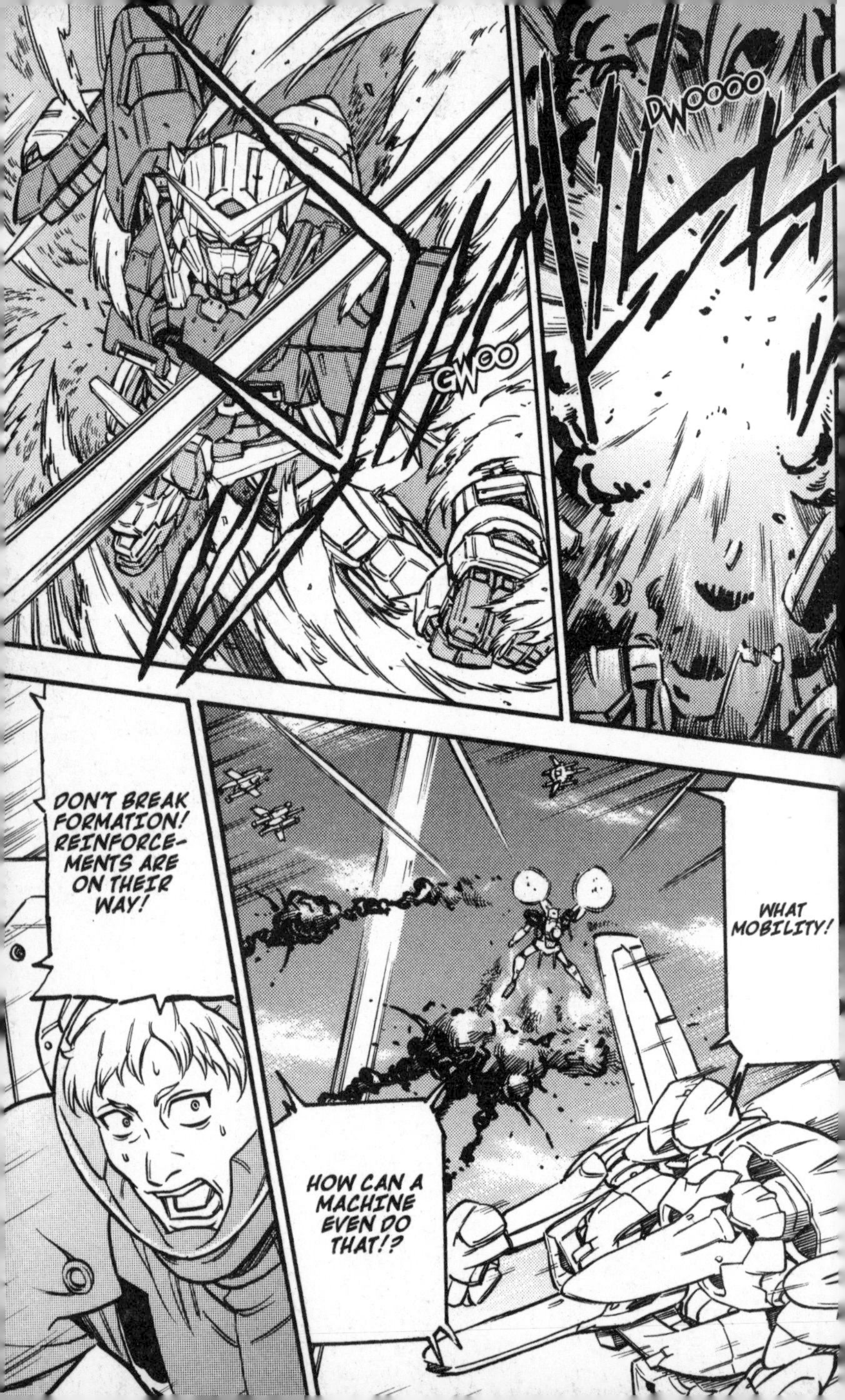
DWOOOO
GWOO
WHAT MOBILITY!
DON'T BREAK FORMATION! REINFORCEMENTS ARE ON THEIR WAY!
HOW CAN A MACHINE EVEN DO THAT!?

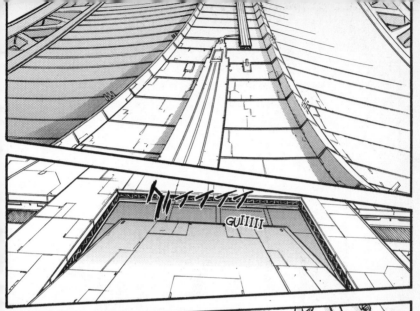

GUIIIII

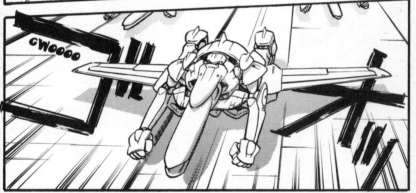

GWOOOO

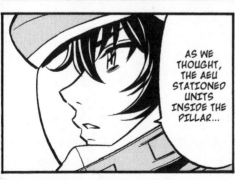

AS WE THOUGHT, THE AEU STATIONED UNITS INSIDE THE PILLAR...

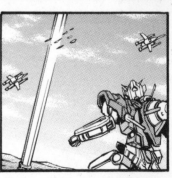

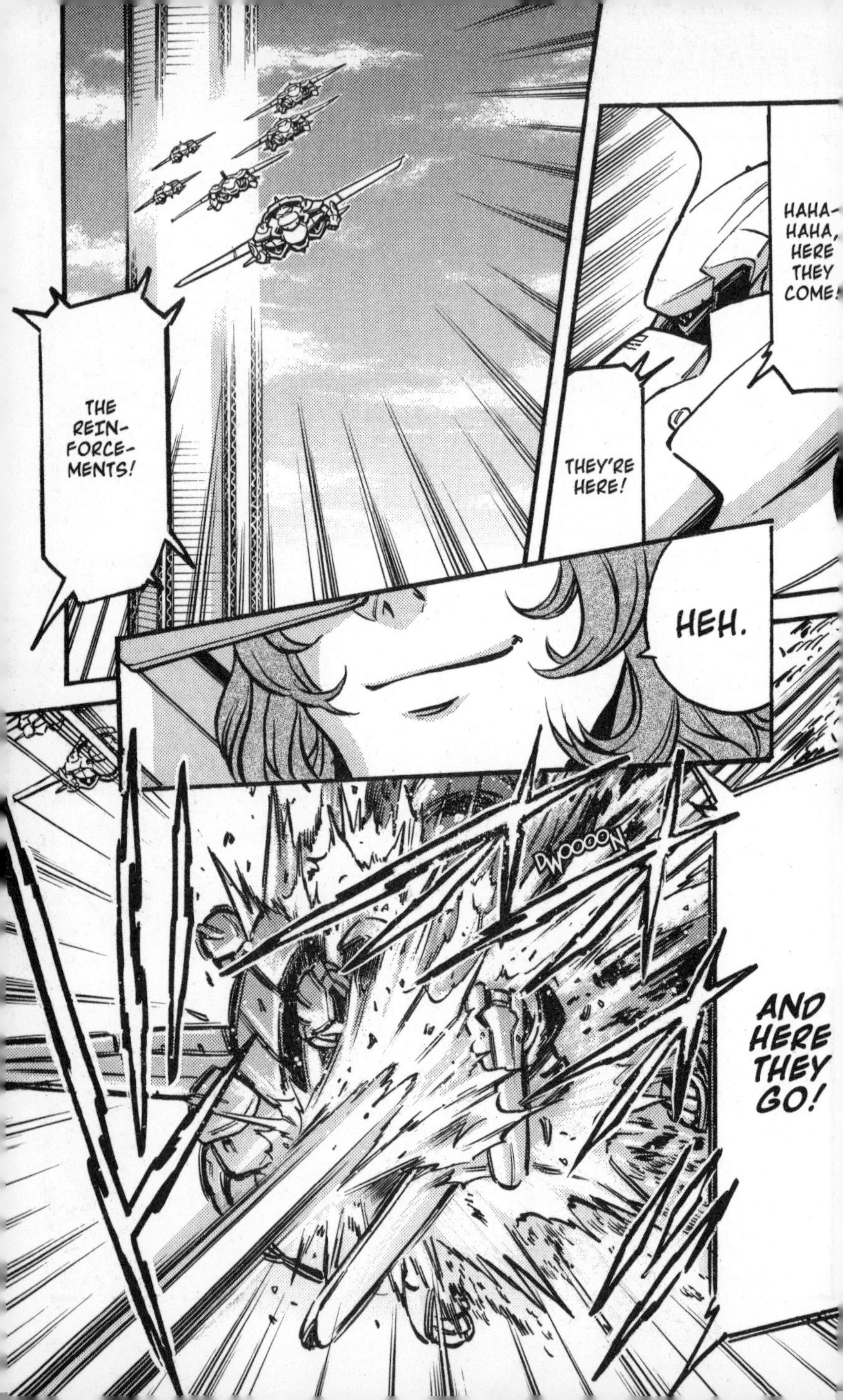
HAHA-HAHA, HERE THEY COME!
THEY'RE HERE!
THE REIN-FORCE-MENTS!
HEH.
DWOOOON
AND HERE THEY GO!

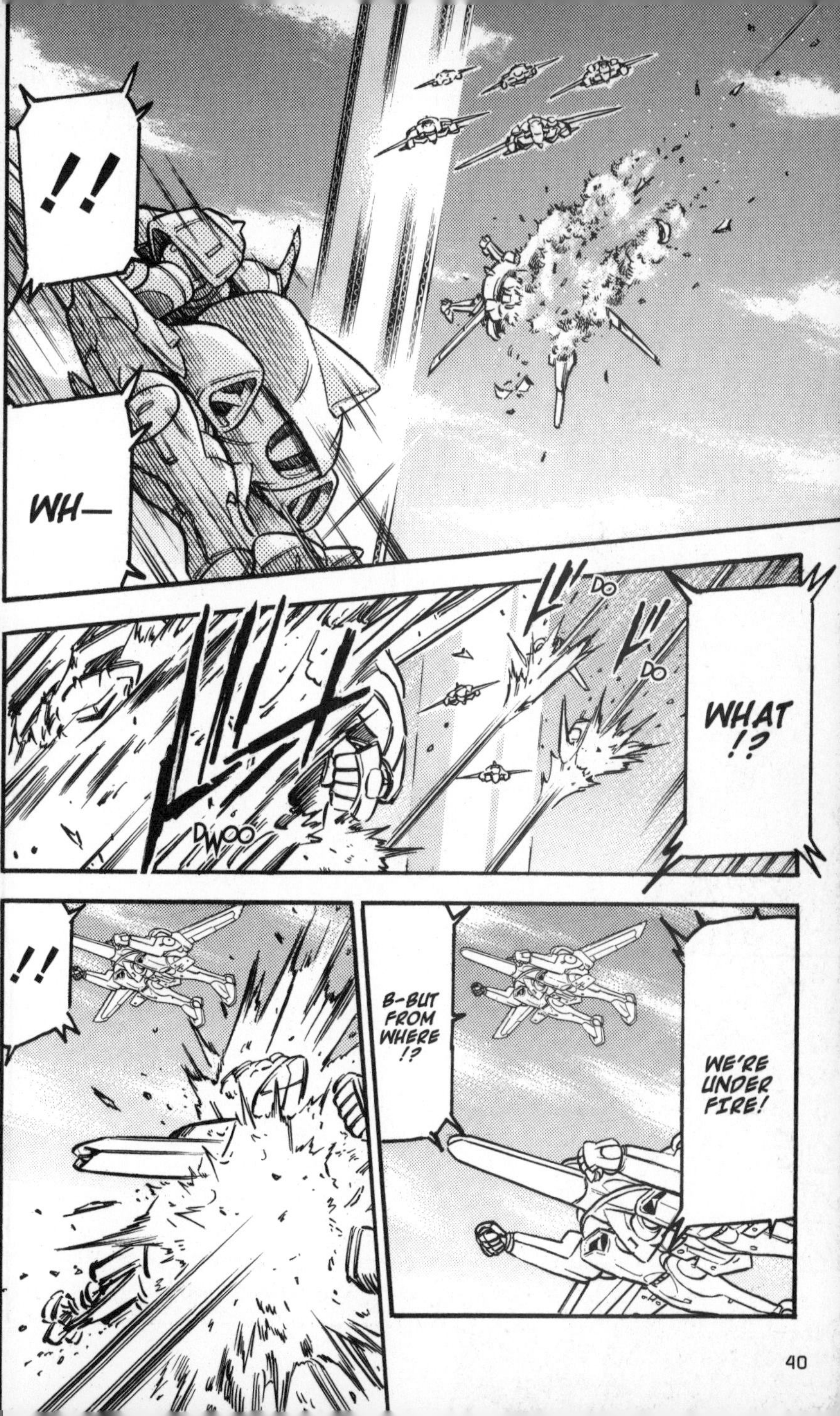
!!
WH—
WHAT!?
DO
DO
DWOO
WE'RE UNDER FIRE!
B-BUT FROM WHERE!?
!!

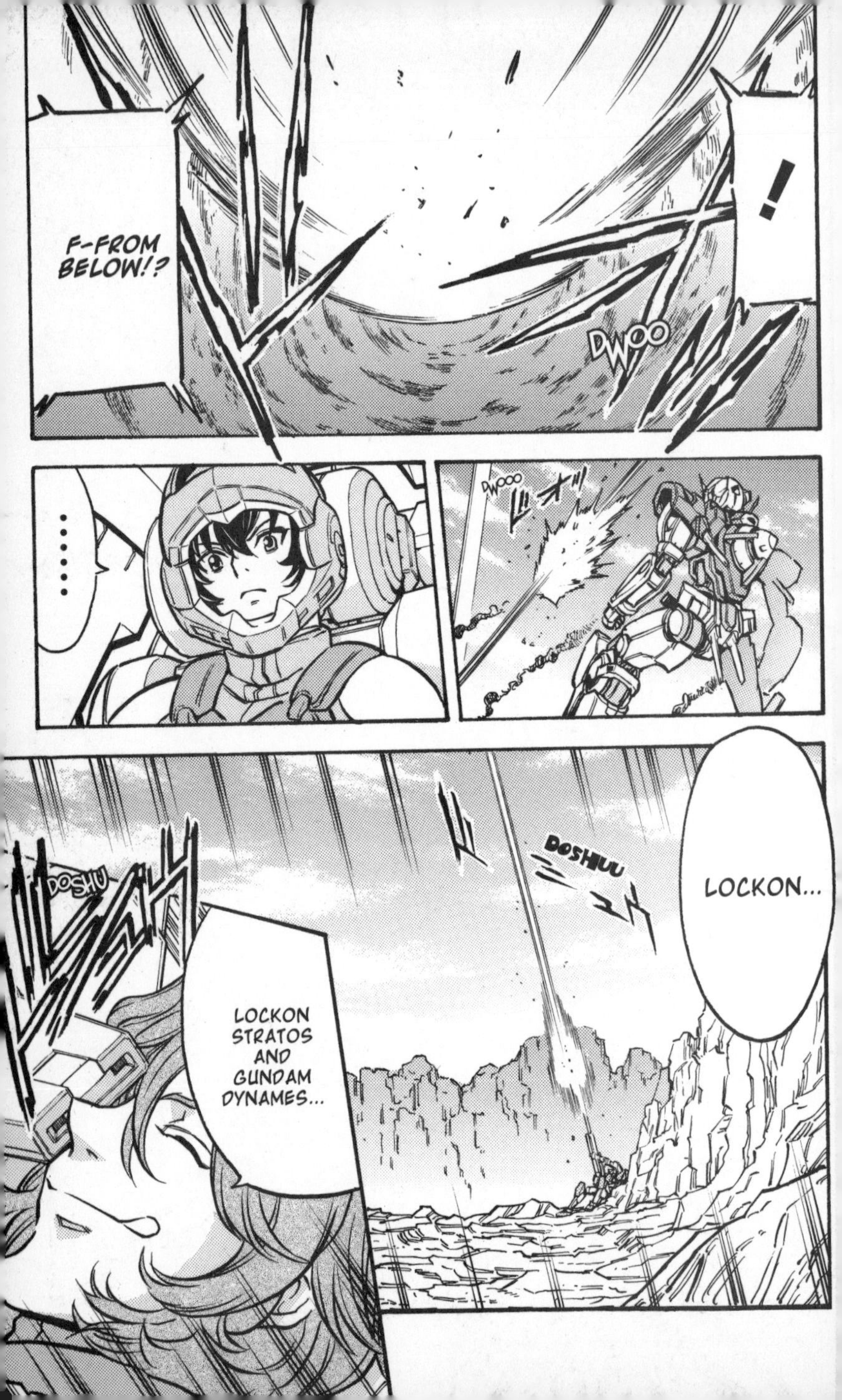
!
DWOO
F-FROM BELOW!?
DWOOO
......
LOCKON...
DOSHUU
DOSHU
LOCKON STRATOS AND GUNDAM DYNAMES...

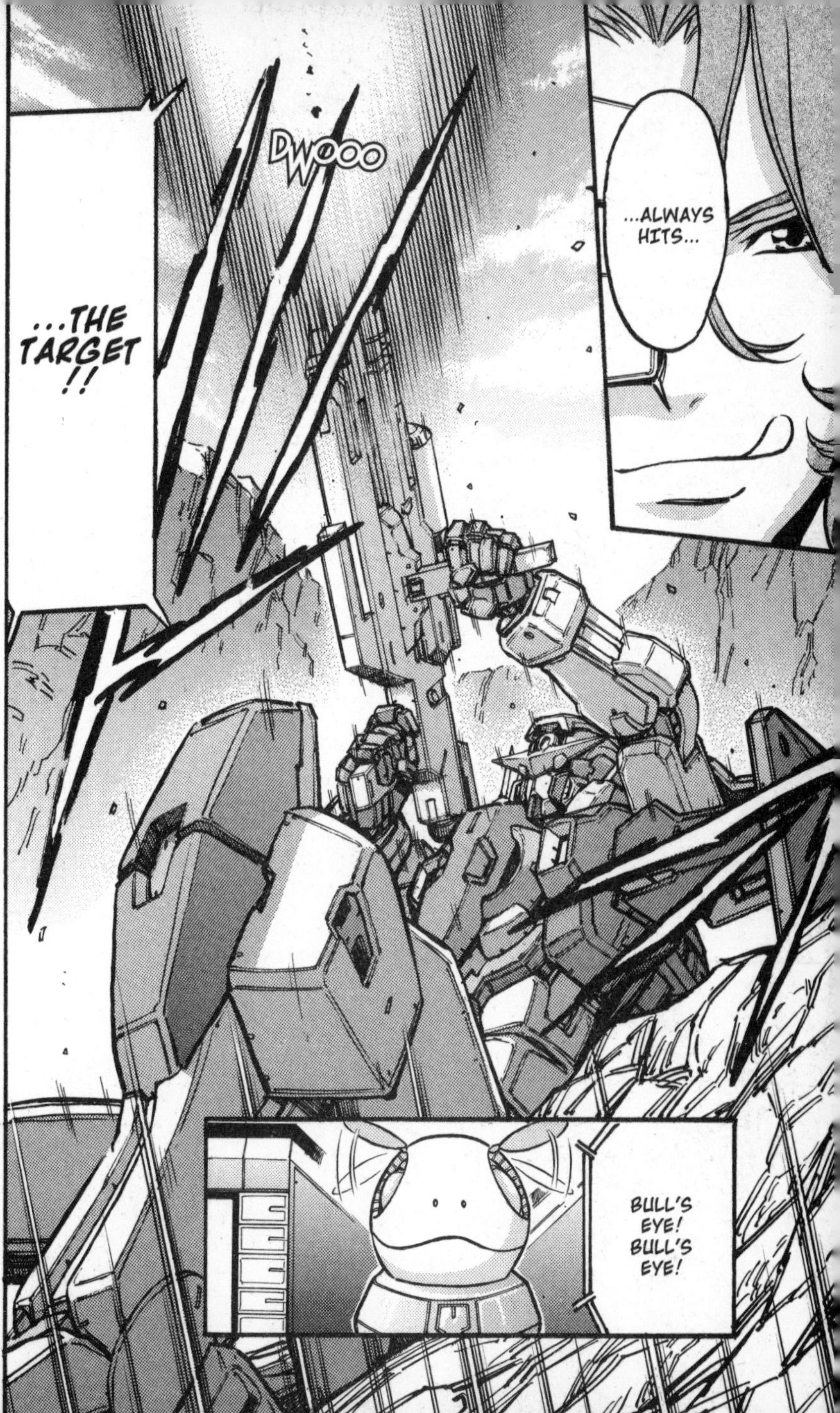
...ALWAYS HITS...
...THE TARGET!!
DWOOO
BULL'S EYE! BULL'S EYE!

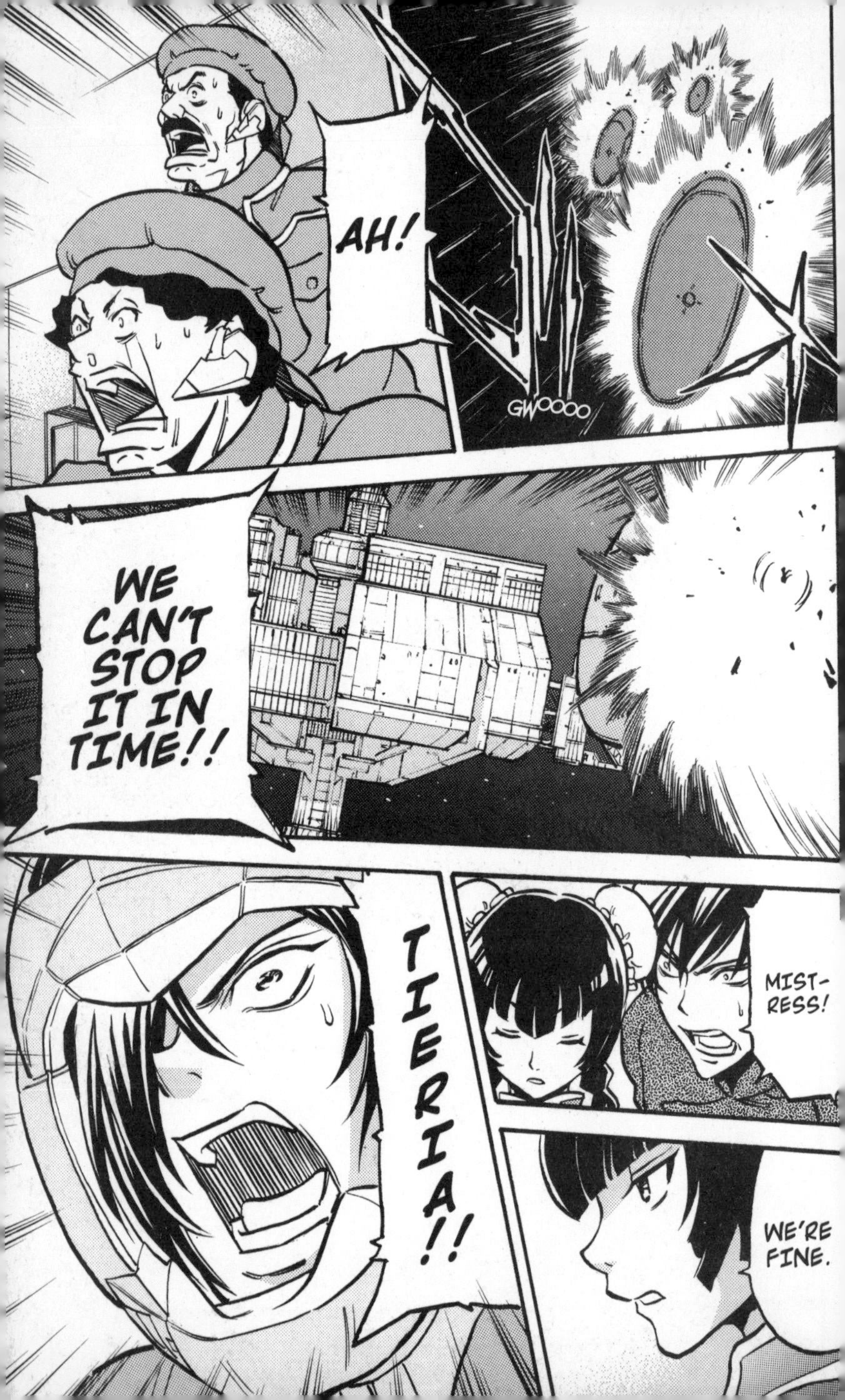
AH!
GWOOOO
WE CAN'T STOP IT IN TIME!!
MIST-RESS!
WE'RE FINE.
TIERIA!!

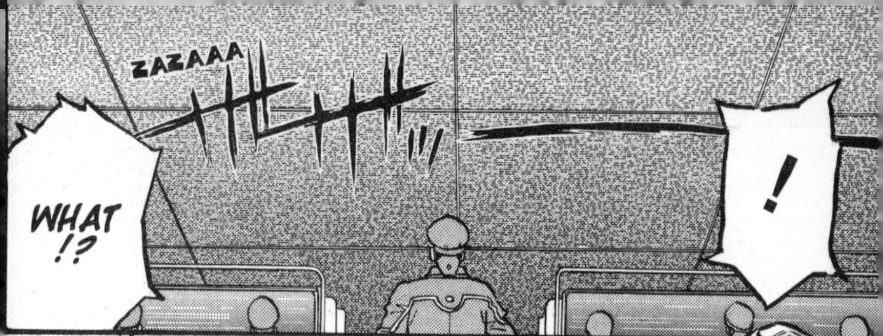
!
ZAZAAA
WHAT !?
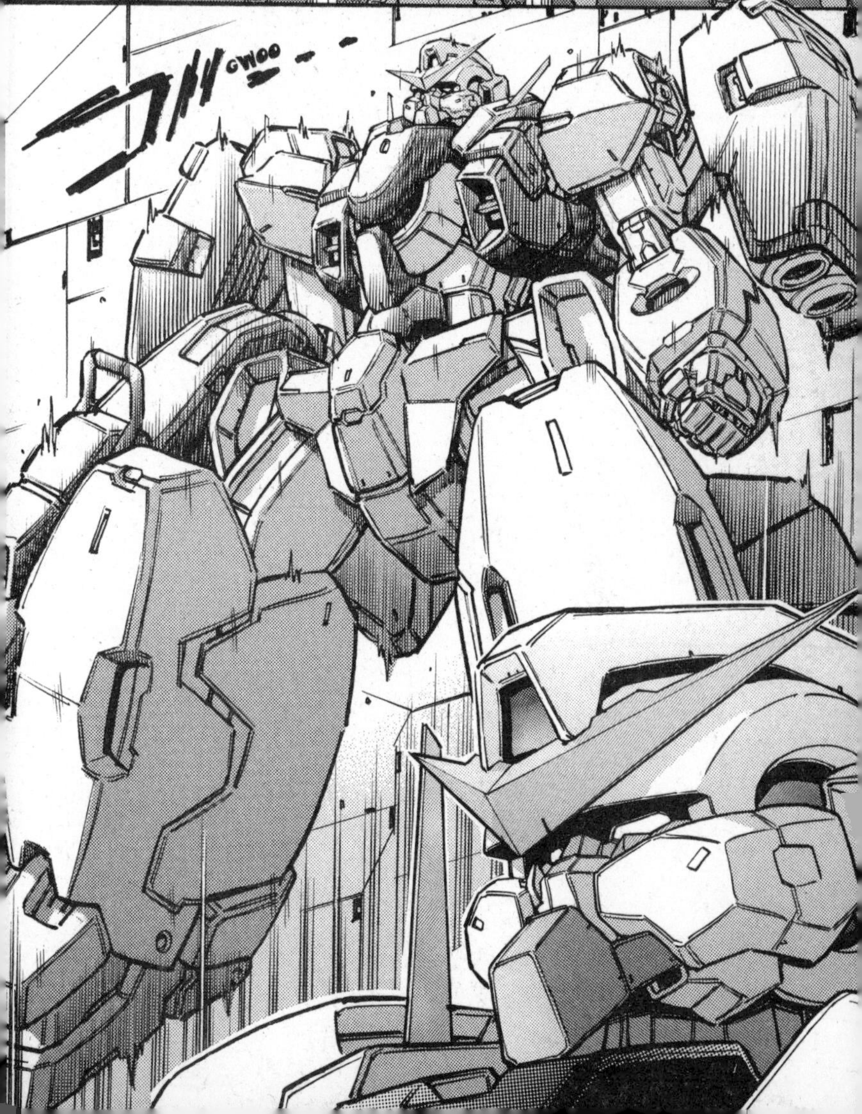
GWOO

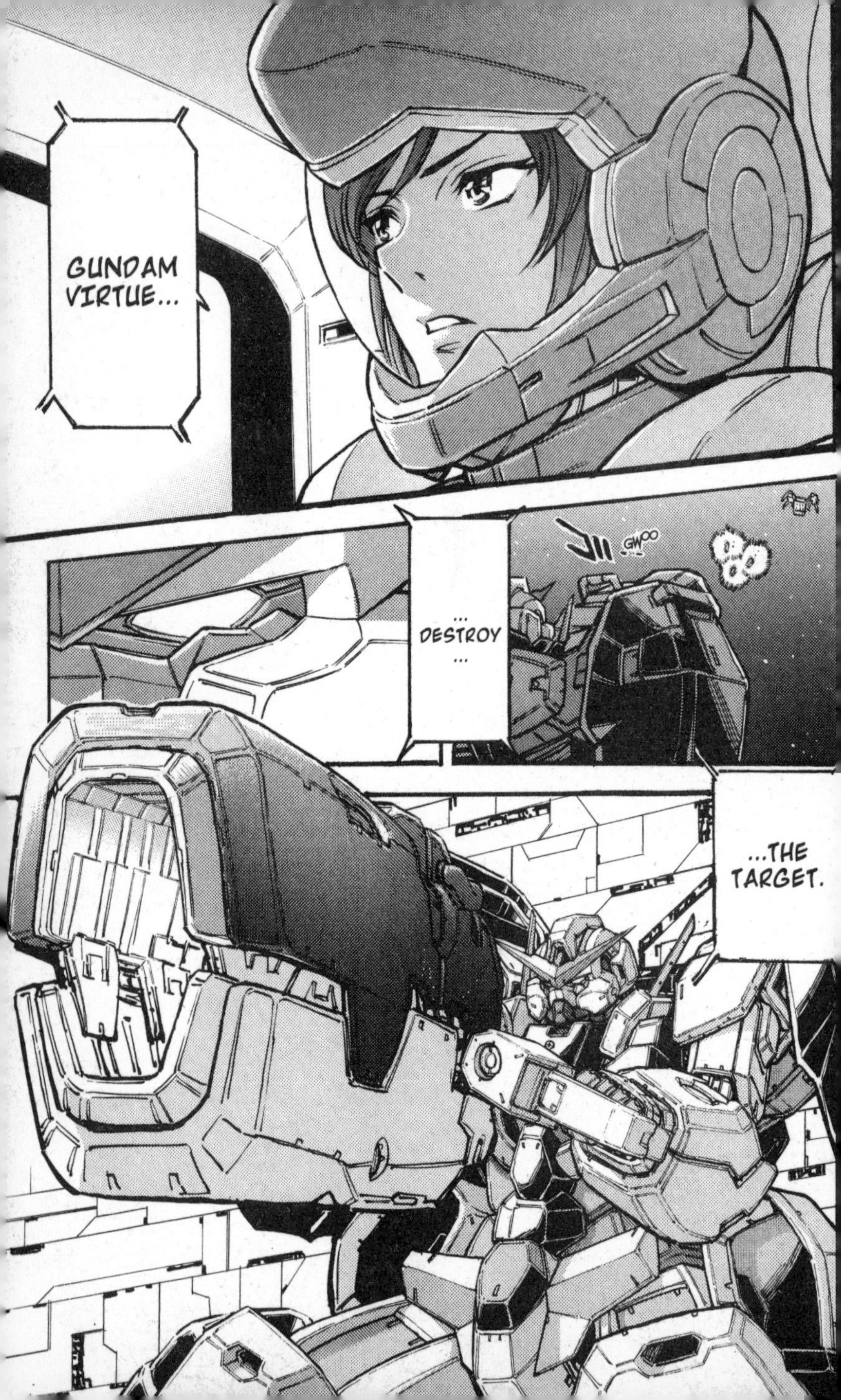
GUNDAM VIRTUE...
GWOO
...DESTROY...
...THE TARGET.

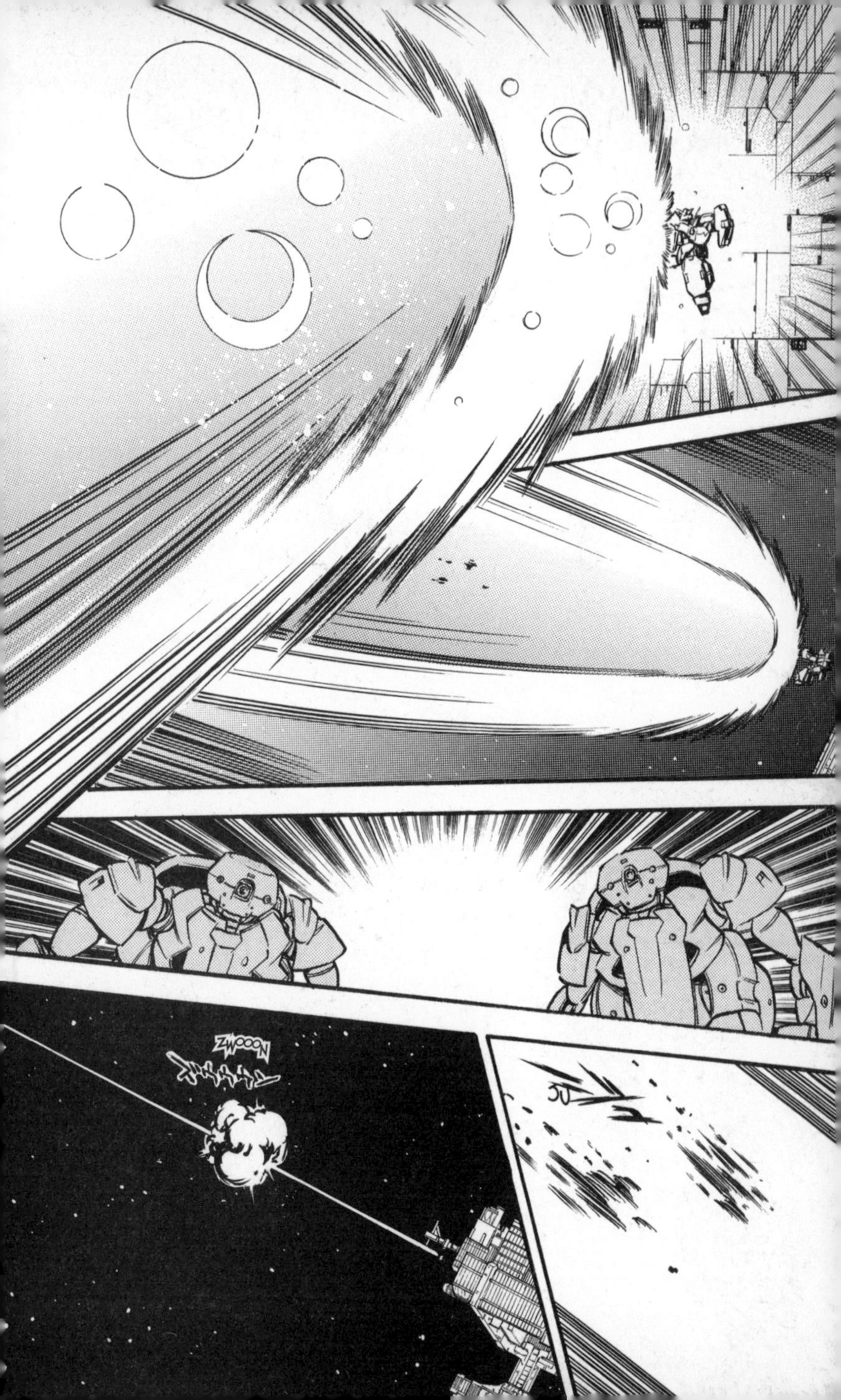
ZWOOON

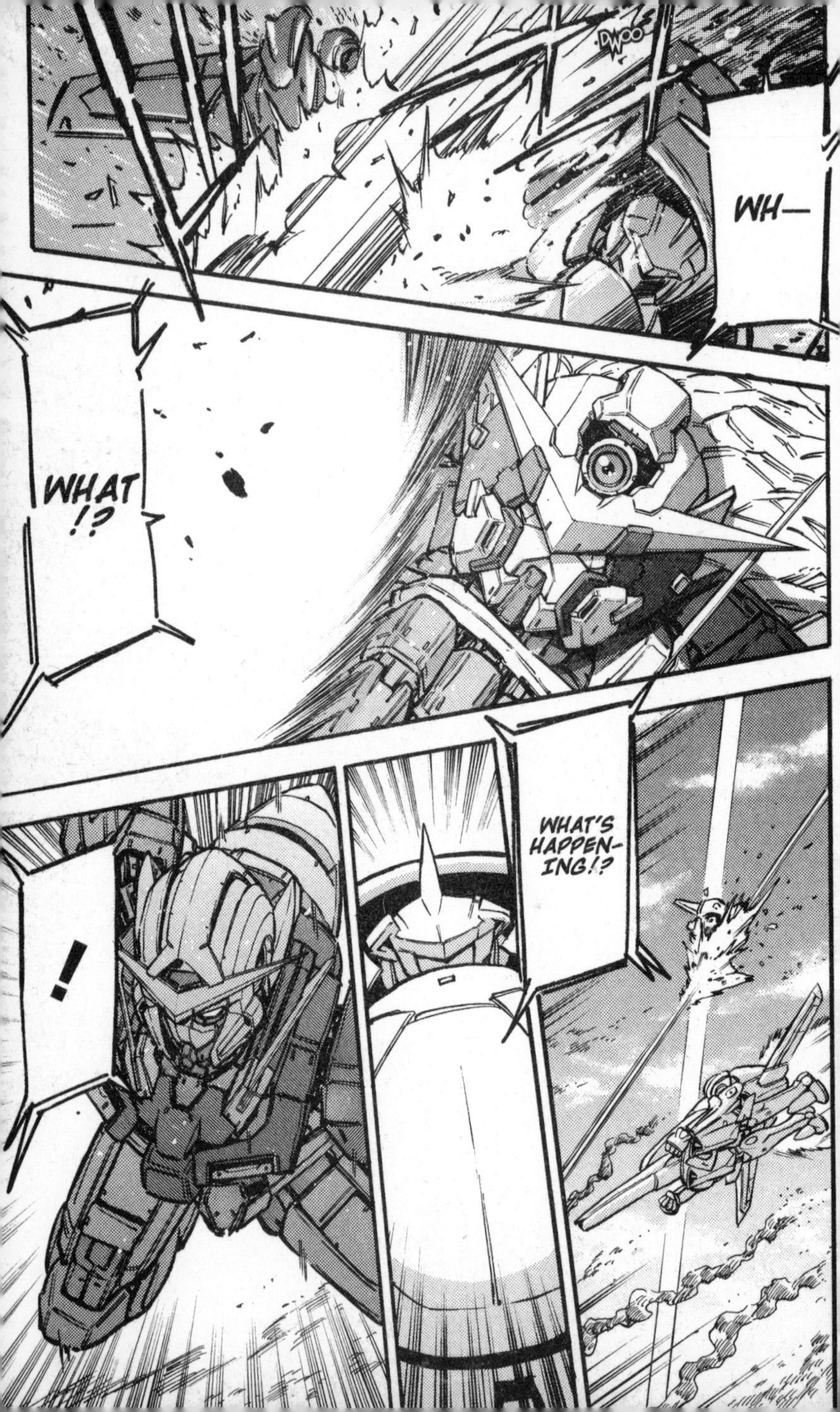
DWOO
WH—
WHAT !?
WHAT'S HAPPEN-ING!?
!

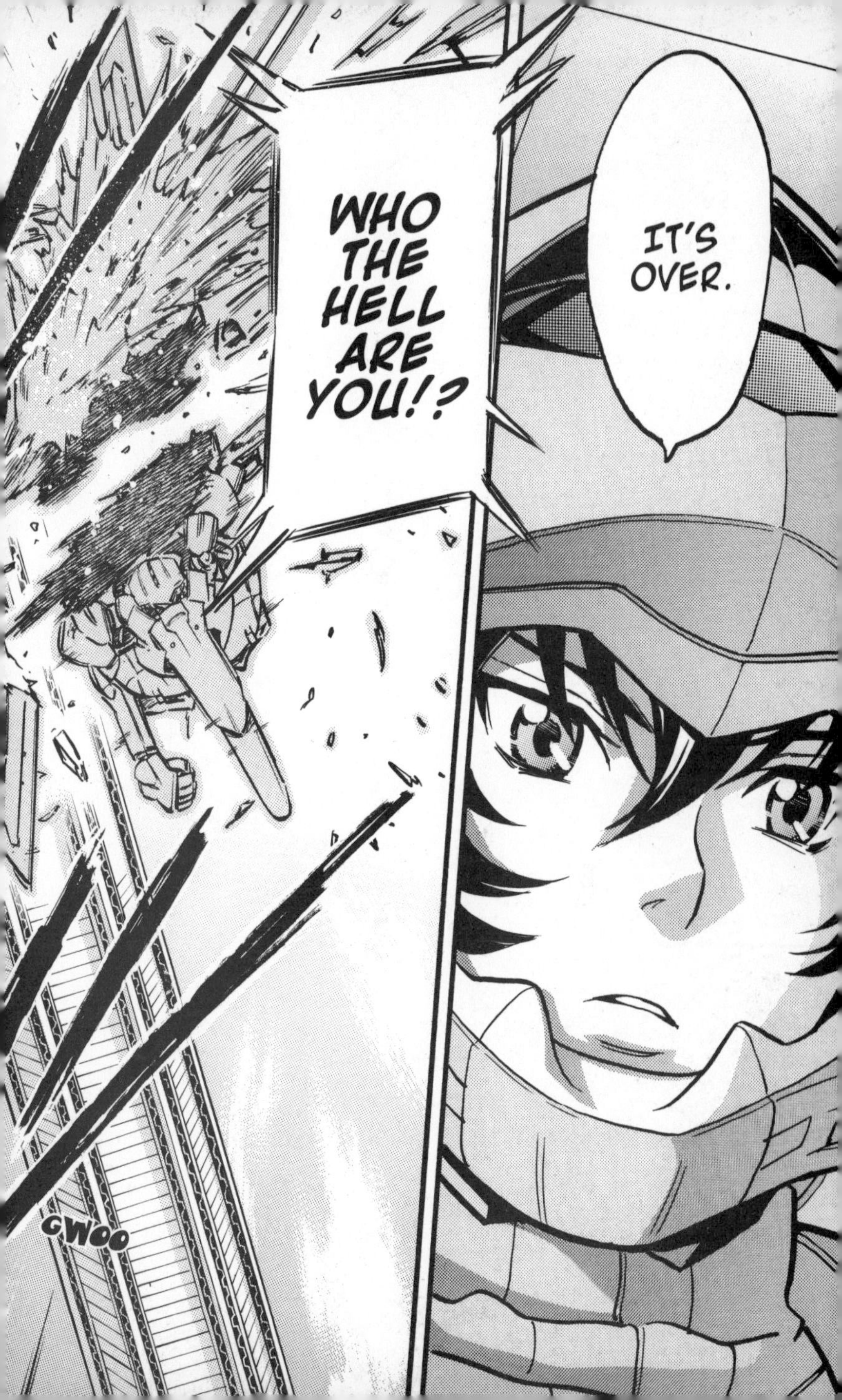
IT'S OVER.
WHO THE HELL ARE YOU!?
GWOO

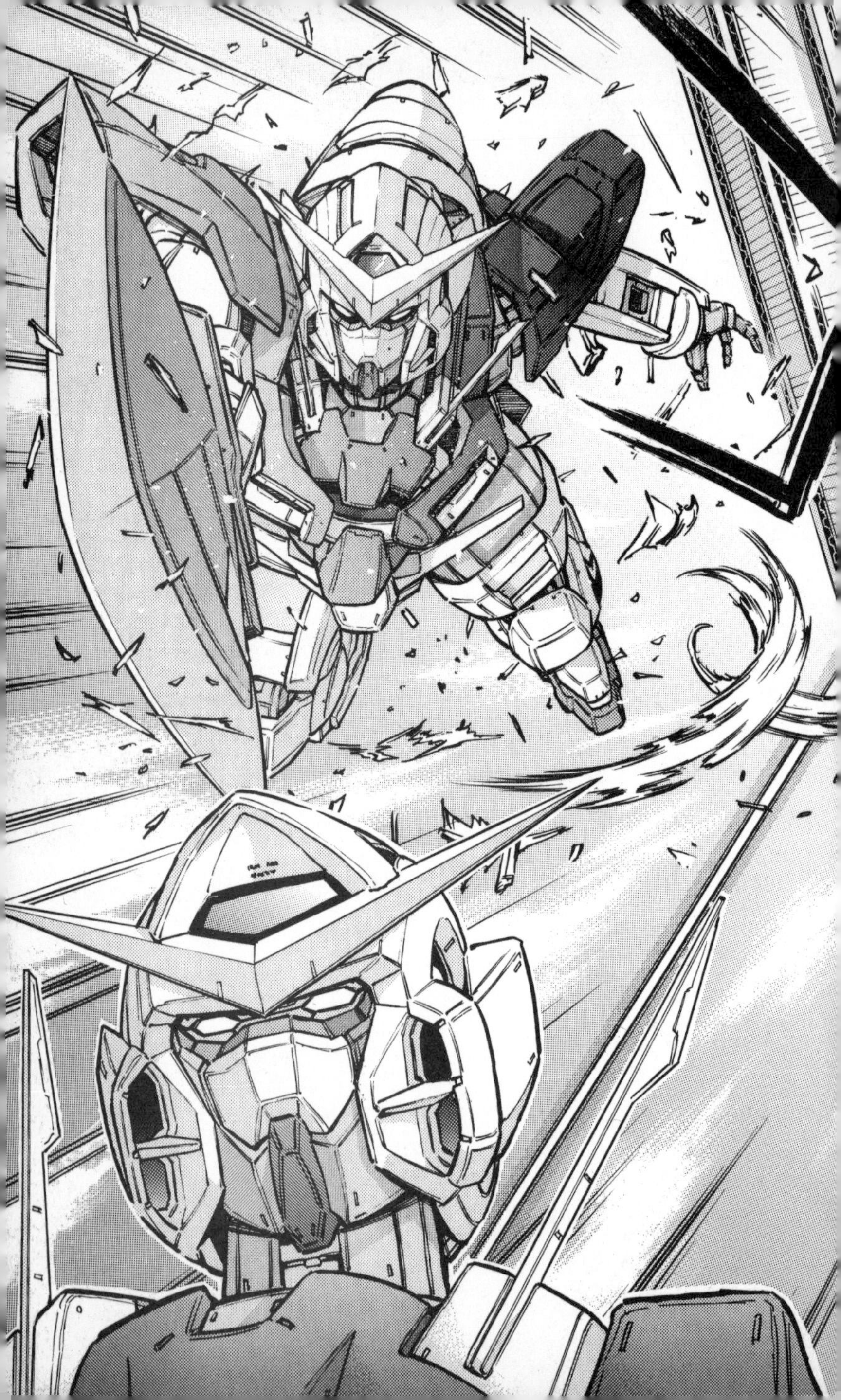

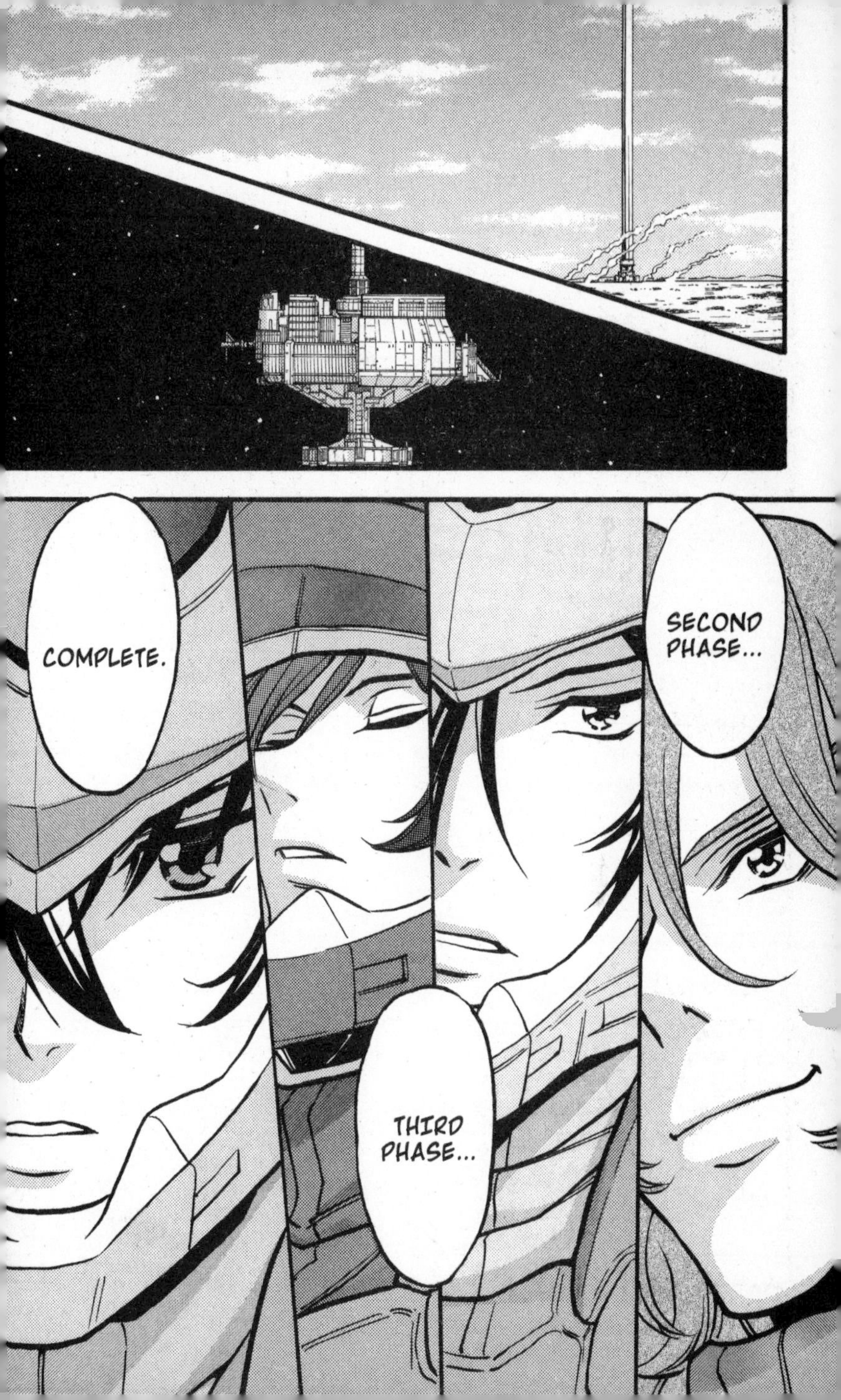
SECOND PHASE...
THIRD PHASE...
COMPLETE.

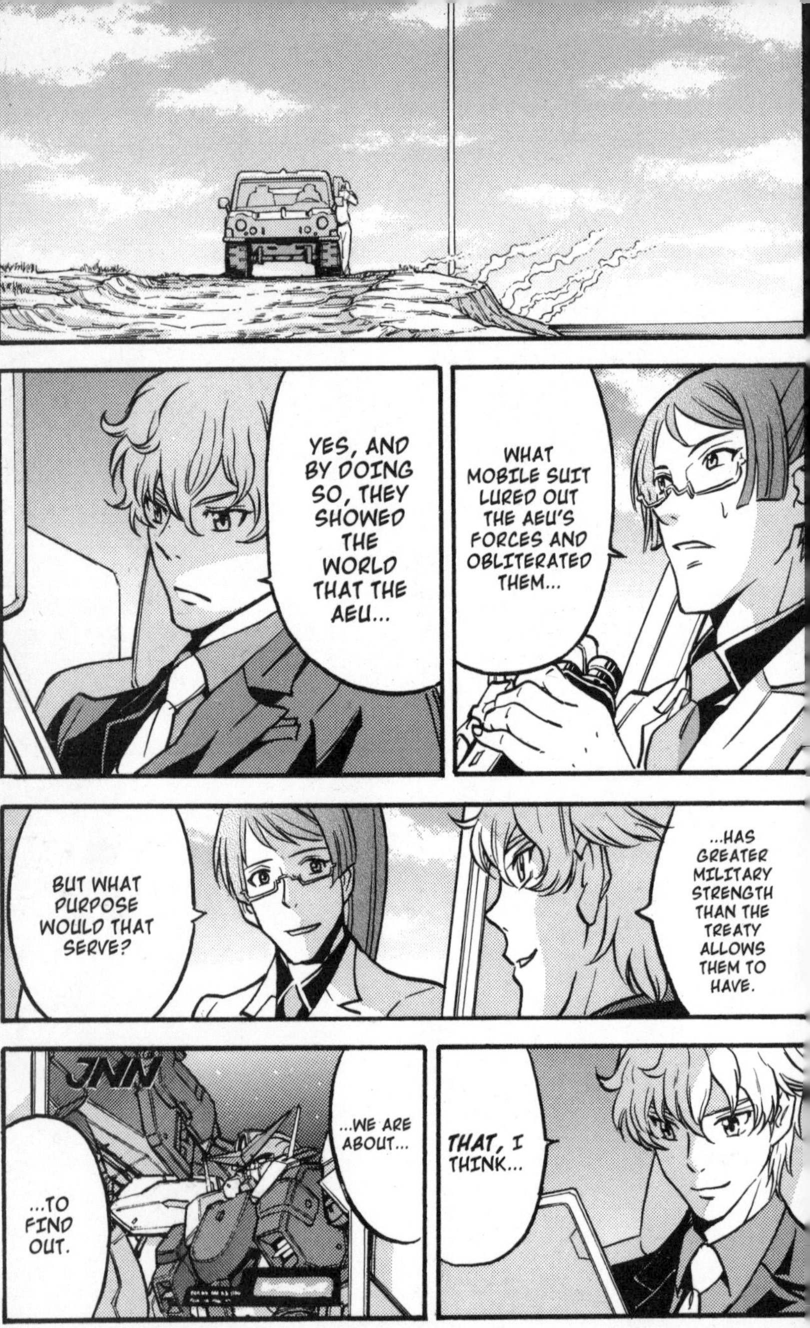
WHAT MOBILE SUIT LURED OUT THE AEU'S FORCES AND OBLITERATED THEM...
YES, AND BY DOING SO, THEY SHOWED THE WORLD THAT THE AEU...
...HAS GREATER MILITARY STRENGTH THAN THE TREATY ALLOWS THEM TO HAVE.
BUT WHAT PURPOSE WOULD THAT SERVE?
THAT, I THINK...
...WE ARE ABOUT...
JNN
...TO FIND OUT.

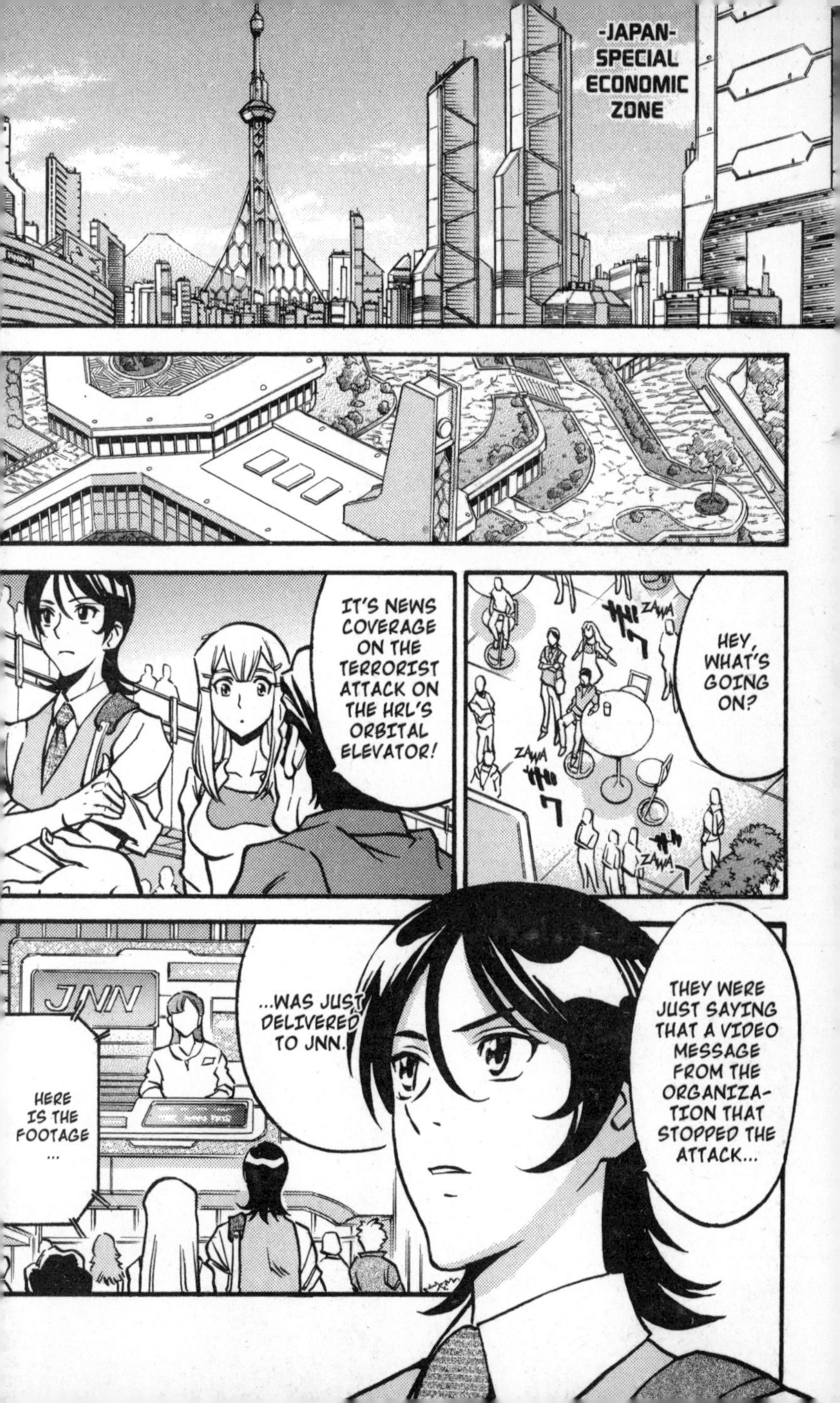
-JAPAN-
SPECIAL ECONOMIC ZONE
HEY, WHAT'S GOING ON?
ZAWA
ZAWA
ZAWA
IT'S NEWS COVERAGE ON THE TERRORIST ATTACK ON THE HRL'S ORBITAL ELEVATOR!
THEY WERE JUST SAYING THAT A VIDEO MESSAGE FROM THE ORGANIZATION THAT STOPPED THE ATTACK...
...WAS JUST DELIVERED TO JNN.
JNN
HERE IS THE FOOTAGE...

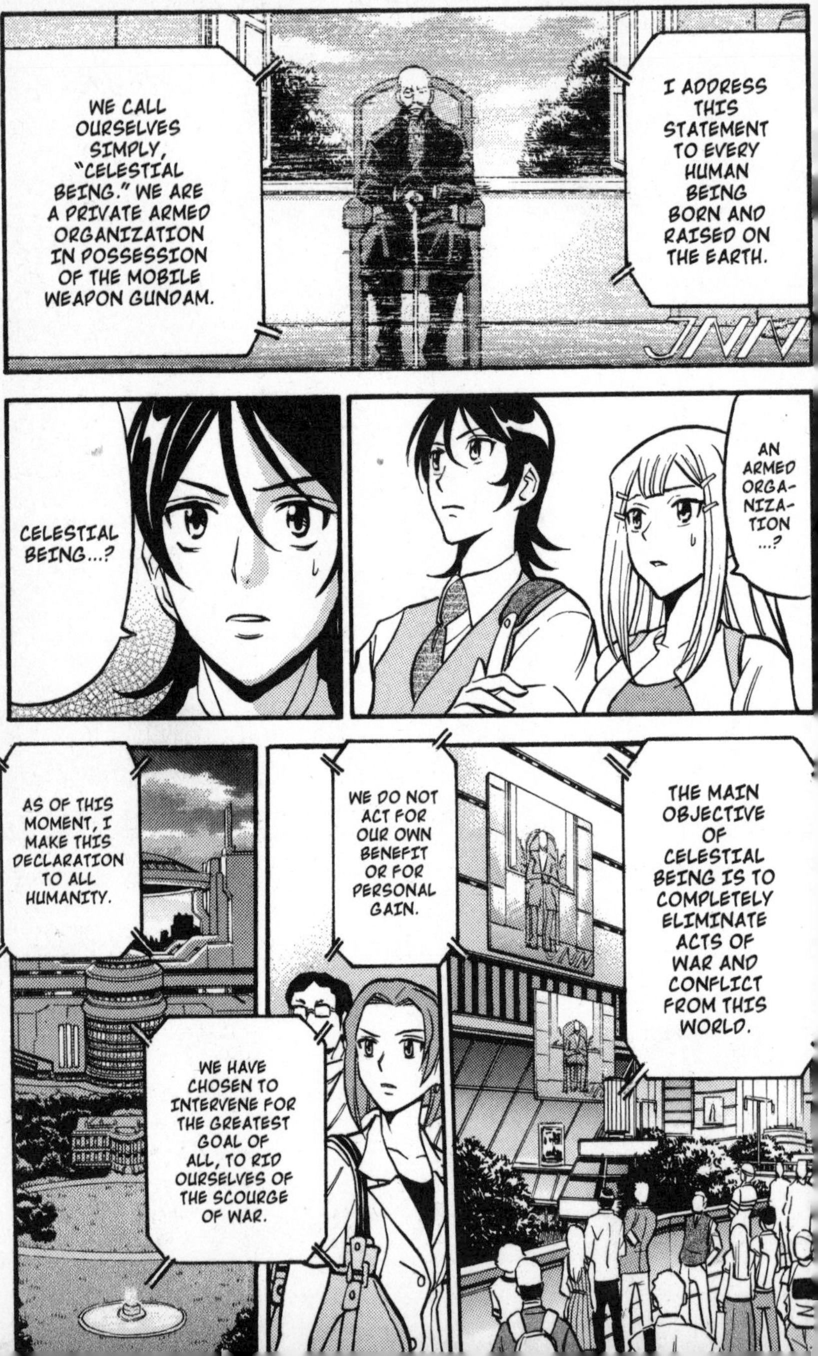
I ADDRESS THIS STATEMENT TO EVERY HUMAN BEING BORN AND RAISED ON THE EARTH.
WE CALL OURSELVES SIMPLY, "CELESTIAL BEING." WE ARE A PRIVATE ARMED ORGANIZATION IN POSSESSION OF THE MOBILE WEAPON GUNDAM.
JNN
AN ARMED ORGA-NIZA-TION ...?
CELESTIAL BEING...?
THE MAIN OBJECTIVE OF CELESTIAL BEING IS TO COMPLETELY ELIMINATE ACTS OF WAR AND CONFLICT FROM THIS WORLD.
WE DO NOT ACT FOR OUR OWN BENEFIT OR FOR PERSONAL GAIN.
AS OF THIS MOMENT, I MAKE THIS DECLARATION TO ALL HUMANITY.
WE HAVE CHOSEN TO INTERVENE FOR THE GREATEST GOAL OF ALL, TO RID OURSELVES OF THE SCOURGE OF WAR.

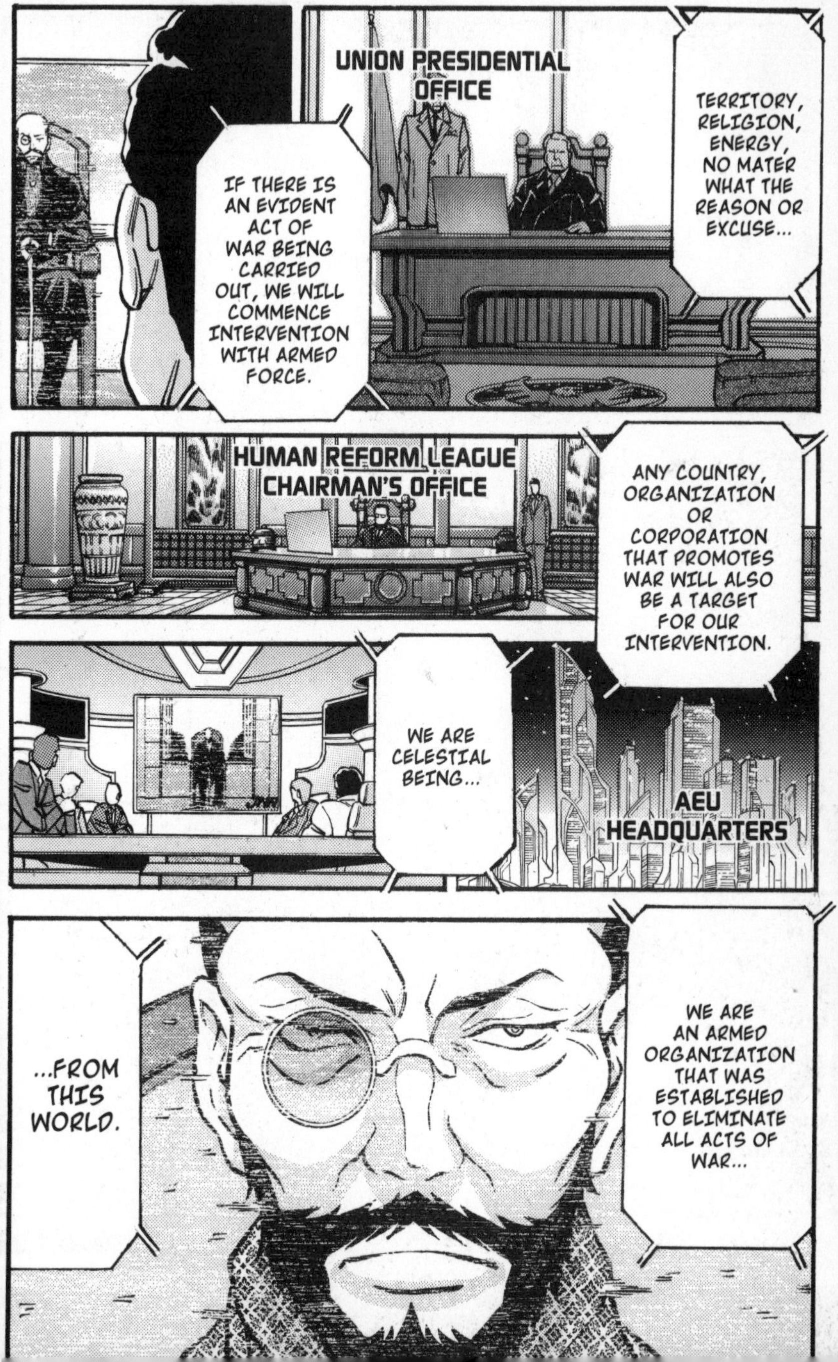
UNION PRESIDENTIAL OFFICE
TERRITORY, RELIGION, ENERGY, NO MATER WHAT THE REASON OR EXCUSE...
IF THERE IS AN EVIDENT ACT OF WAR BEING CARRIED OUT, WE WILL COMMENCE INTERVENTION WITH ARMED FORCE.
HUMAN REFORM LEAGUE CHAIRMAN'S OFFICE
ANY COUNTRY, ORGANIZATION OR CORPORATION THAT PROMOTES WAR WILL ALSO BE A TARGET FOR OUR INTERVENTION.
AEU HEADQUARTERS
WE ARE CELESTIAL BEING...
WE ARE AN ARMED ORGANIZATION THAT WAS ESTABLISHED TO ELIMINATE ALL ACTS OF WAR...
...FROM THIS WORLD.

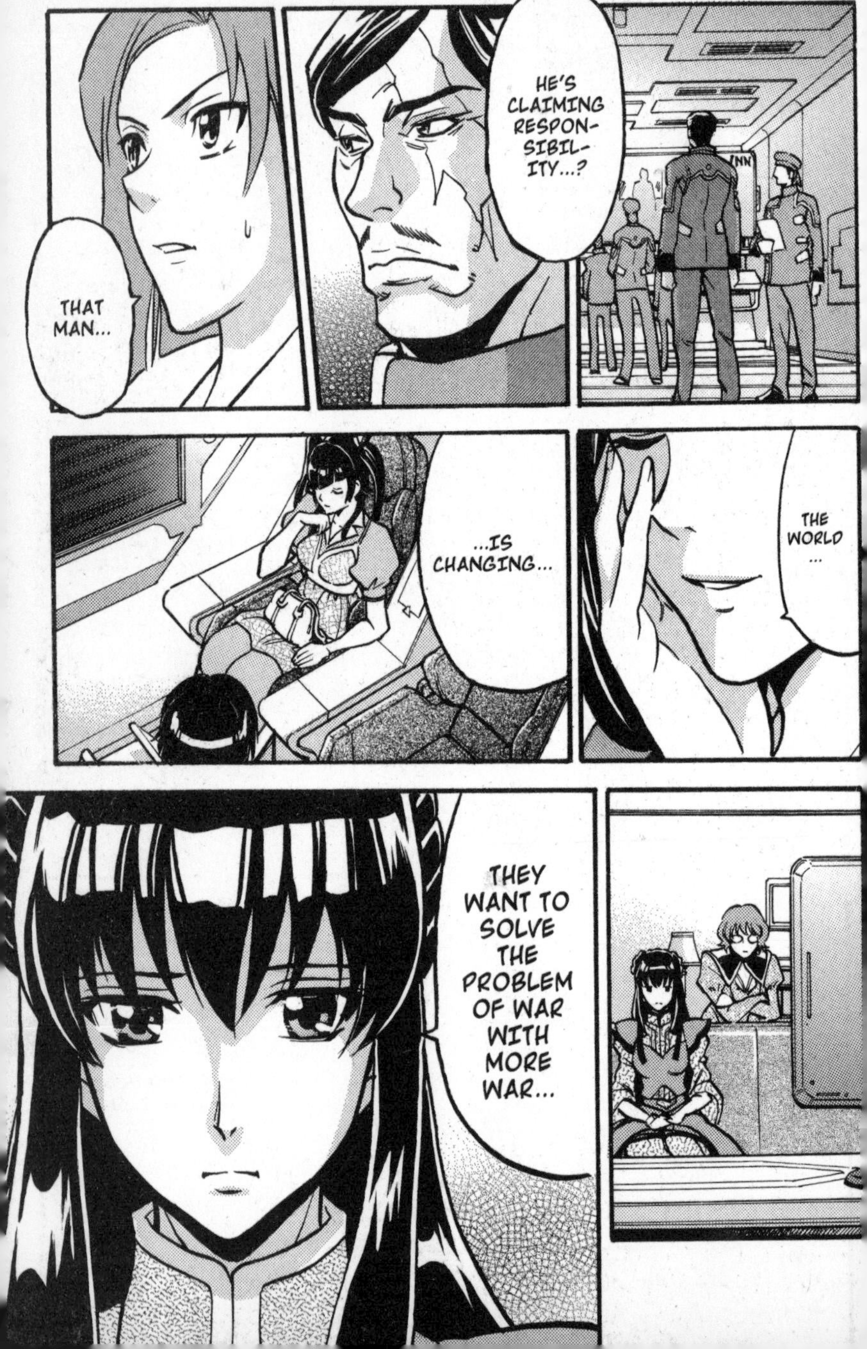
HE'S CLAIMING RESPON-SIBIL-ITY...?
THAT MAN...
THE WORLD ...
...IS CHANGING...
THEY WANT TO SOLVE THE PROBLEM OF WAR WITH MORE WAR...

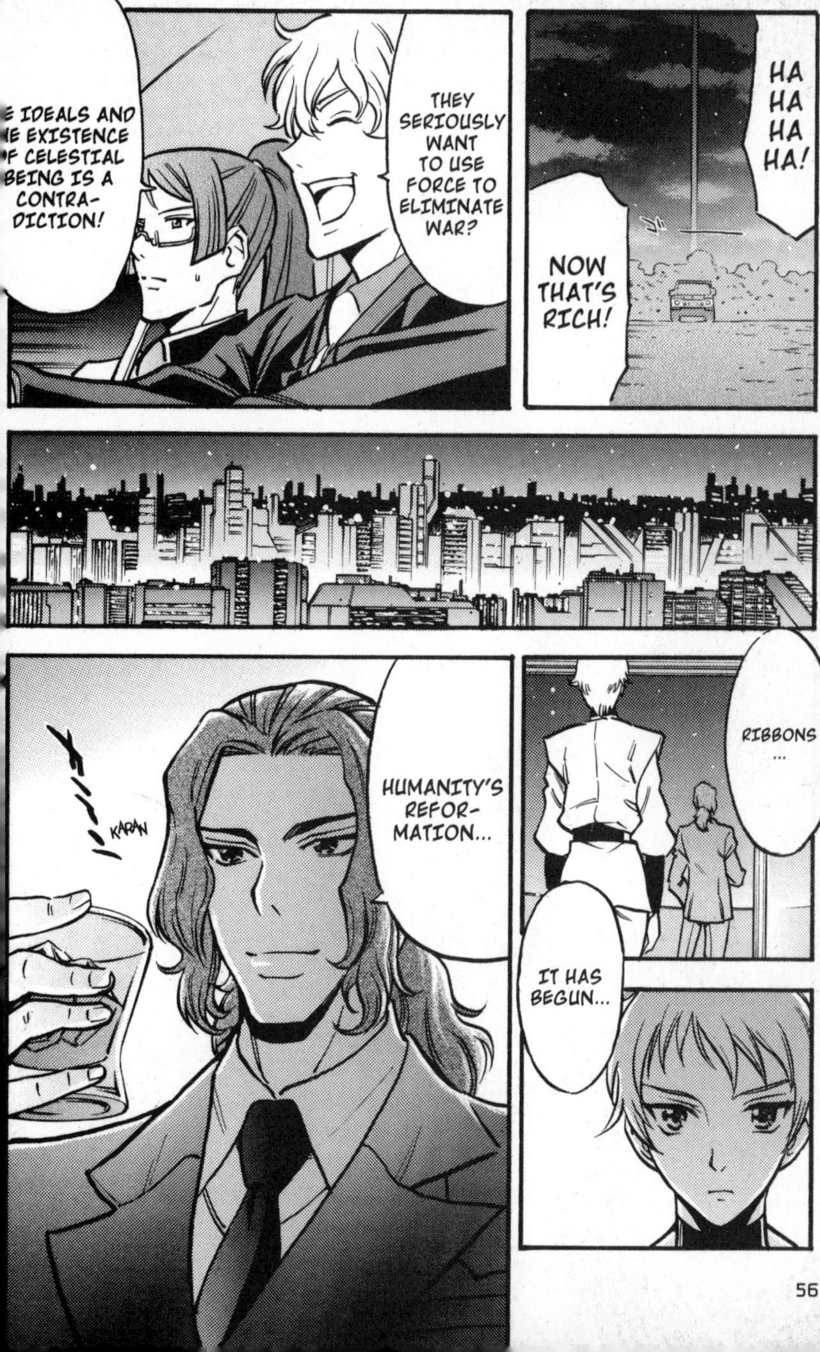
HA HA HA HA!
NOW THAT'S RICH!
THEY SERIOUSLY WANT TO USE FORCE TO ELIMINATE WAR?
E IDEALS AND E EXISTENCE F CELESTIAL BEING IS A CONTRA-DICTION!
RIBBONS ...
IT HAS BEGUN...
HUMANITY'S REFOR-MATION...
KARAN

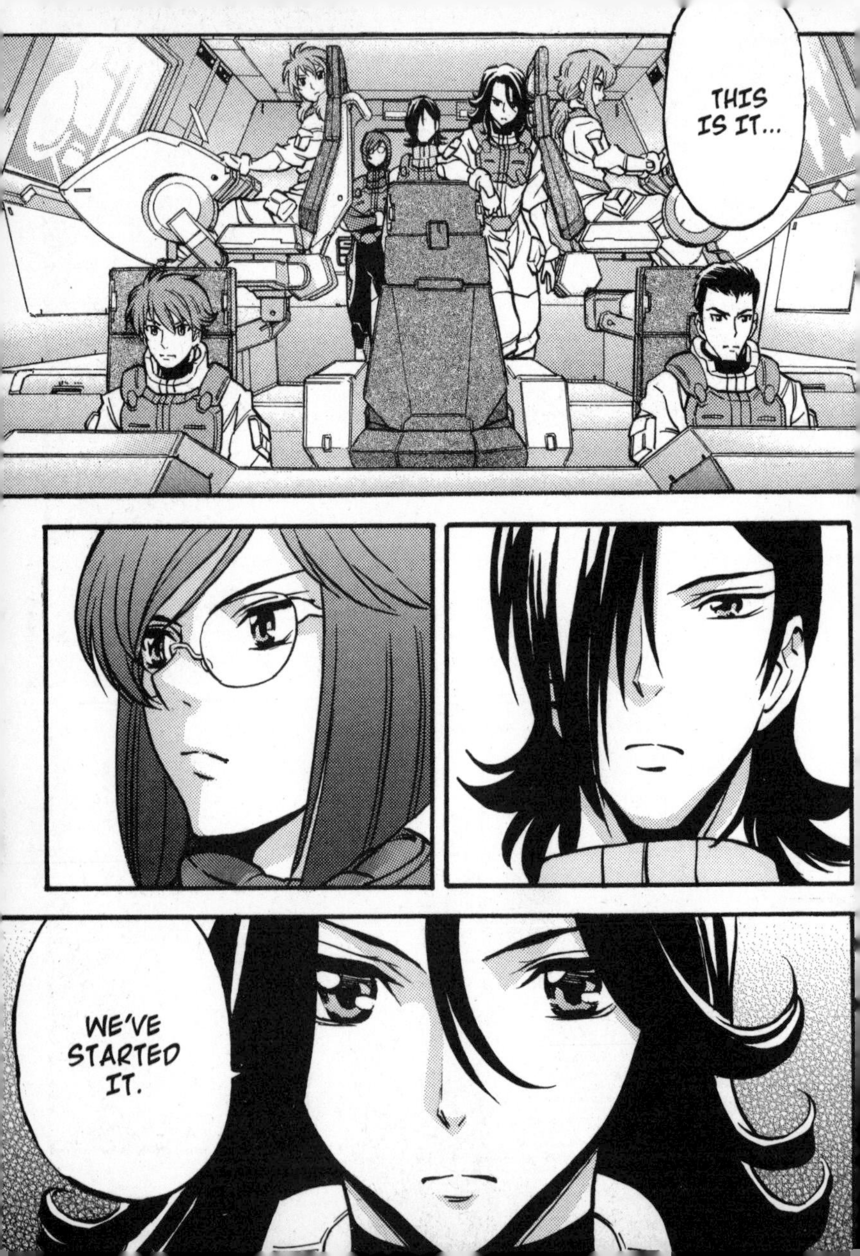
THIS IS IT...
WE'VE STARTED IT.

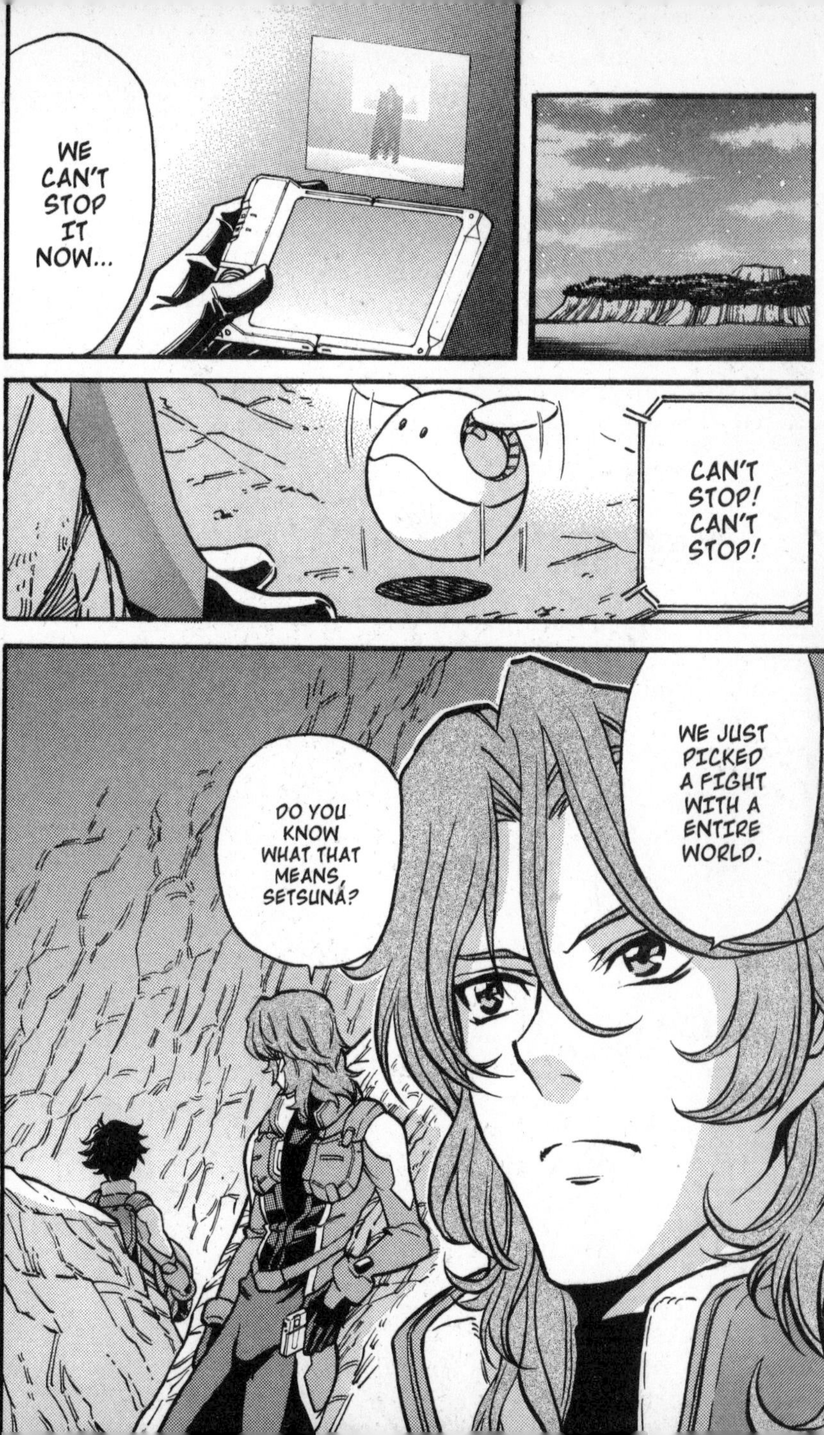
WE CAN'T STOP IT NOW...
CAN'T STOP! CAN'T STOP!
WE JUST PICKED A FIGHT WITH A ENTIRE WORLD.
DO YOU KNOW WHAT THAT MEANS, SETSUNA?

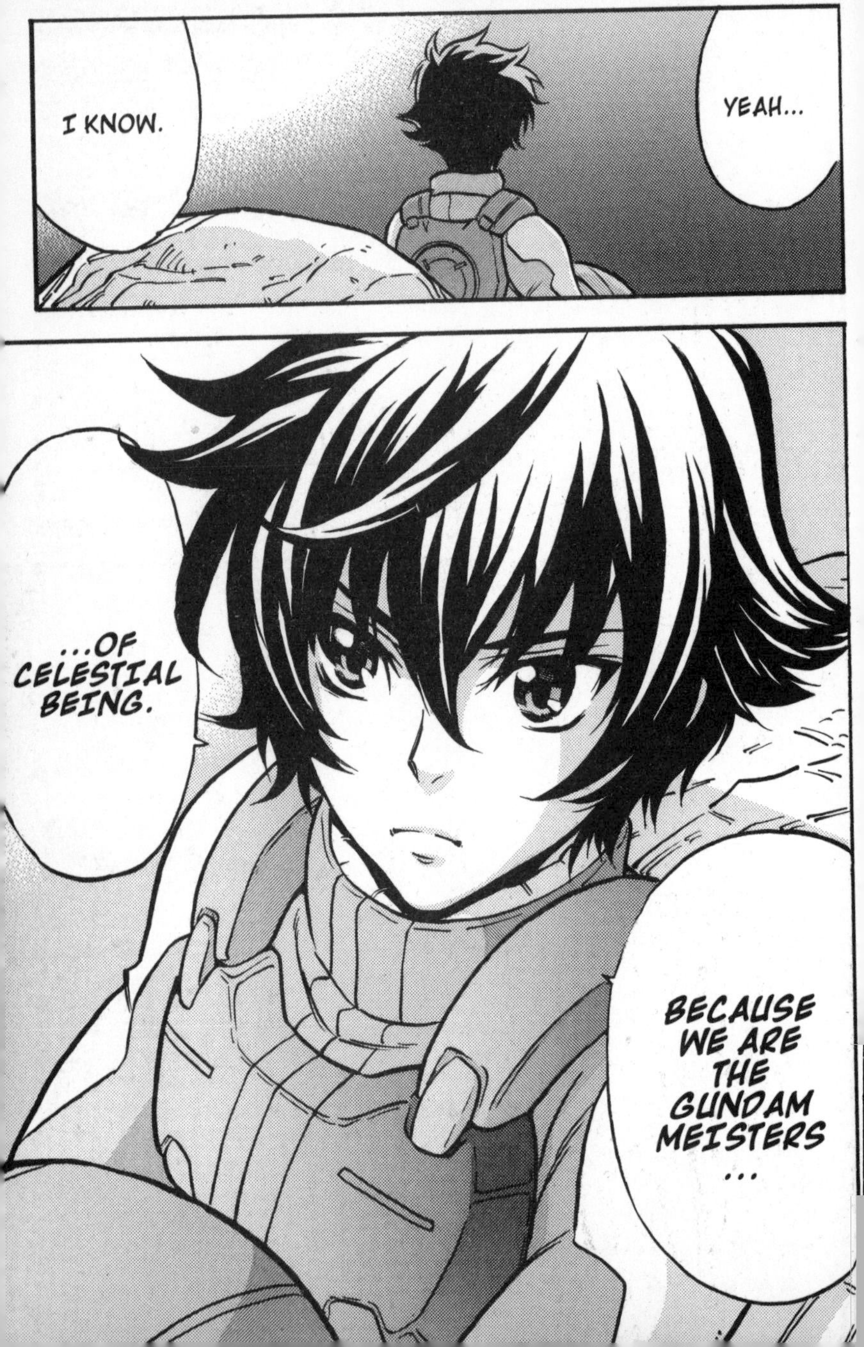
YEAH...
I KNOW.
BECAUSE WE ARE THE GUNDAM MEISTERS ...
...OF CELESTIAL BEING.

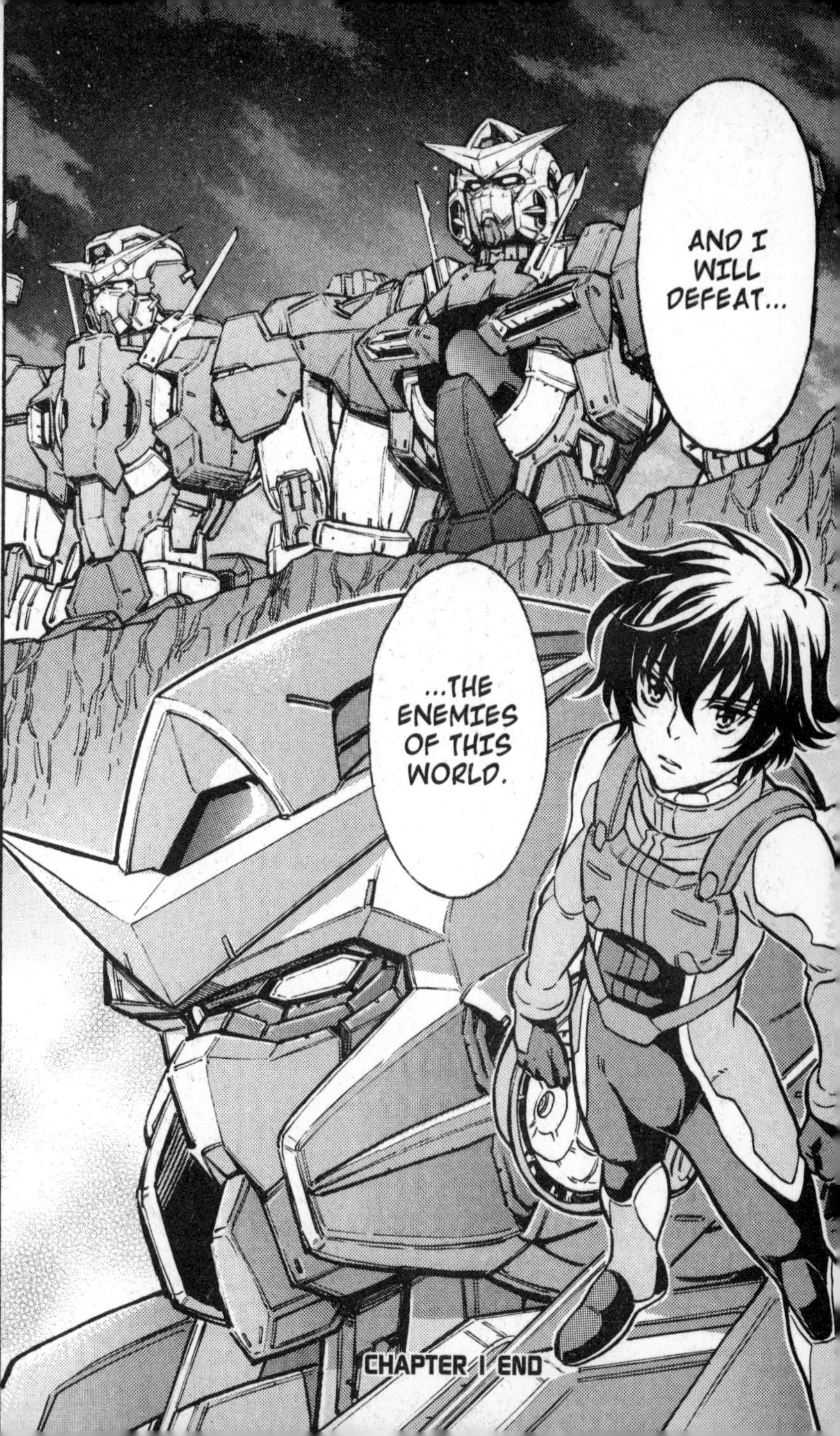
AND I WILL DEFEAT...
...THE ENEMIES OF THIS WORLD.
CHAPTER 1 END

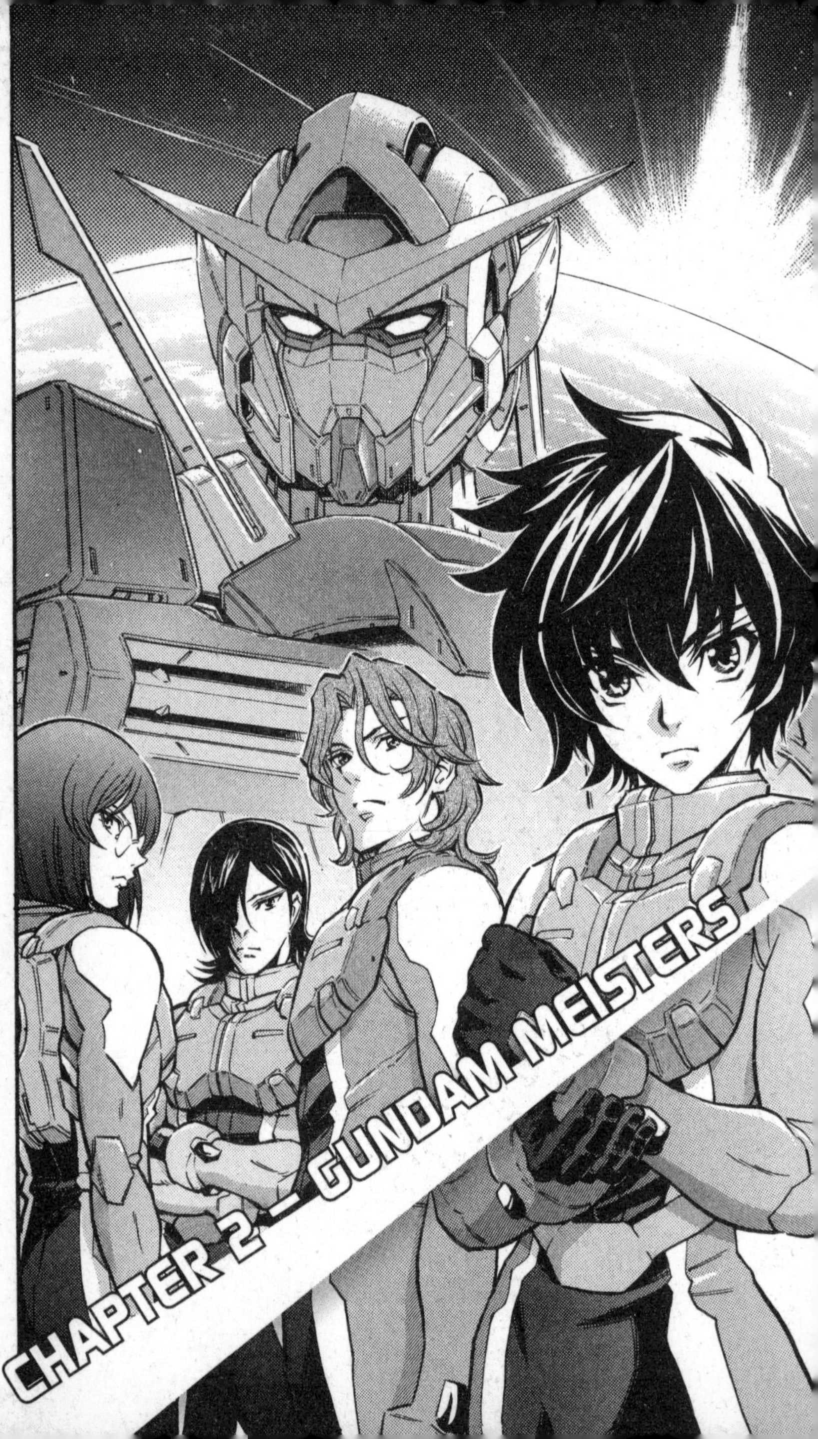
CHAPTER 2 — GUNDAM MEISTERS

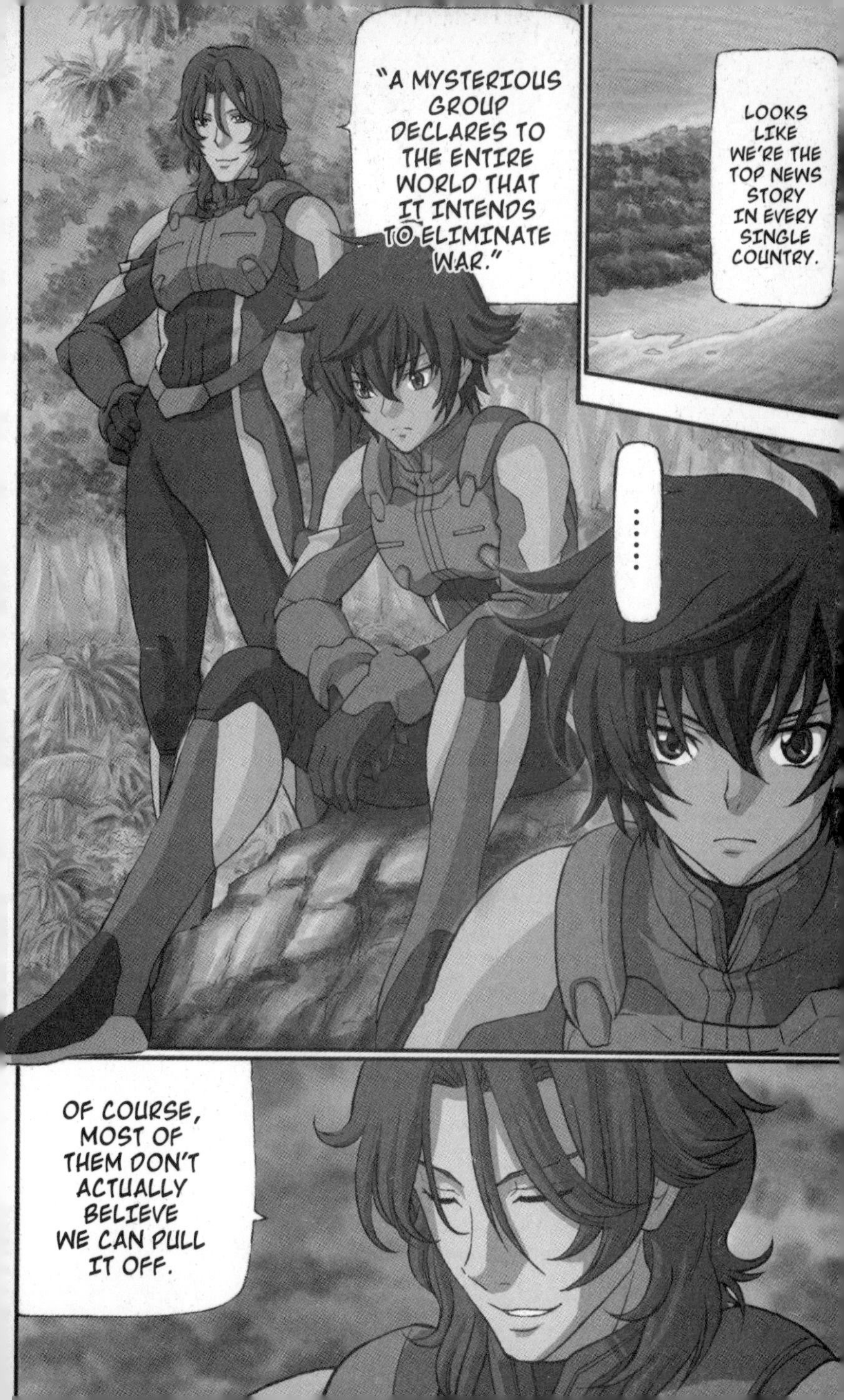
LOOKS LIKE WE'RE THE TOP NEWS STORY IN EVERY SINGLE COUNTRY.
"A MYSTERIOUS GROUP DECLARES TO THE ENTIRE WORLD THAT IT INTENDS TO ELIMINATE WAR."
......
OF COURSE, MOST OF THEM DON'T ACTUALLY BELIEVE WE CAN PULL IT OFF.

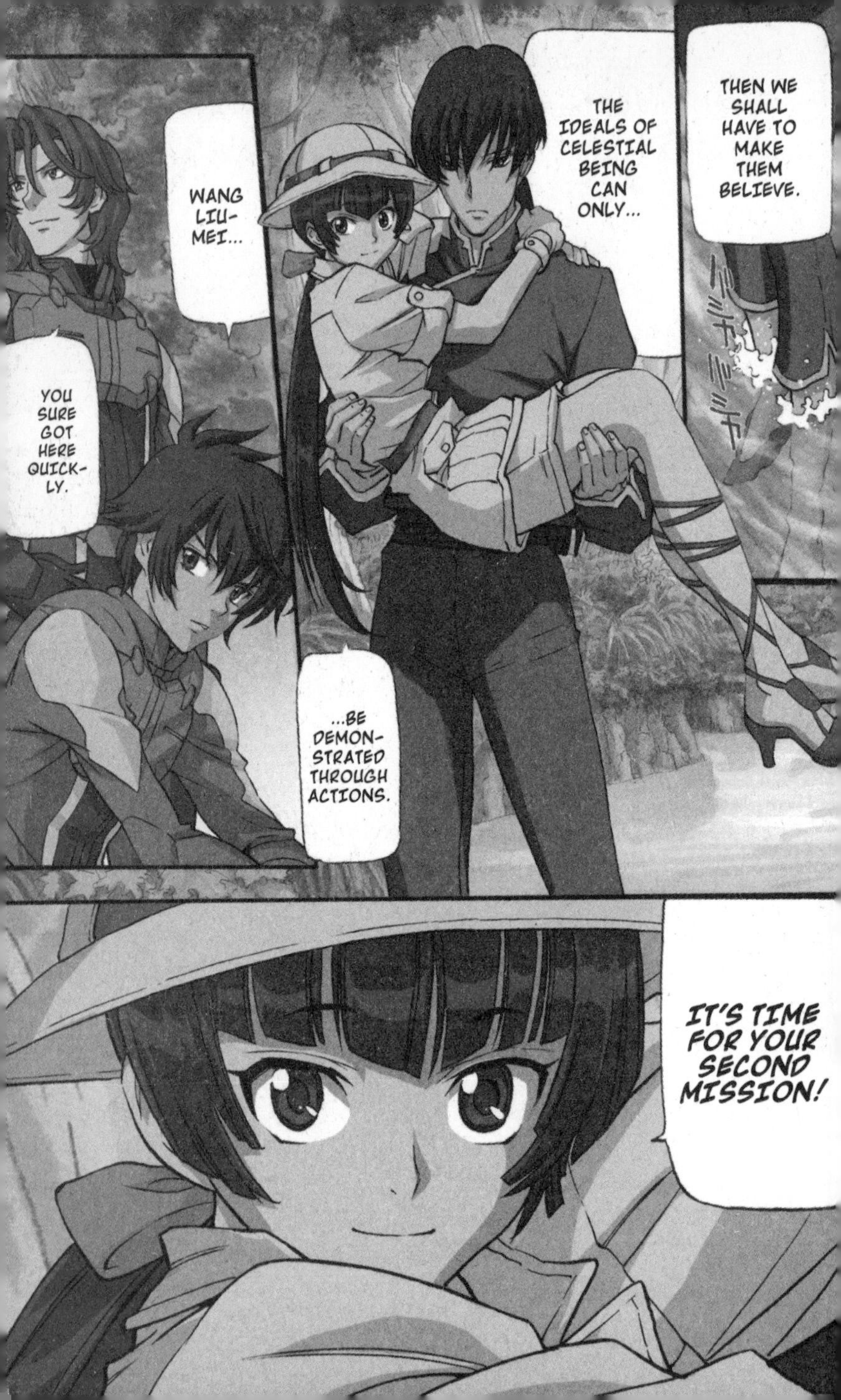
THEN WE SHALL HAVE TO MAKE THEM BELIEVE.
バシャ バシャ
THE IDEALS OF CELESTIAL BEING CAN ONLY...
...BE DEMONSTRATED THROUGH ACTIONS.
WANG LIU-MEI...
YOU SURE GOT HERE QUICKLY.
IT'S TIME FOR YOUR SECOND MISSION!

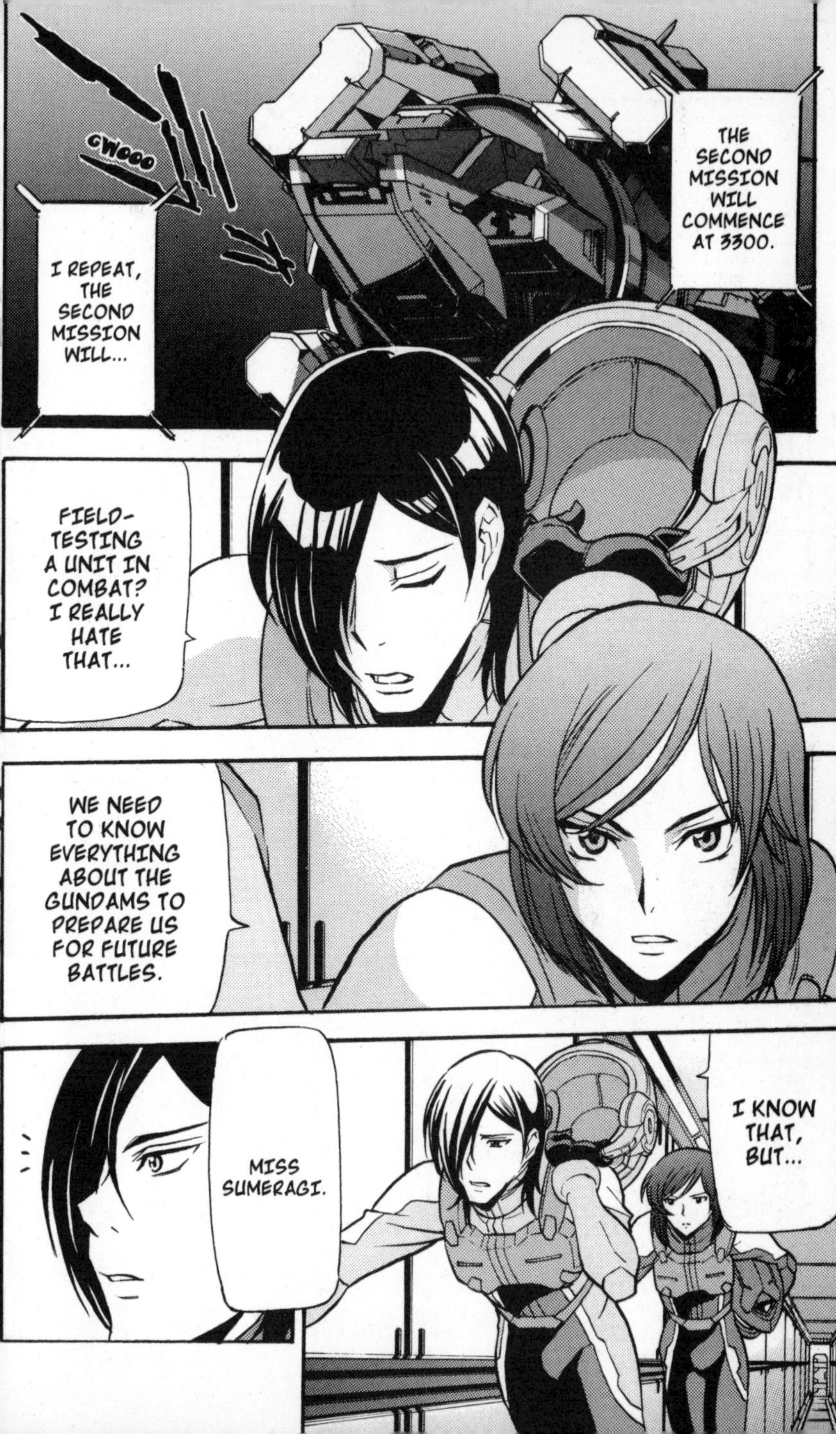
THE SECOND MISSION WILL COMMENCE AT 3300.
GWOOO
I REPEAT, THE SECOND MISSION WILL...
FIELD-TESTING A UNIT IN COMBAT? I REALLY HATE THAT...
WE NEED TO KNOW EVERYTHING ABOUT THE GUNDAMS TO PREPARE US FOR FUTURE BATTLES.
I KNOW THAT, BUT...
MISS SUMERAGI.

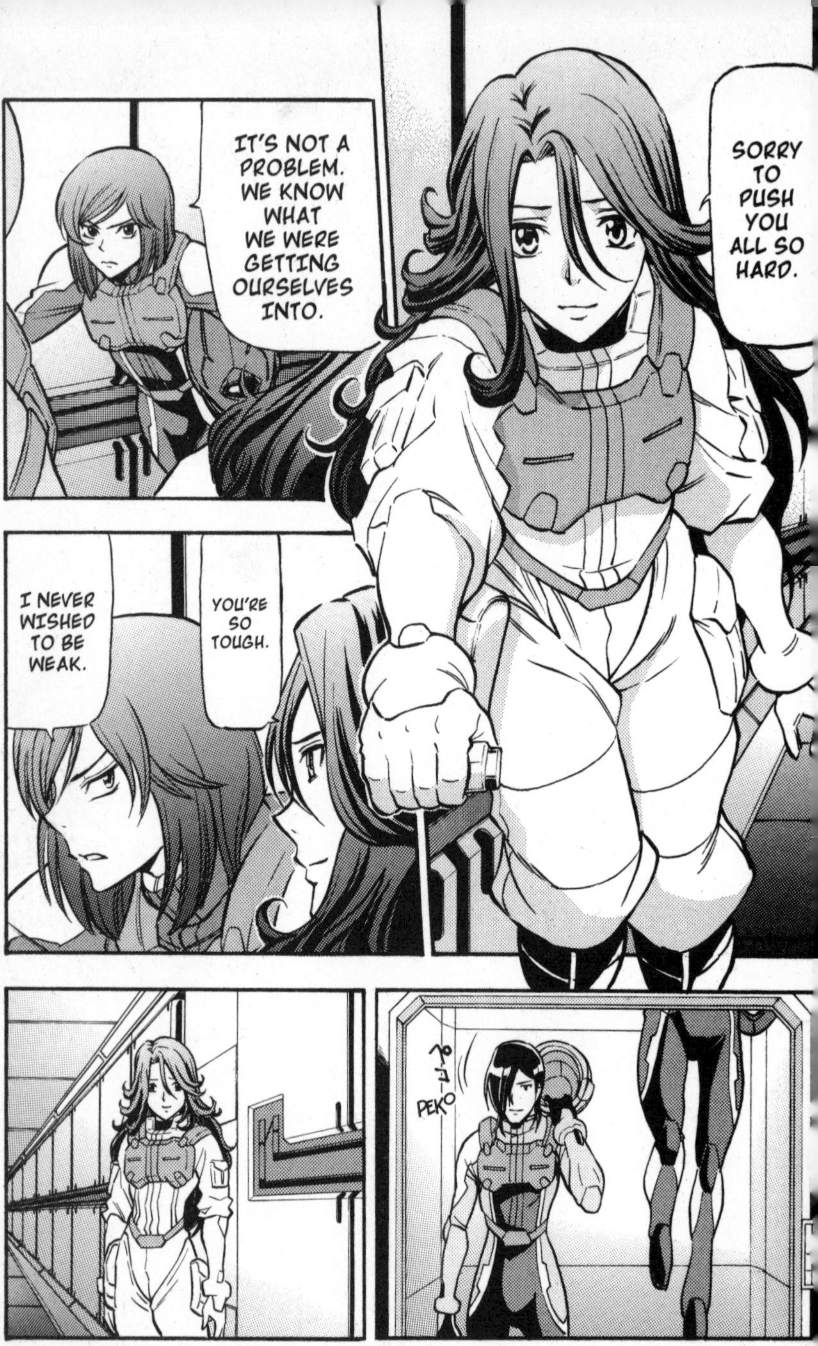
SORRY TO PUSH YOU ALL SO HARD.
IT'S NOT A PROBLEM. WE KNOW WHAT WE WERE GETTING OURSELVES INTO.
YOU'RE SO TOUGH.
I NEVER WISHED TO BE WEAK.
ペコ
PEKO

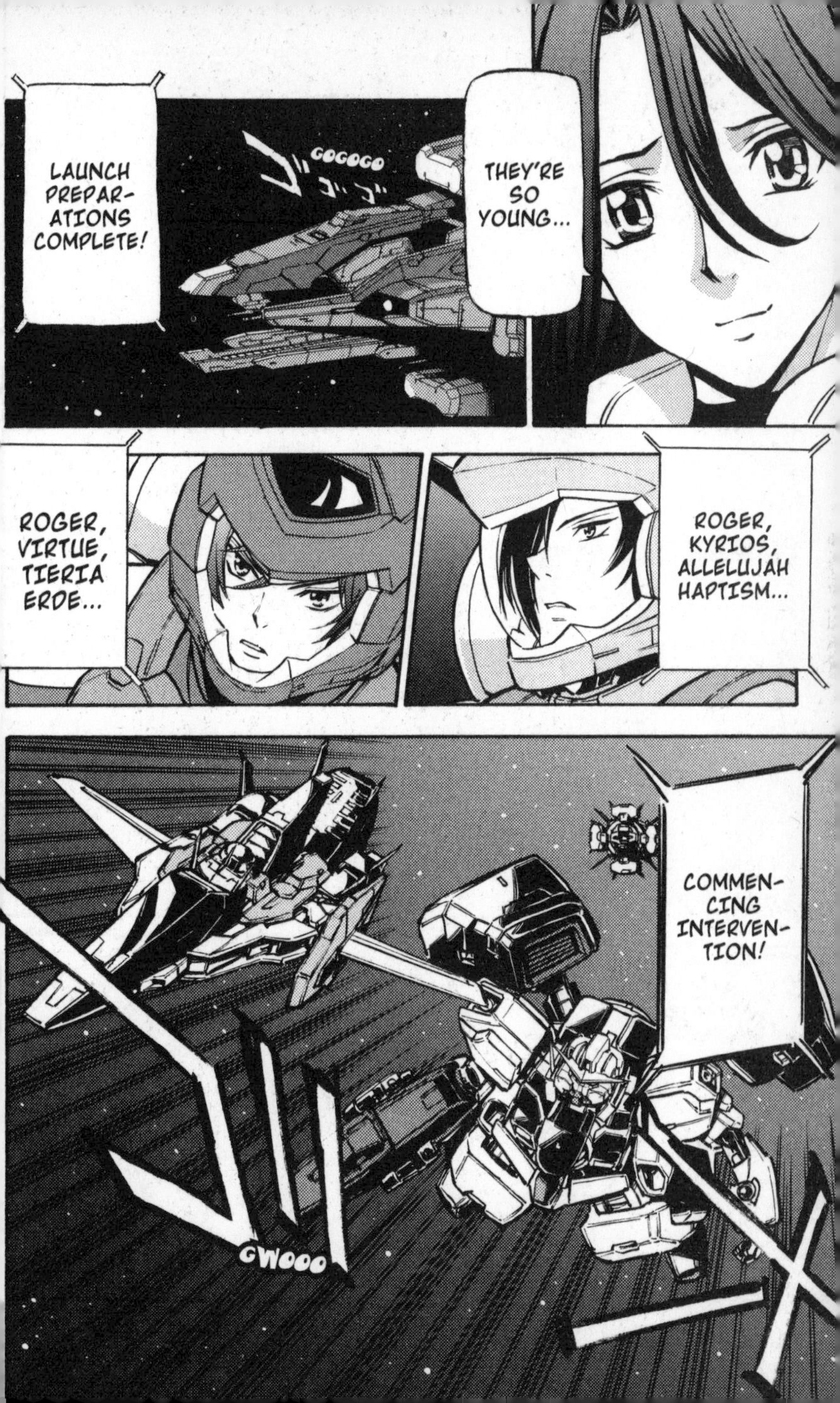
THEY'RE SO YOUNG...
LAUNCH PREPAR-ATIONS COMPLETE!
GOGOGO
ROGER, KYRIOS, ALLELUJAH HAPTISM...
ROGER, VIRTUE, TIERIA ERDE...
COMMEN-CING INTERVEN-TION!
GWOOO

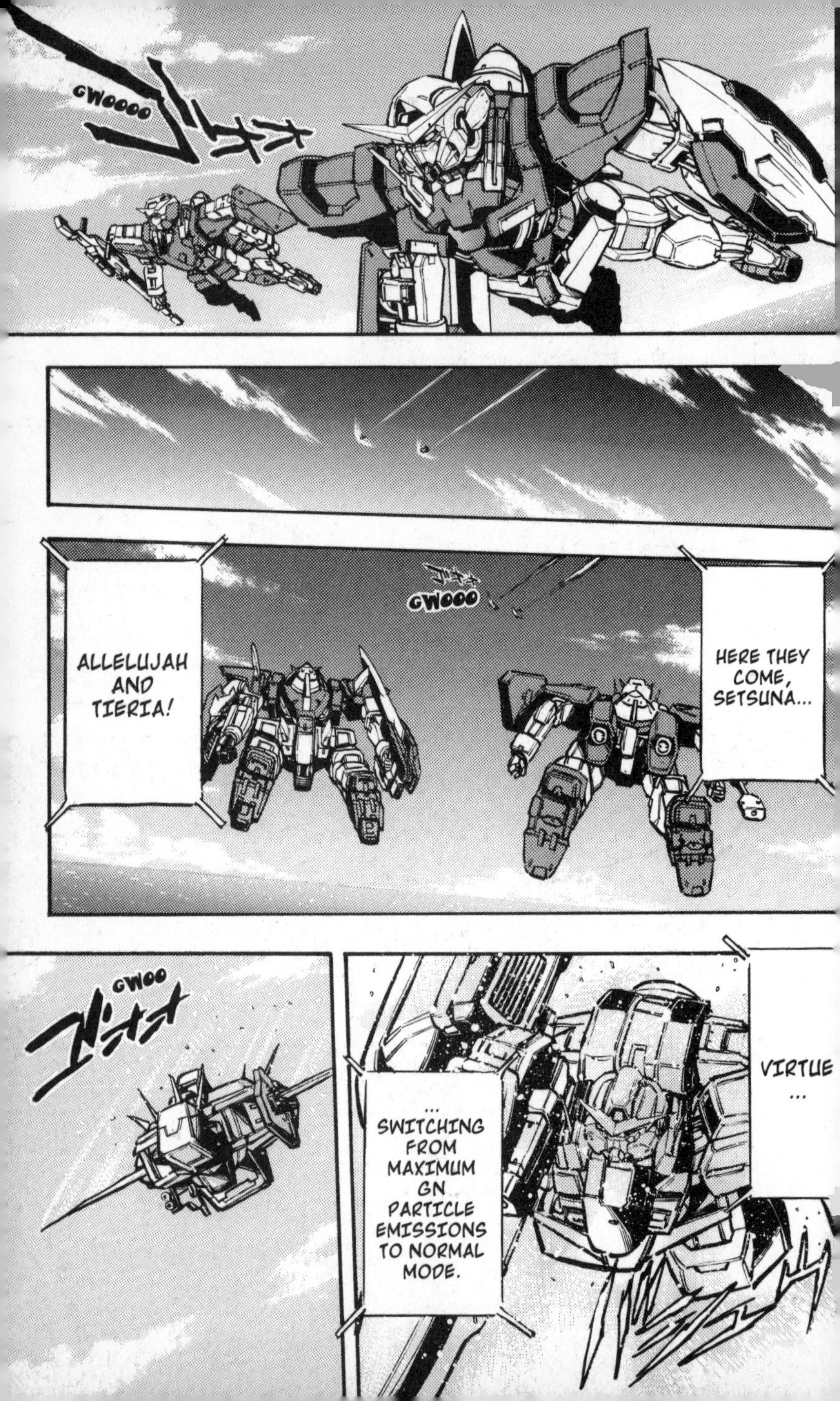
GWOOOO
HERE THEY COME, SETSUNA...
GWOOO
ALLELUJAH AND TIERIA!
VIRTUE ...
... SWITCHING FROM MAXIMUM GN PARTICLE EMISSIONS TO NORMAL MODE.
GWOO

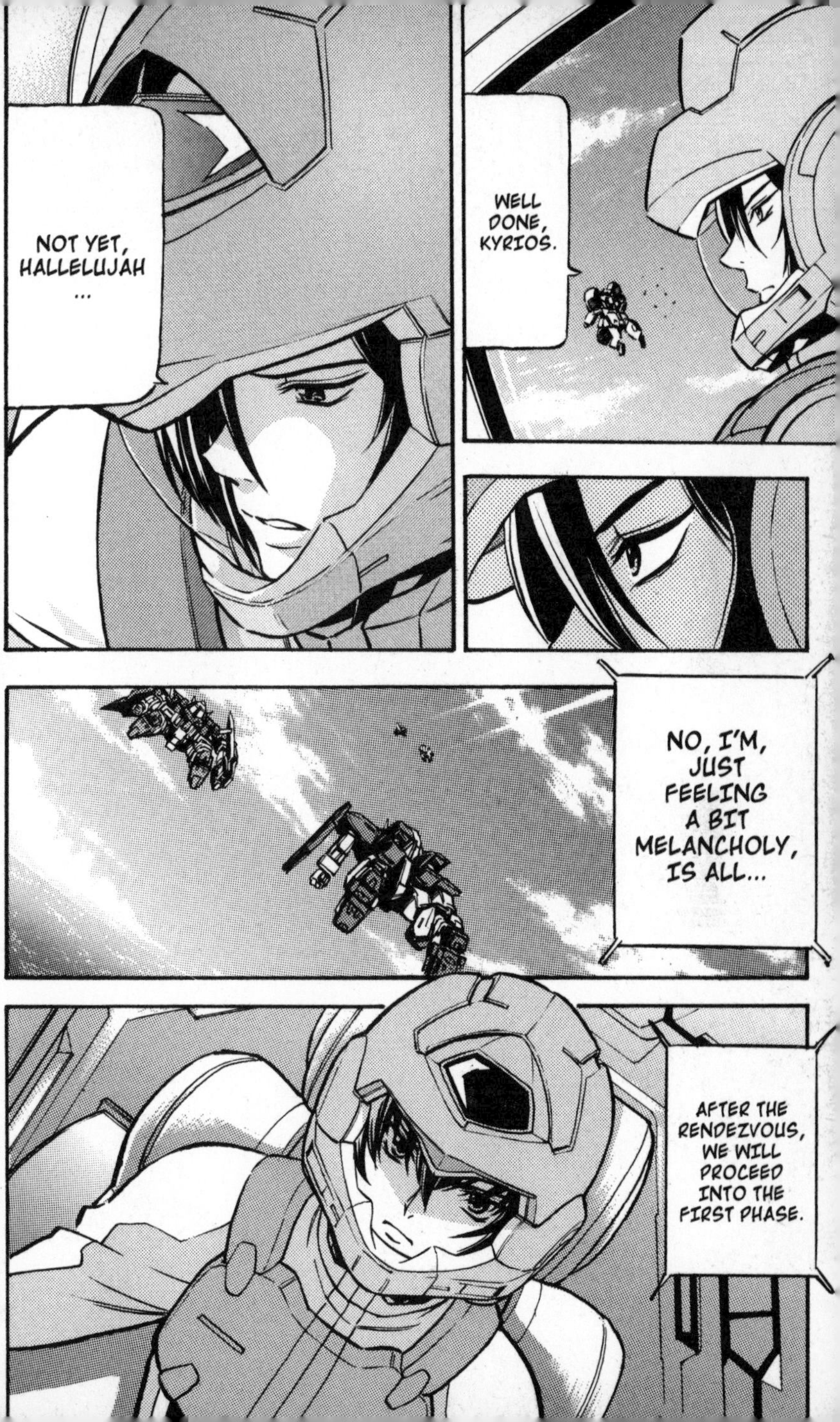
WELL DONE, KYRIOS.
NOT YET, HALLELUJAH ...
NO, I'M, JUST FEELING A BIT MELANCHOLY, IS ALL...
AFTER THE RENDEZVOUS, WE WILL PROCEED INTO THE FIRST PHASE.

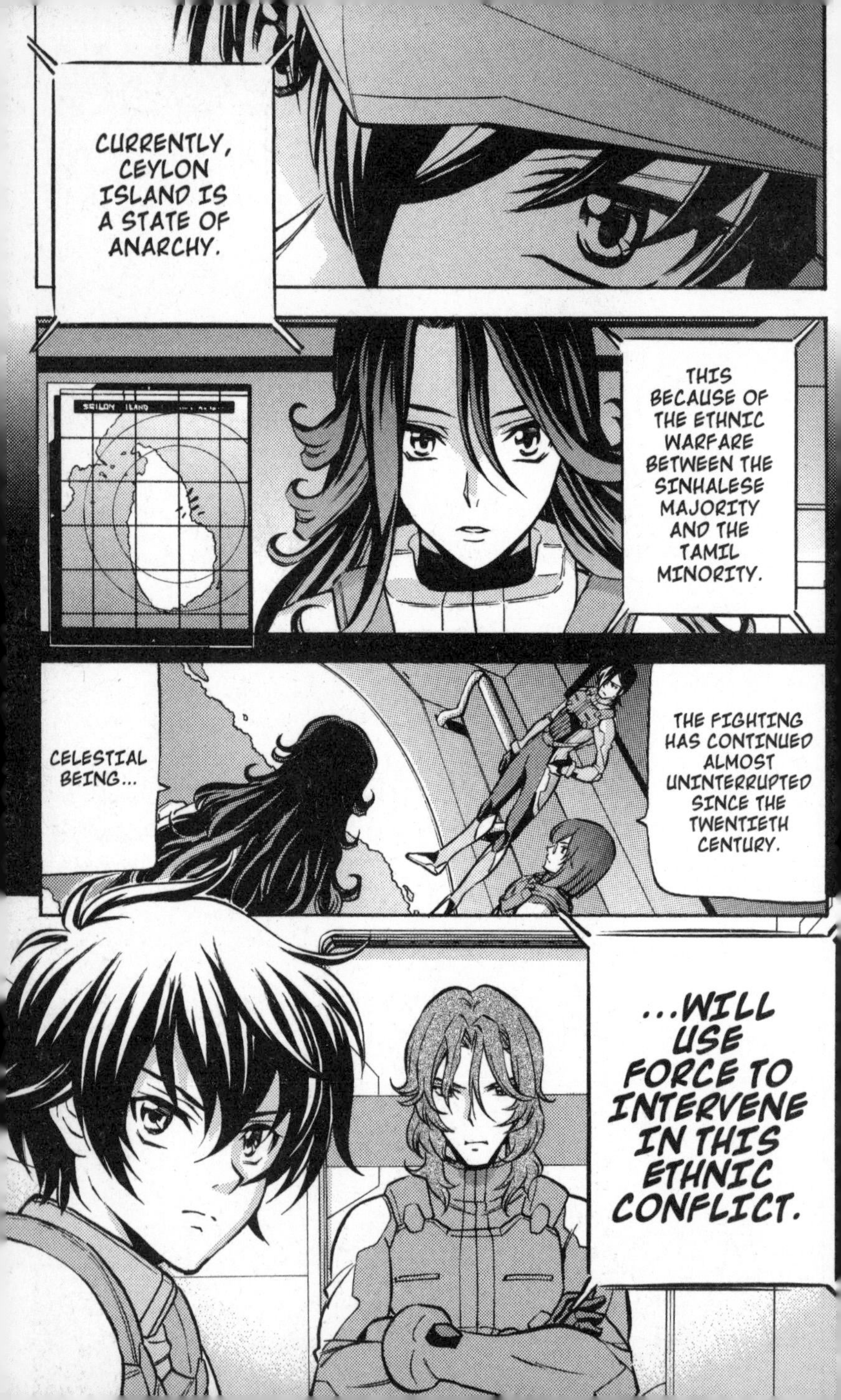

CURRENTLY, CEYLON ISLAND IS A STATE OF ANARCHY.
THIS BECAUSE OF THE ETHNIC WARFARE BETWEEN THE SINHALESE MAJORITY AND THE TAMIL MINORITY.
THE FIGHTING HAS CONTINUED ALMOST UNINTERRUPTED SINCE THE TWENTIETH CENTURY.
CELESTIAL BEING...
...WILL USE FORCE TO INTERVENE IN THIS ETHNIC CONFLICT.

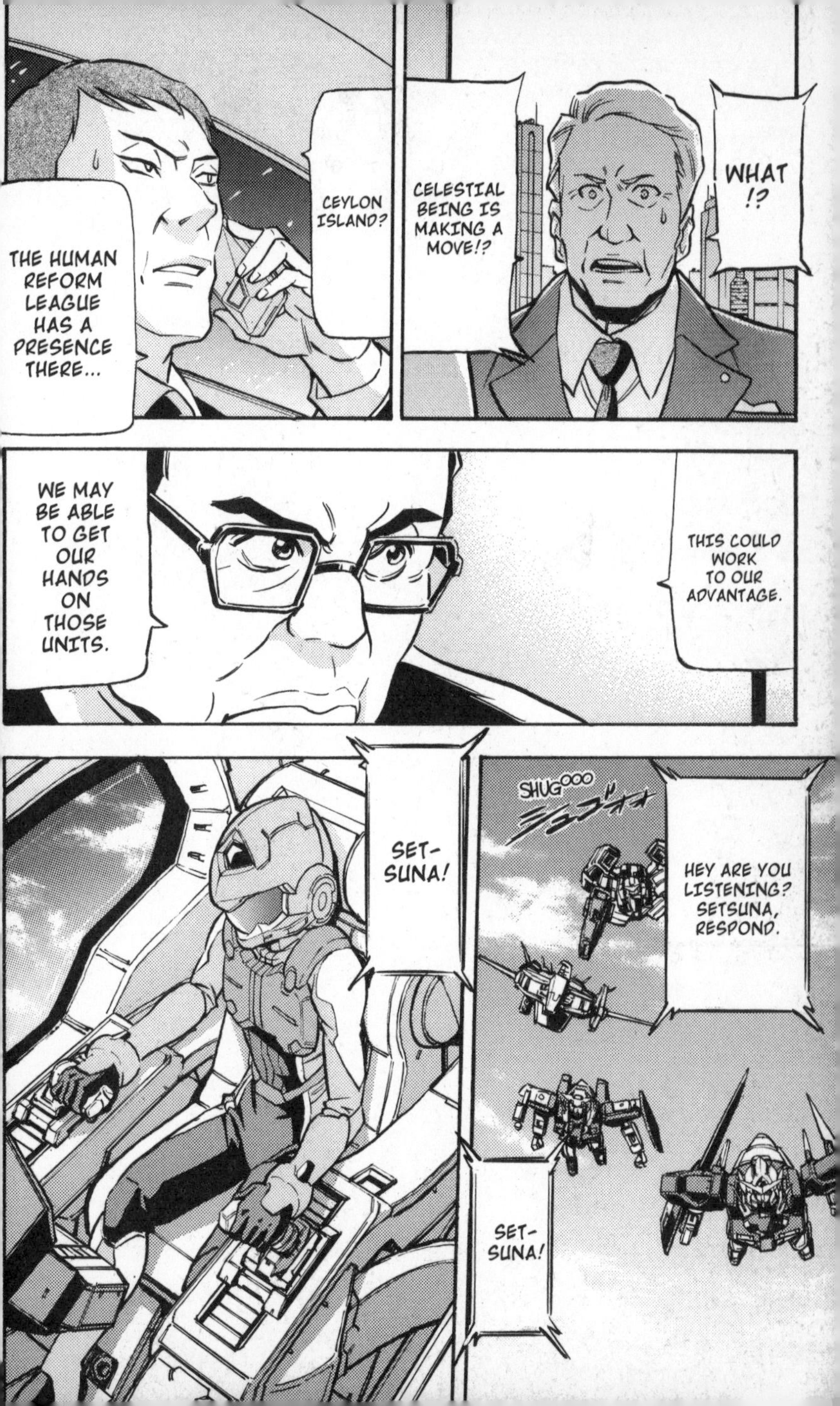
WHAT!?
CELESTIAL BEING IS MAKING A MOVE!?
CEYLON ISLAND?
THE HUMAN REFORM LEAGUE HAS A PRESENCE THERE...
THIS COULD WORK TO OUR ADVANTAGE.
WE MAY BE ABLE TO GET OUR HANDS ON THOSE UNITS.
SHUGOOO
HEY ARE YOU LISTENING? SETSUNA, RESPOND.
SET-SUNA!
SET-SUNA!

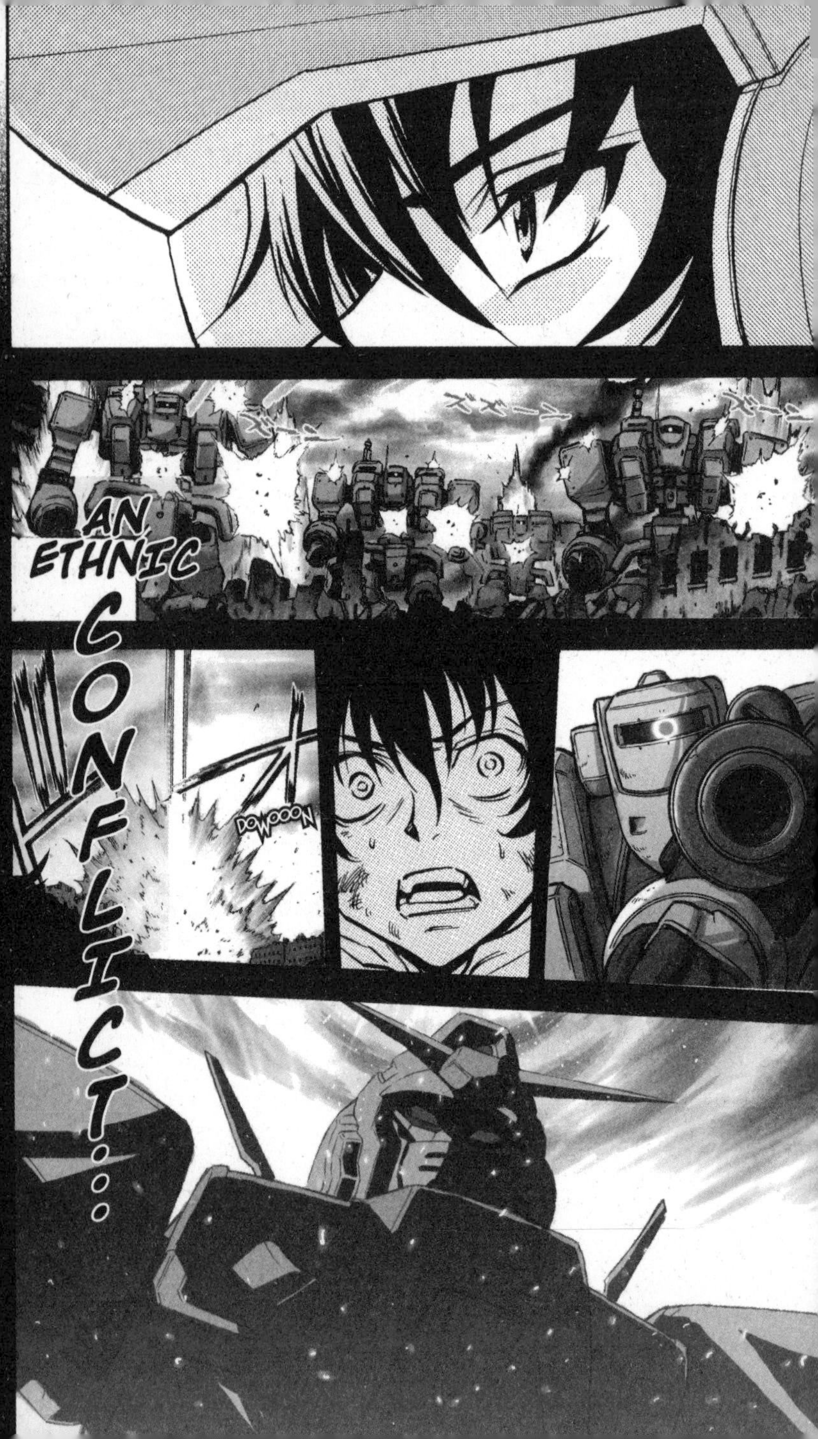
AN ETHNIC CONFLICT...
DOWOOON

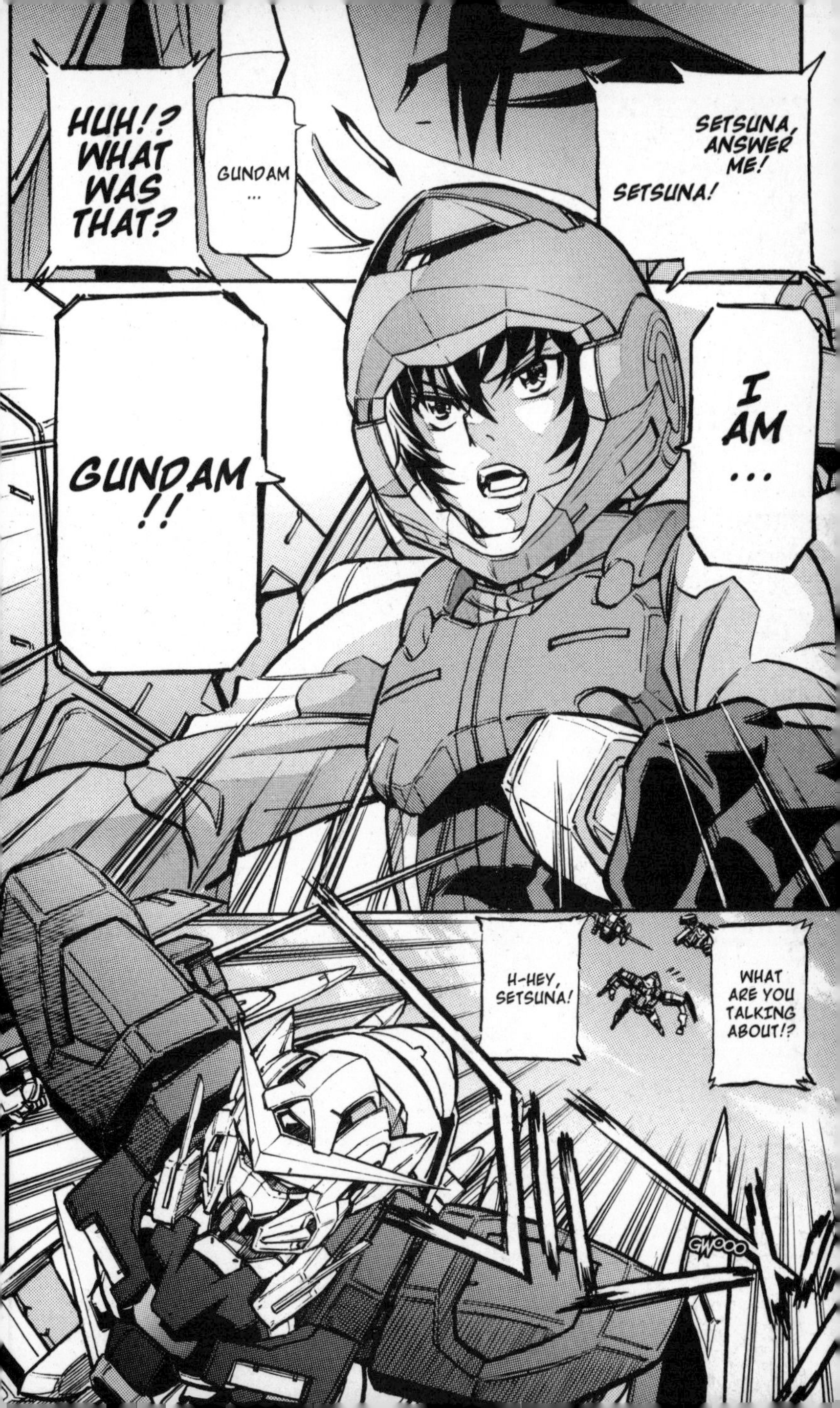
SETSUNA, ANSWER ME!
SETSUNA!
GUNDAM ...
HUH!? WHAT WAS THAT?
I AM ...
GUNDAM !!
WHAT ARE YOU TALKING ABOUT!?
H-HEY, SETSUNA!
GWOOO

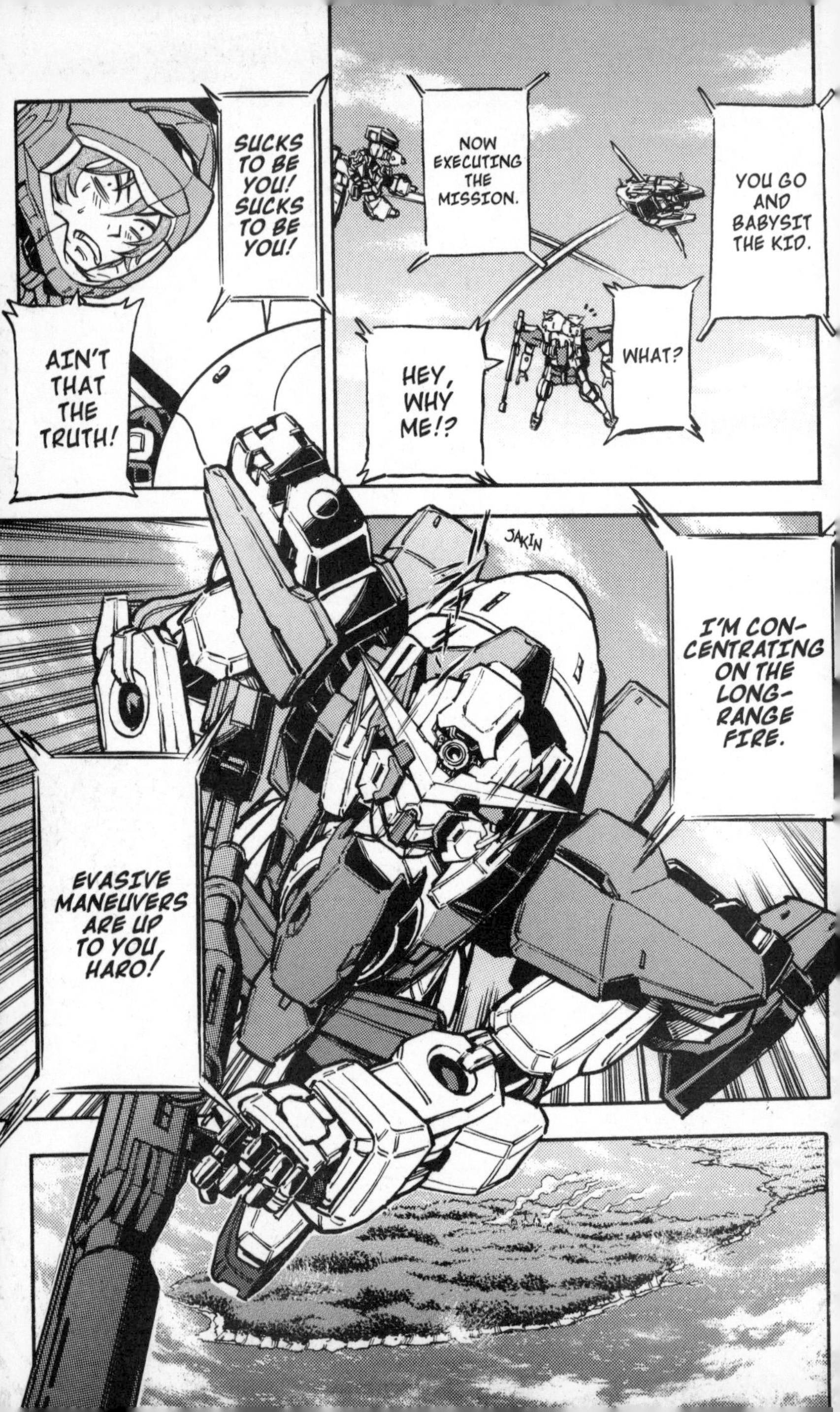
YOU GO AND BABYSIT THE KID.
NOW EXECUTING THE MISSION.
WHAT?
HEY, WHY ME!?
SUCKS TO BE YOU! SUCKS TO BE YOU!
AIN'T THAT THE TRUTH!
JAKIN
I'M CONCENTRATING ON THE LONG-RANGE FIRE.
EVASIVE MANEUVERS ARE UP TO YOU, HARO!

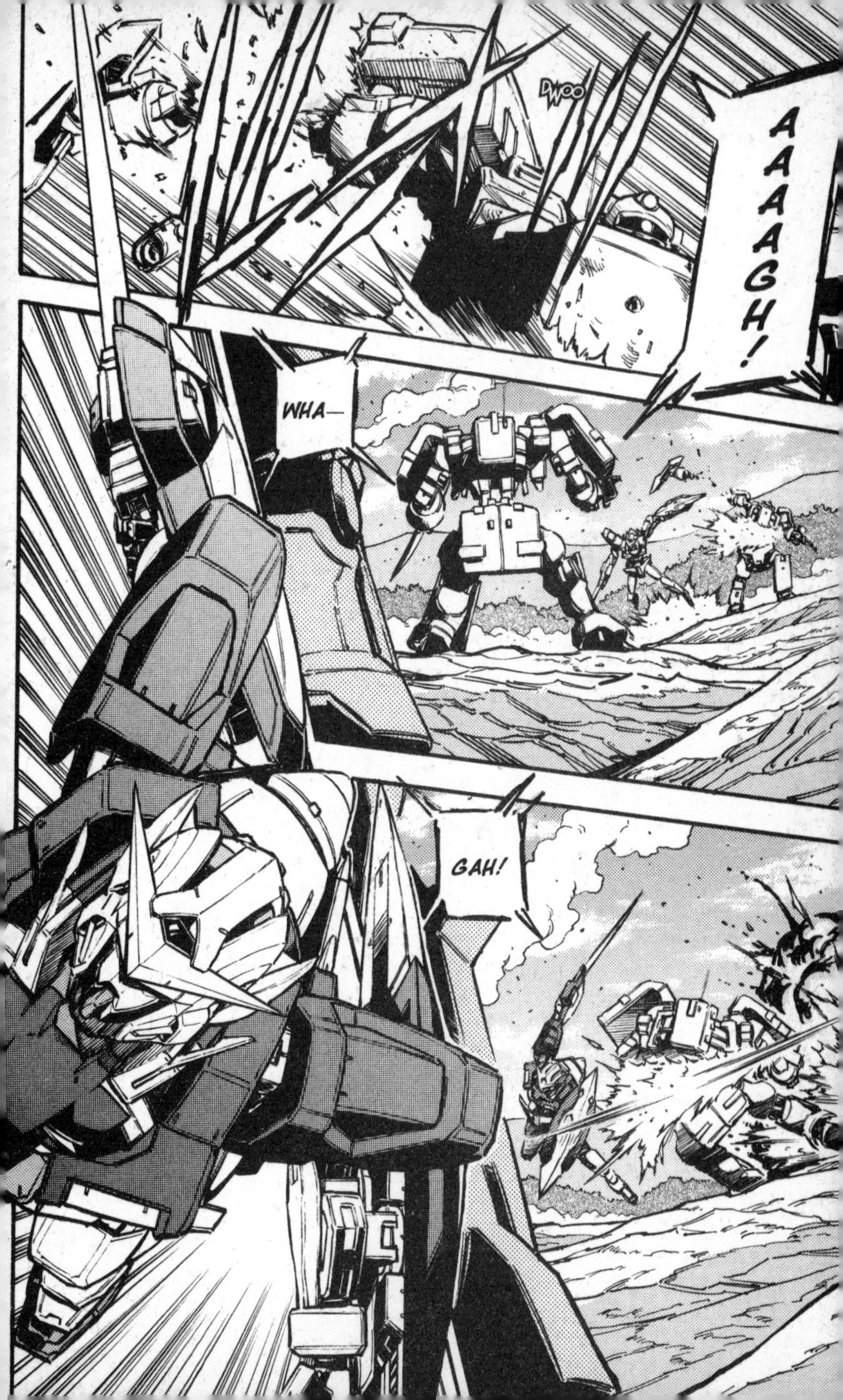
AAAAAGH!
DWOO
WHA—
GAH!

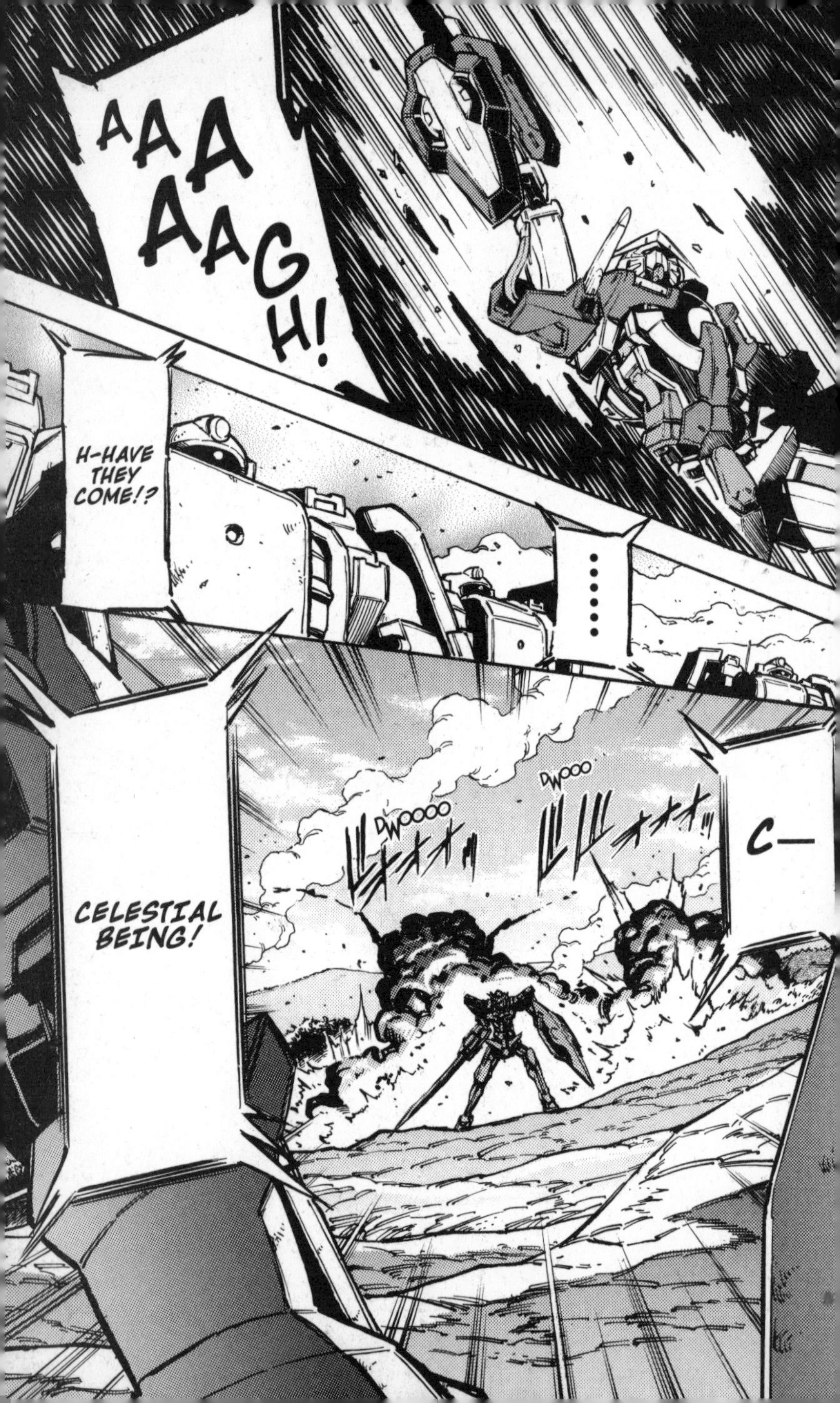

AAAAAAGH!
H-HAVE THEY COME!?
......
C—
DWOOO
DWOOOO
CELESTIAL BEING!

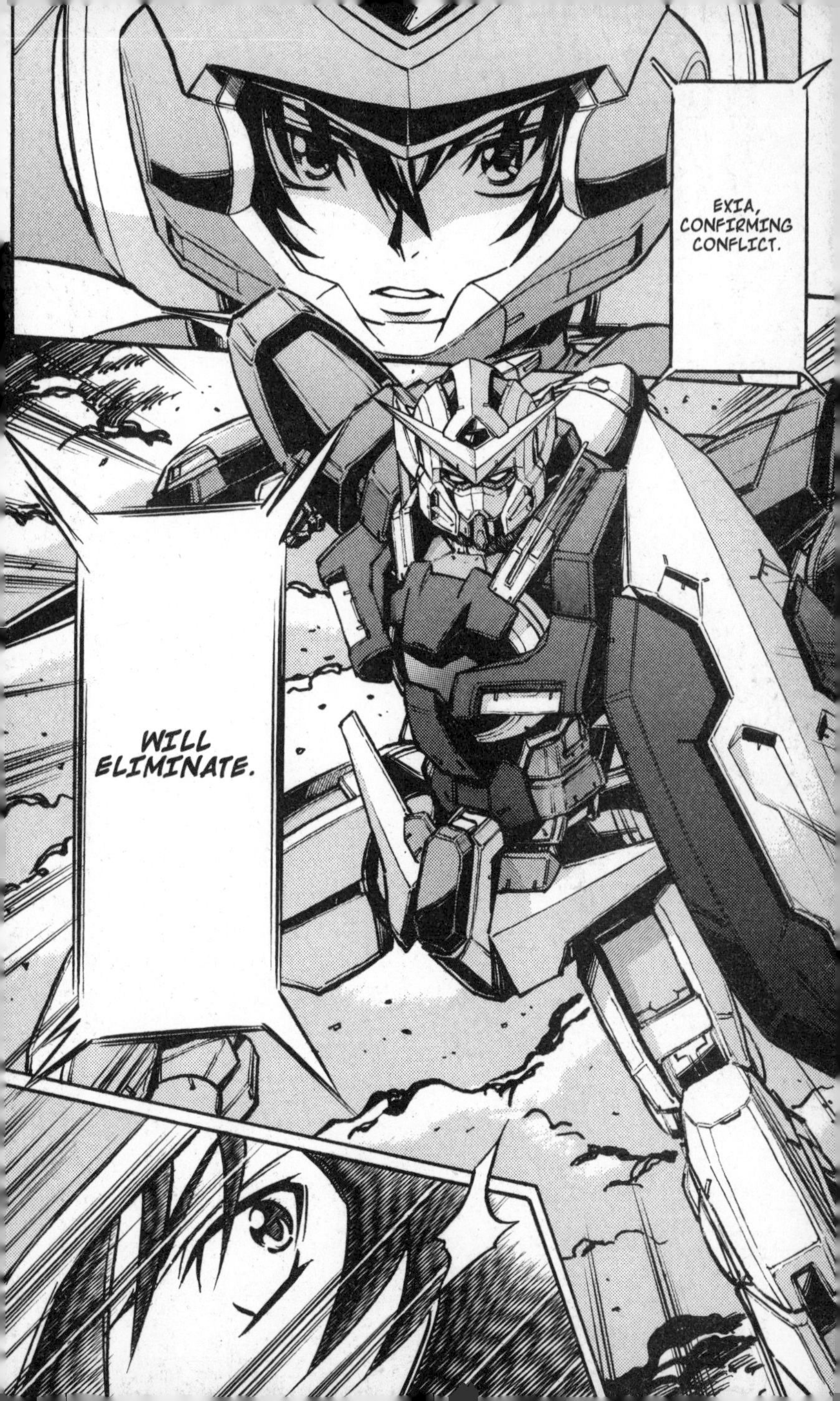
EXIA, CONFIRMING CONFLICT.
WILL ELIMINATE.

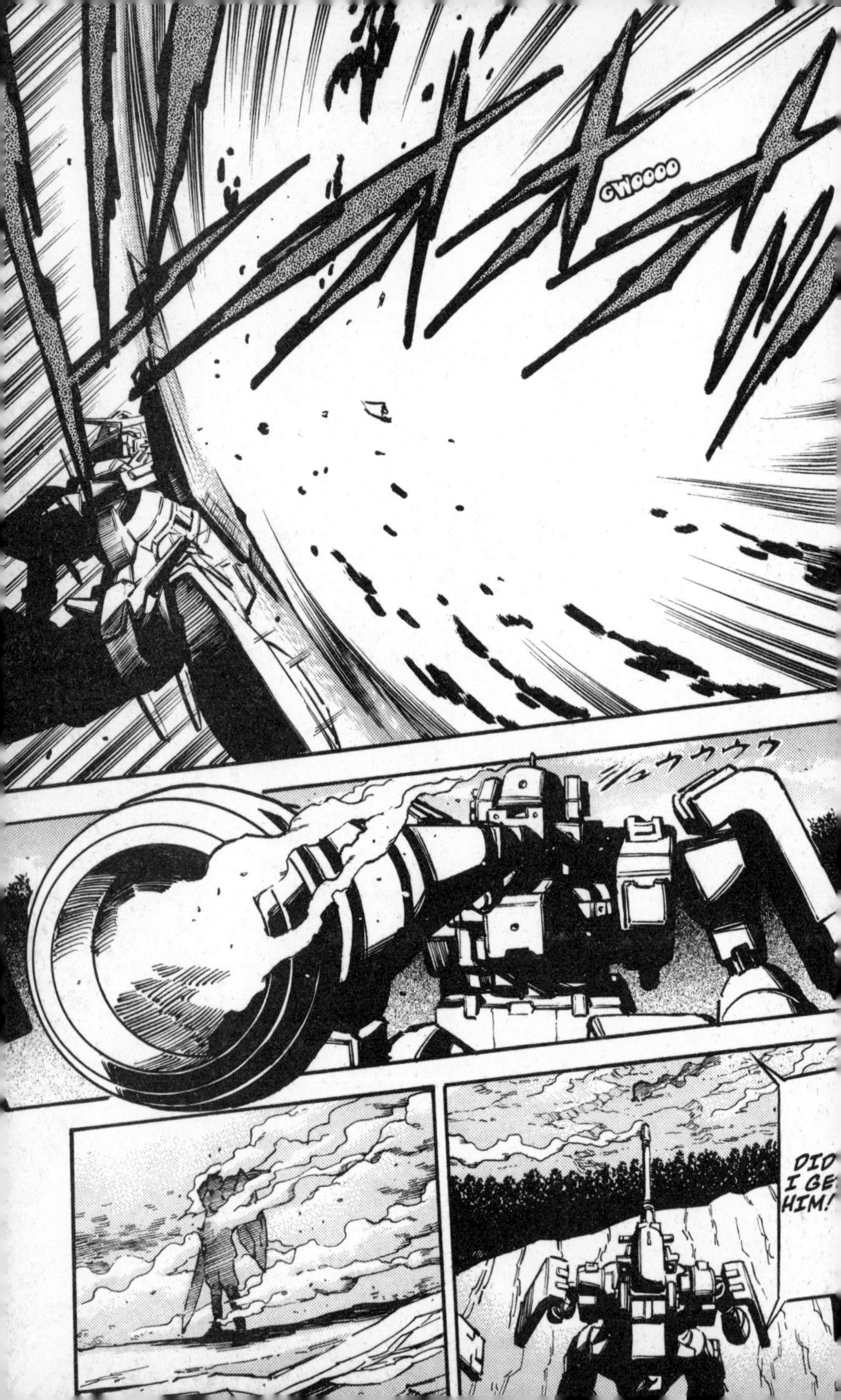
GWOOOO
シュウウウウ
DID I GE HIM!

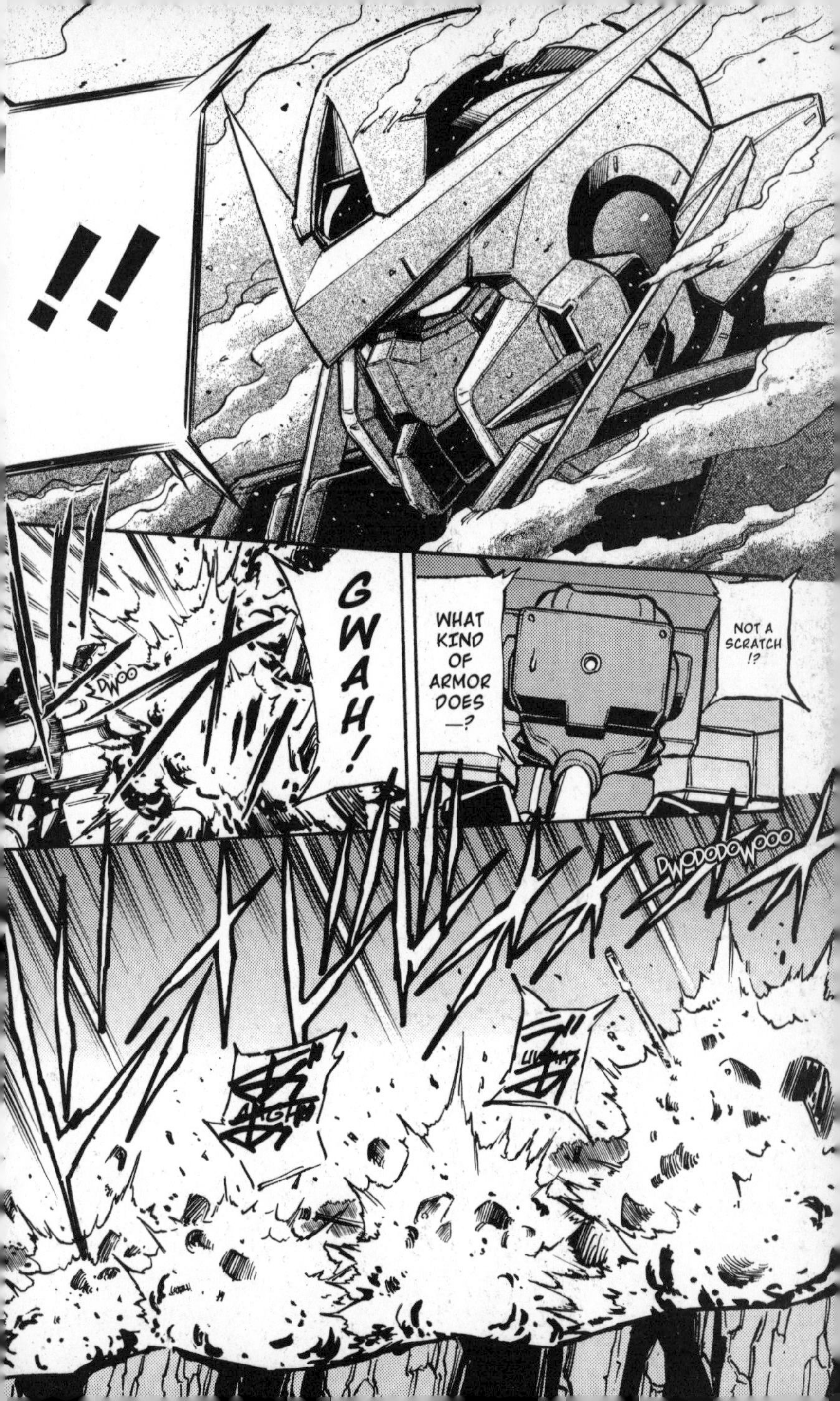
!!
NOT A SCRATCH !?
WHAT KIND OF ARMOR DOES —?
GWAH!
DWOO
DWODODOWOOO

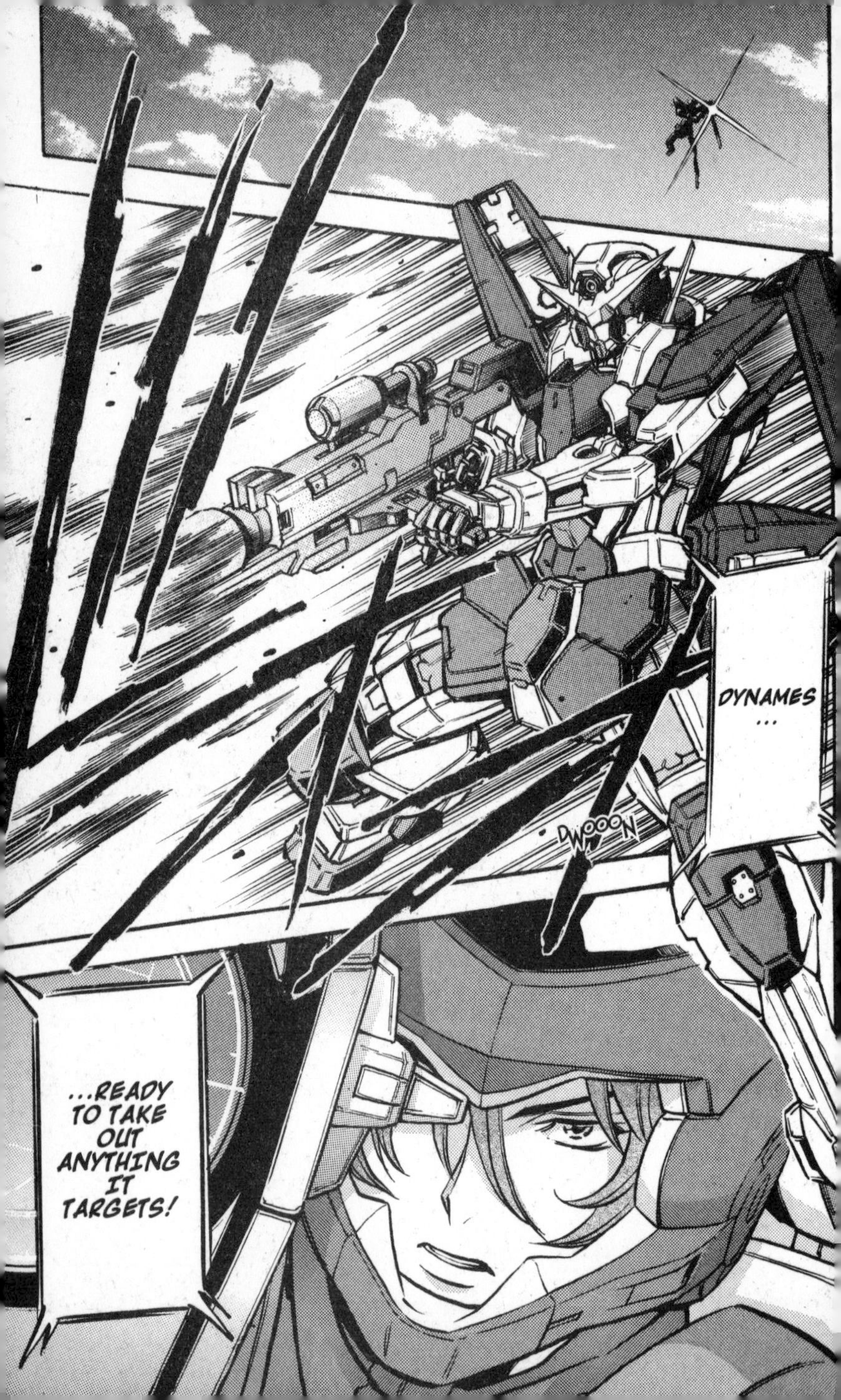
DYNAMES ...
DWOOON
...READY TO TAKE OUT ANYTHING IT TARGETS!

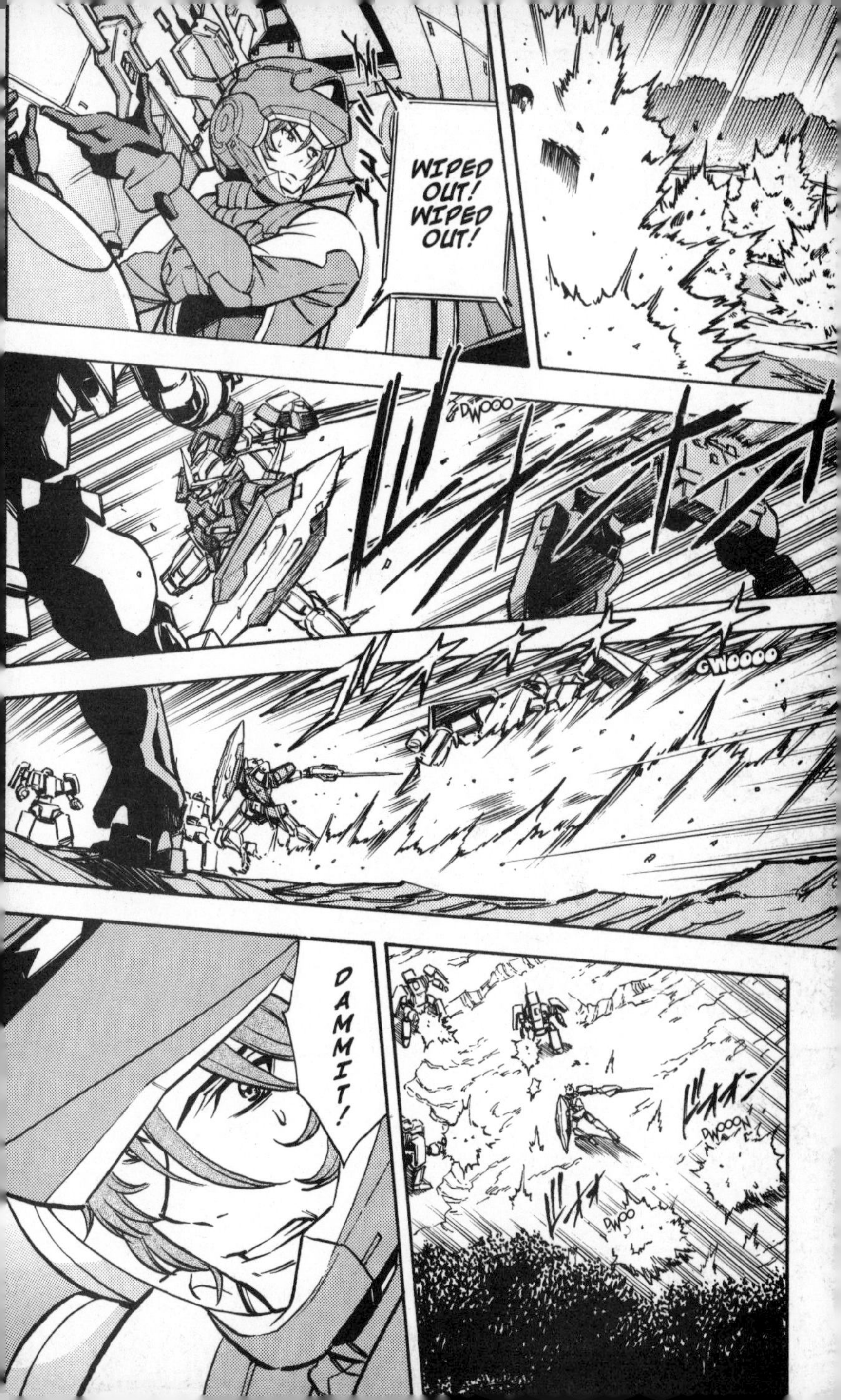
WIPED OUT! WIPED OUT!
DWOOO
GWOOOO
DWOOON
DWOO
DAMMIT!

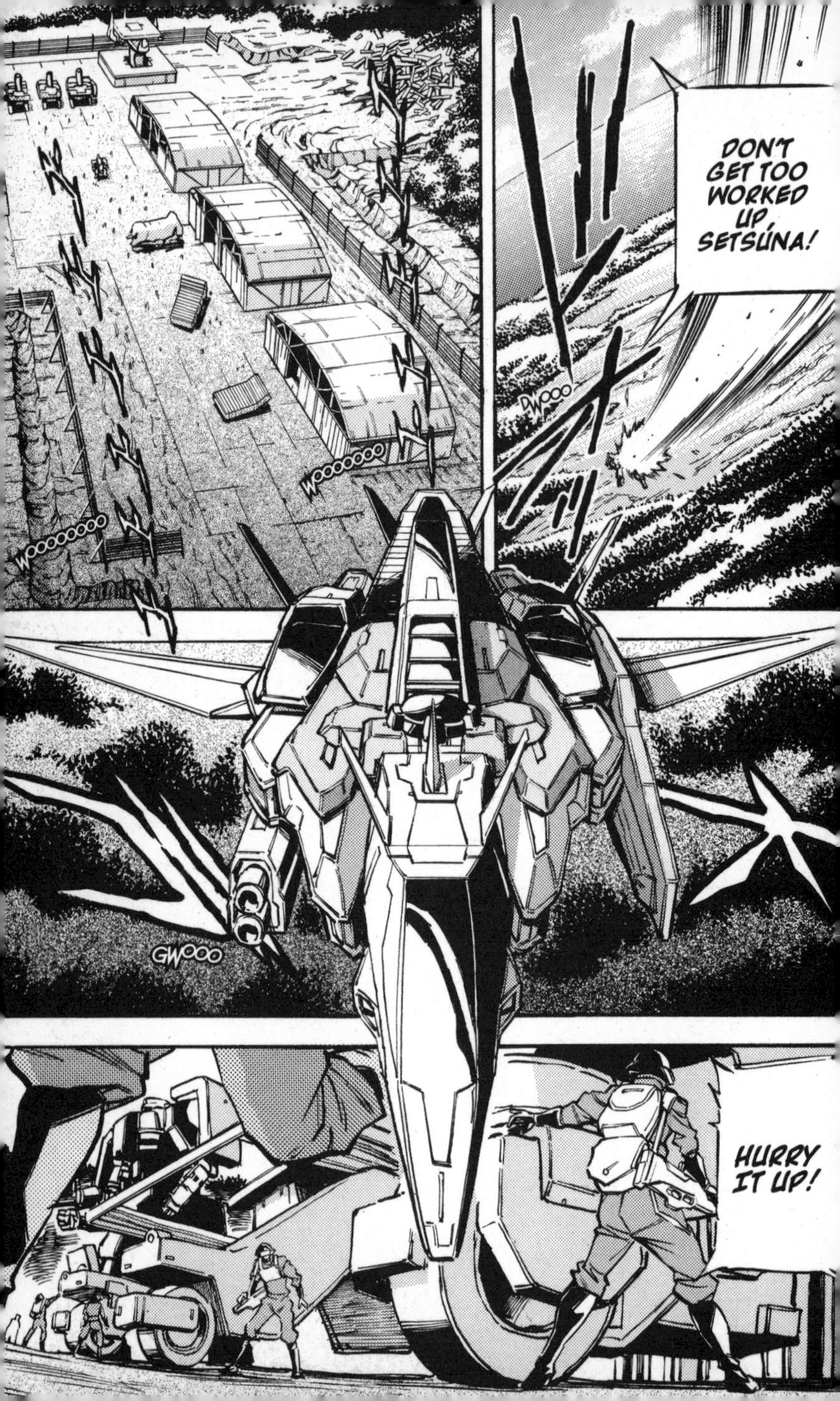
DON'T GET TOO WORKED UP, SETSUNA!
DWOOO
WOOOOOOO
WOOOOOOOOO
GWOOO
HURRY IT UP!

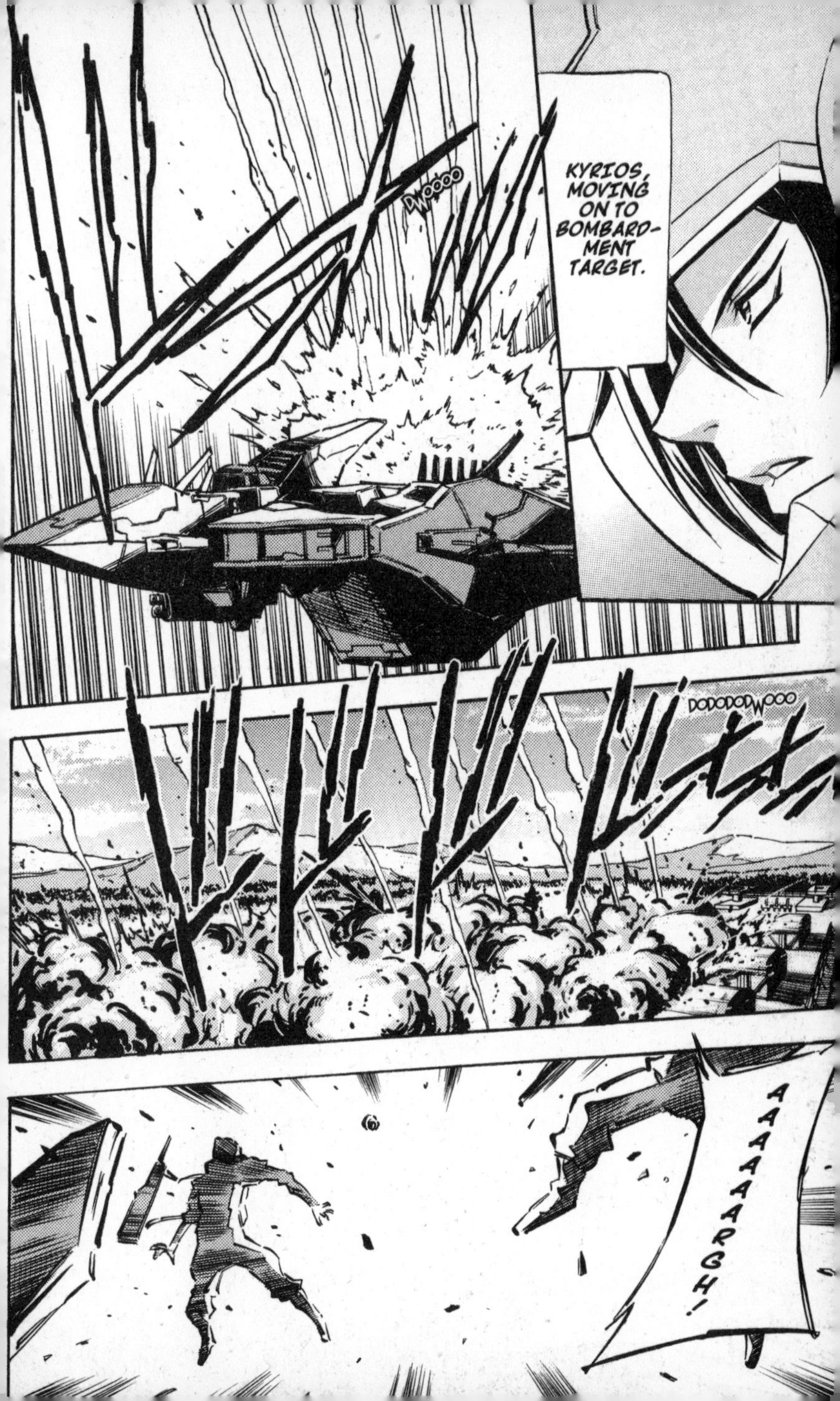
KYRIOS, MOVING ON TO BOMBARD-MENT TARGET.
DWOOOO
DODODODWOOO
AAAAAARGH!

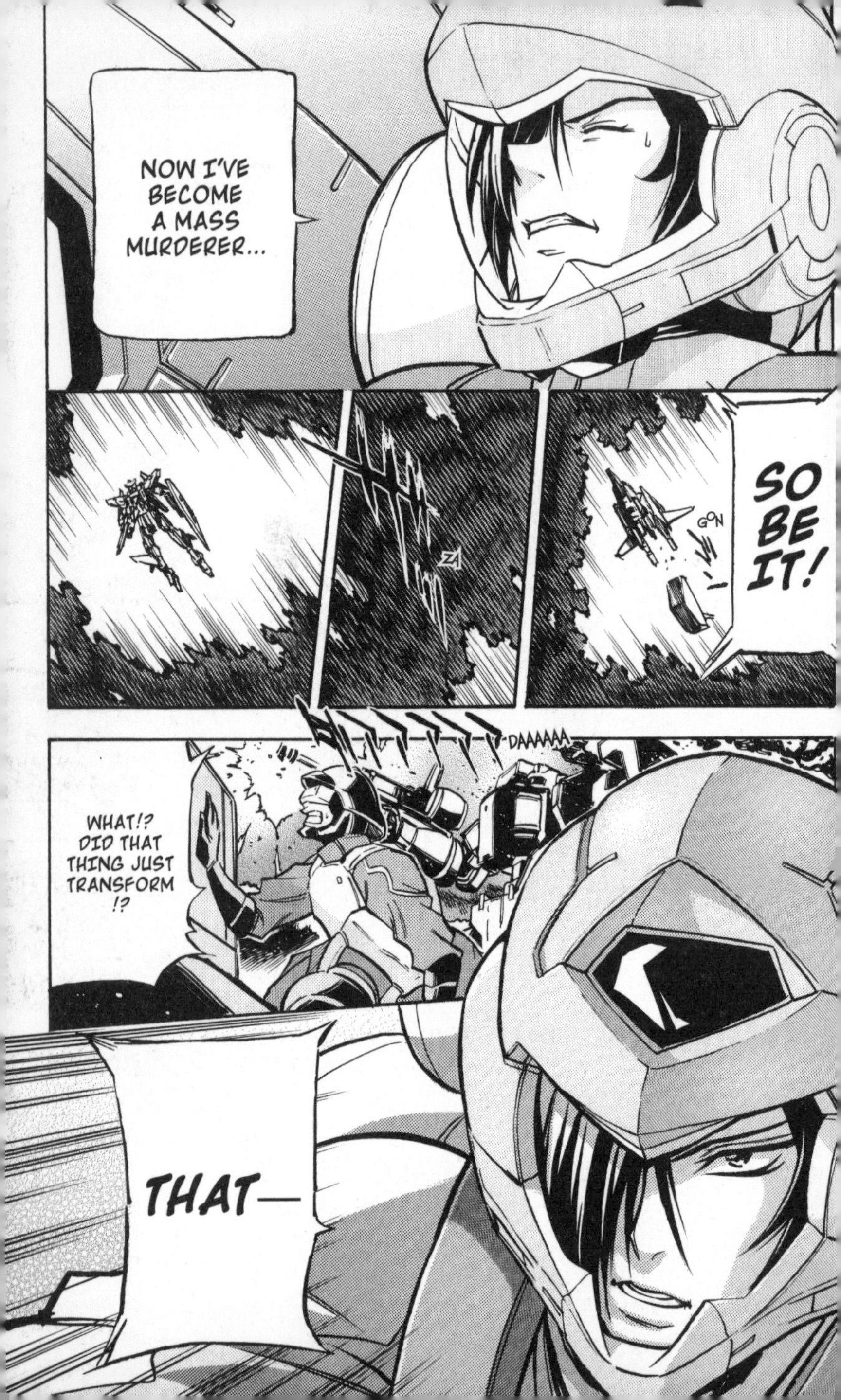
NOW I'VE BECOME A MASS MURDERER...
SO BE IT!
GON
ZA
DAAAAAA
WHAT!? DID THAT THING JUST TRANSFORM !?
THAT—

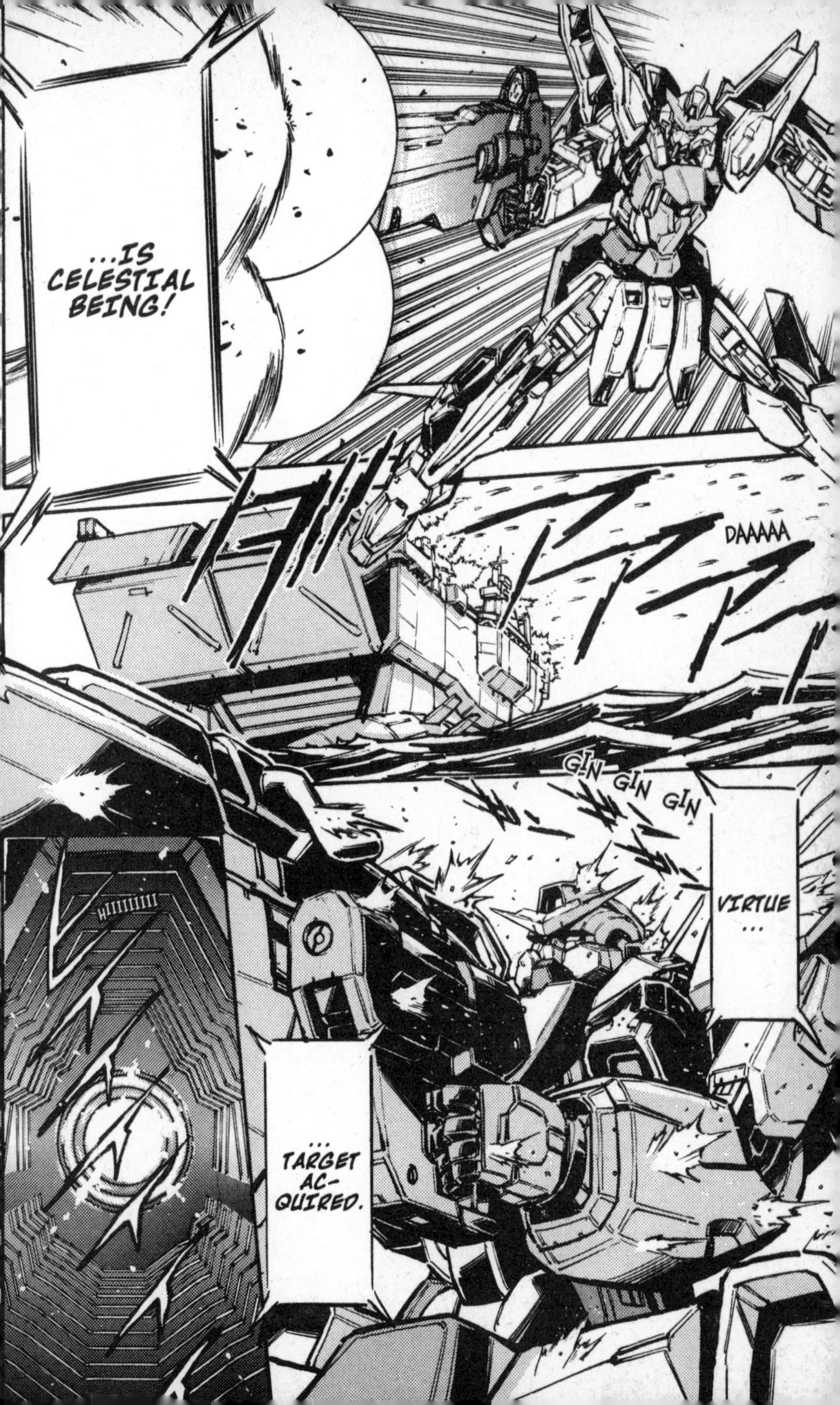
...IS CELESTIAL BEING!
DAAAAA
GIN GIN GIN
VIRTUE ...
... TARGET AC-QUIRED.

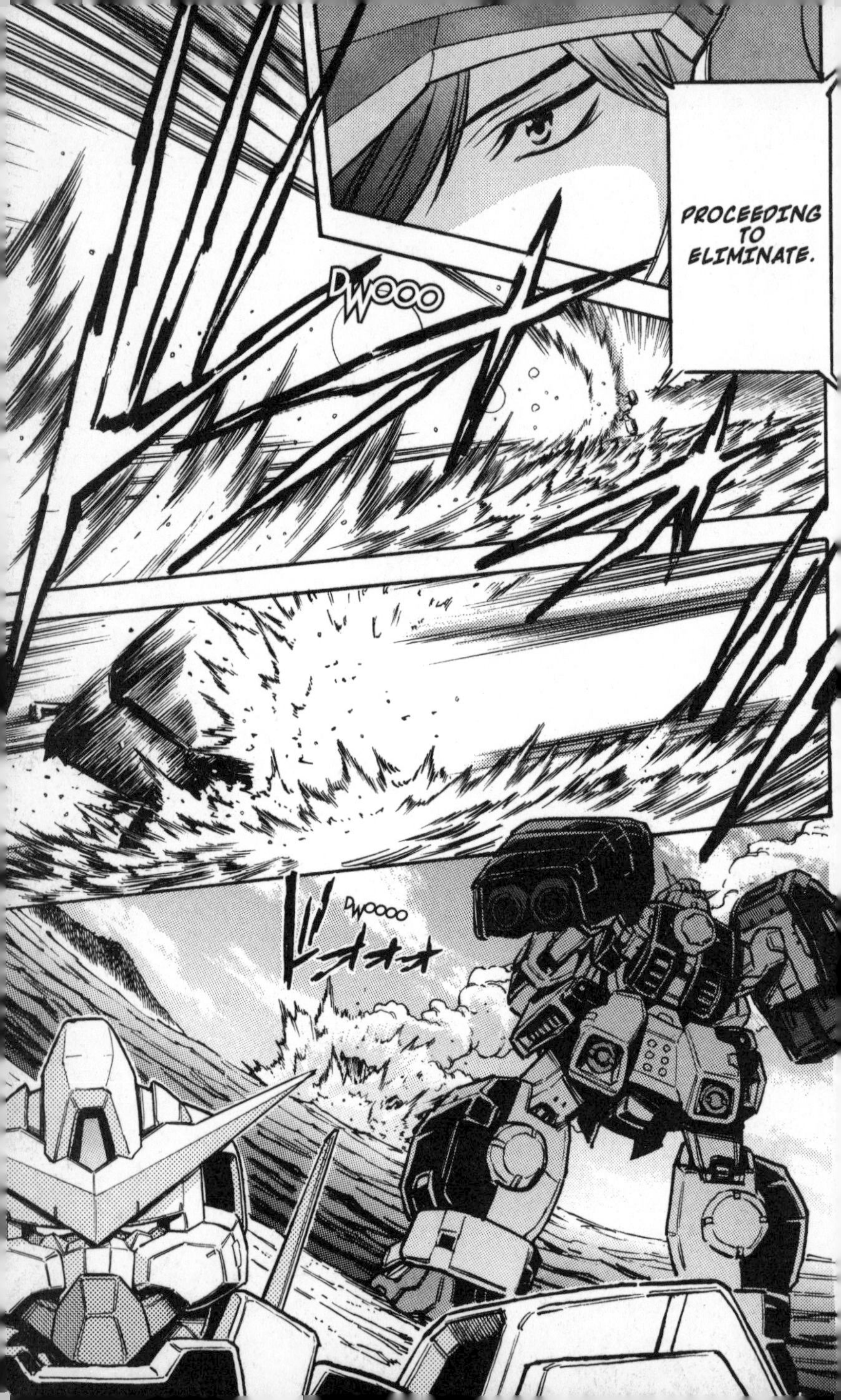
PROCEEDING TO ELIMINATE.
DWOOO
ドオオオ
DWOOOO

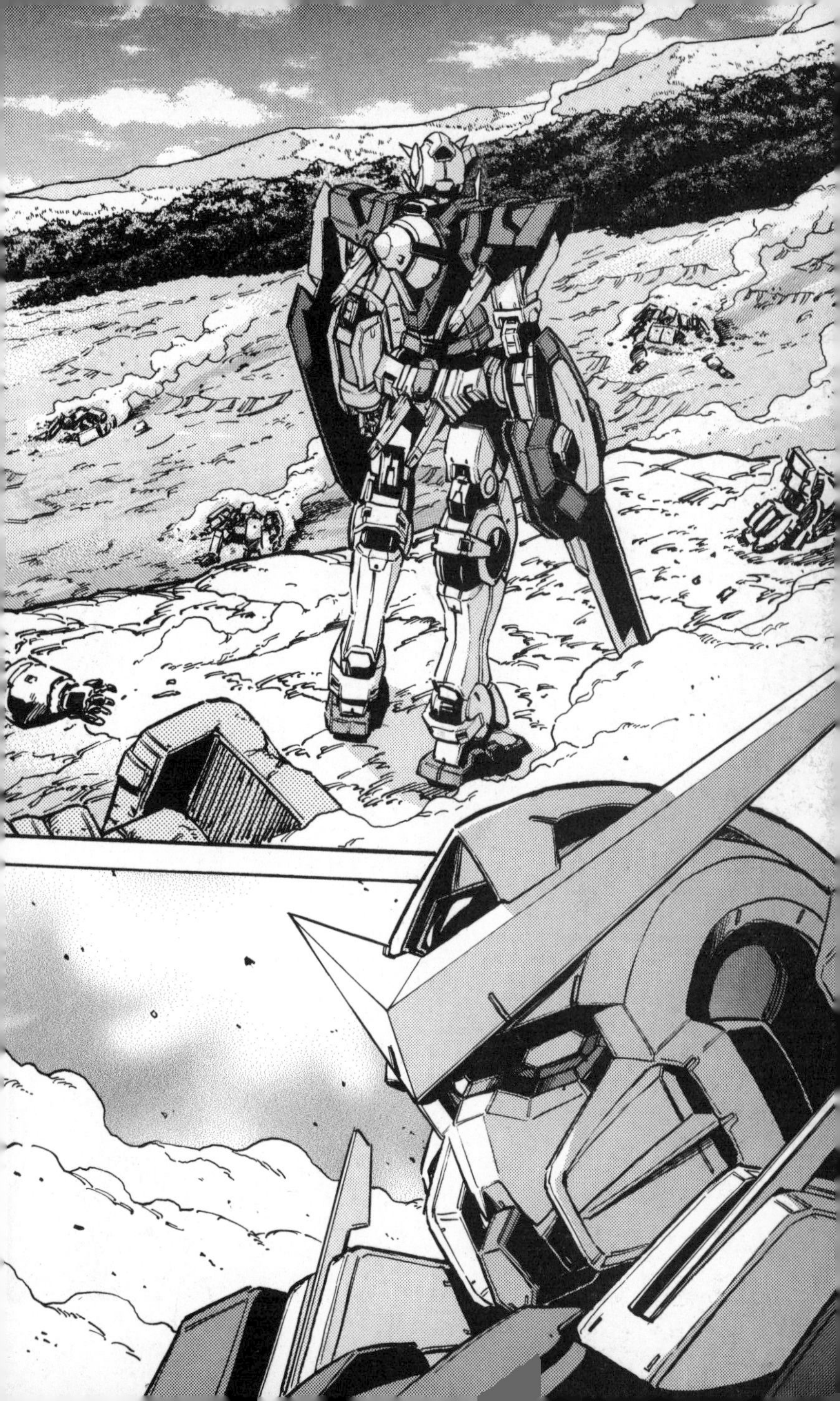

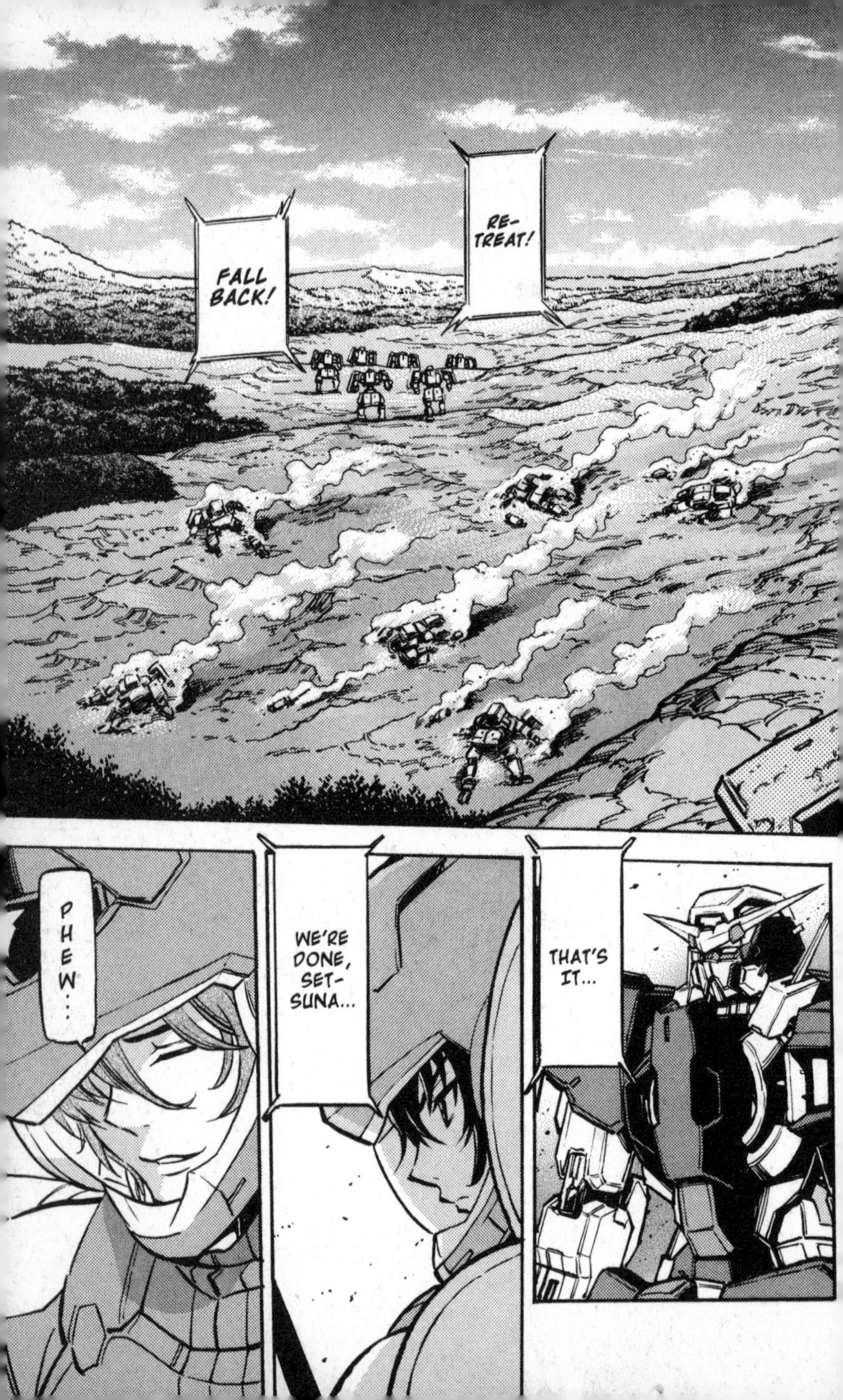
RE-TREAT!
FALL BACK!
THAT'S IT...
WE'RE DONE, SET-SUNA...
PHEW...

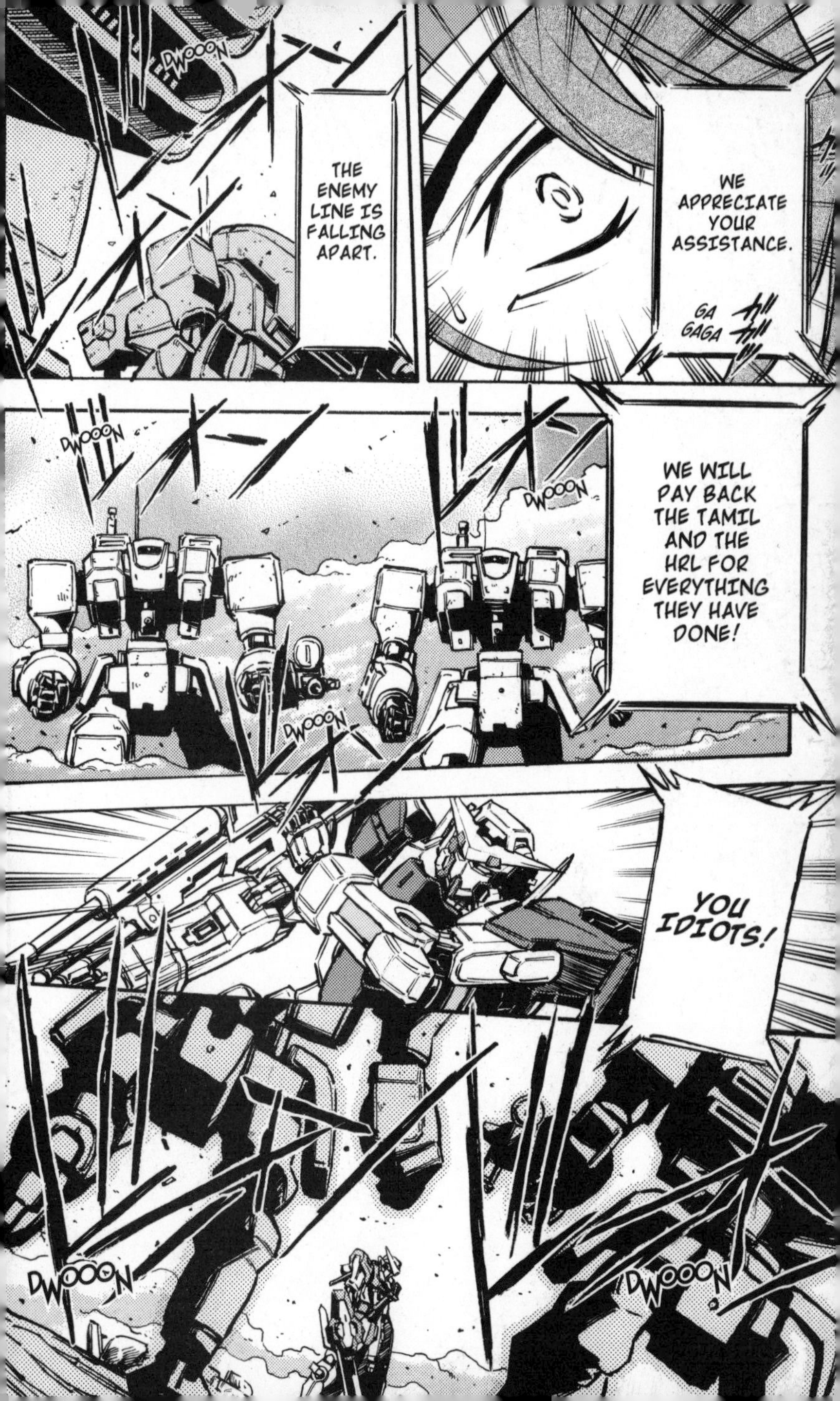
WE APPRECIATE YOUR ASSISTANCE.
GA GAGA
THE ENEMY LINE IS FALLING APART.
DWOOON
WE WILL PAY BACK THE TAMIL AND THE HRL FOR EVERYTHING THEY HAVE DONE!
DWOOON
DWOOON
DWOOON
YOU IDIOTS!
DWOOON
DWOOON

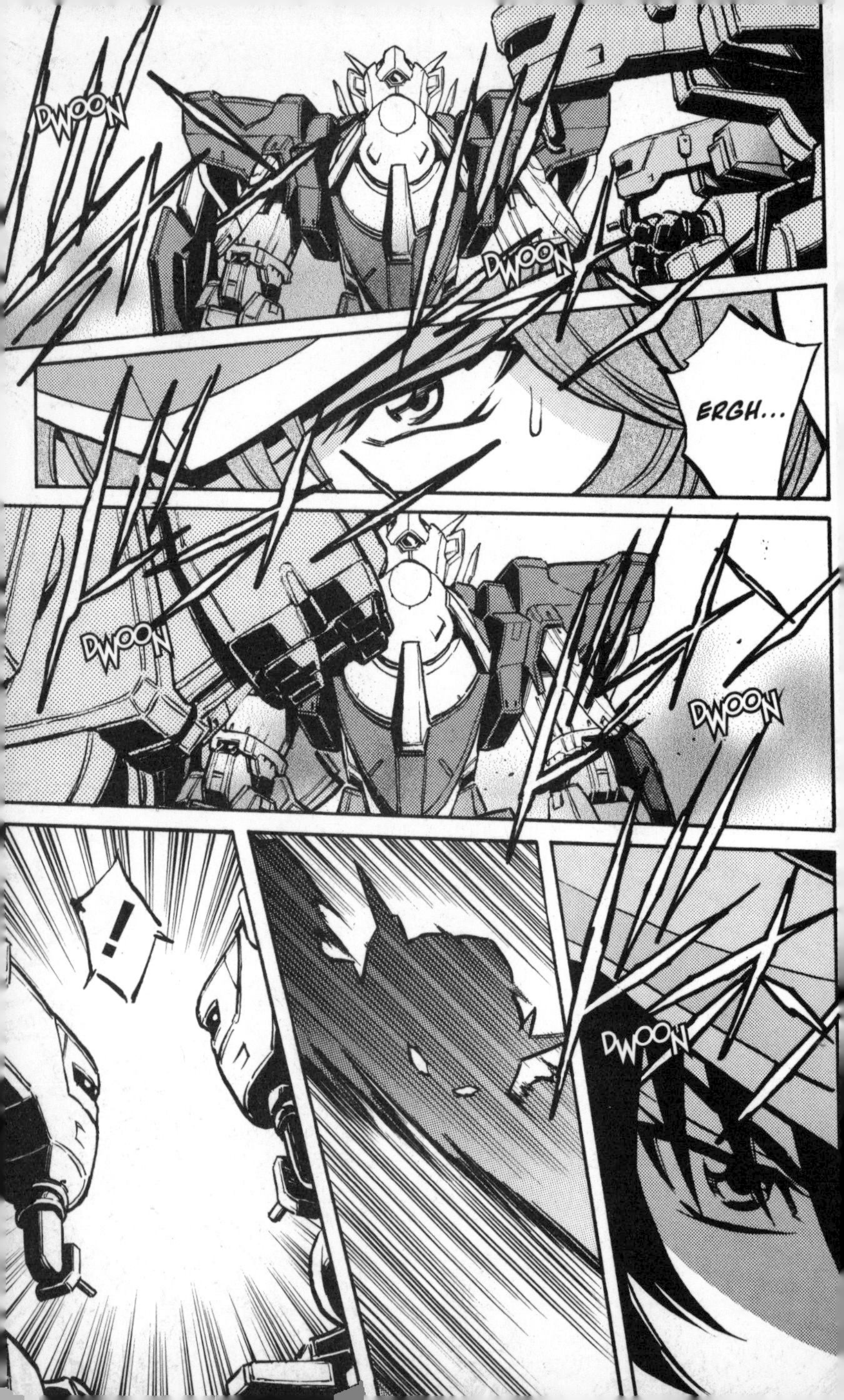
DWOON
DWOON
ERGH...
DWOON
DWOON
DWOON
!

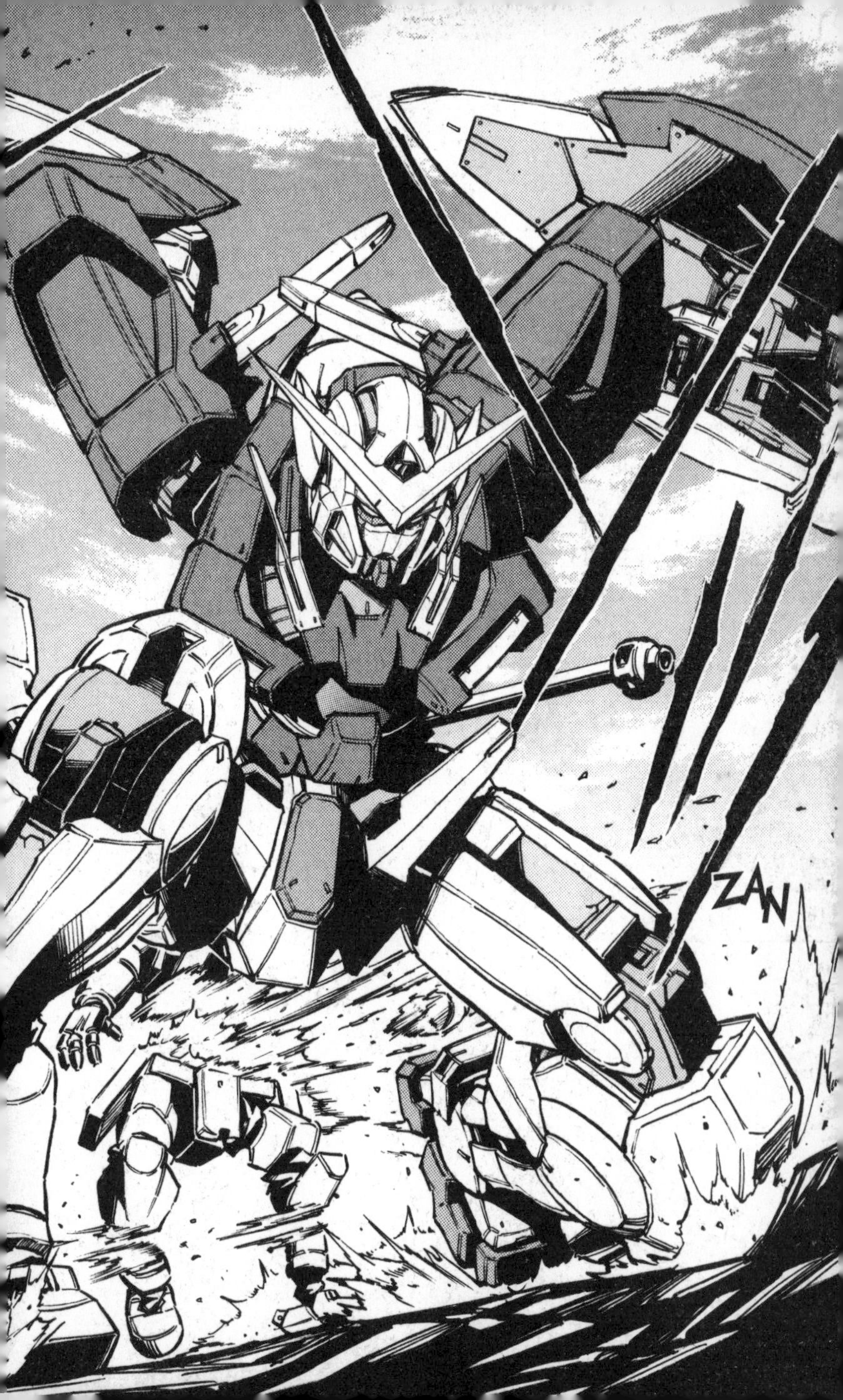
ZAN

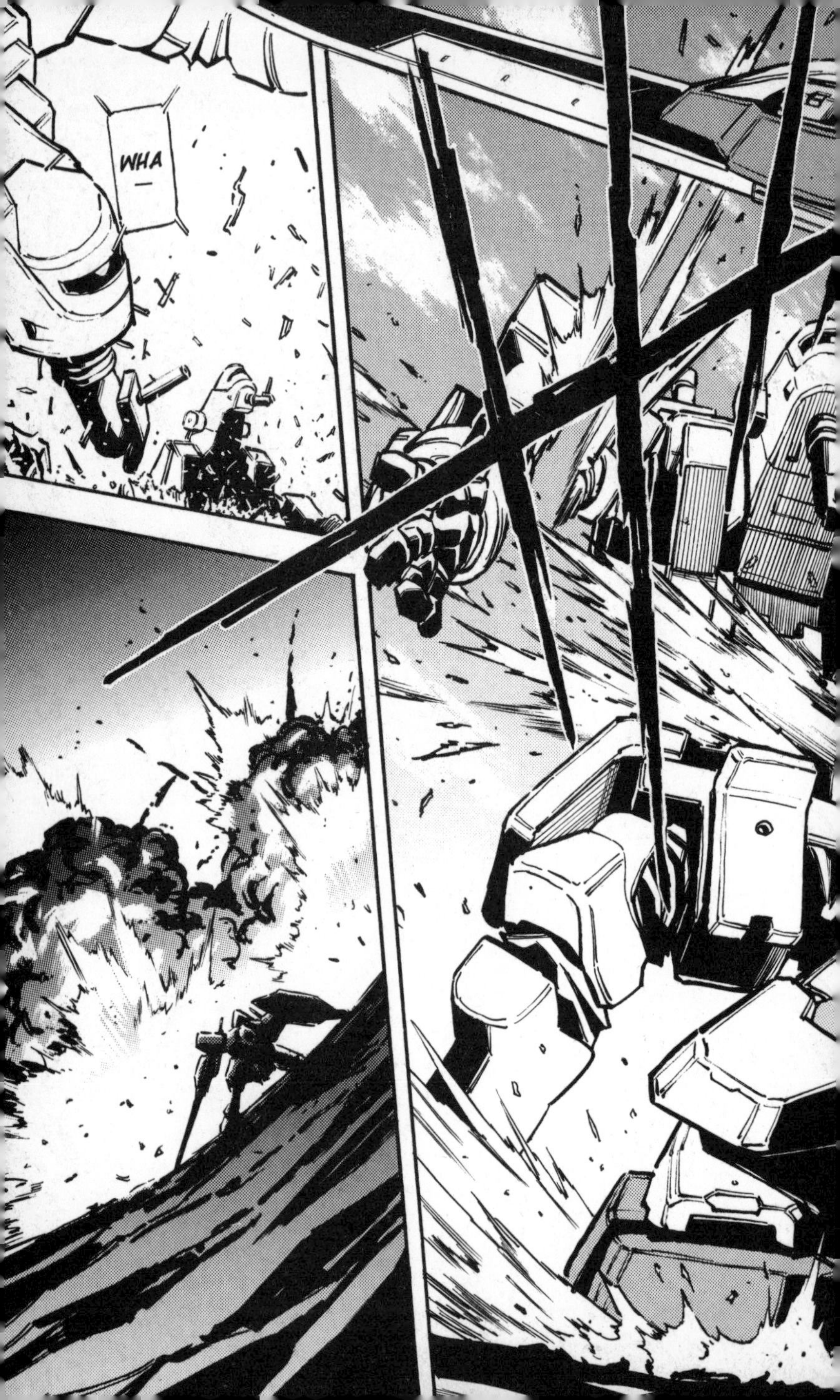
WHA

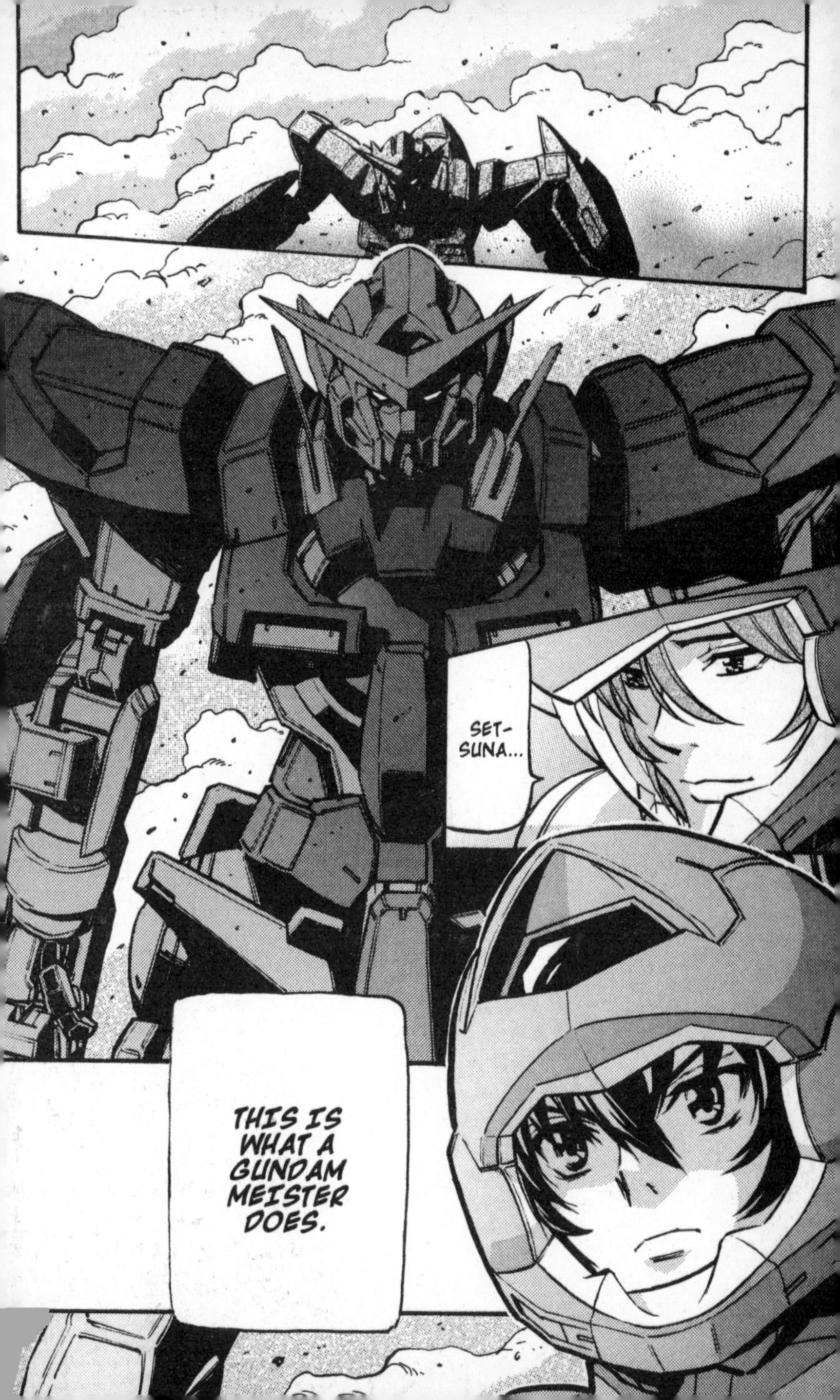
SET-SUNA...
THIS IS WHAT A GUNDAM MEISTER DOES.

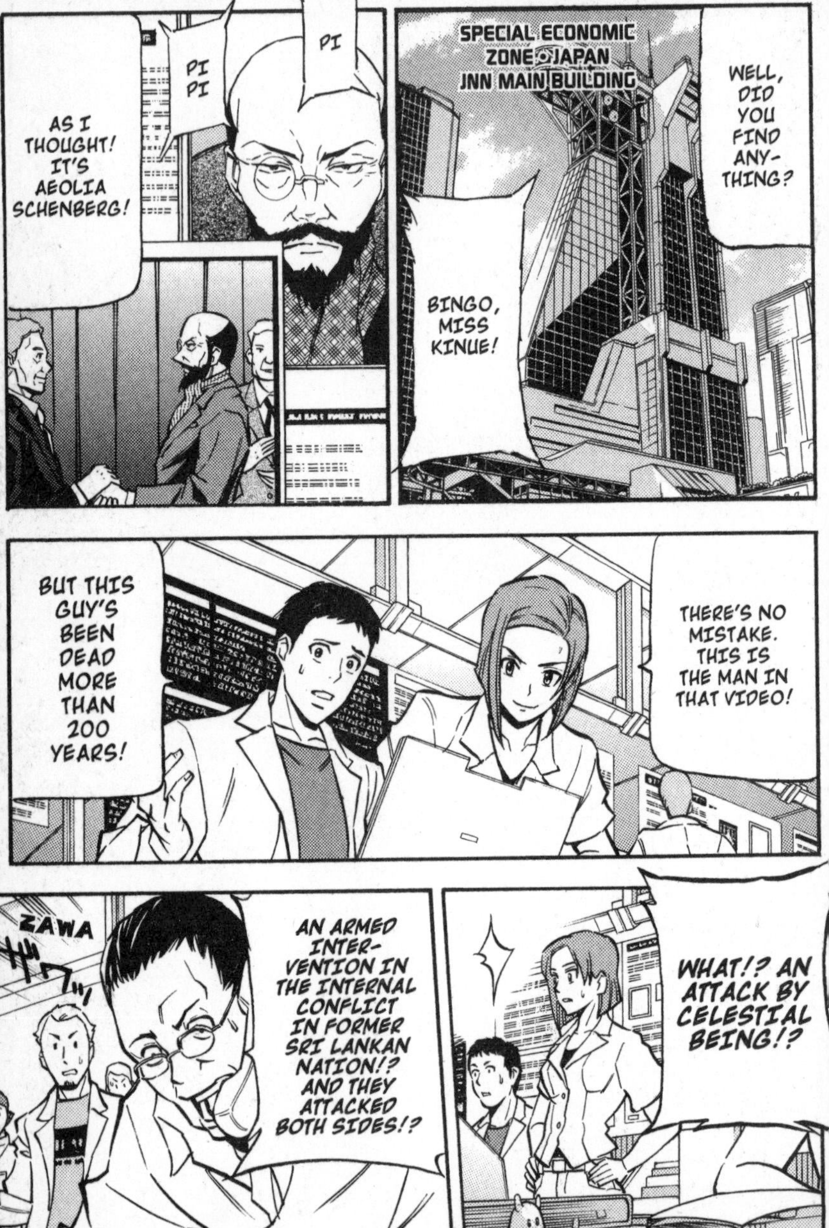
SPECIAL ECONOMIC ZONE JAPAN JNN MAIN BUILDING
WELL, DID YOU FIND ANY-THING?
BINGO, MISS KINUE!
PI
PI PI
AS I THOUGHT! IT'S AEOLIA SCHENBERG!
THERE'S NO MISTAKE. THIS IS THE MAN IN THAT VIDEO!
BUT THIS GUY'S BEEN DEAD MORE THAN 200 YEARS!
WHAT!? AN ATTACK BY CELESTIAL BEING!?
AN ARMED INTER-VENTION IN THE INTERNAL CONFLICT IN FORMER SRI LANKAN NATION!? AND THEY ATTACKED BOTH SIDES!?
ZAWA

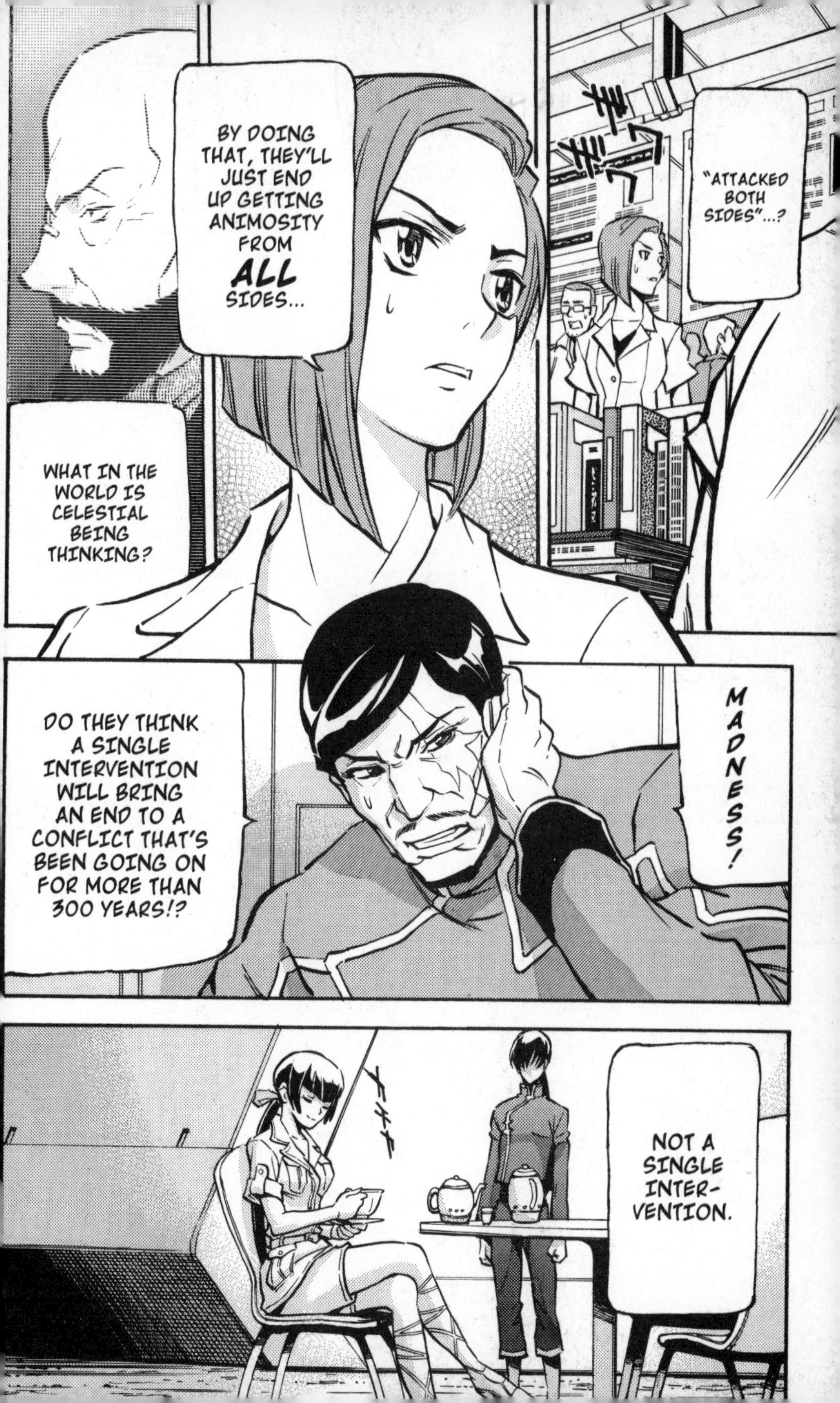
"ATTACKED BOTH SIDES"...?
BY DOING THAT, THEY'LL JUST END UP GETTING ANIMOSITY FROM **ALL** SIDES...
WHAT IN THE WORLD IS CELESTIAL BEING THINKING?
MADNESS!
DO THEY THINK A SINGLE INTERVENTION WILL BRING AN END TO A CONFLICT THAT'S BEEN GOING ON FOR MORE THAN 300 YEARS!?
NOT A SINGLE INTER-VENTION.

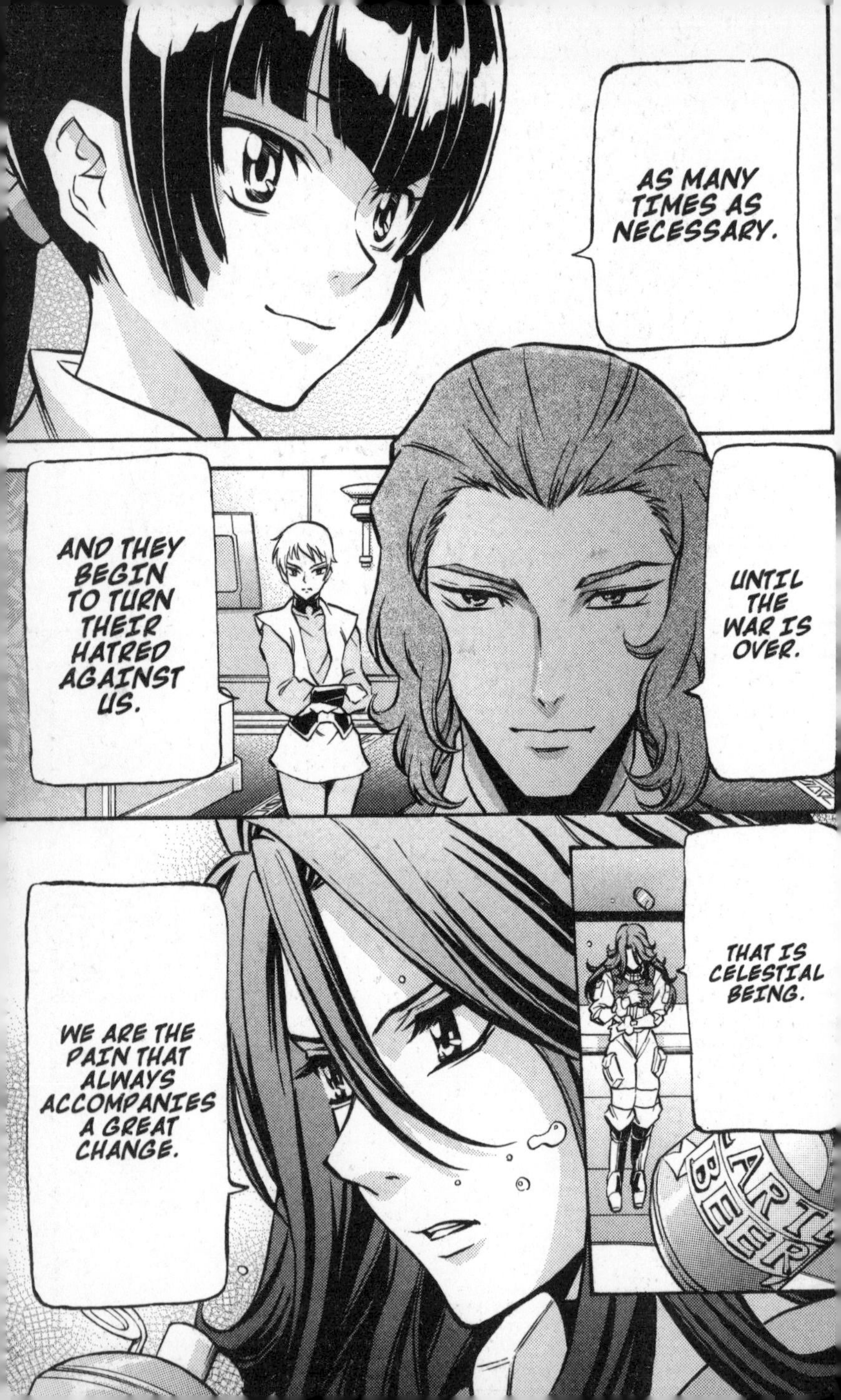
AS MANY TIMES AS NECESSARY.
UNTIL THE WAR IS OVER.
AND THEY BEGIN TO TURN THEIR HATRED AGAINST US.
THAT IS CELESTIAL BEING.
WE ARE THE PAIN THAT ALWAYS ACCOMPANIES A GREAT CHANGE.

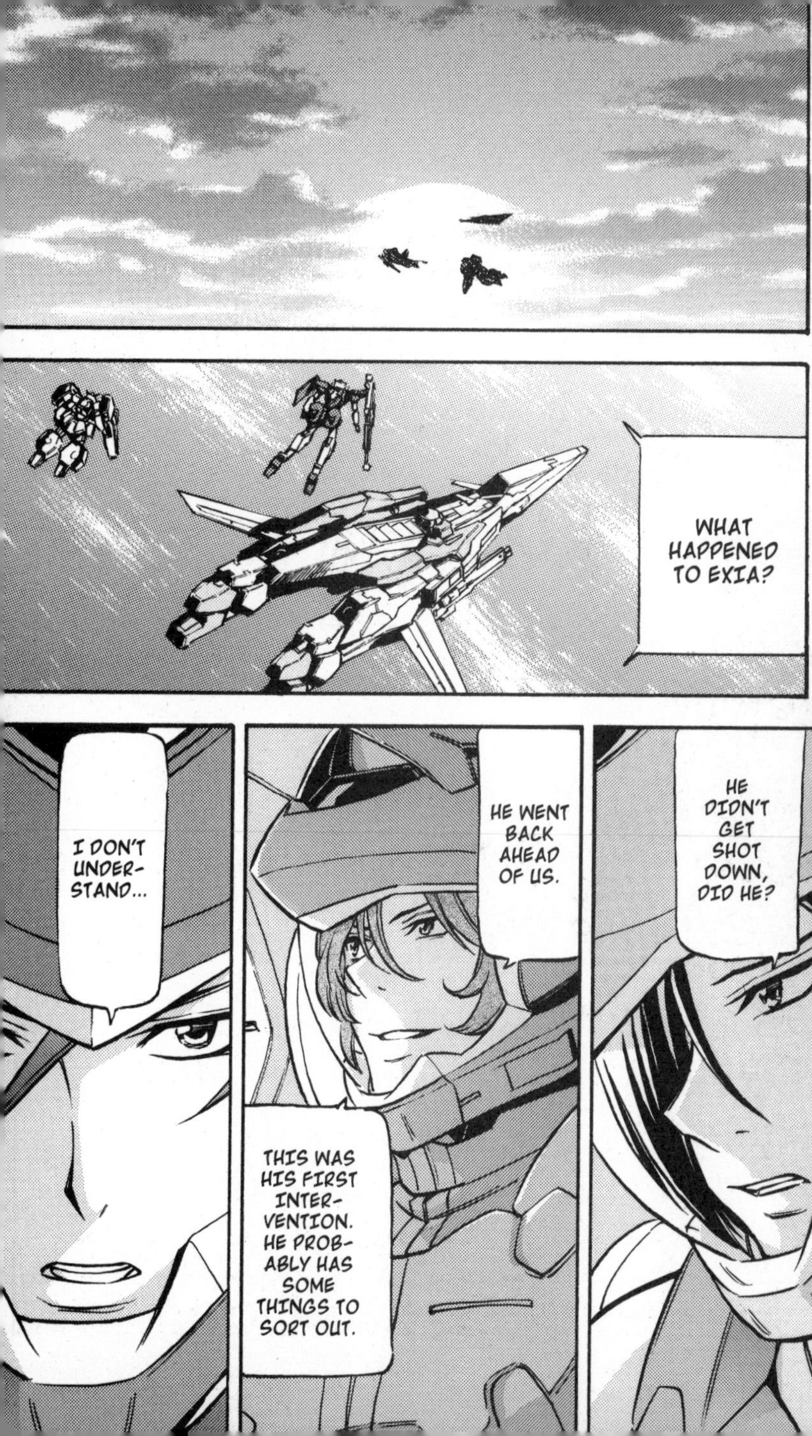
WHAT HAPPENED TO EXIA?
HE DIDN'T GET SHOT DOWN, DID HE?
HE WENT BACK AHEAD OF US.
THIS WAS HIS FIRST INTER-VENTION. HE PROB-ABLY HAS SOME THINGS TO SORT OUT.
I DON'T UNDER-STAND...

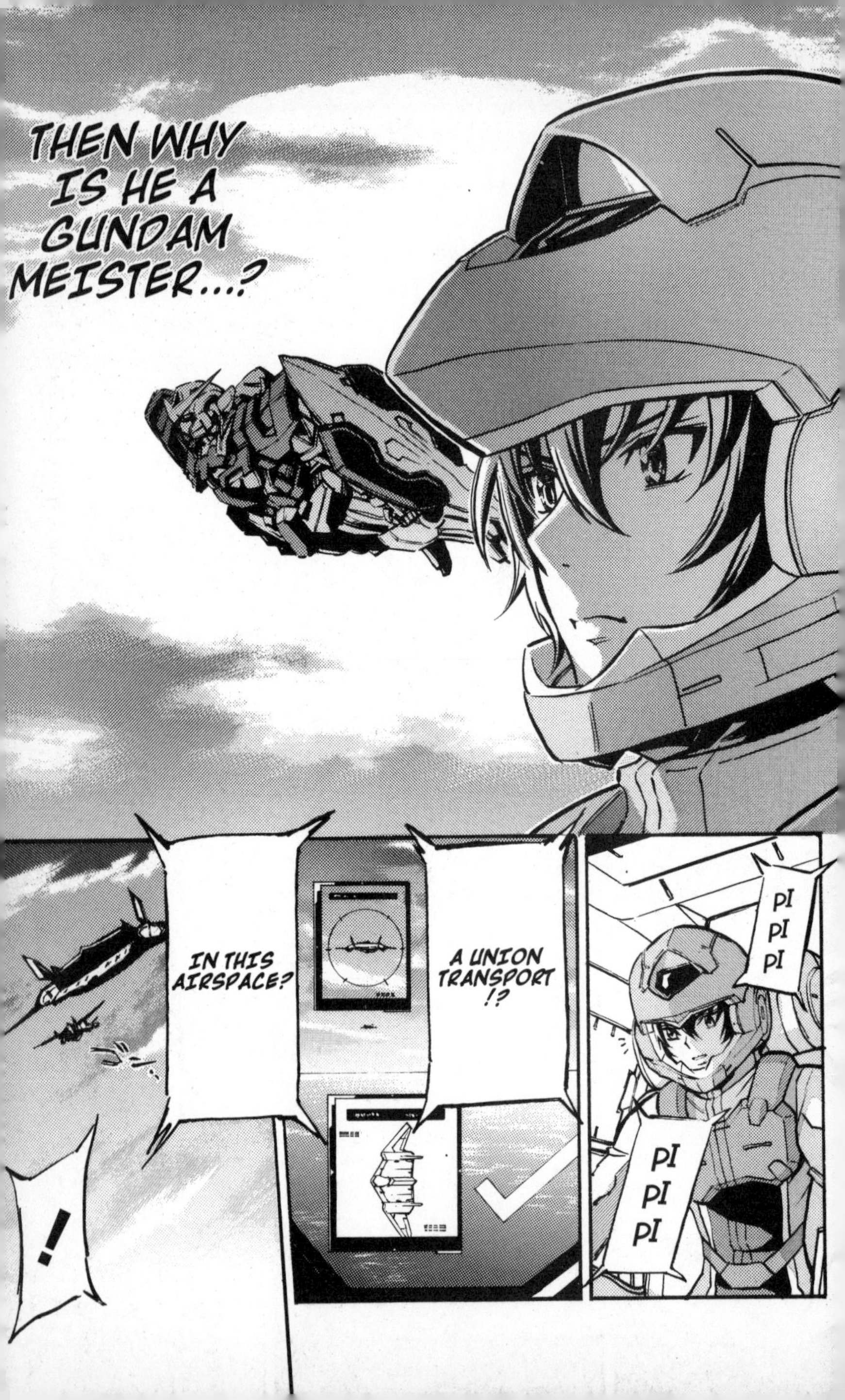
THEN WHY IS HE A GUNDAM MEISTER...?
PI PI PI
PI PI PI
A UNION TRANSPORT !?
IN THIS AIRSPACE?
!

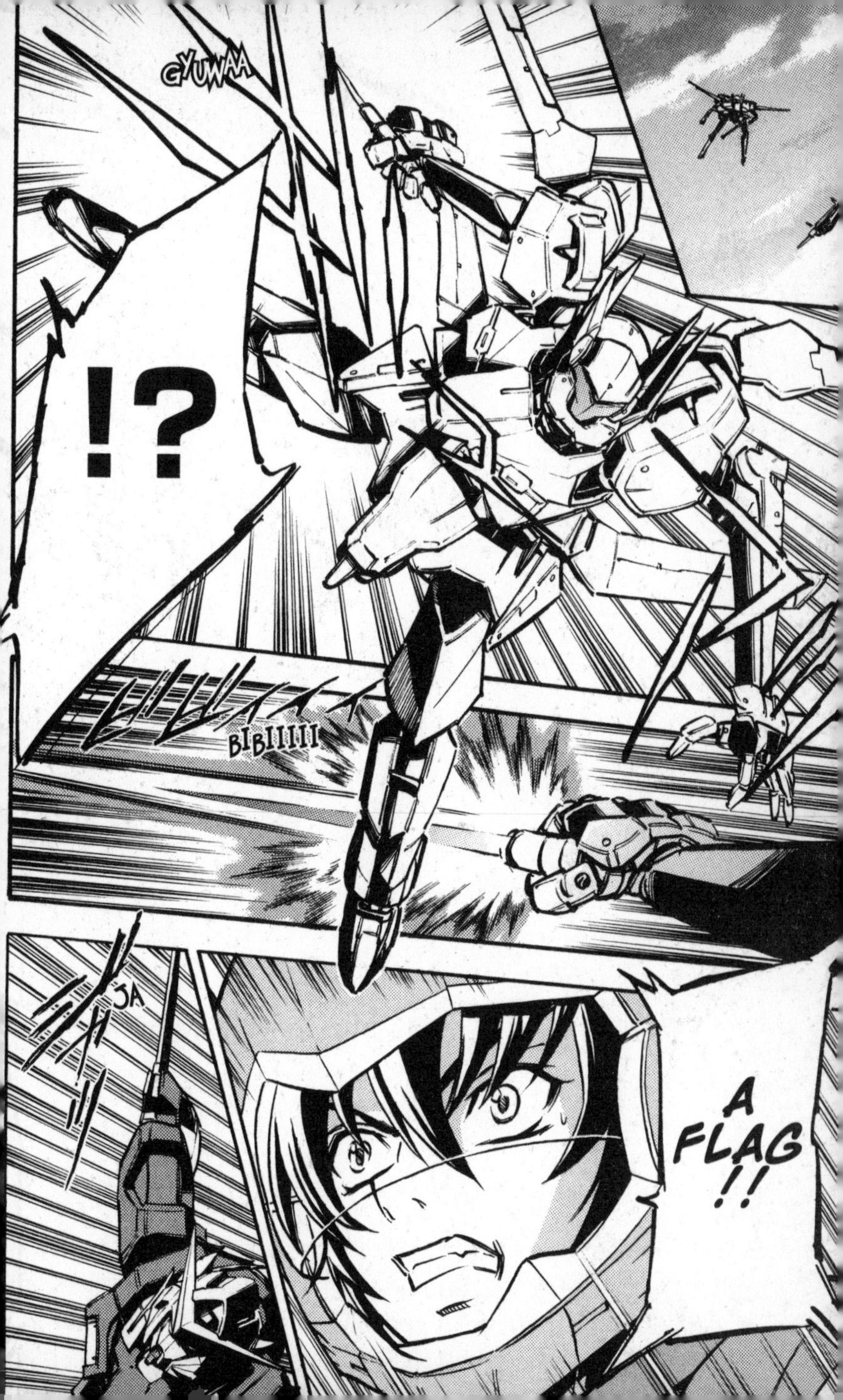
GYUWAA
!?
BIBIIIII
A FLAG!!
JA

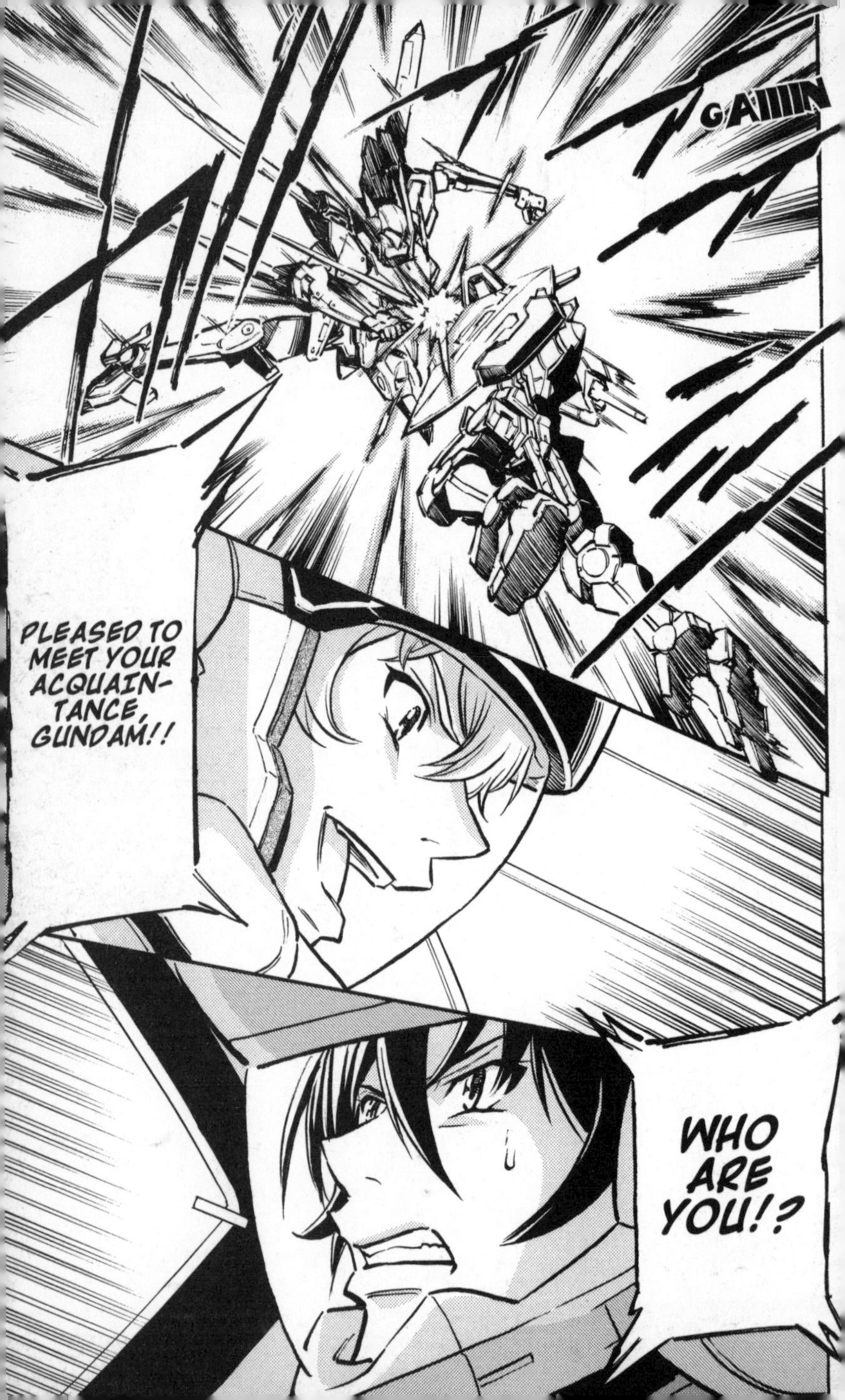
GAIIIIN
PLEASED TO MEET YOUR ACQUAIN-TANCE, GUNDAM!!
WHO ARE YOU!?

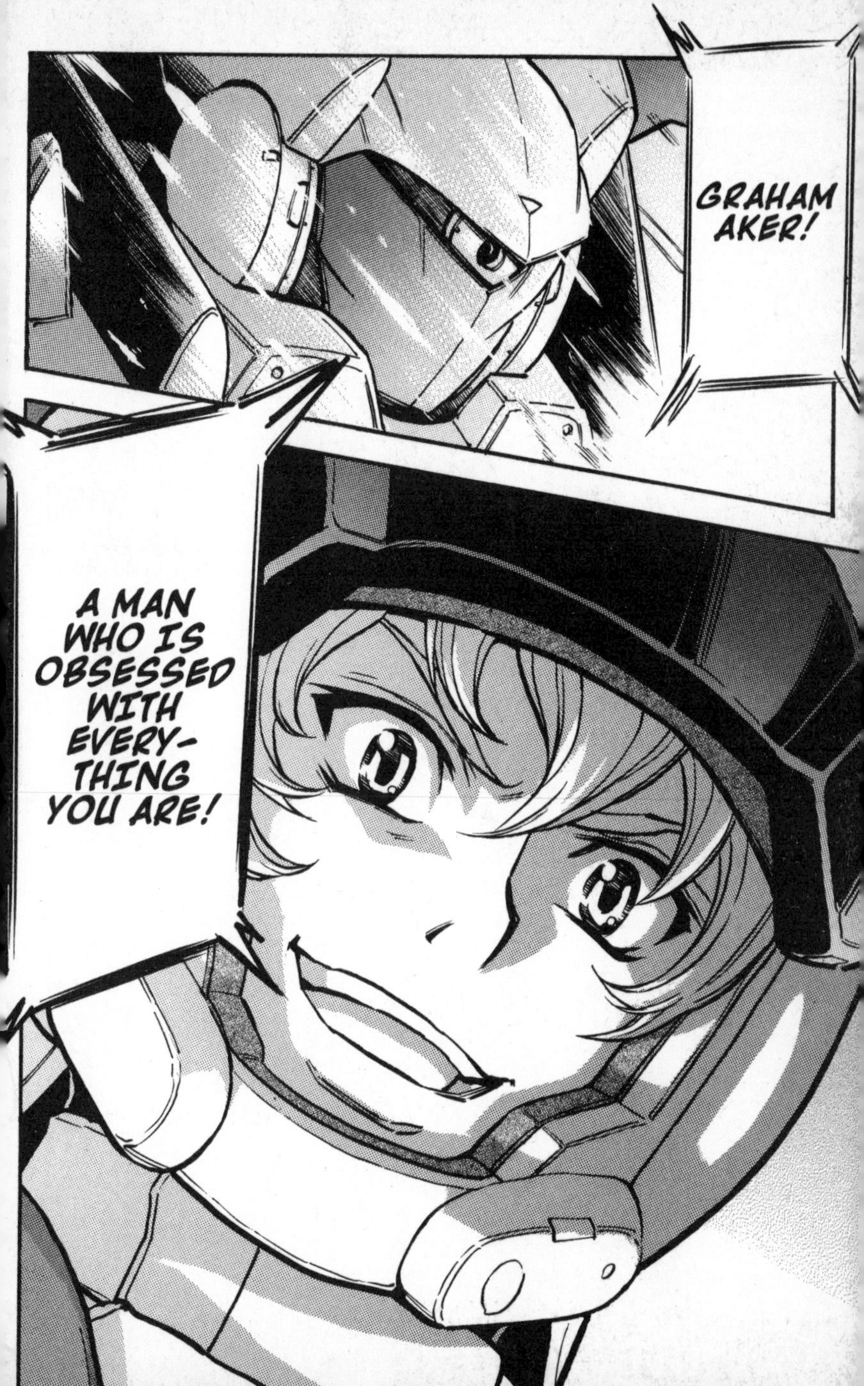
GRAHAM AKER!
A MAN WHO IS OBSESSED WITH EVERY-THING YOU ARE!

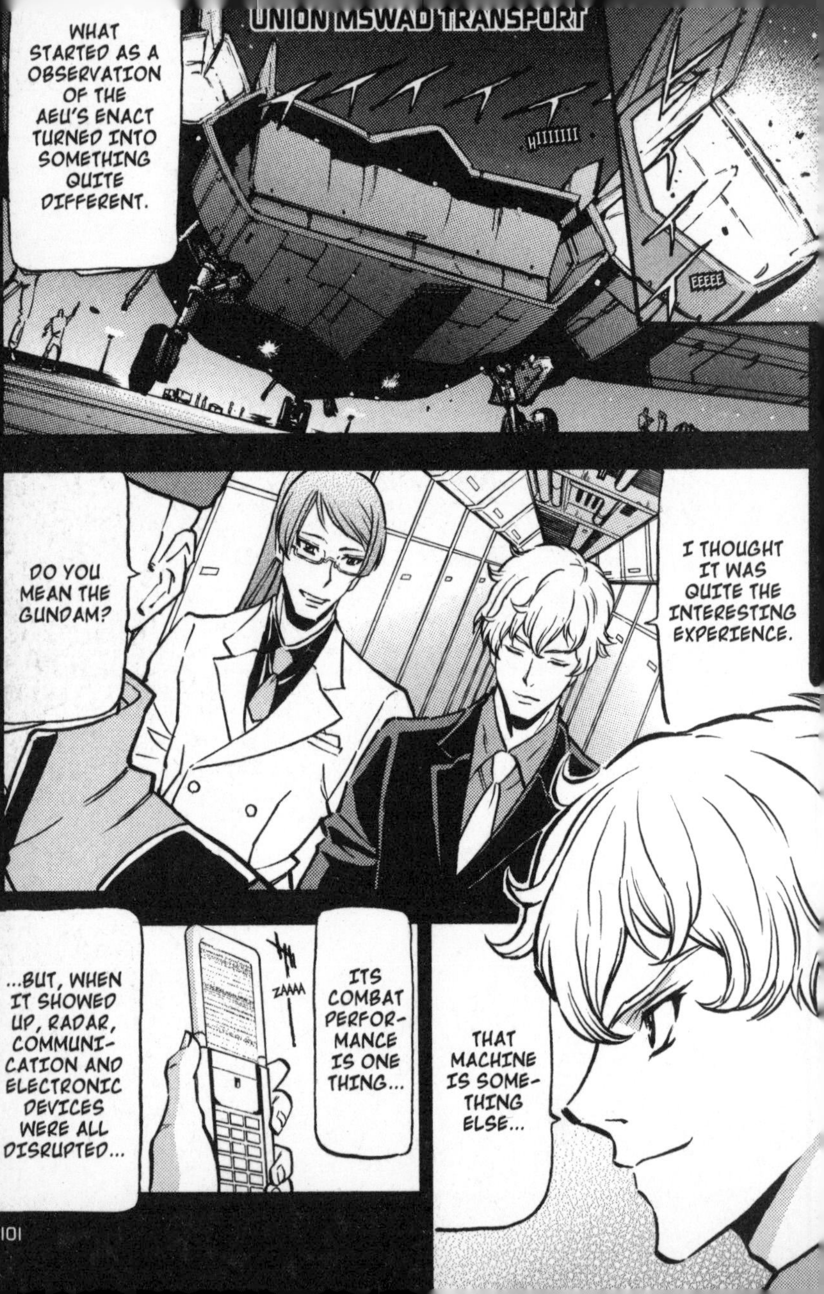
UNION MSWAD TRANSPORT
HIIIIIII
EEEEE
WHAT STARTED AS A OBSERVATION OF THE AEU'S ENACT TURNED INTO SOMETHING QUITE DIFFERENT.
I THOUGHT IT WAS QUITE THE INTERESTING EXPERIENCE.
DO YOU MEAN THE GUNDAM?
THAT MACHINE IS SOME-THING ELSE...
ITS COMBAT PERFOR-MANCE IS ONE THING...
ZAAAA
...BUT, WHEN IT SHOWED UP, RADAR, COMMUNI-CATION AND ELECTRONIC DEVICES WERE ALL DISRUPTED...

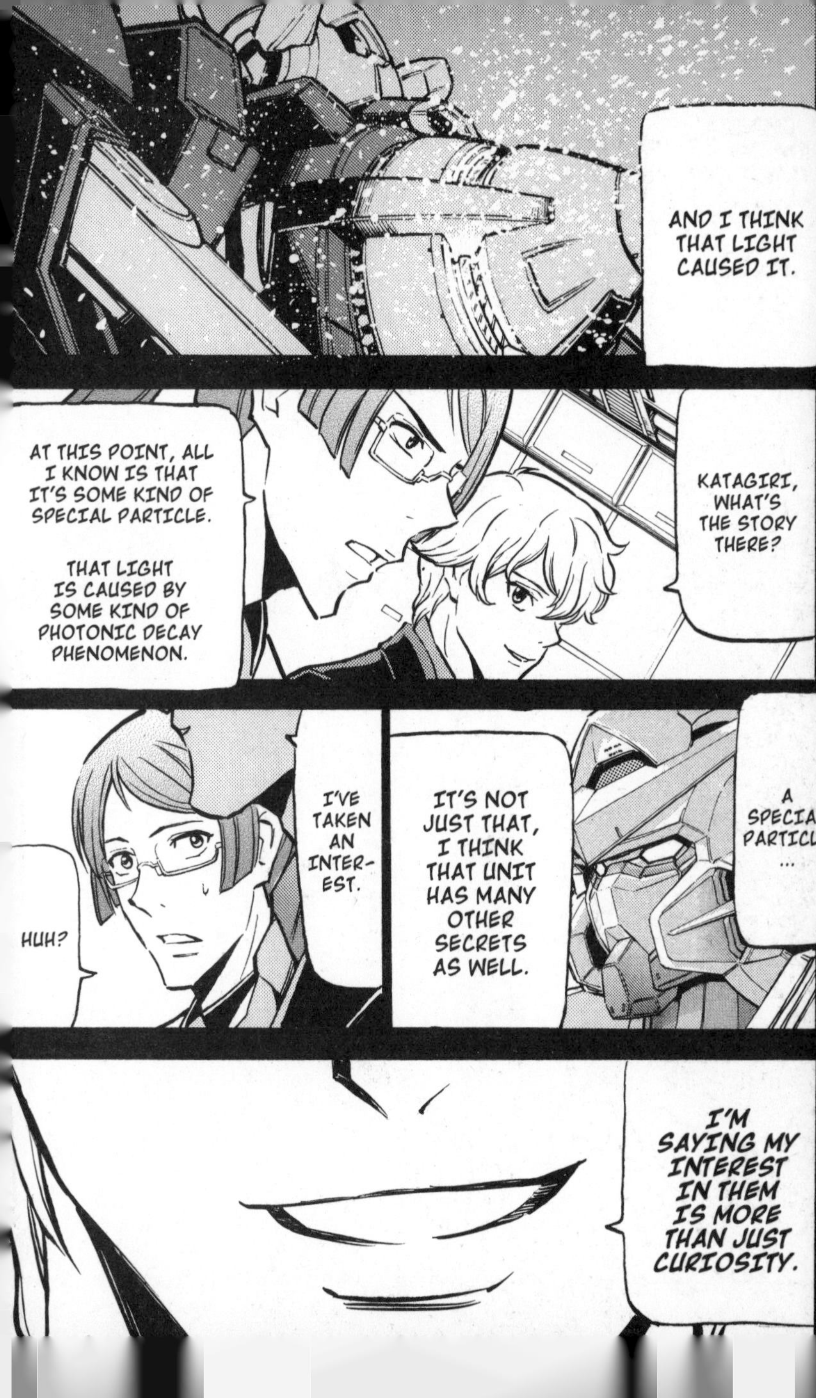
AND I THINK THAT LIGHT CAUSED IT.
KATAGIRI, WHAT'S THE STORY THERE?
AT THIS POINT, ALL I KNOW IS THAT IT'S SOME KIND OF SPECIAL PARTICLE.
THAT LIGHT IS CAUSED BY SOME KIND OF PHOTONIC DECAY PHENOMENON.
A SPECIAL PARTICLE ...
IT'S NOT JUST THAT, I THINK THAT UNIT HAS MANY OTHER SECRETS AS WELL.
I'VE TAKEN AN INTER-EST.
HUH?
I'M SAYING MY INTEREST IN THEM IS MORE THAN JUST CURIOSITY.

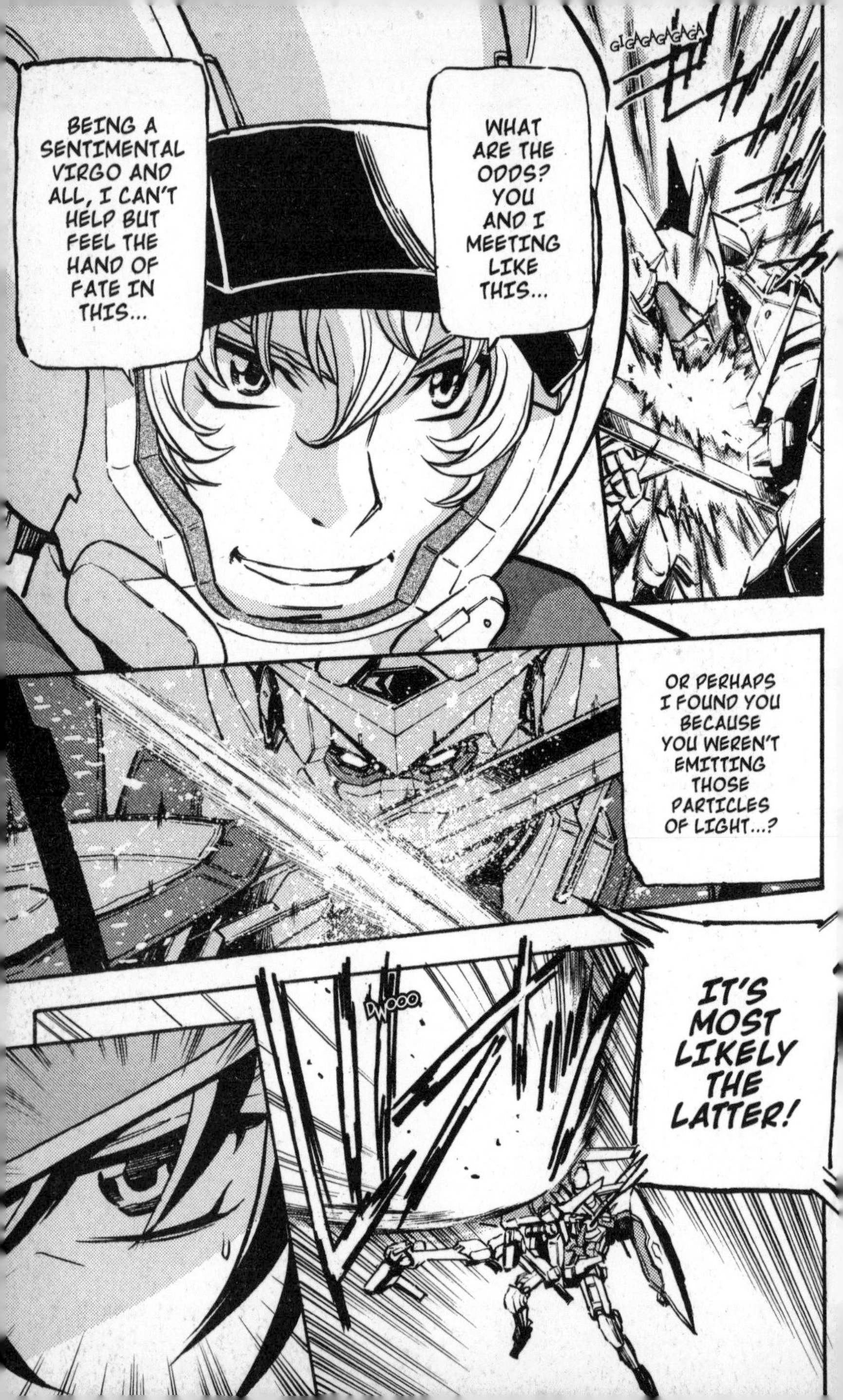
GIGAGAGAGAGA
WHAT ARE THE ODDS? YOU AND I MEETING LIKE THIS...
BEING A SENTIMENTAL VIRGO AND ALL, I CAN'T HELP BUT FEEL THE HAND OF FATE IN THIS...
OR PERHAPS I FOUND YOU BECAUSE YOU WEREN'T EMITTING THOSE PARTICLES OF LIGHT...?
IT'S MOST LIKELY THE LATTER!
DWOOO

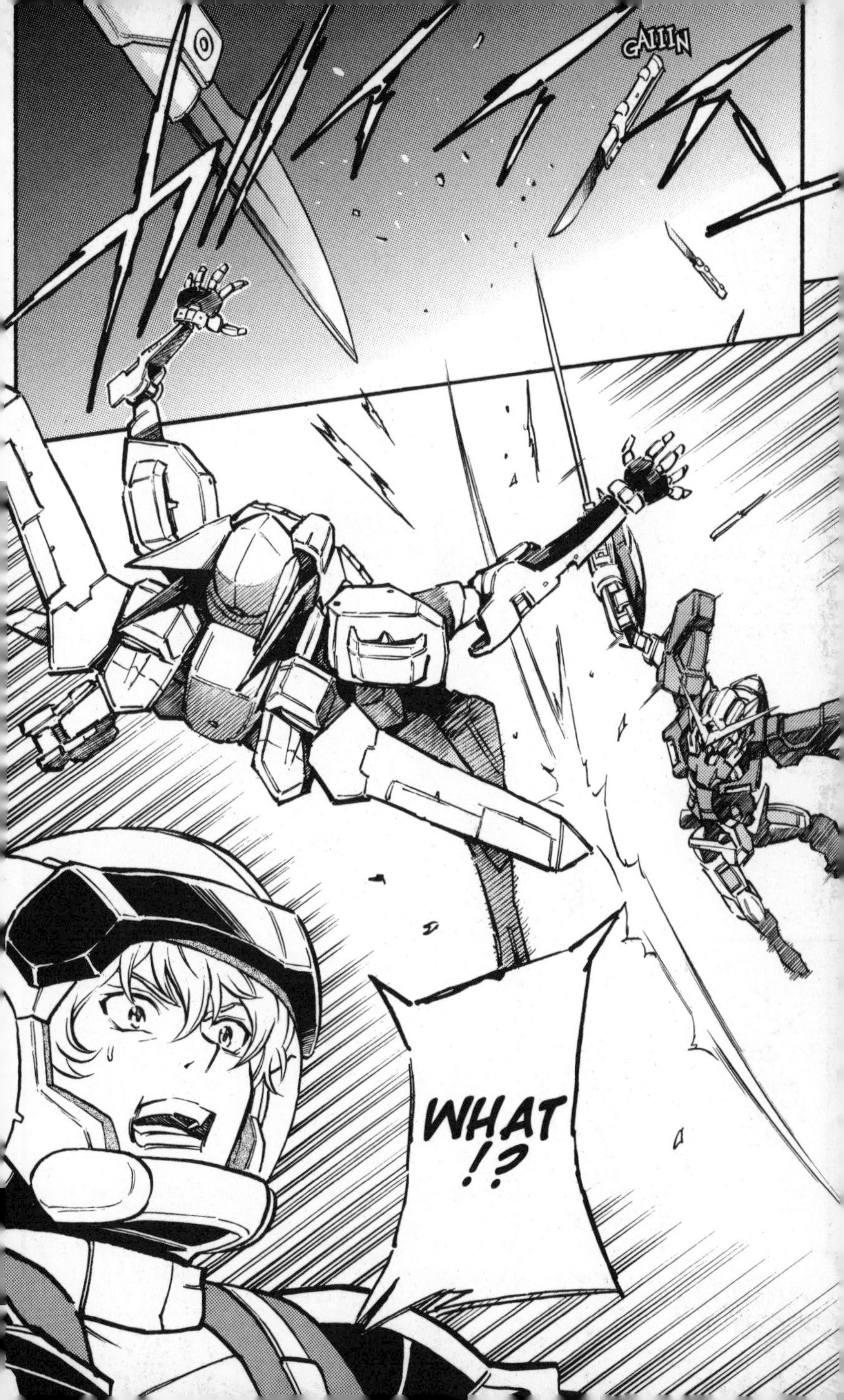
GAIIIN
WHAT!?

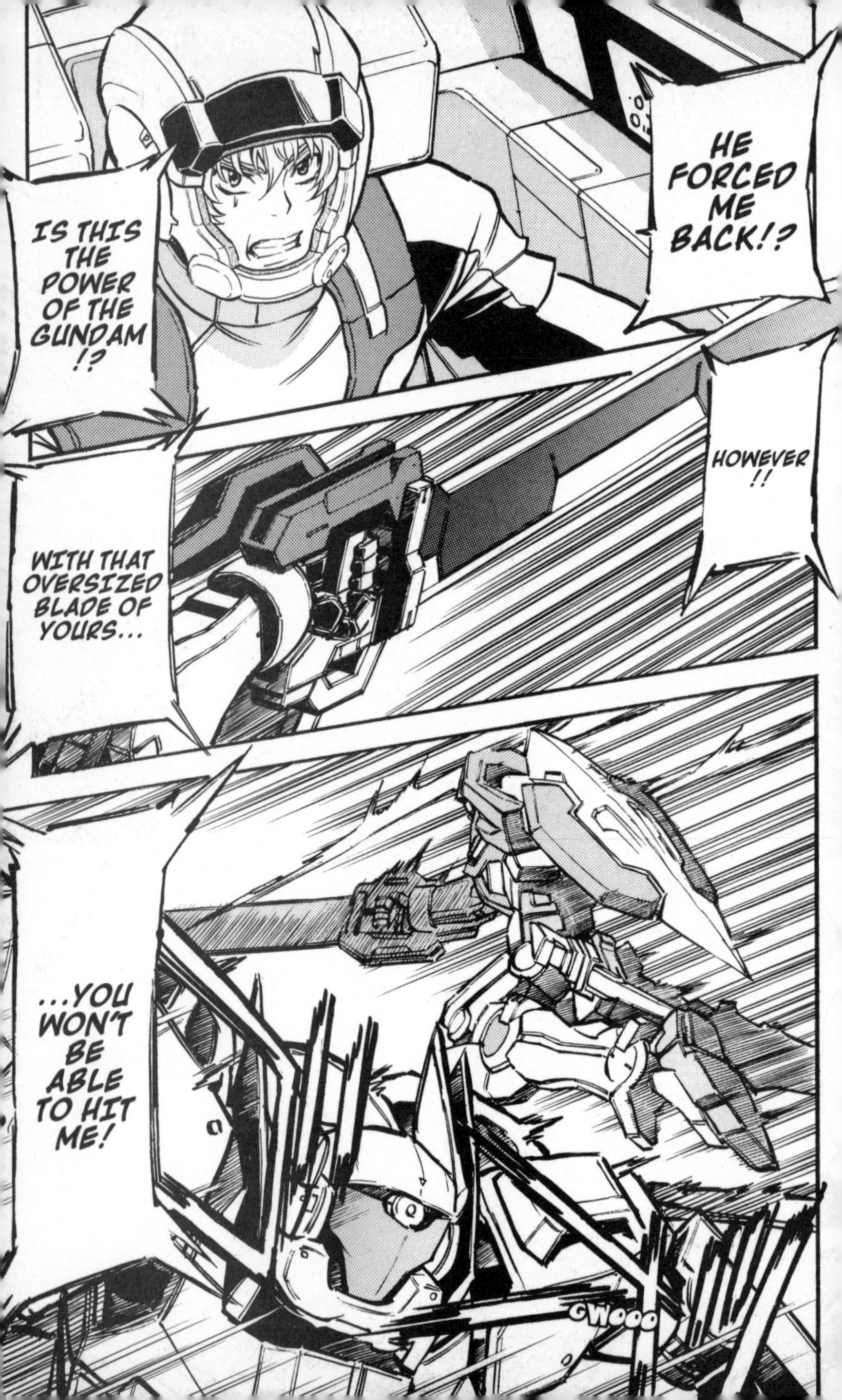
HE FORCED ME BACK!?
IS THIS THE POWER OF THE GUNDAM!?
HOWEVER!!
WITH THAT OVERSIZED BLADE OF YOURS...
...YOU WON'T BE ABLE TO HIT ME!
GWOOO

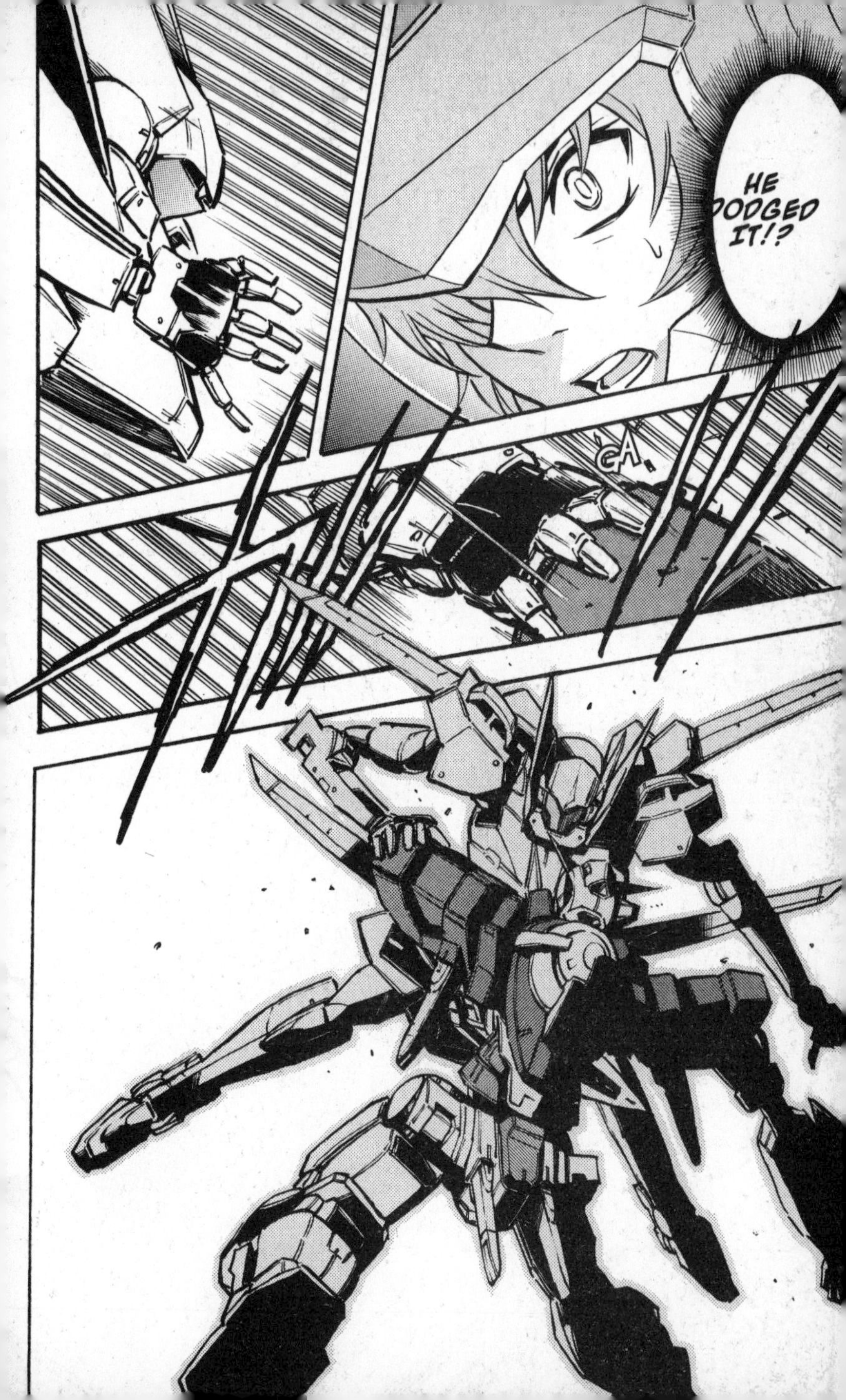
HE DODGED IT!?
GA

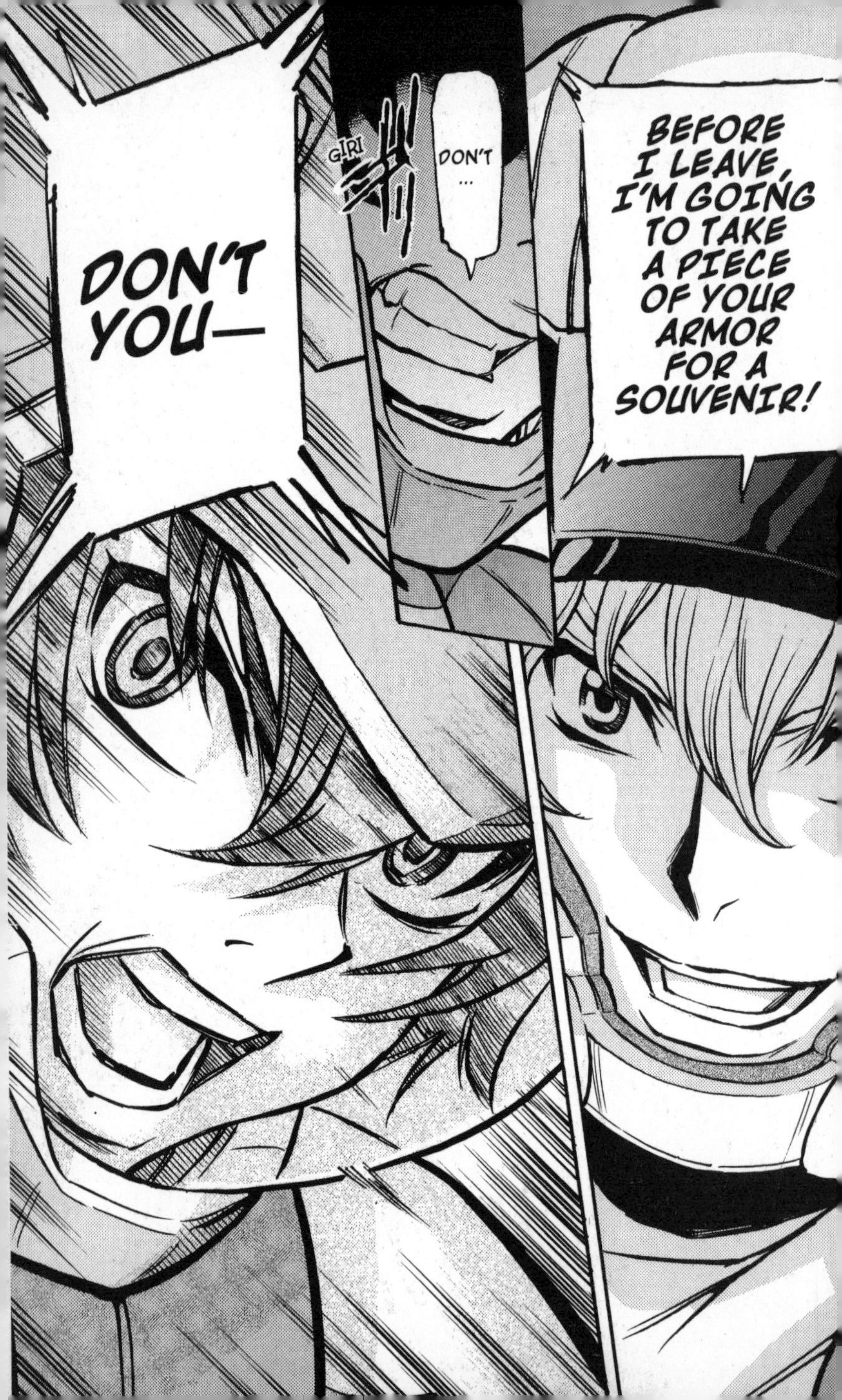
BEFORE I LEAVE, I'M GOING TO TAKE A PIECE OF YOUR ARMOR FOR A SOUVENIR!
DON'T ...
GIRI
DON'T YOU—

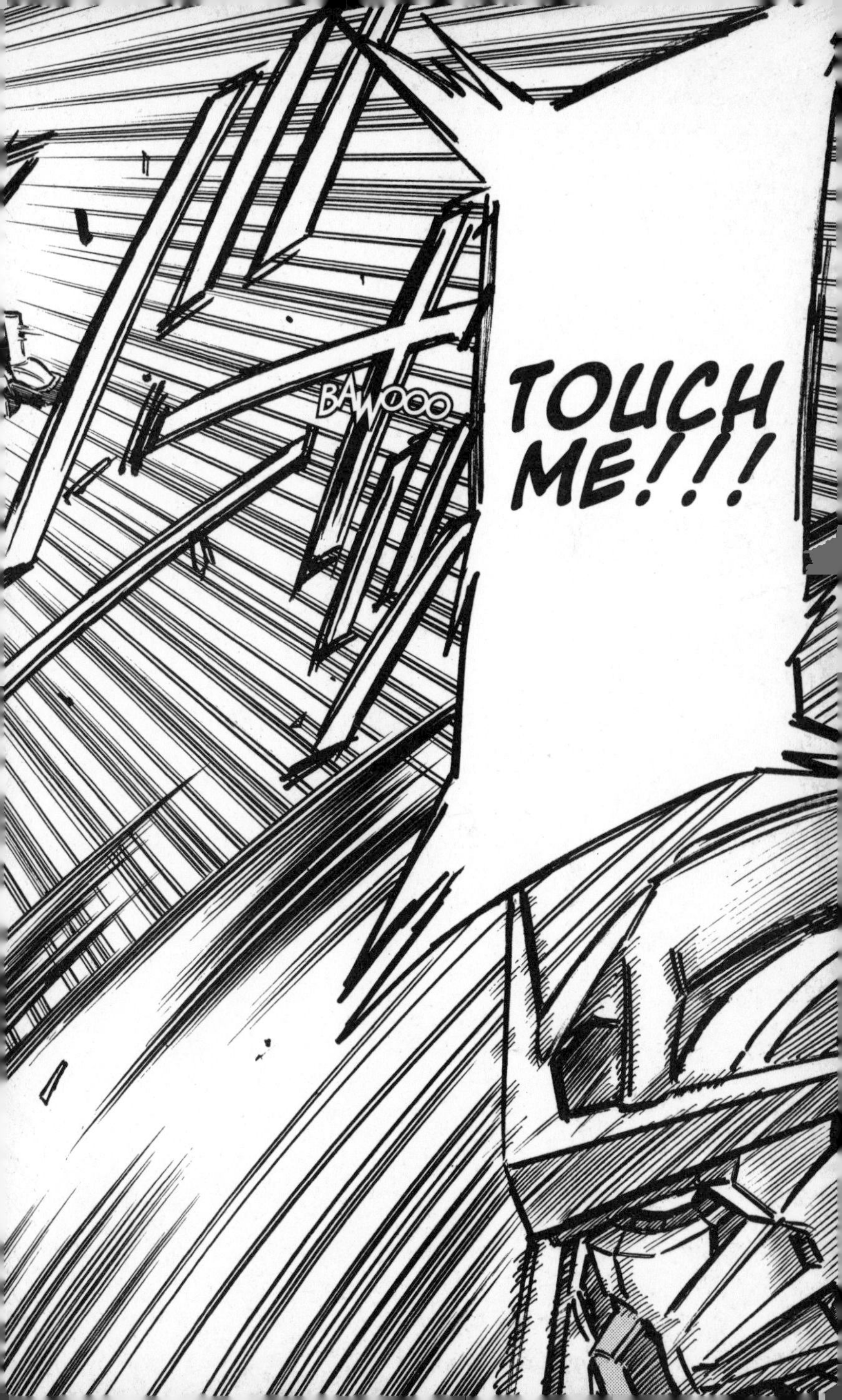
TOUCH ME!!!
BAWOOO

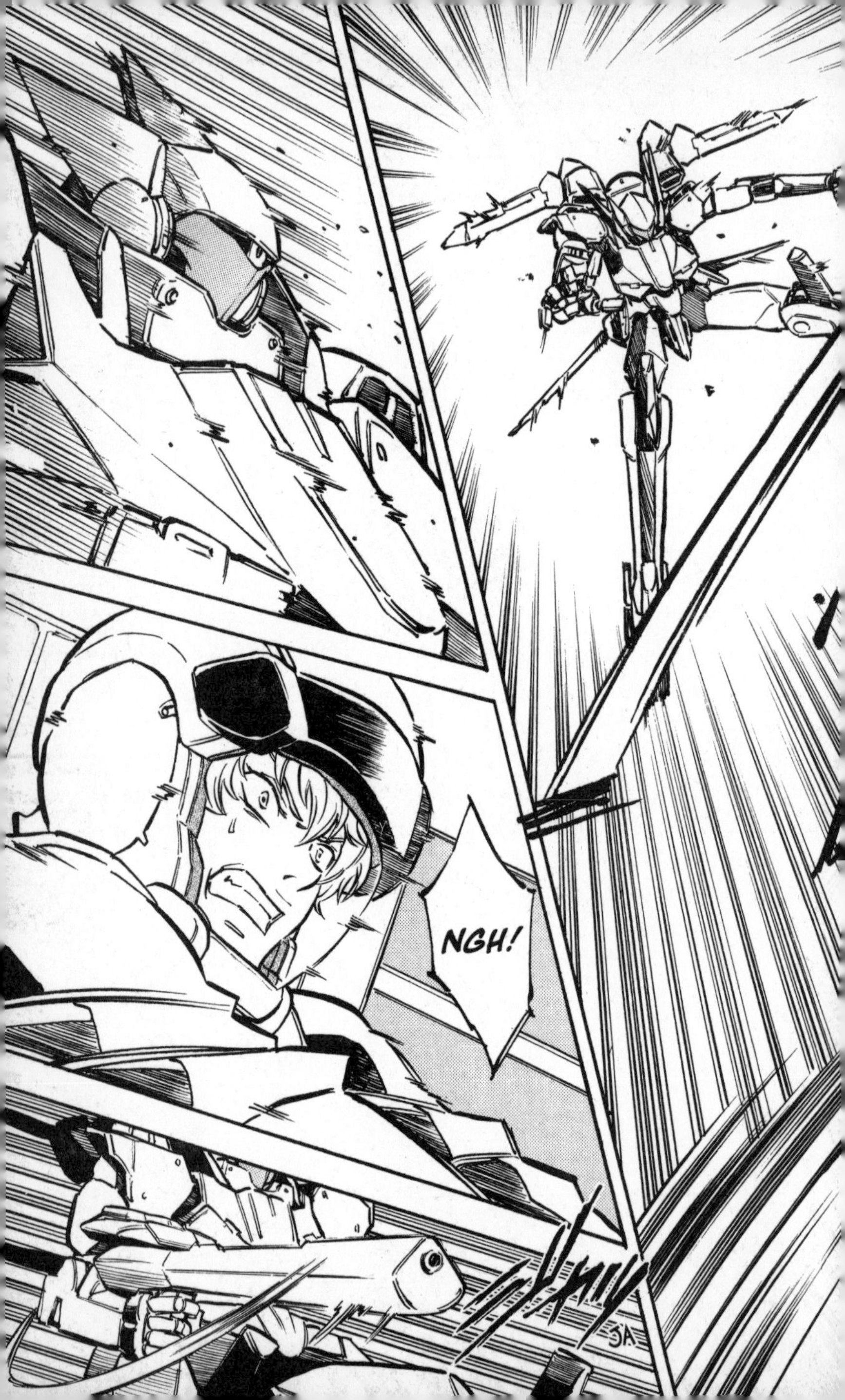
NGH!

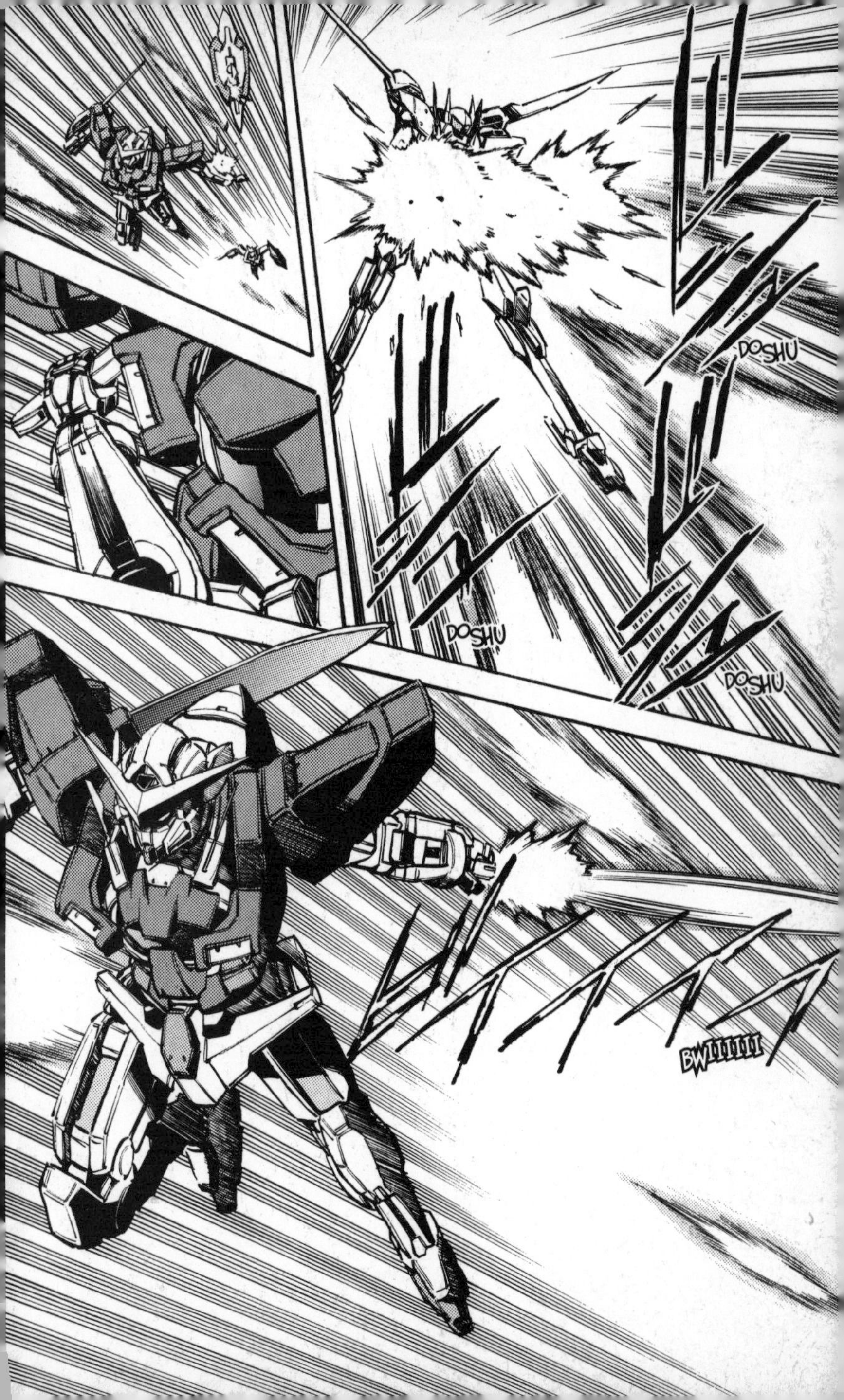
DOSHU
DOSHU
DOSHU
BWIIIIII

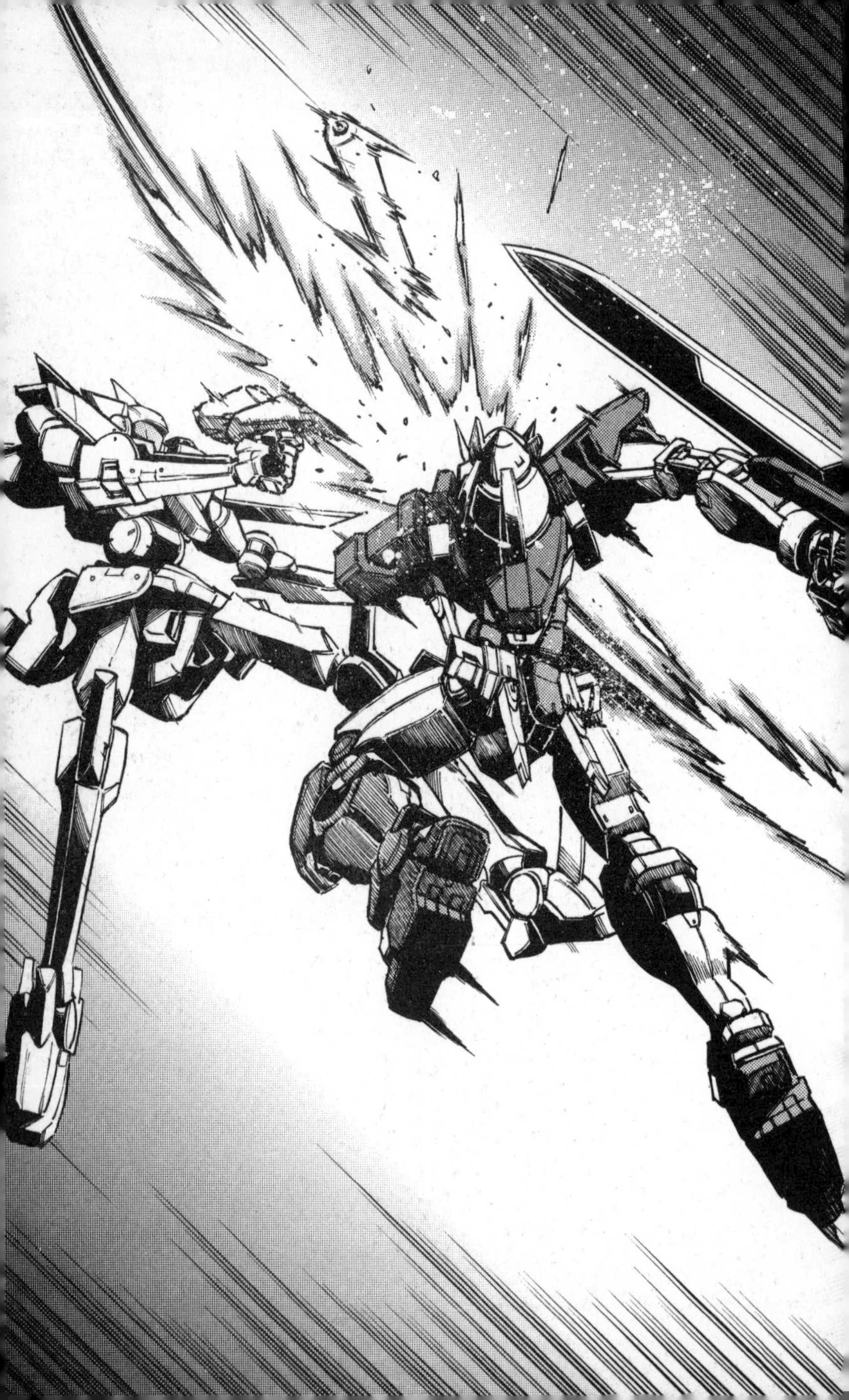

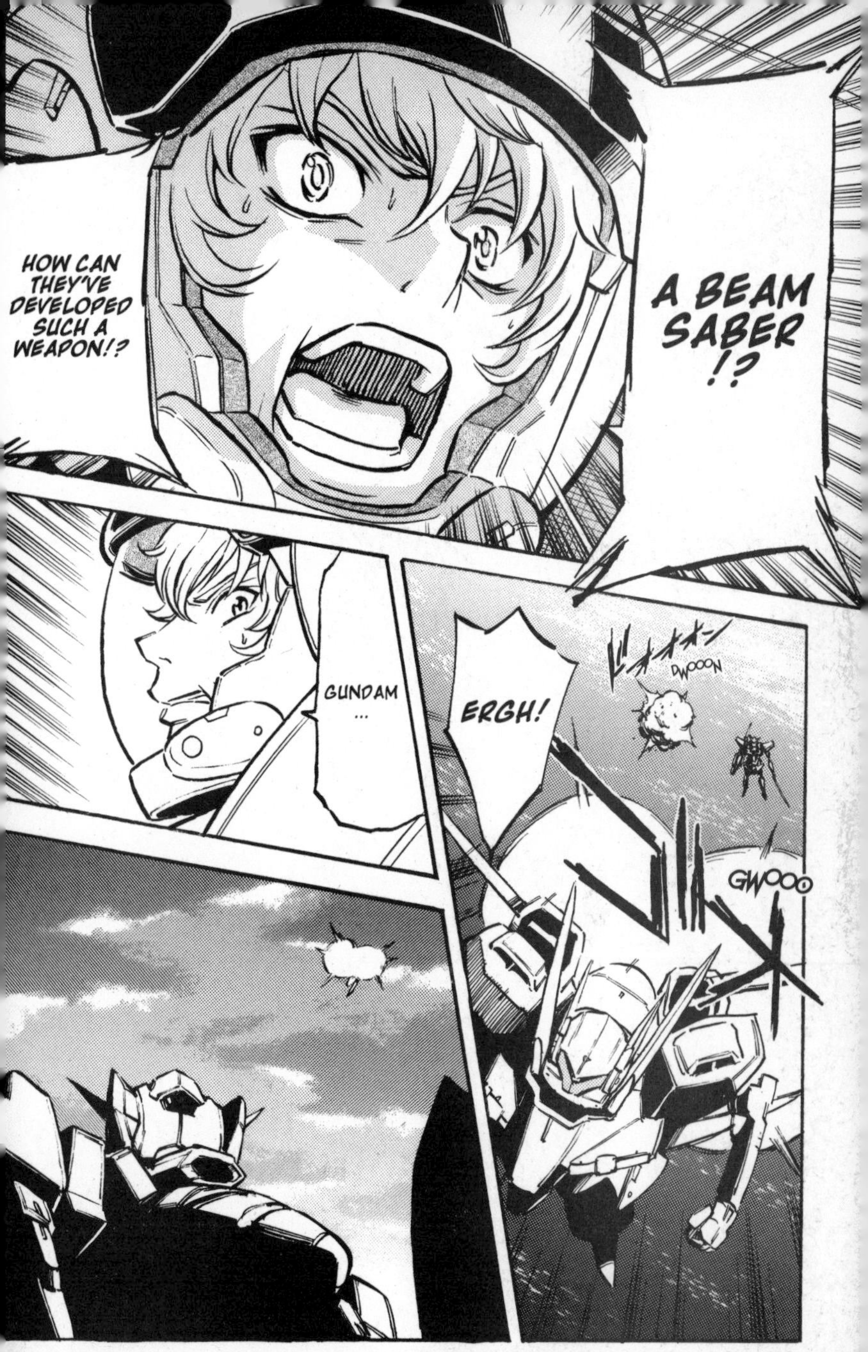
A BEAM SABER!?
HOW CAN THEY'VE DEVELOPED SUCH A WEAPON!?
DWOOON
ERGH!
GUNDAM ...
GWOOO

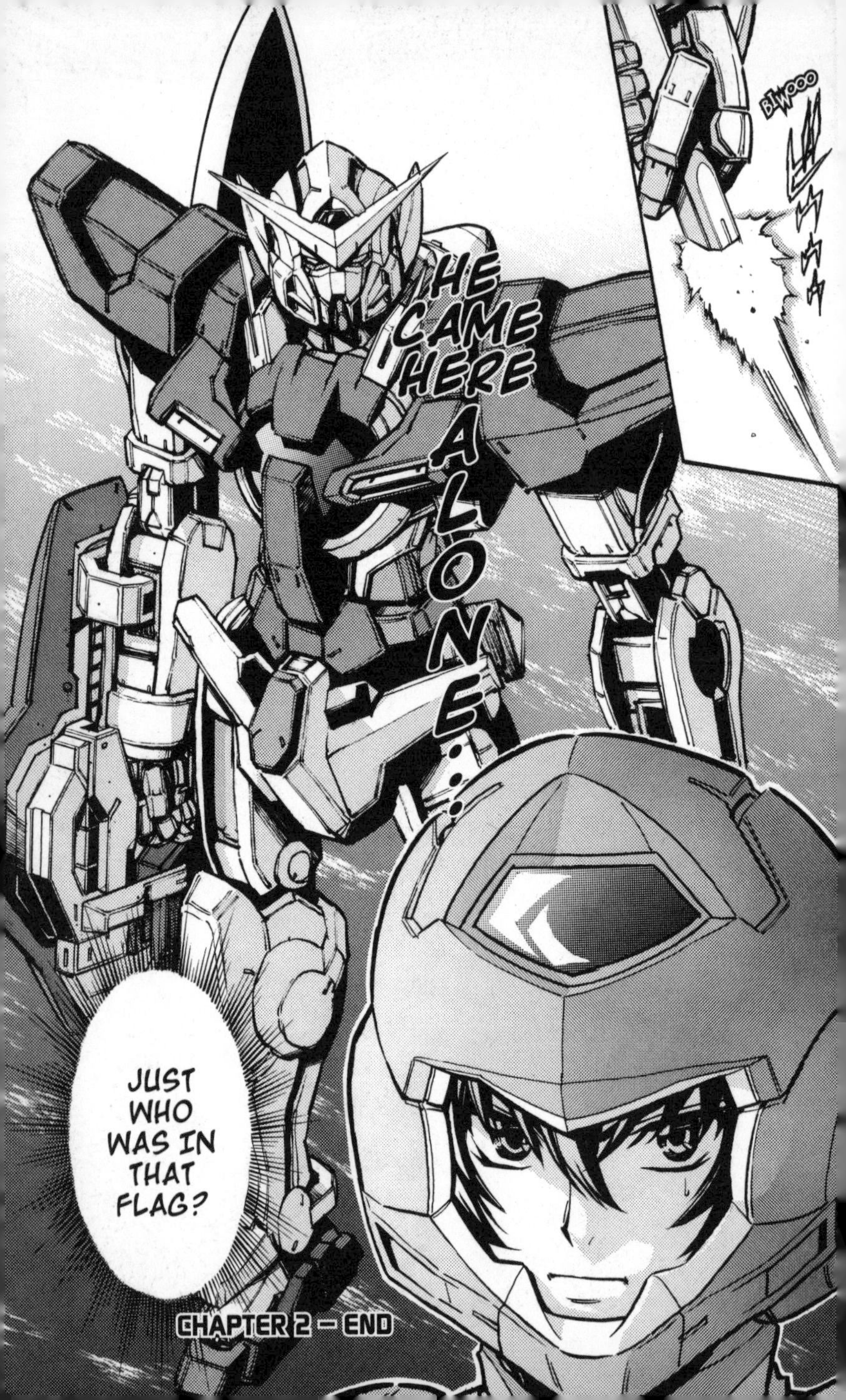
BIWOOO
HE CAME HERE ALONE...
JUST WHO WAS IN THAT FLAG?
CHAPTER 2 — END

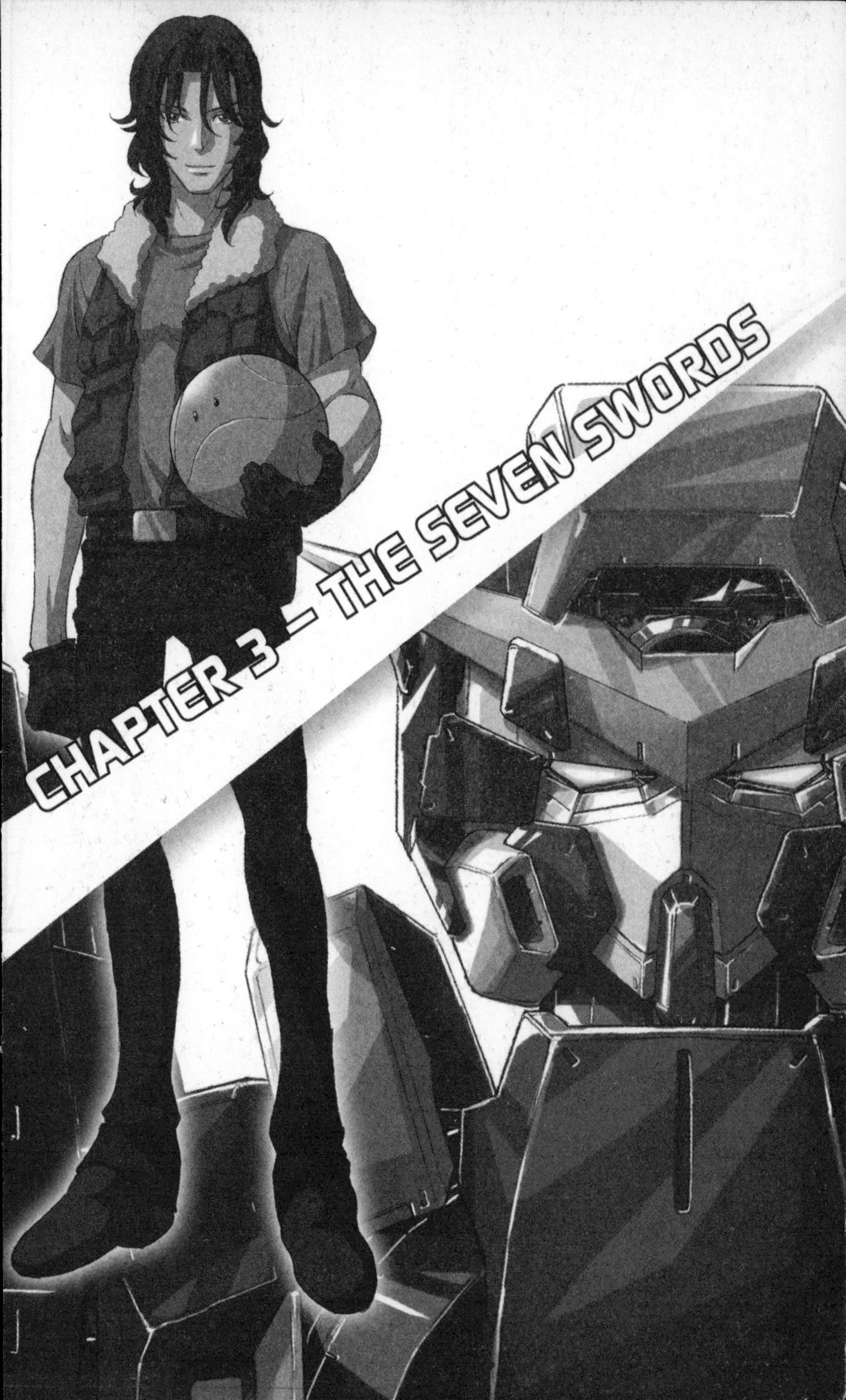
CHAPTER 3 – THE SEVEN SWORDS

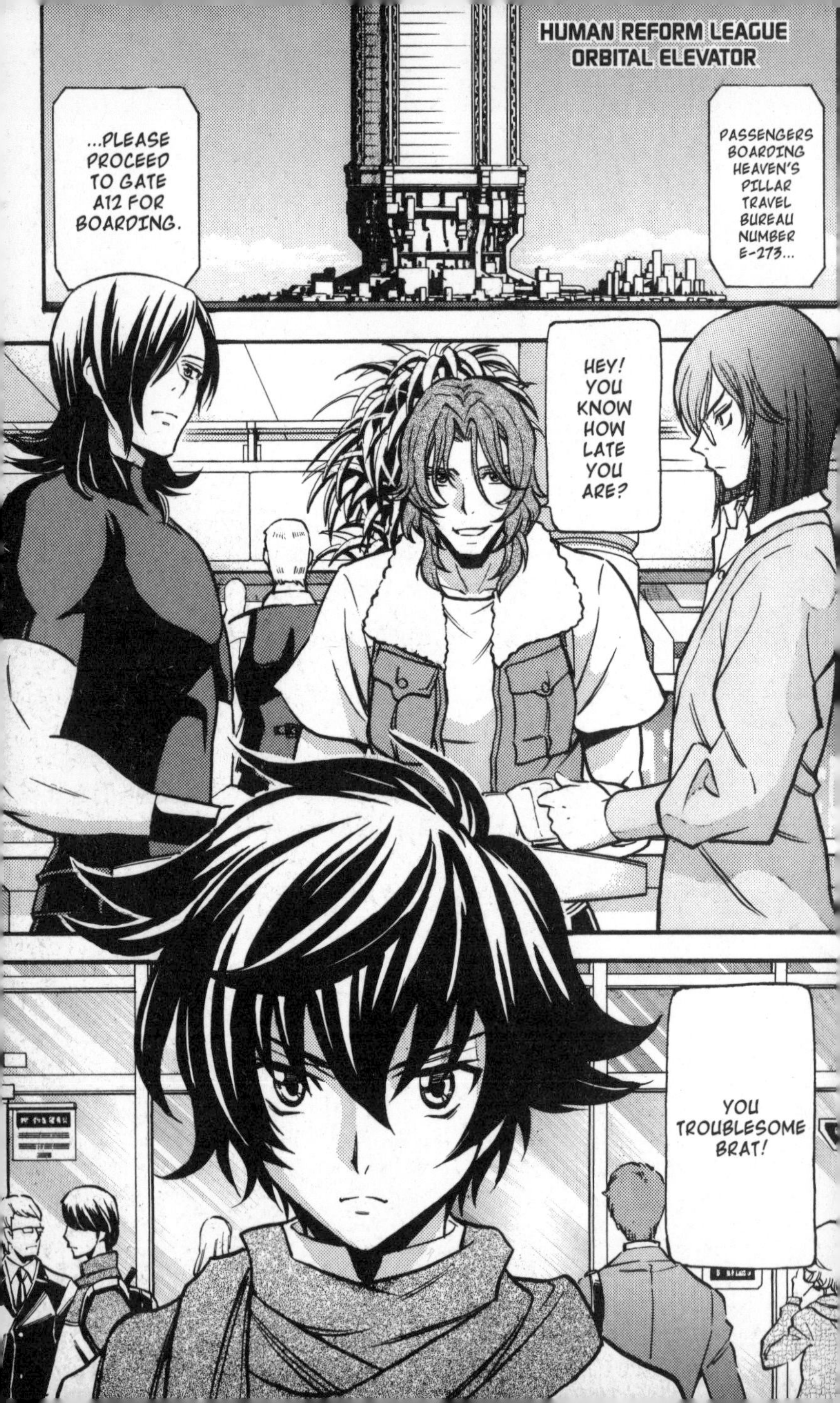
HUMAN REFORM LEAGUE ORBITAL ELEVATOR
PASSENGERS BOARDING HEAVEN'S PILLAR TRAVEL BUREAU NUMBER E-273...
...PLEASE PROCEED TO GATE A12 FOR BOARDING.
HEY! YOU KNOW HOW LATE YOU ARE?
YOU TROUBLESOME BRAT!

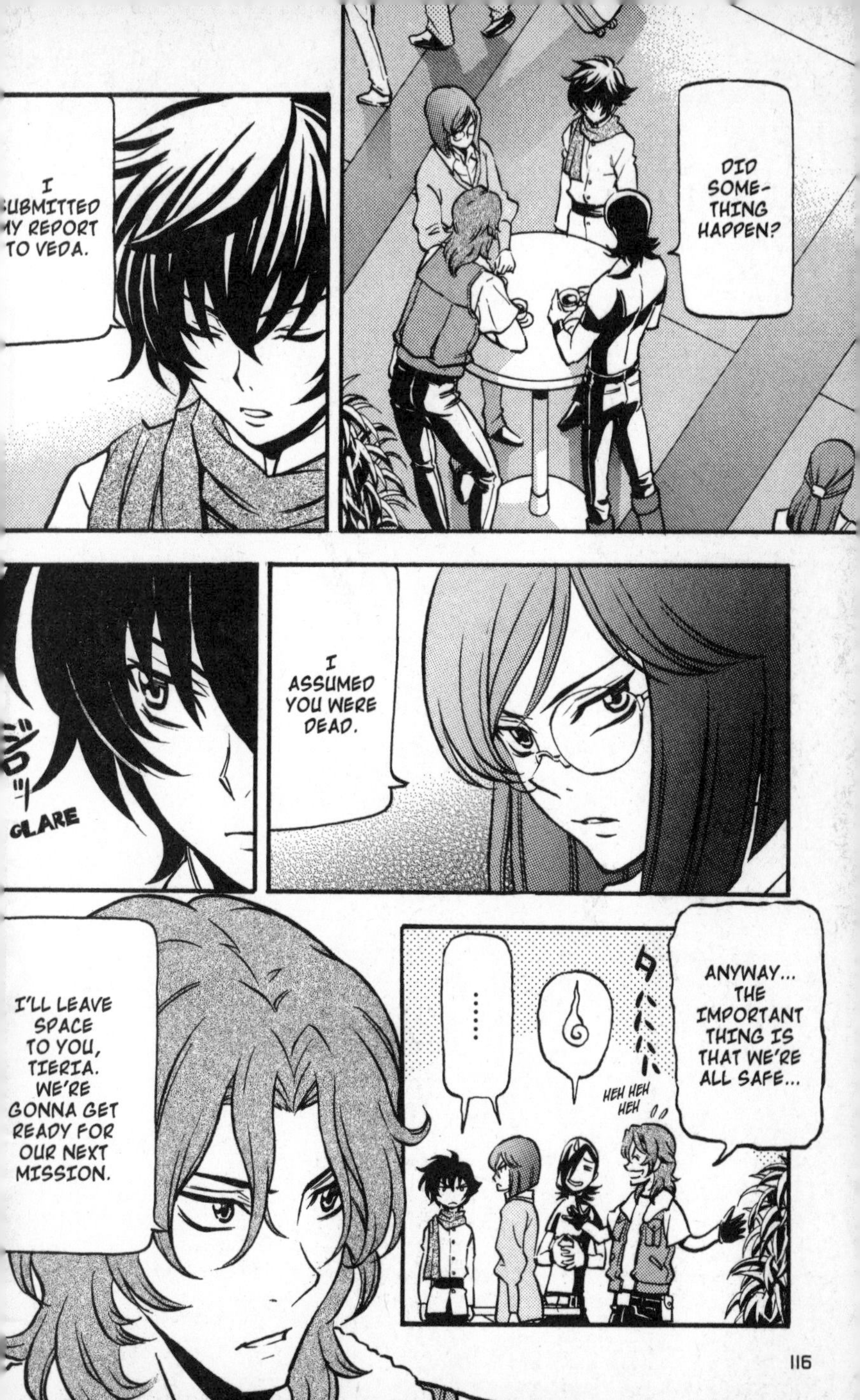
DID SOMETHING HAPPEN?
I SUBMITTED MY REPORT TO VEDA.
I ASSUMED YOU WERE DEAD.
ジロッ
GLARE
ANYWAY... THE IMPORTANT THING IS THAT WE'RE ALL SAFE...
HEH HEH HEH
......
I'LL LEAVE SPACE TO YOU, TIERIA. WE'RE GONNA GET READY FOR OUR NEXT MISSION.

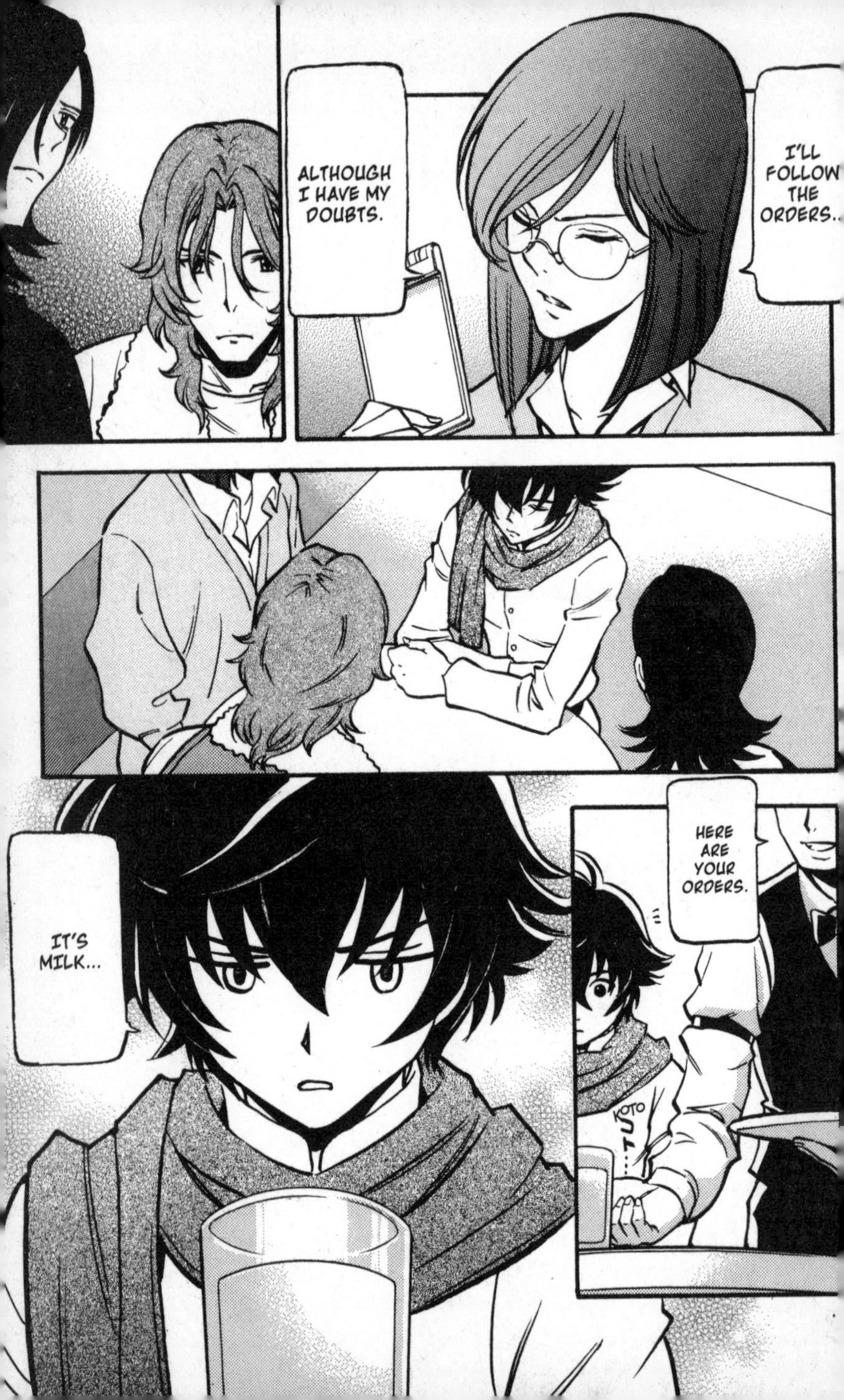
I'LL FOLLOW THE ORDERS..
ALTHOUGH I HAVE MY DOUBTS.
HERE ARE YOUR ORDERS.
KOTO
IT'S MILK...

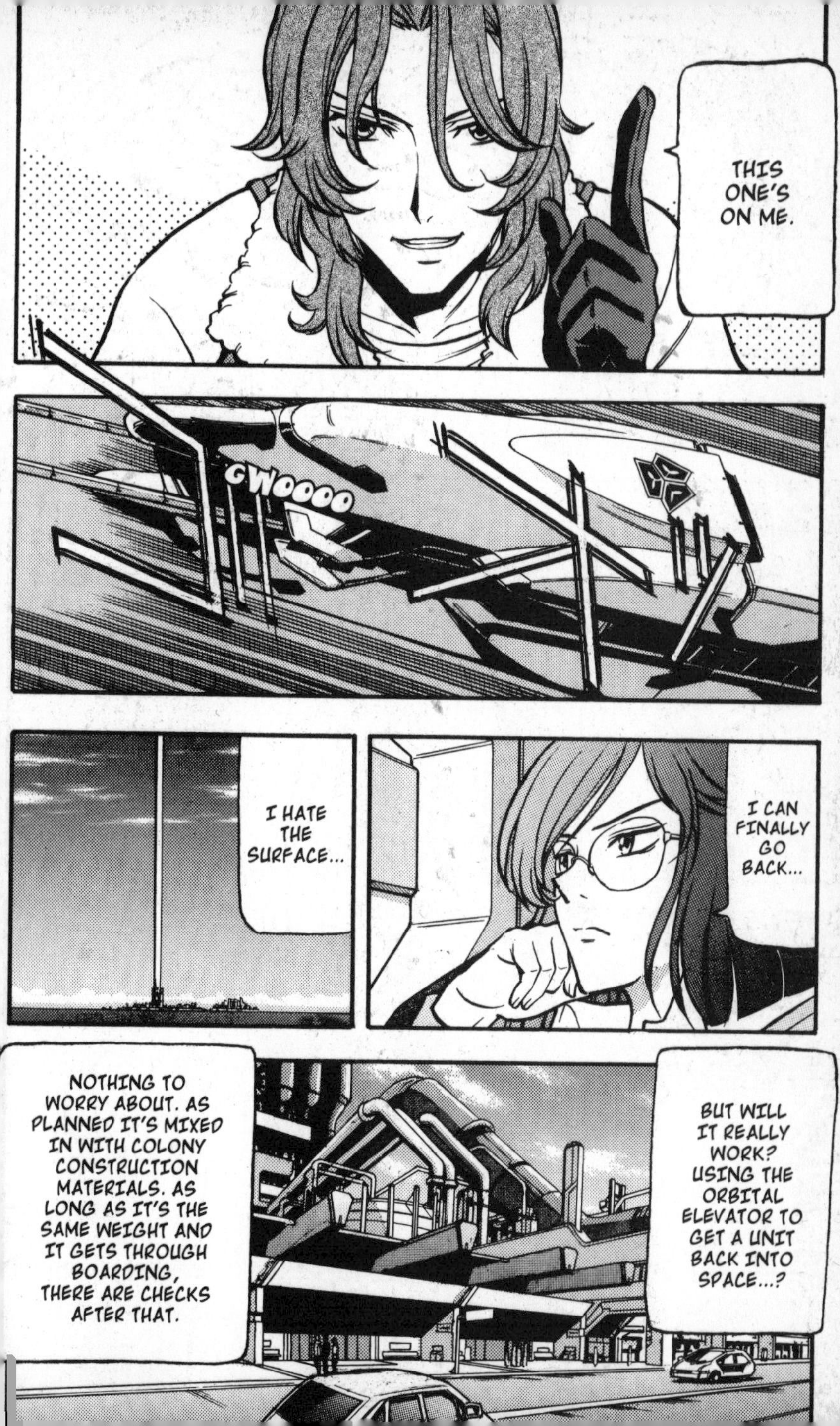
THIS ONE'S ON ME.
GWOOOO
I CAN FINALLY GO BACK...
I HATE THE SURFACE...
BUT WILL IT REALLY WORK? USING THE ORBITAL ELEVATOR TO GET A UNIT BACK INTO SPACE...?
NOTHING TO WORRY ABOUT. AS PLANNED IT'S MIXED IN WITH COLONY CONSTRUCTION MATERIALS. AS LONG AS IT'S THE SAME WEIGHT AND IT GETS THROUGH BOARDING, THERE ARE CHECKS AFTER THAT.

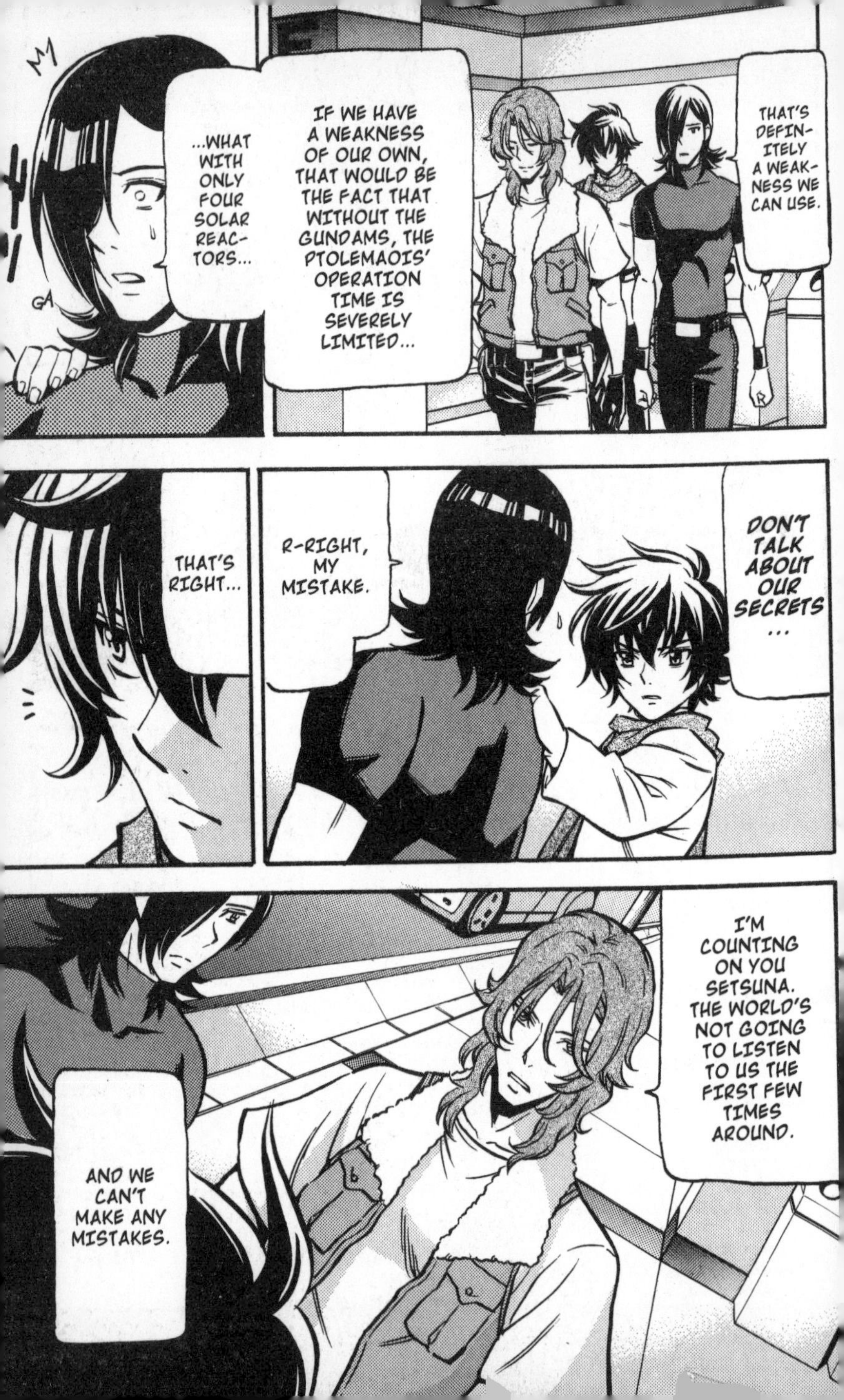
THAT'S DEFIN-ITELY A WEAK-NESS WE CAN USE.
IF WE HAVE A WEAKNESS OF OUR OWN, THAT WOULD BE THE FACT THAT WITHOUT THE GUNDAMS, THE PTOLEMAOIS' OPERATION TIME IS SEVERELY LIMITED...
...WHAT WITH ONLY FOUR SOLAR REAC-TORS...
GA
DON'T TALK ABOUT OUR SECRETS...
R-RIGHT, MY MISTAKE.
THAT'S RIGHT...
I'M COUNTING ON YOU SETSUNA. THE WORLD'S NOT GOING TO LISTEN TO US THE FIRST FEW TIMES AROUND.
AND WE CAN'T MAKE ANY MISTAKES.

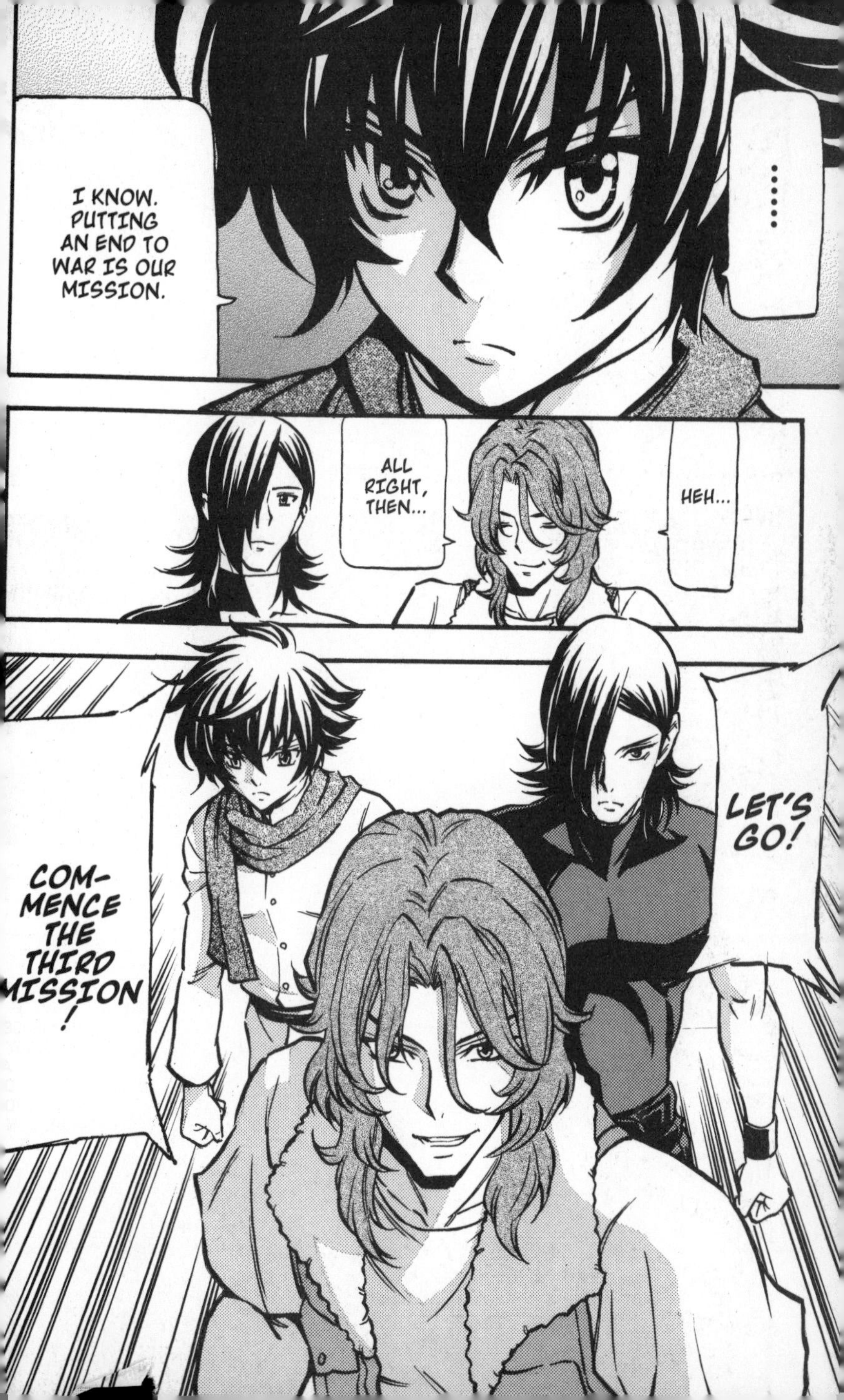
......
I KNOW. PUTTING AN END TO WAR IS OUR MISSION.
HEH...
ALL RIGHT, THEN...
LET'S GO!
COM-MENCE THE THIRD MISSION!

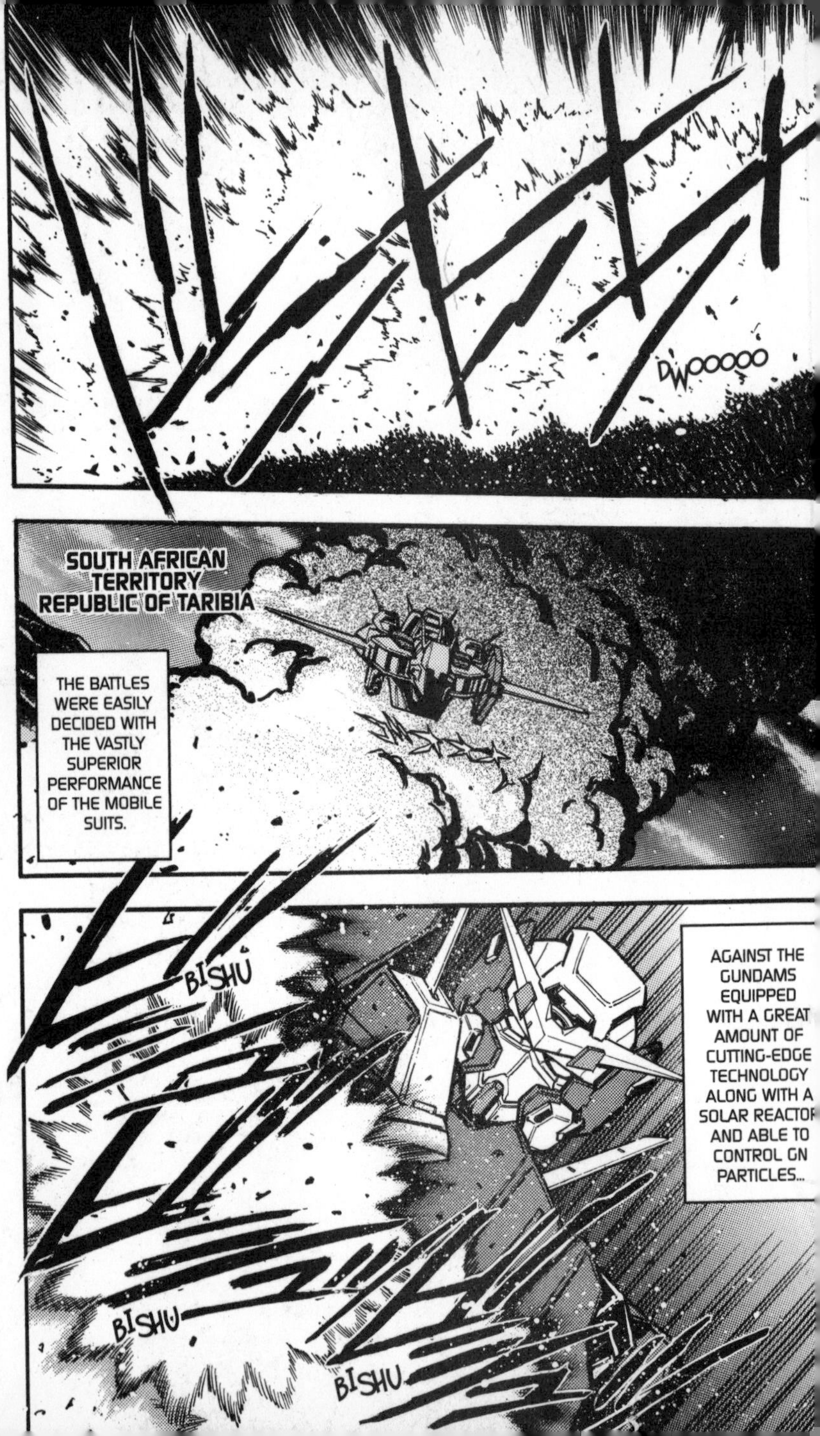
DWOOOOO
SOUTH AFRICAN TERRITORY REPUBLIC OF TARIBIA
THE BATTLES WERE EASILY DECIDED WITH THE VASTLY SUPERIOR PERFORMANCE OF THE MOBILE SUITS.
AGAINST THE GUNDAMS EQUIPPED WITH A GREAT AMOUNT OF CUTTING-EDGE TECHNOLOGY ALONG WITH A SOLAR REACTOR AND ABLE TO CONTROL GN PARTICLES...
BISHU
BISHU
BISHU

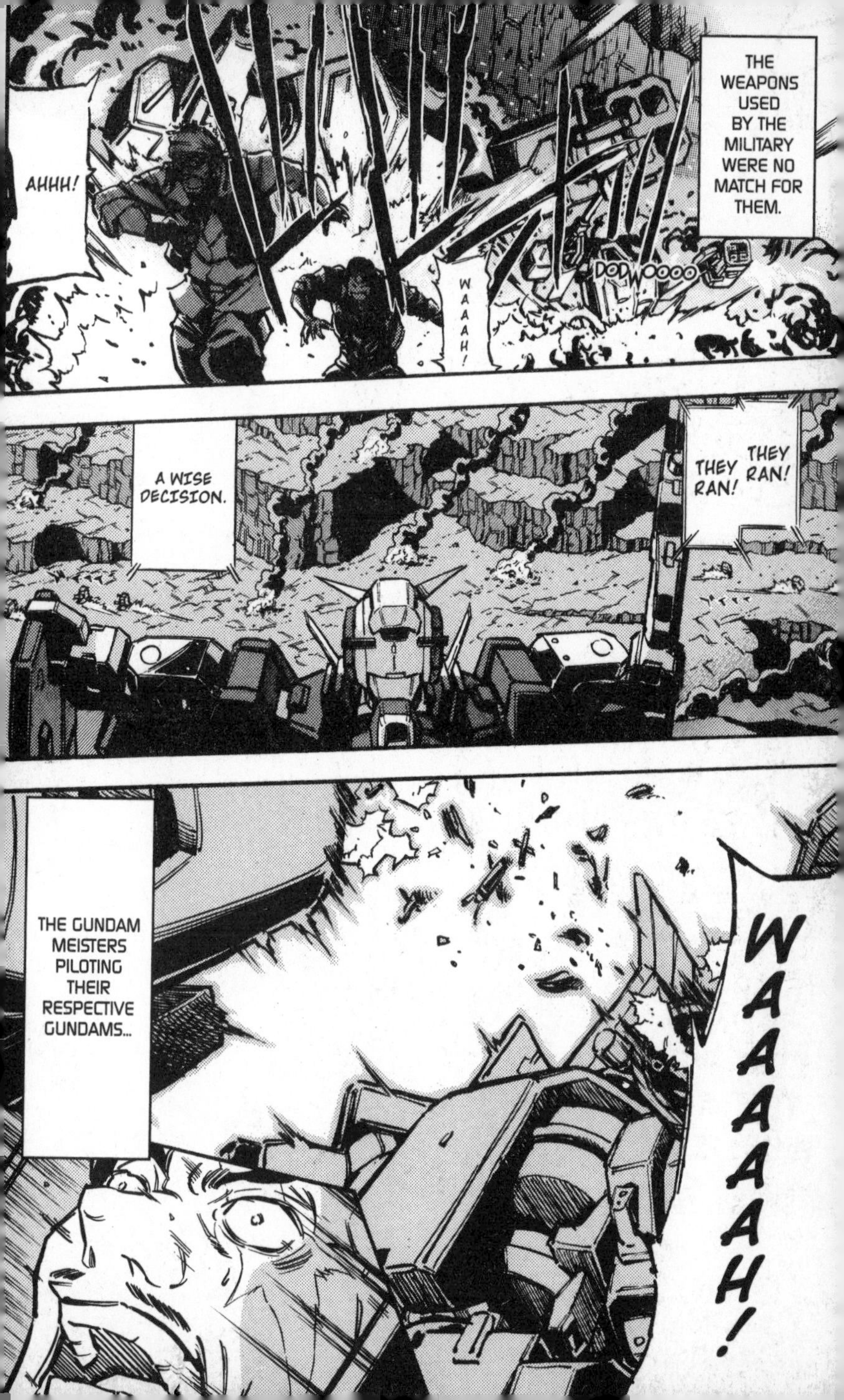
THE WEAPONS USED BY THE MILITARY WERE NO MATCH FOR THEM.
DODWOOOO
WAAAAH!
AHHH!
THEY RAN!
THEY RAN!
A WISE DECISION.
WAAAAAH!
THE GUNDAM MEISTERS PILOTING THEIR RESPECTIVE GUNDAMS...

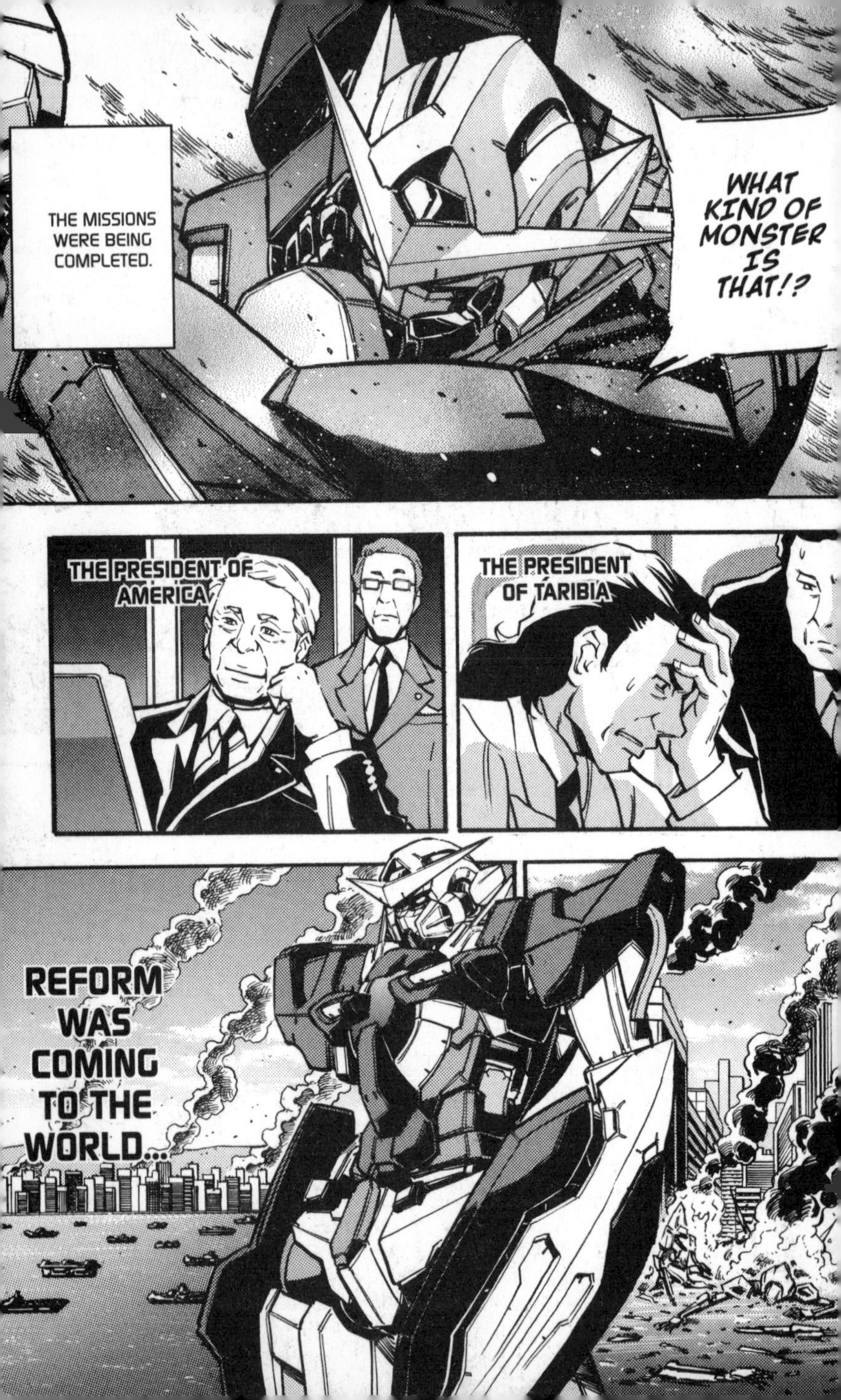

WHAT KIND OF MONSTER IS THAT!?
THE MISSIONS WERE BEING COMPLETED.
THE PRESIDENT OF TARIBIA
THE PRESIDENT OF AMERICA
REFORM WAS COMING TO THE WORLD...

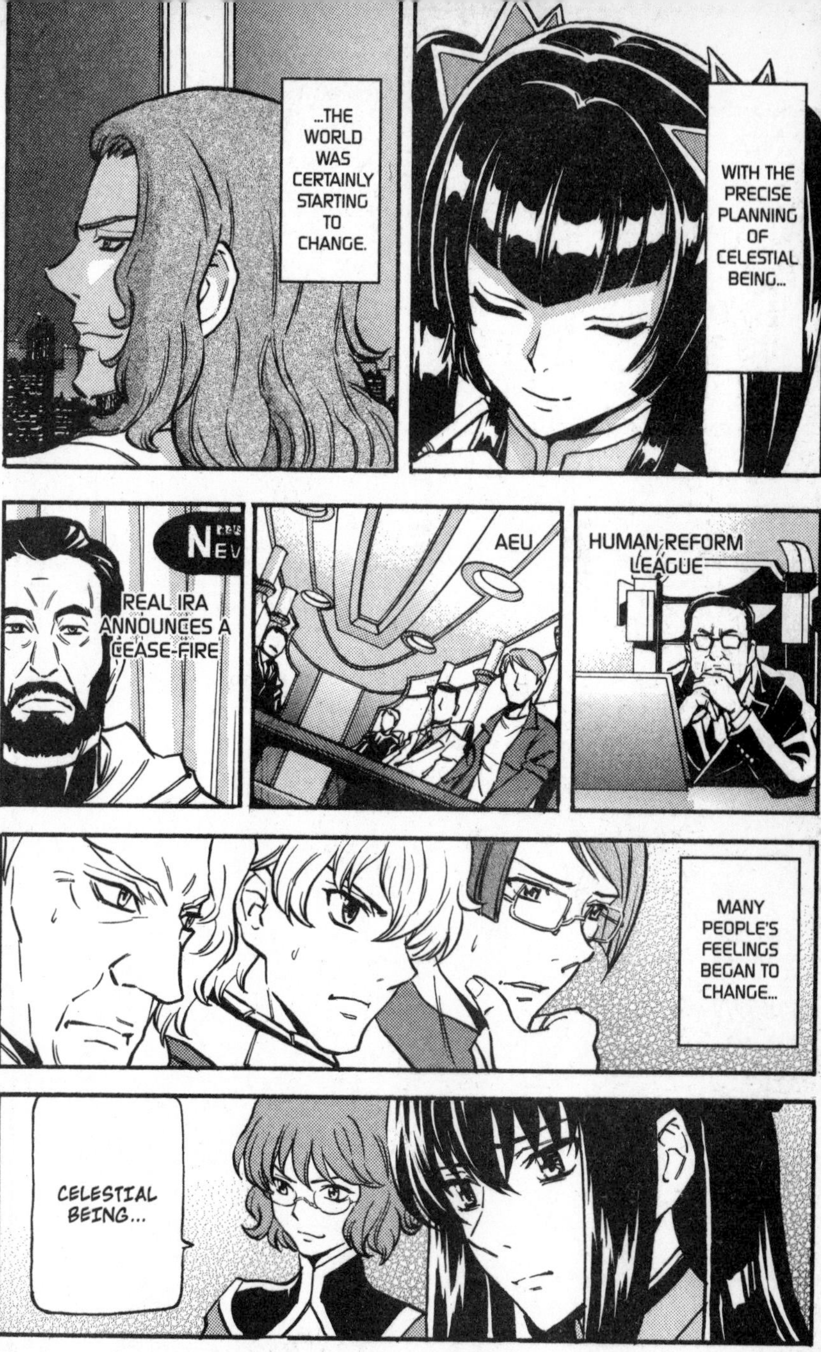
WITH THE PRECISE PLANNING OF CELESTIAL BEING...
...THE WORLD WAS CERTAINLY STARTING TO CHANGE.
HUMAN-REFORM LEAGUE
AEU
REAL IRA ANNOUNCES A CEASE-FIRE
MANY PEOPLE'S FEELINGS BEGAN TO CHANGE...
CELESTIAL BEING...

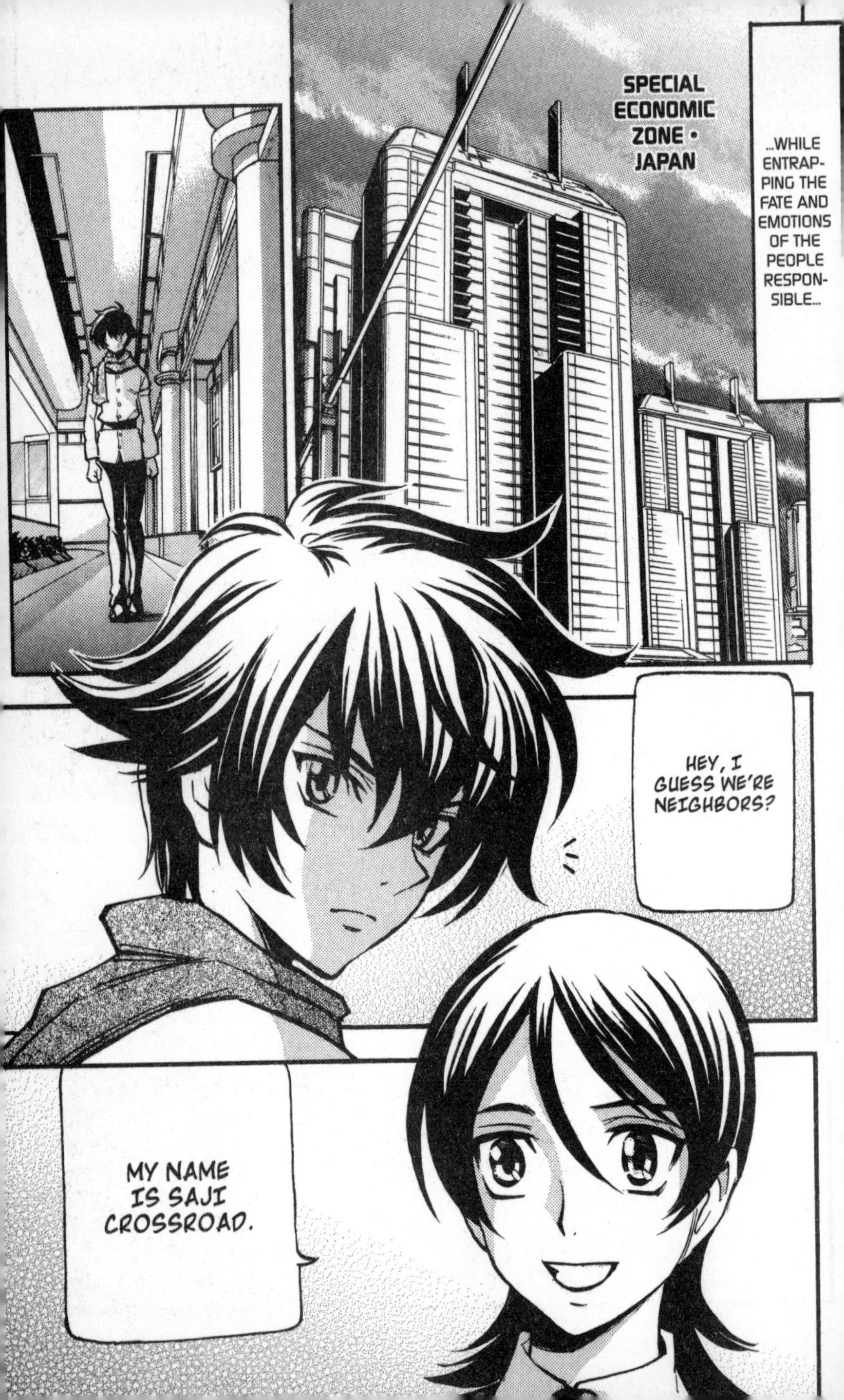
...WHILE ENTRAPPING THE FATE AND EMOTIONS OF THE PEOPLE RESPONSIBLE...
SPECIAL ECONOMIC ZONE • JAPAN
HEY, I GUESS WE'RE NEIGHBORS?
MY NAME IS SAJI CROSSROAD.

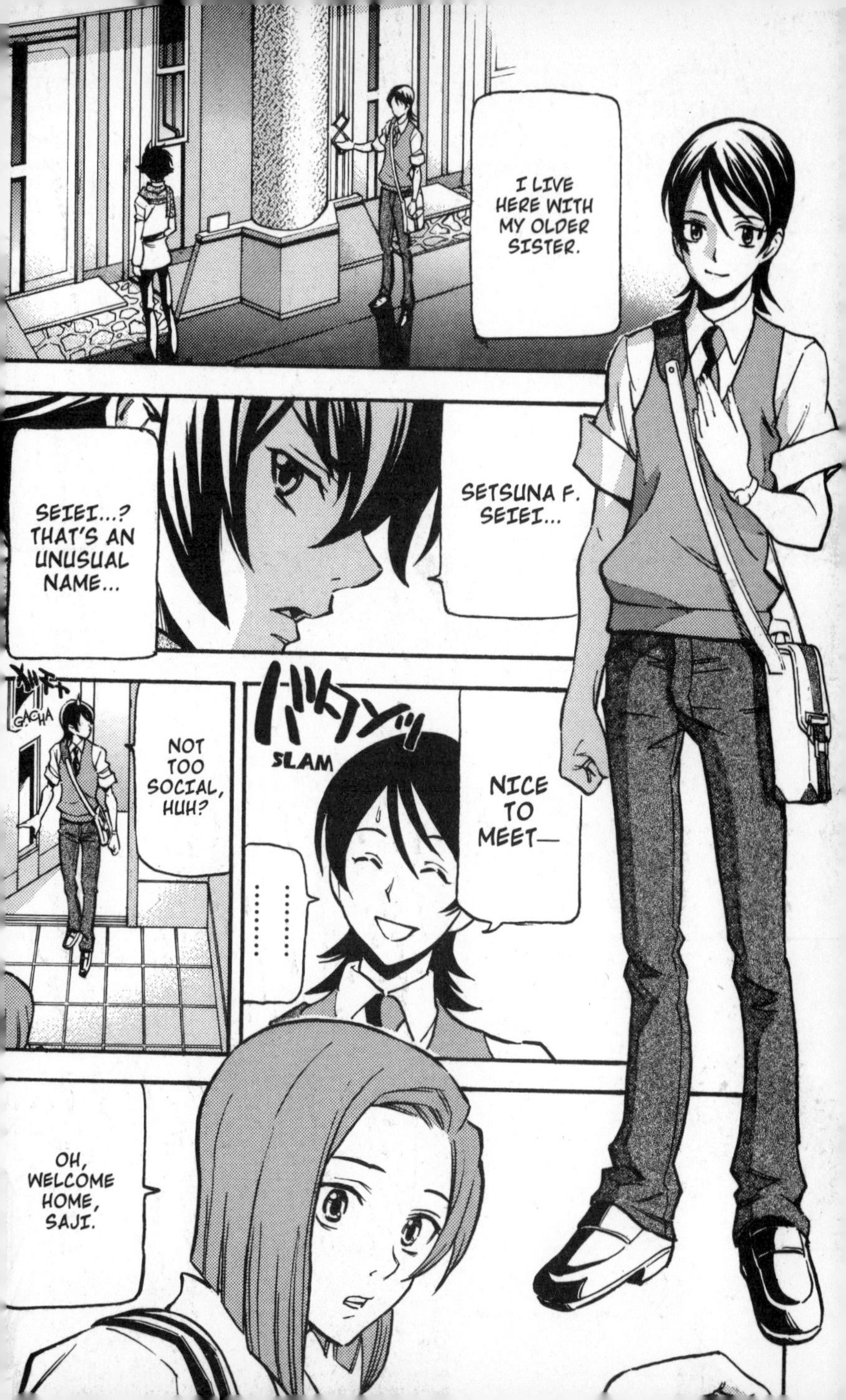
I LIVE HERE WITH MY OLDER SISTER.
SETSUNA F. SEIEI...
SEIEI...? THAT'S AN UNUSUAL NAME...
SLAM
NICE TO MEET—
......
GACHA
NOT TOO SOCIAL, HUH?
OH, WELCOME HOME, SAJI.

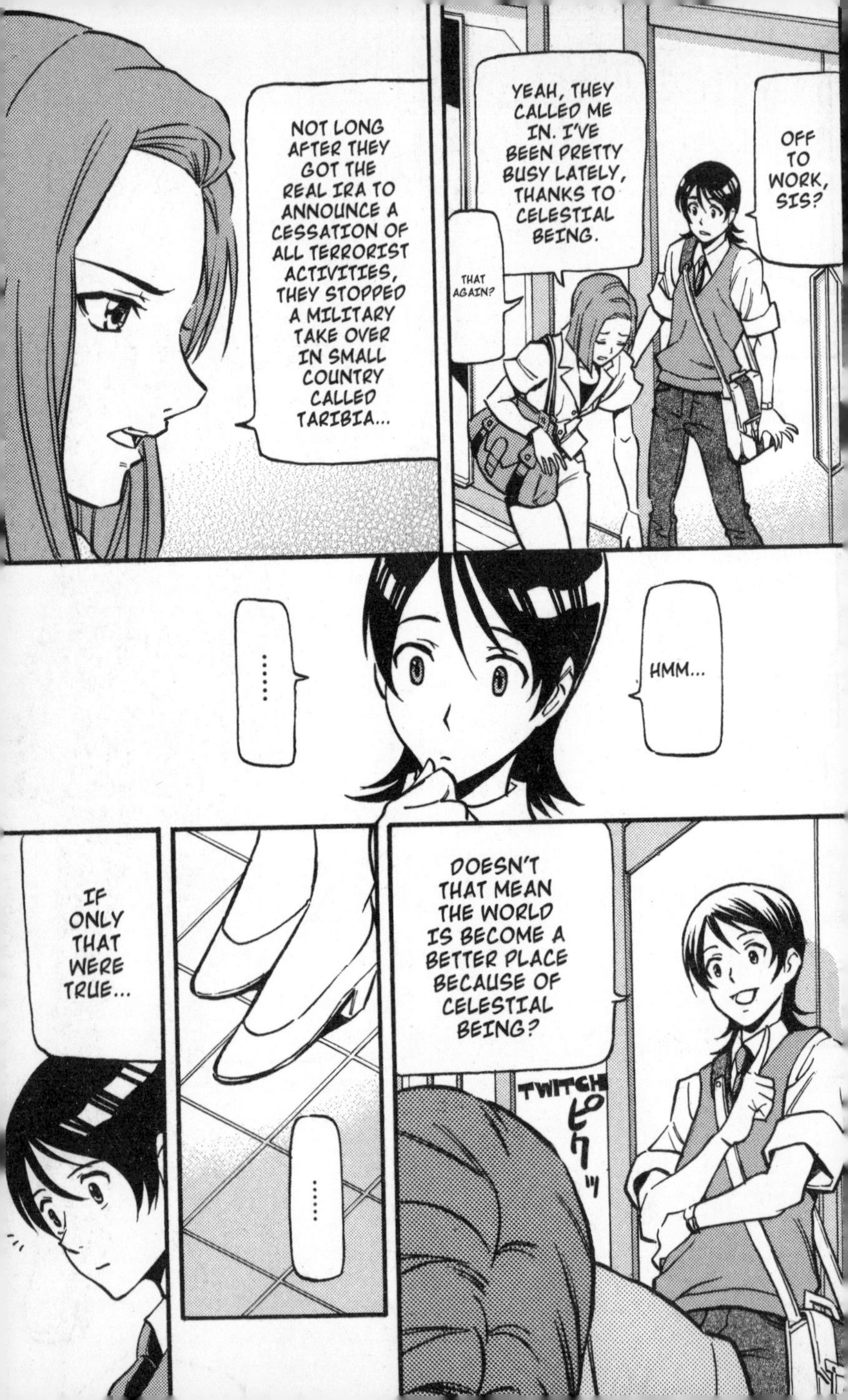
OFF TO WORK, SIS?
YEAH, THEY CALLED ME IN. I'VE BEEN PRETTY BUSY LATELY, THANKS TO CELESTIAL BEING.
THAT AGAIN?
NOT LONG AFTER THEY GOT THE REAL IRA TO ANNOUNCE A CESSATION OF ALL TERRORIST ACTIVITIES, THEY STOPPED A MILITARY TAKE OVER IN SMALL COUNTRY CALLED TARIBIA...
HMM...
......
DOESN'T THAT MEAN THE WORLD IS BECOME A BETTER PLACE BECAUSE OF CELESTIAL BEING?
TWITCH
ピクッ
......
IF ONLY THAT WERE TRUE...

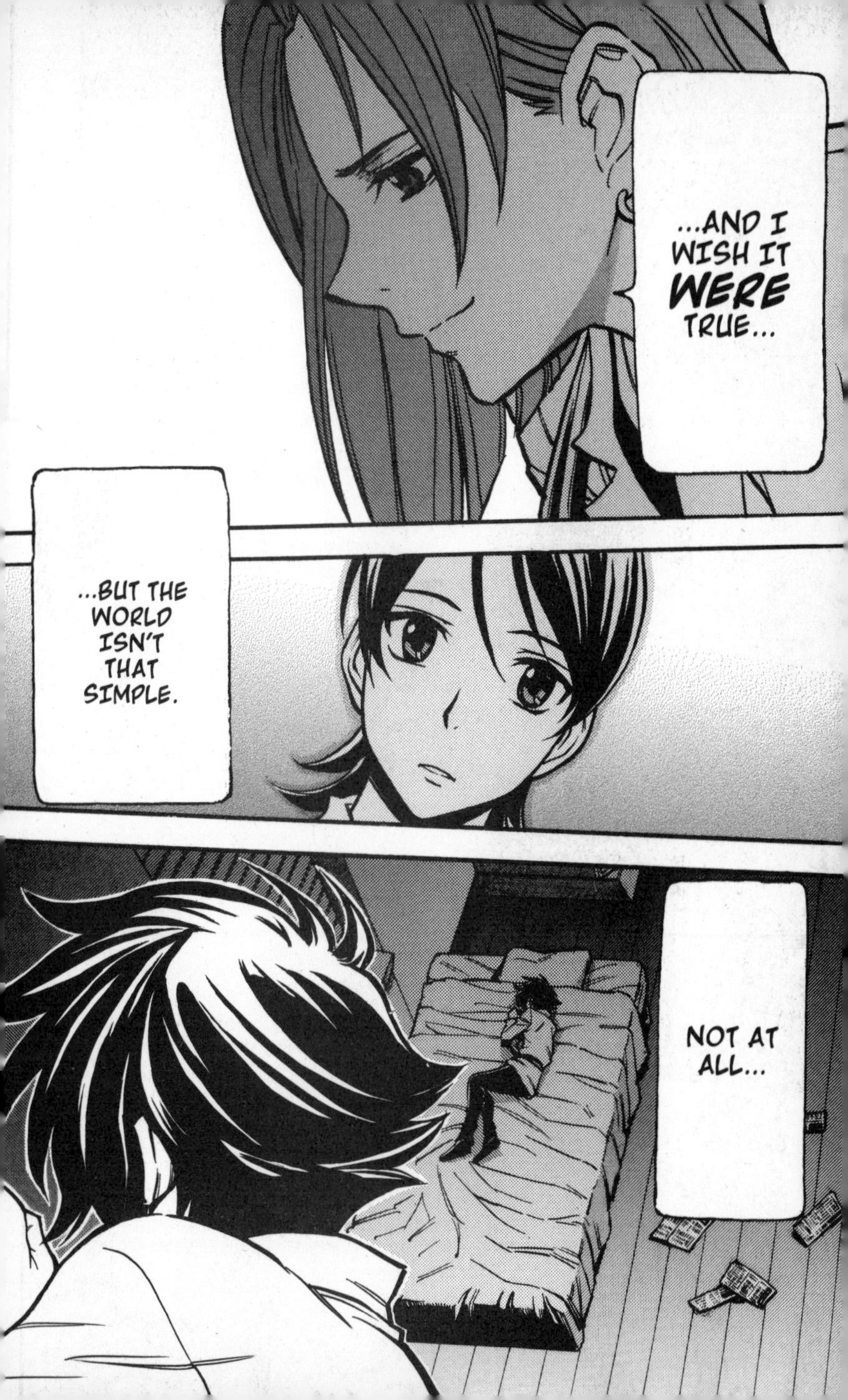
...AND I WISH IT WERE TRUE...
...BUT THE WORLD ISN'T THAT SIMPLE.
NOT AT ALL...

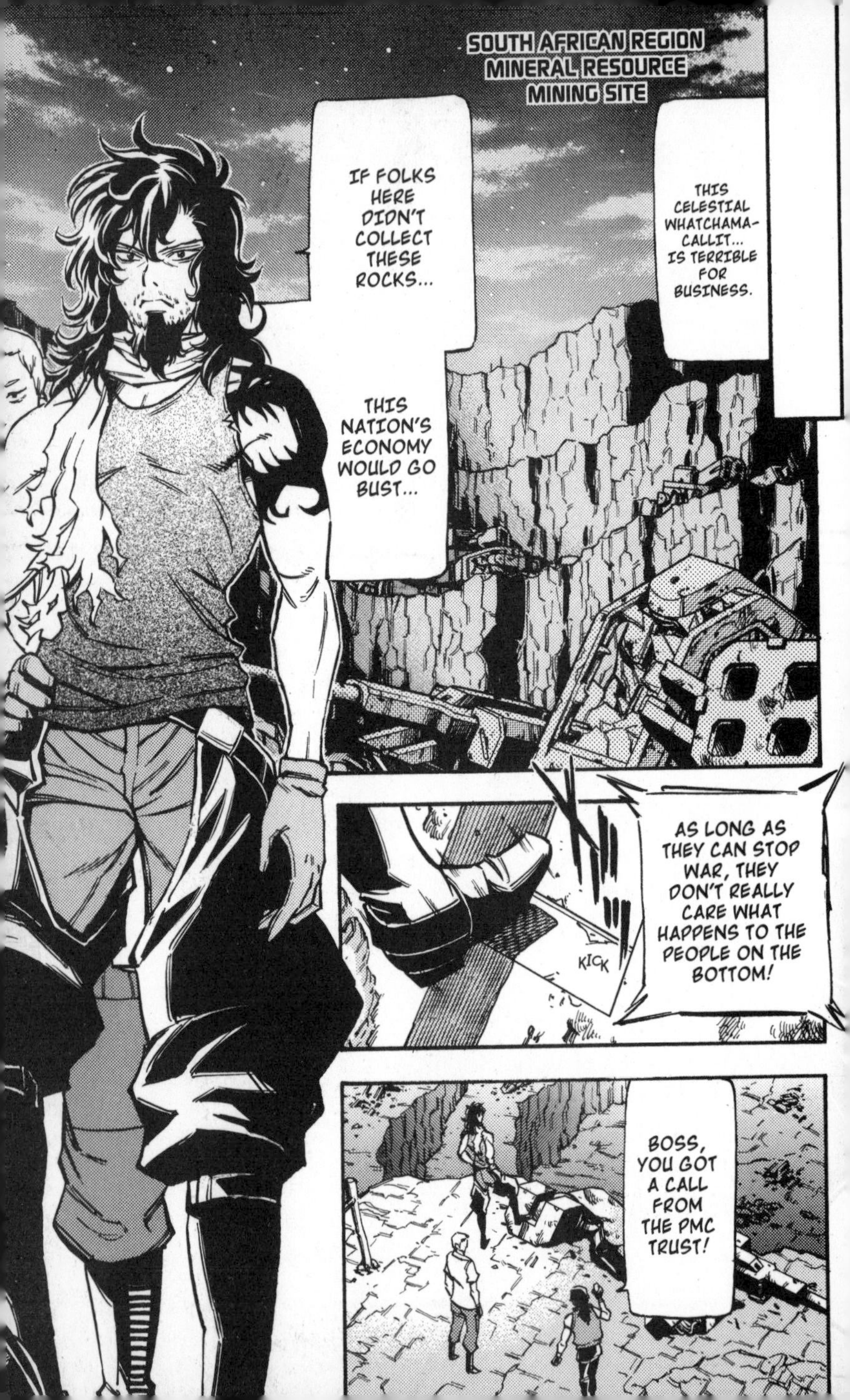
SOUTH AFRICAN REGION MINERAL RESOURCE MINING SITE
THIS CELESTIAL WHATCHAMA-CALLIT... IS TERRIBLE FOR BUSINESS.
IF FOLKS HERE DIDN'T COLLECT THESE ROCKS...
THIS NATION'S ECONOMY WOULD GO BUST...
AS LONG AS THEY CAN STOP WAR, THEY DON'T REALLY CARE WHAT HAPPENS TO THE PEOPLE ON THE BOTTOM!
KICK
BOSS, YOU GOT A CALL FROM THE PMC TRUST!

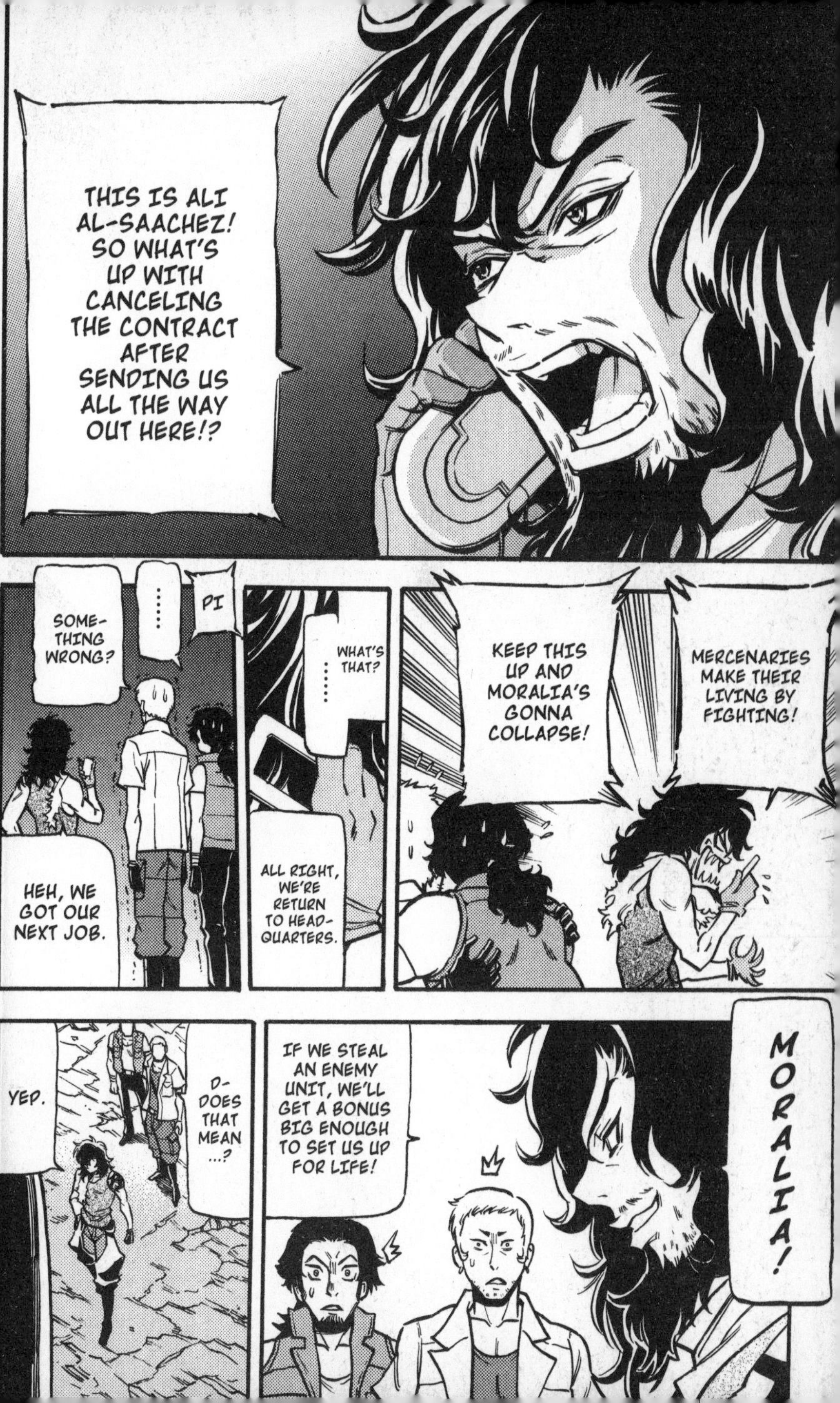
THIS IS ALI AL-SAACHEZ! SO WHAT'S UP WITH CANCELING THE CONTRACT AFTER SENDING US ALL THE WAY OUT HERE!?
MERCENARIES MAKE THEIR LIVING BY FIGHTING!
KEEP THIS UP AND MORALIA'S GONNA COLLAPSE!
WHAT'S THAT?
......
ALL RIGHT, WE'RE RETURN TO HEAD-QUARTERS.
PI
......
SOME-THING WRONG?
HEH, WE GOT OUR NEXT JOB.
MORALIA!
IF WE STEAL AN ENEMY UNIT, WE'LL GET A BONUS BIG ENOUGH TO SET US UP FOR LIFE!
D-DOES THAT MEAN ...?
YEP.

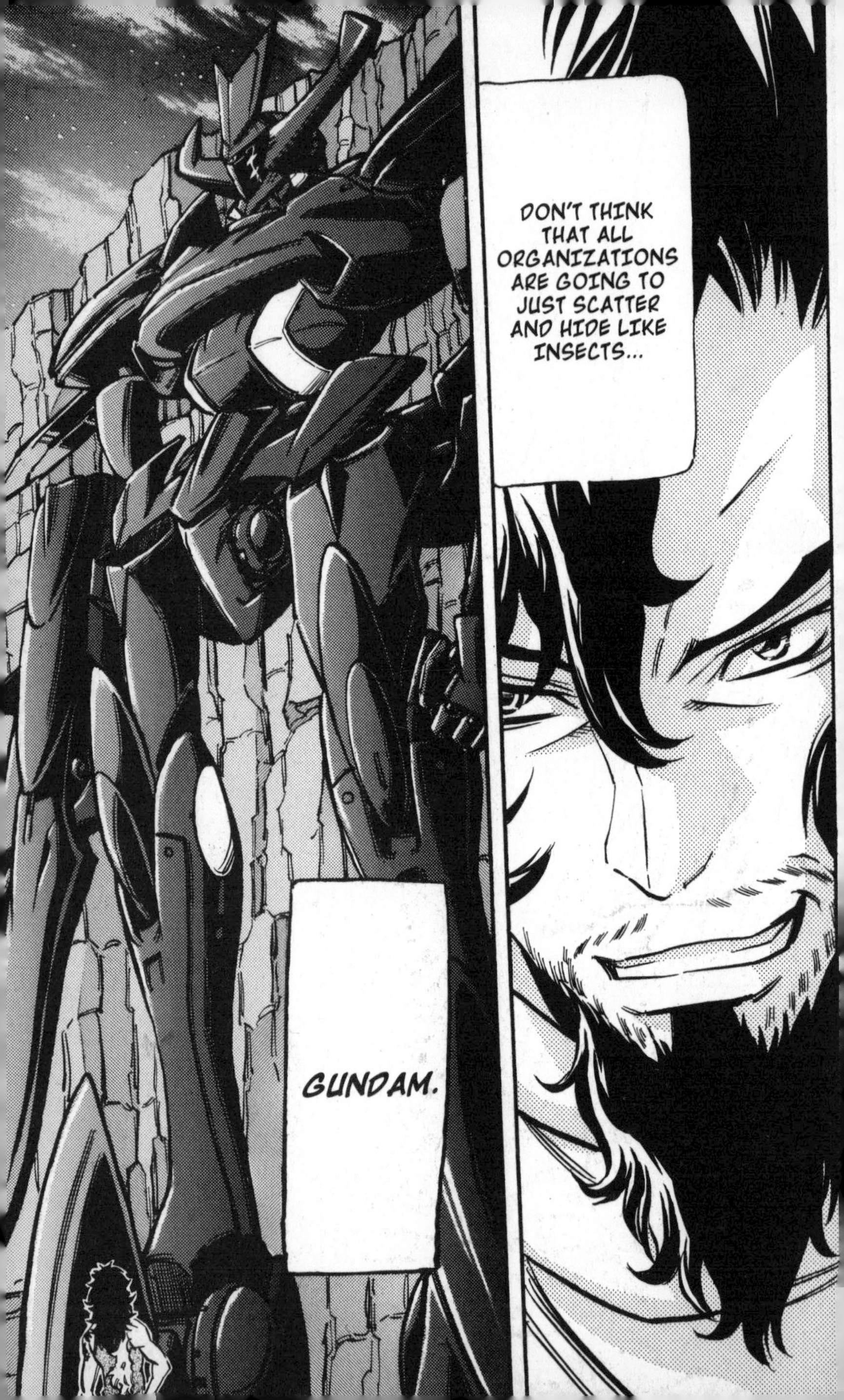
DON'T THINK THAT ALL ORGANIZATIONS ARE GOING TO JUST SCATTER AND HIDE LIKE INSECTS...
GUNDAM.

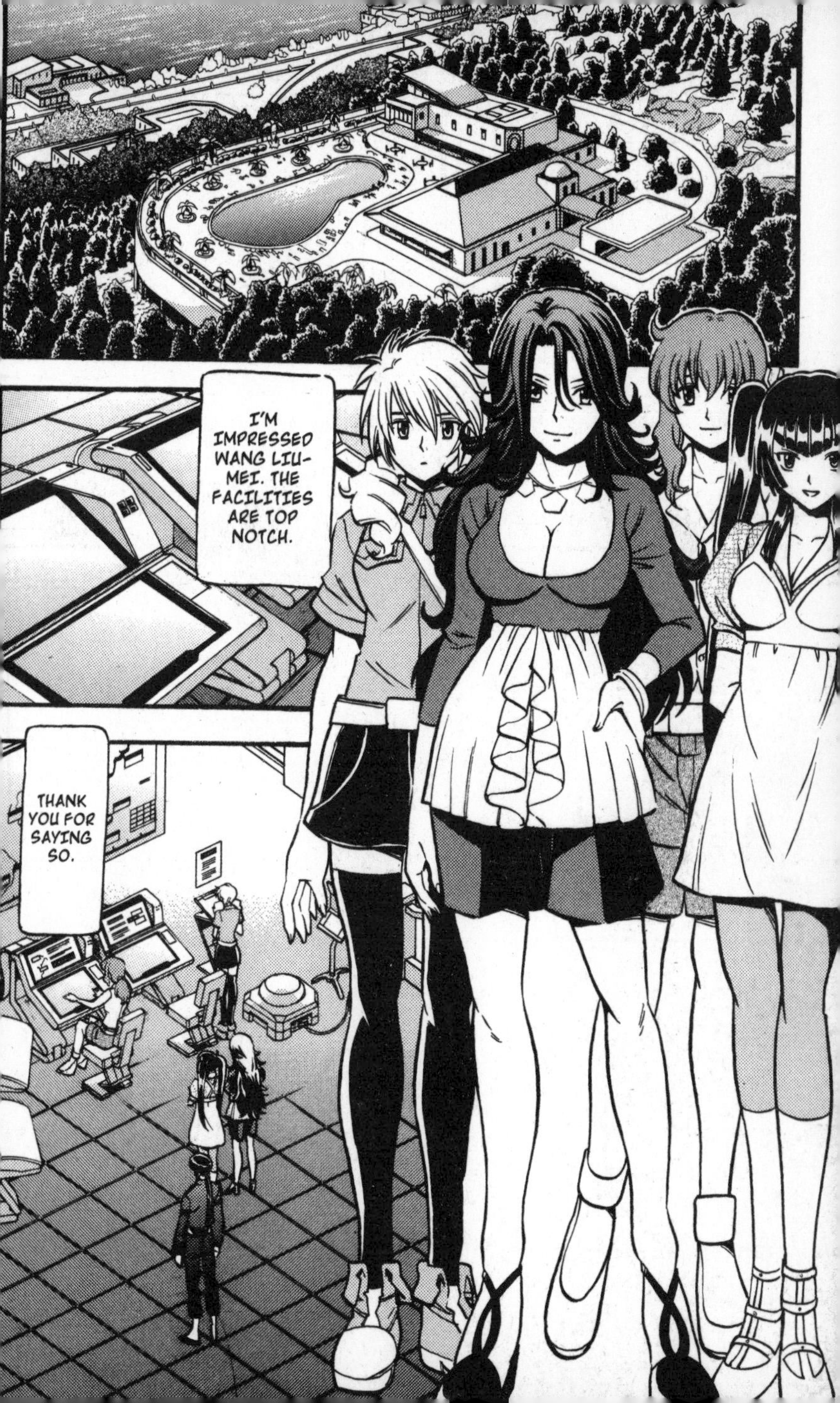
I'M IMPRESSED WANG LIU-MEI. THE FACILITIES ARE TOP NOTCH.
THANK YOU FOR SAYING SO.

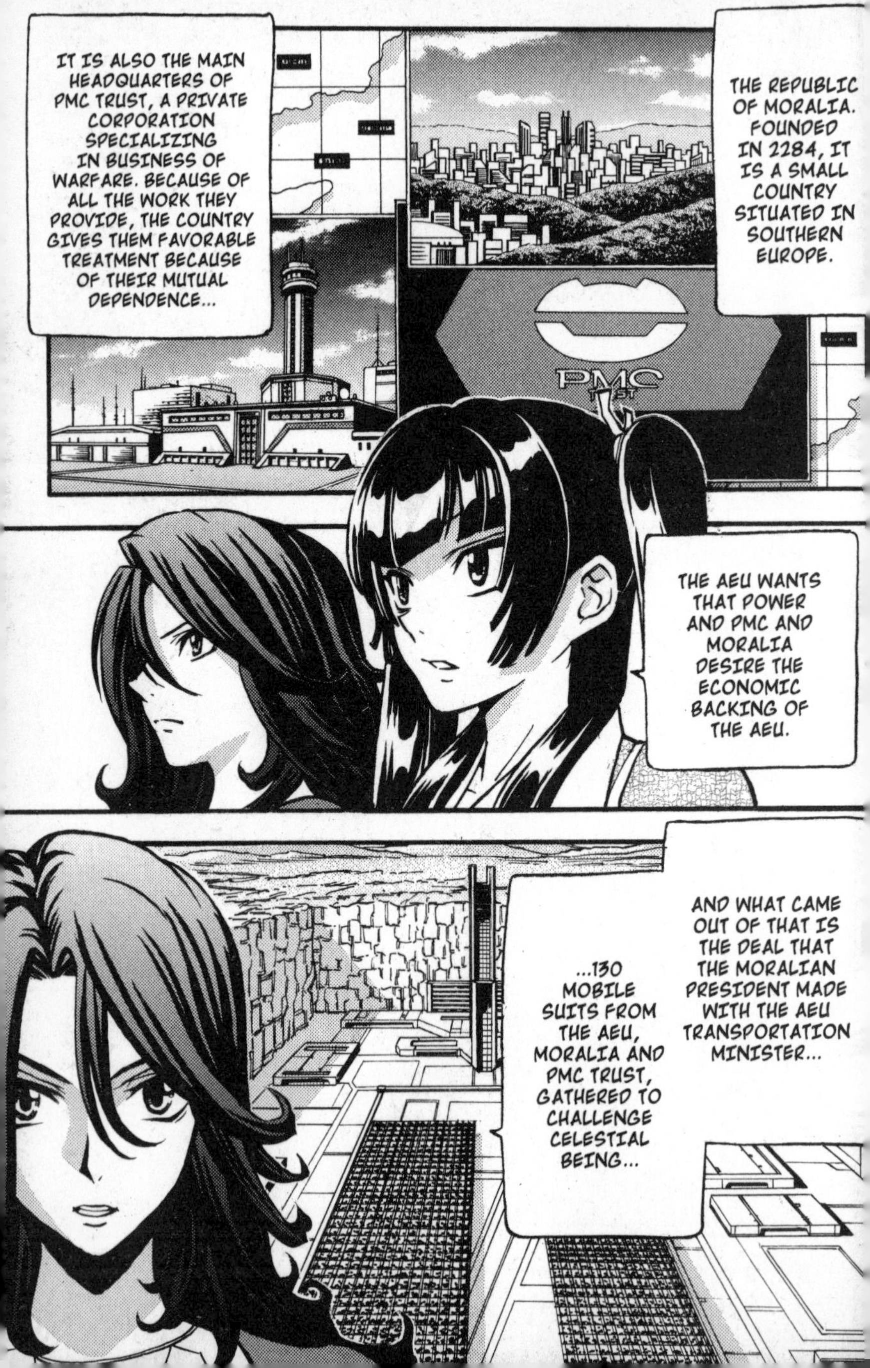
THE REPUBLIC OF MORALIA. FOUNDED IN 2284, IT IS A SMALL COUNTRY SITUATED IN SOUTHERN EUROPE.
IT IS ALSO THE MAIN HEADQUARTERS OF PMC TRUST, A PRIVATE CORPORATION SPECIALIZING IN BUSINESS OF WARFARE. BECAUSE OF ALL THE WORK THEY PROVIDE, THE COUNTRY GIVES THEM FAVORABLE TREATMENT BECAUSE OF THEIR MUTUAL DEPENDENCE...
THE AEU WANTS THAT POWER AND PMC AND MORALIA DESIRE THE ECONOMIC BACKING OF THE AEU.
AND WHAT CAME OUT OF THAT IS THE DEAL THAT THE MORALIAN PRESIDENT MADE WITH THE AEU TRANSPORTATION MINISTER...
...130 MOBILE SUITS FROM THE AEU, MORALIA AND PMC TRUST, GATHERED TO CHALLENGE CELESTIAL BEING...

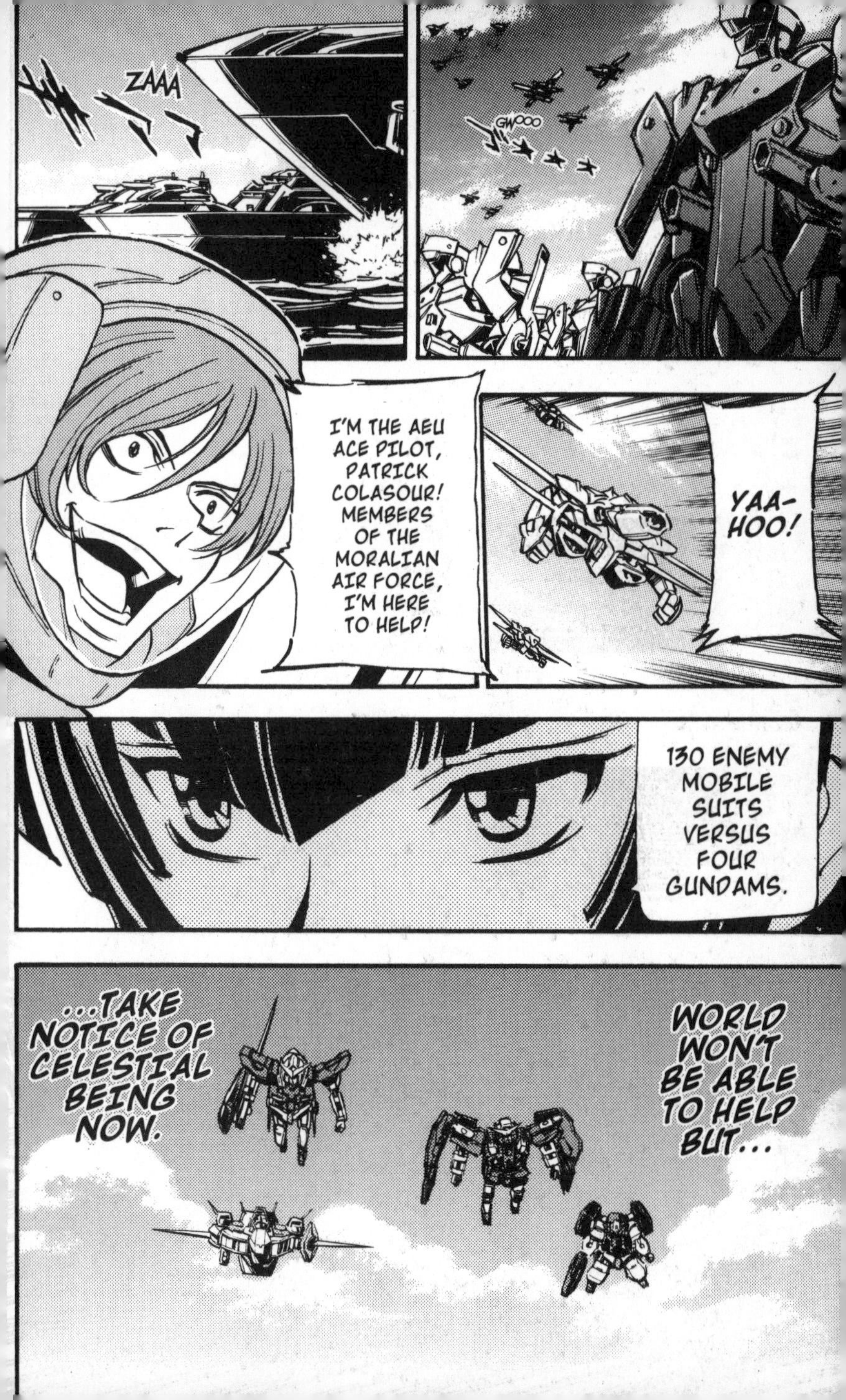
GWOOO
ZAAA
YAA-HOO!
I'M THE AEU ACE PILOT, PATRICK COLASOUR! MEMBERS OF THE MORALIAN AIR FORCE, I'M HERE TO HELP!
130 ENEMY MOBILE SUITS VERSUS FOUR GUNDAMS.
WORLD WON'T BE ABLE TO HELP BUT...
...TAKE NOTICE OF CELESTIAL BEING NOW.

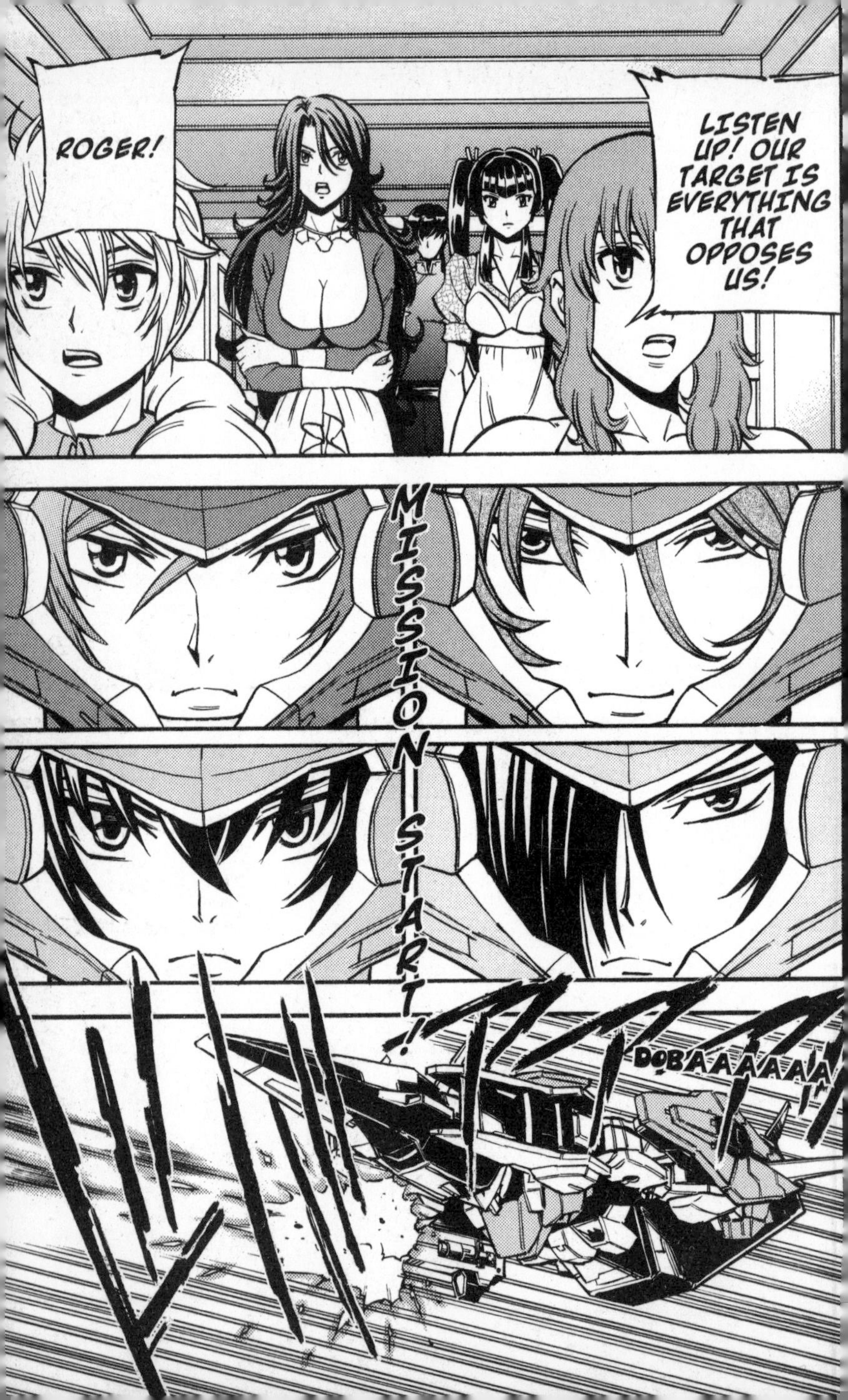
LISTEN UP! OUR TARGET IS EVERYTHING THAT OPPOSES US!
ROGER!
MISSION START!
DOBAAAAAAA!

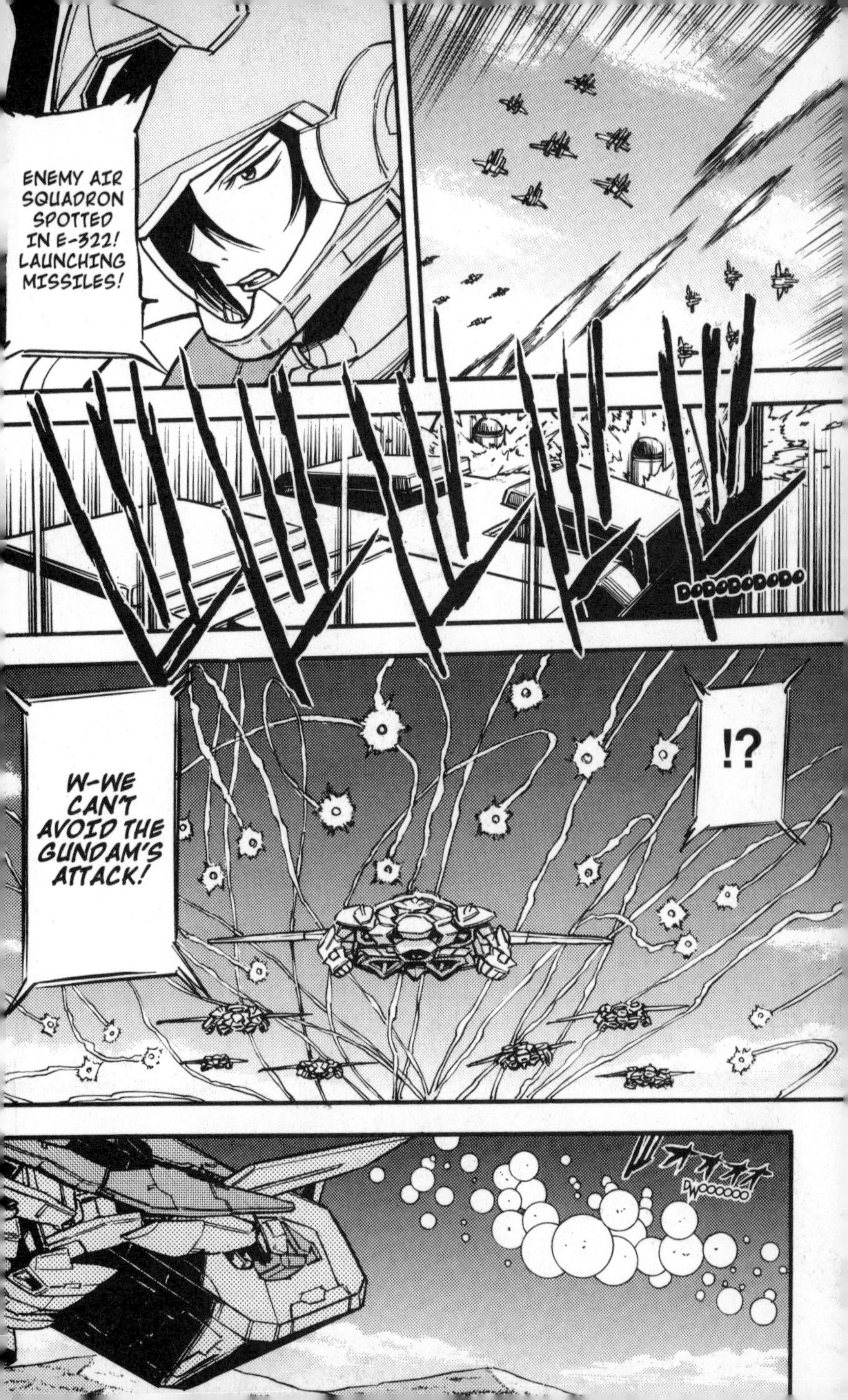
ENEMY AIR SQUADRON SPOTTED IN E-322! LAUNCHING MISSILES!
DODODODODO
!?
W-WE CAN'T AVOID THE GUNDAM'S ATTACK!
DWOOOOOO

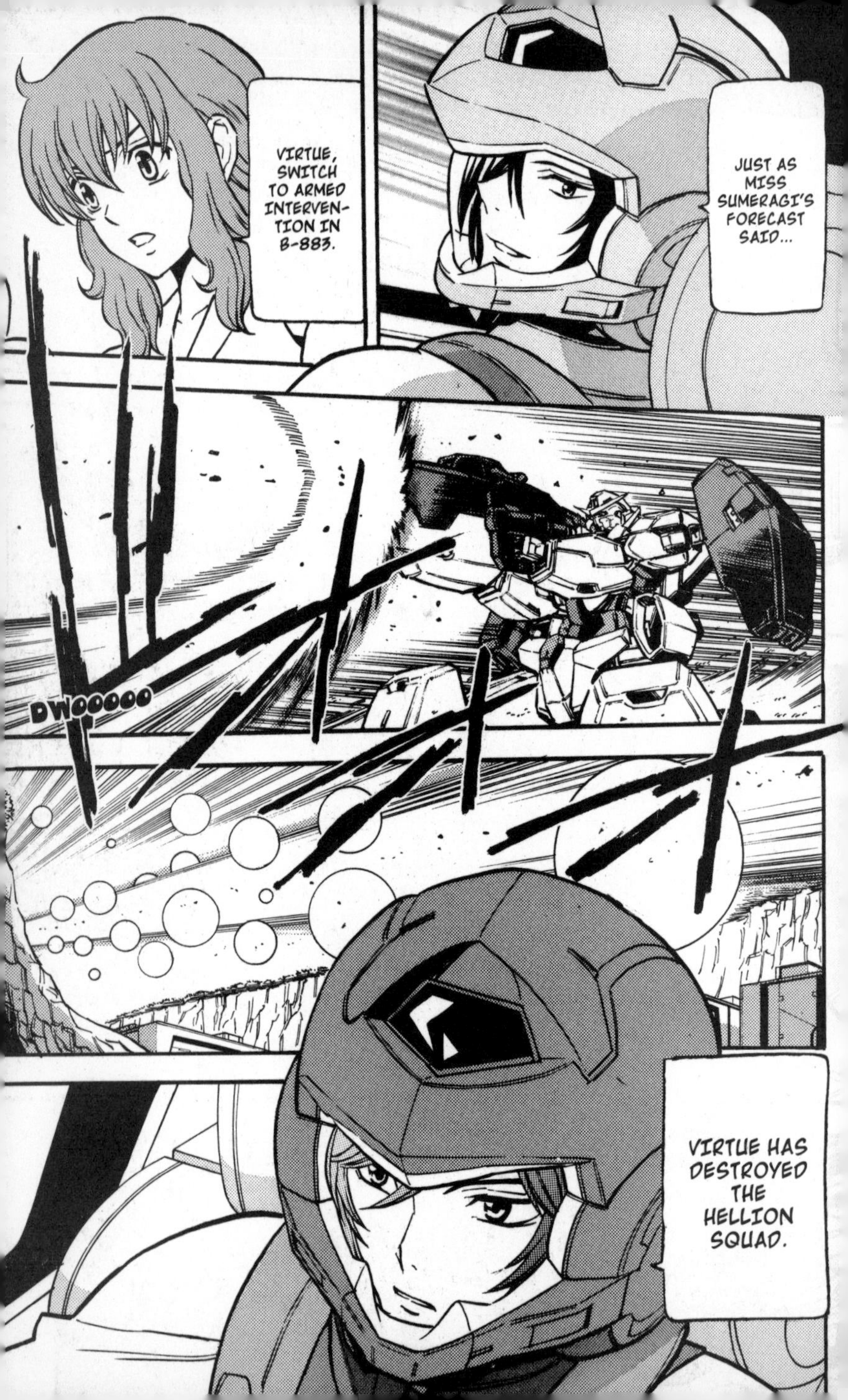
JUST AS MISS SUMERAGI'S FORECAST SAID...
VIRTUE, SWITCH TO ARMED INTERVENTION IN B-883.
DWOOOOO
VIRTUE HAS DESTROYED THE HELLION SQUAD.

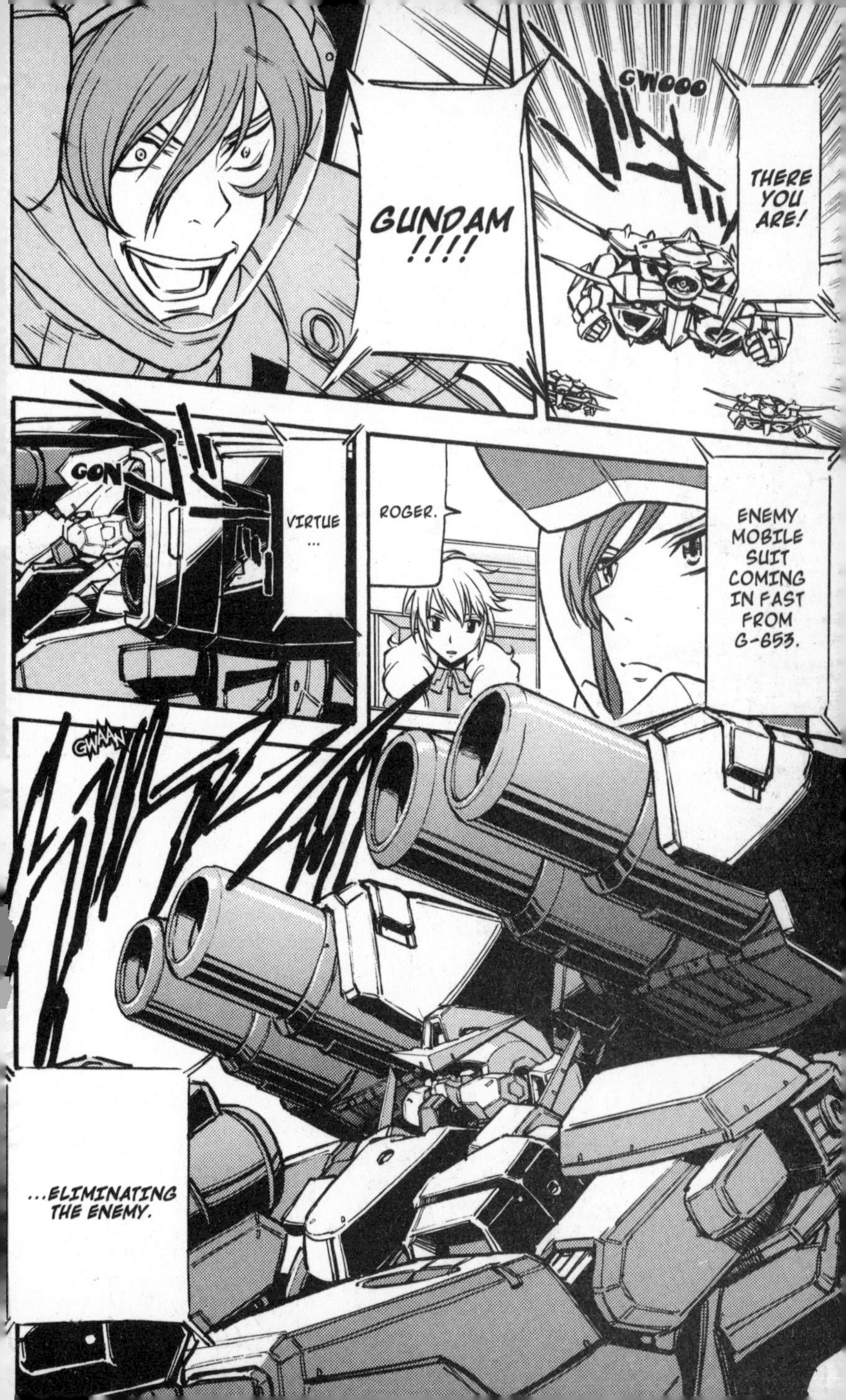
GWOOO
THERE YOU ARE!
GUNDAM !!!!
ENEMY MOBILE SUIT COMING IN FAST FROM G-653.
ROGER.
GON
VIRTUE ...
GWAAN
...ELIMINATING THE ENEMY.

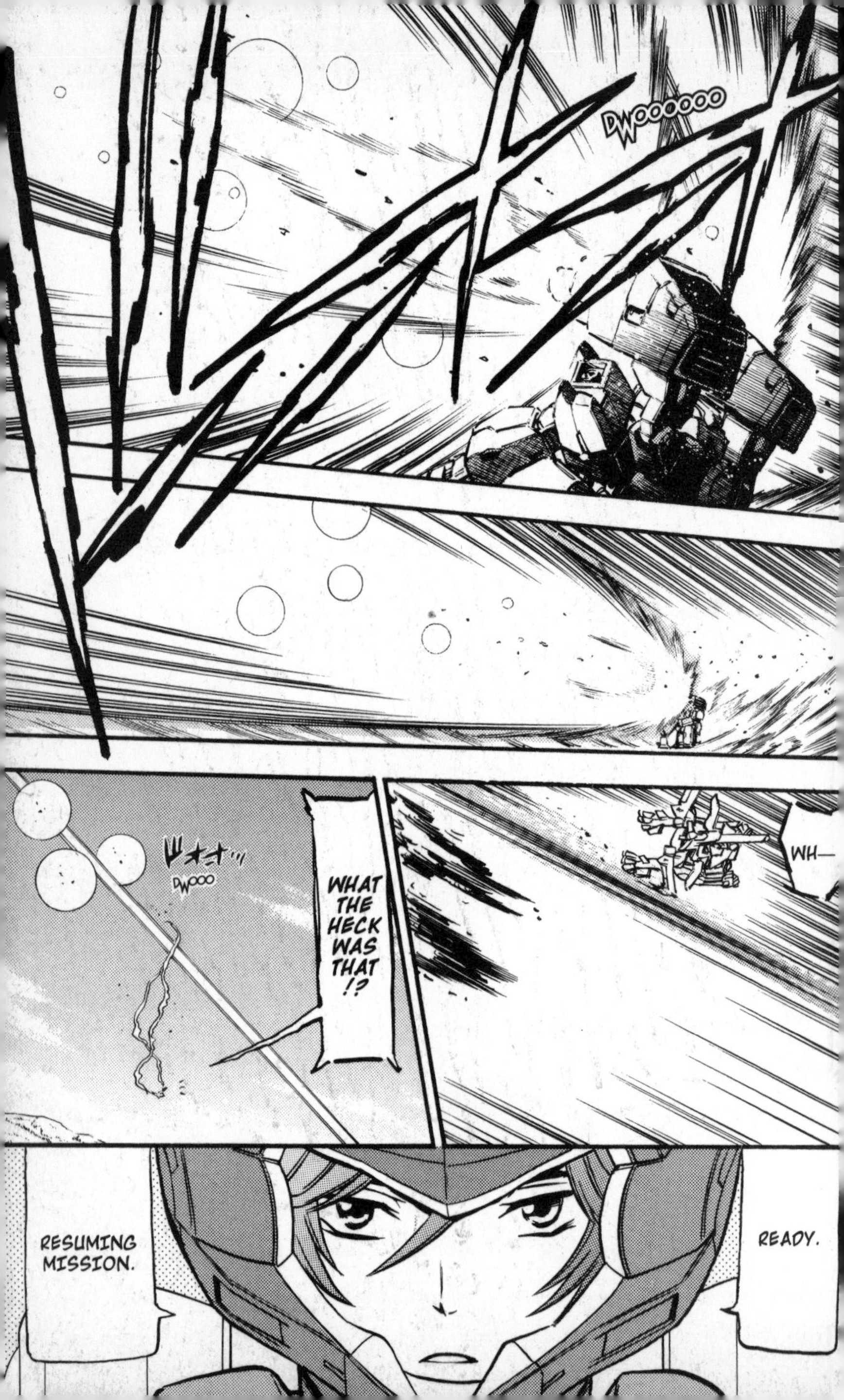
DWOOOOOO
WH—
WHAT THE HECK WAS THAT!?
DWOOO
READY.
RESUMING MISSION.

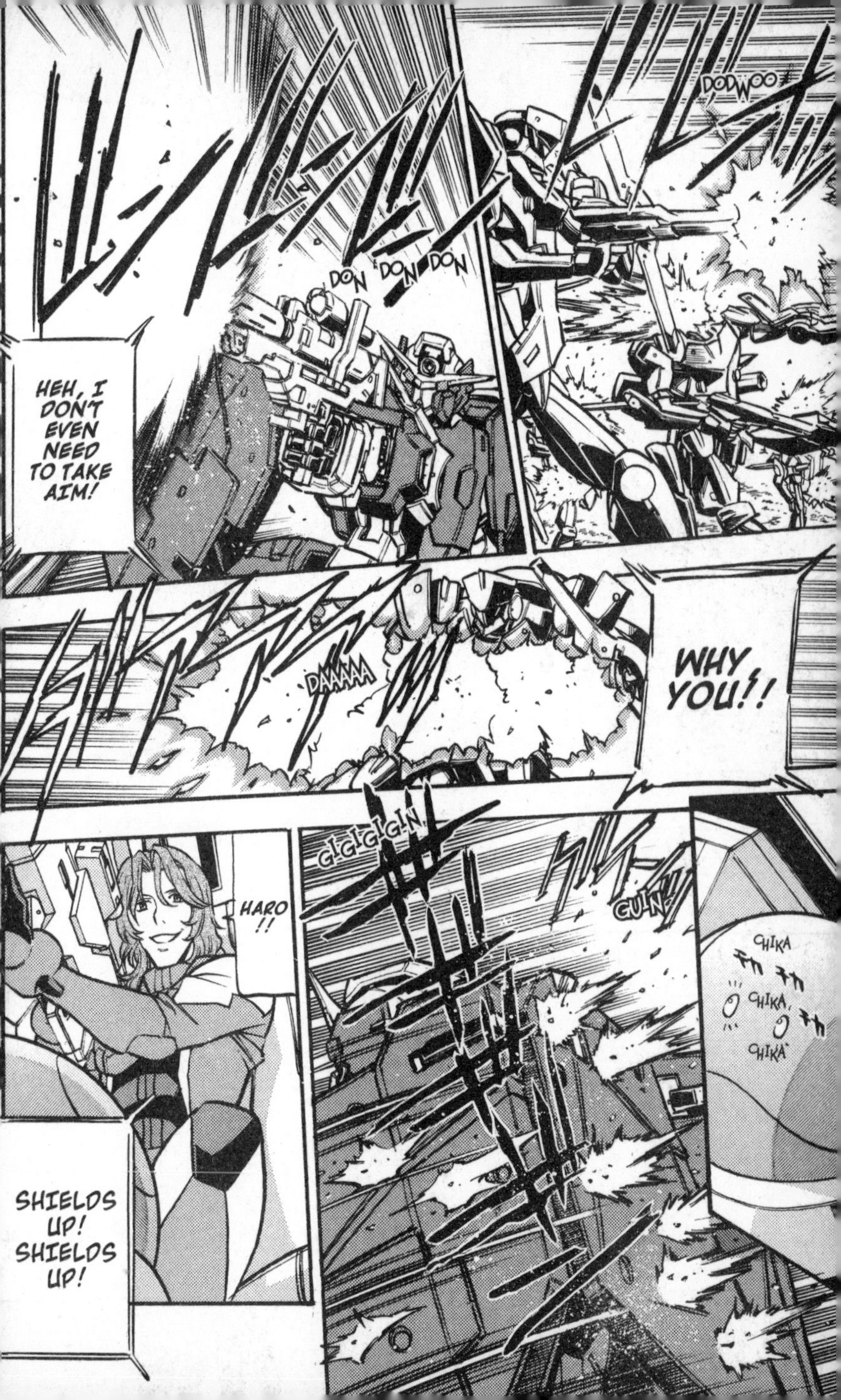
DODWOO
DON DON DON
HEH, I DON'T EVEN NEED TO TAKE AIM!
WHY YOU!!
DAAAAA
CHIKA
チカ チカ
CHIKA
チカ
CHIKA
GUIN!!
GIGIGIGIN
HARO!!
SHIELDS UP! SHIELDS UP!

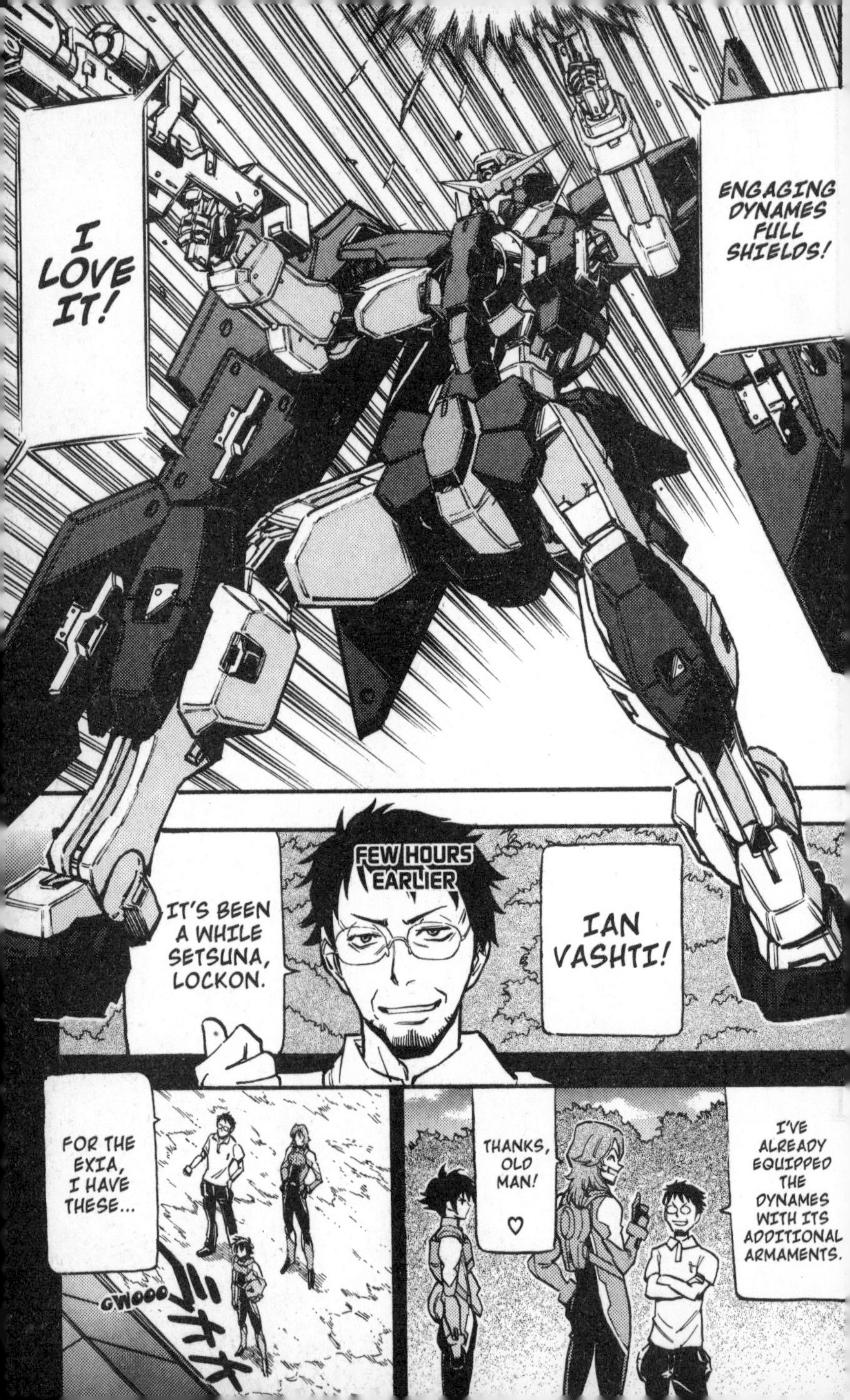
ENGAGING DYNAMES FULL SHIELDS!
I LOVE IT!
FEW HOURS EARLIER
IAN VASHTI!
IT'S BEEN A WHILE SETSUNA, LOCKON.
I'VE ALREADY EQUIPPED THE DYNAMES WITH ITS ADDITIONAL ARMAMENTS.
THANKS, OLD MAN! ♡
FOR THE EXIA, I HAVE THESE...
GWOOO

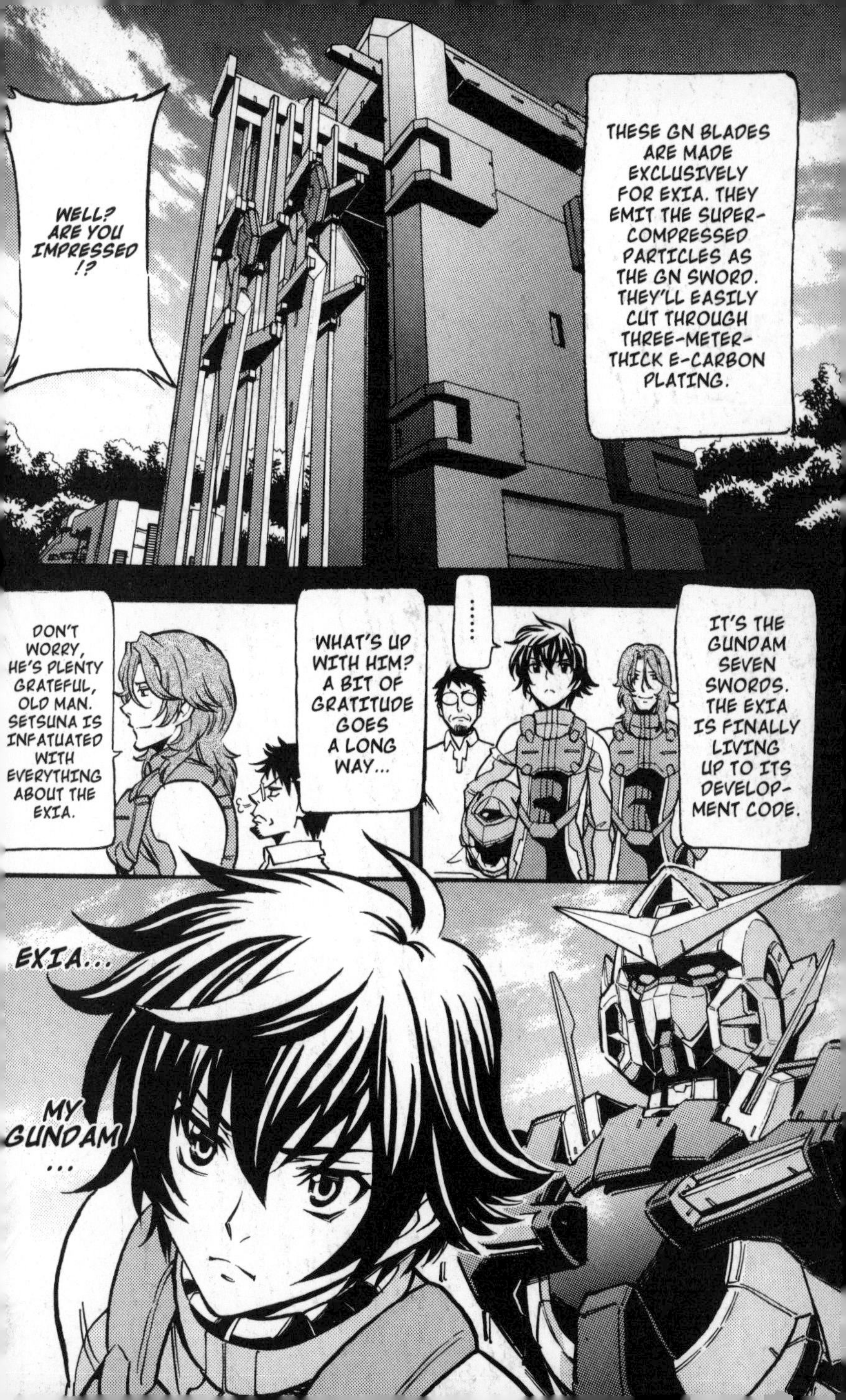
THESE GN BLADES ARE MADE EXCLUSIVELY FOR EXIA. THEY EMIT THE SUPER-COMPRESSED PARTICLES AS THE GN SWORD. THEY'LL EASILY CUT THROUGH THREE-METER-THICK E-CARBON PLATING.
WELL? ARE YOU IMPRESSED!?
IT'S THE GUNDAM SEVEN SWORDS. THE EXIA IS FINALLY LIVING UP TO ITS DEVELOPMENT CODE.
......
WHAT'S UP WITH HIM? A BIT OF GRATITUDE GOES A LONG WAY...
DON'T WORRY, HE'S PLENTY GRATEFUL, OLD MAN. SETSUNA IS INFATUATED WITH EVERYTHING ABOUT THE EXIA.
EXIA...
MY GUNDAM...

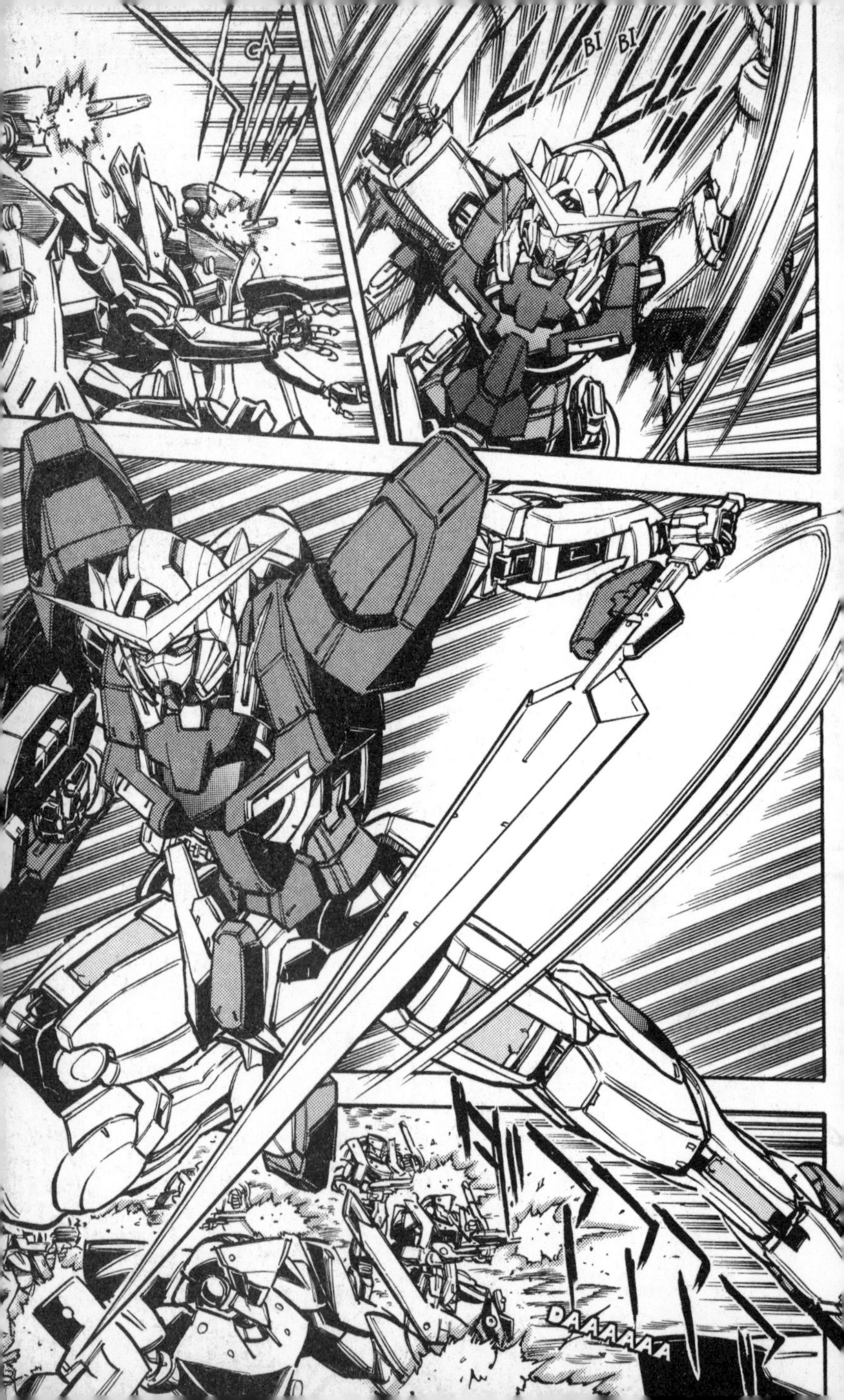
BI BI
CA
DAAAAAA

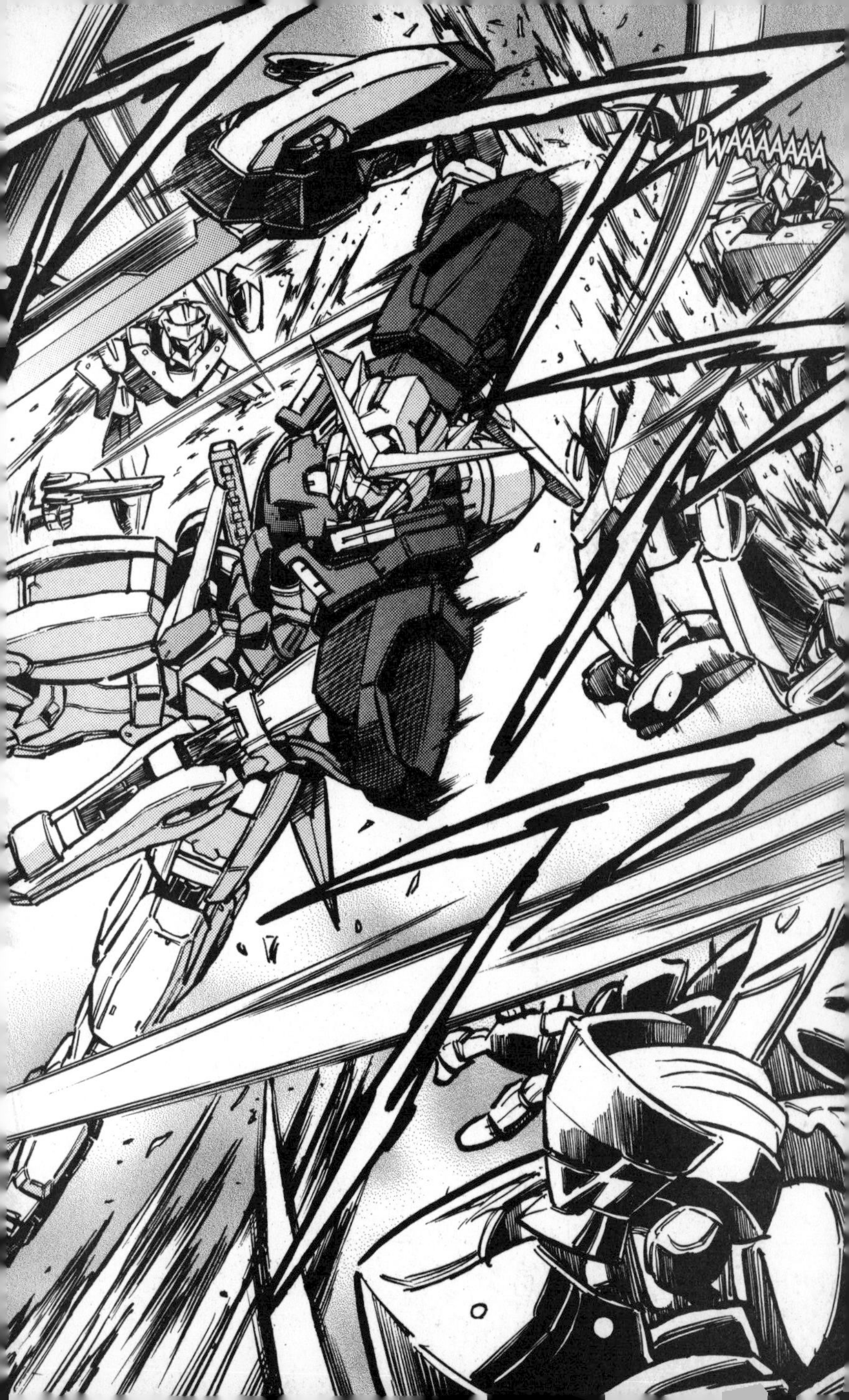
DWAAAAAAA

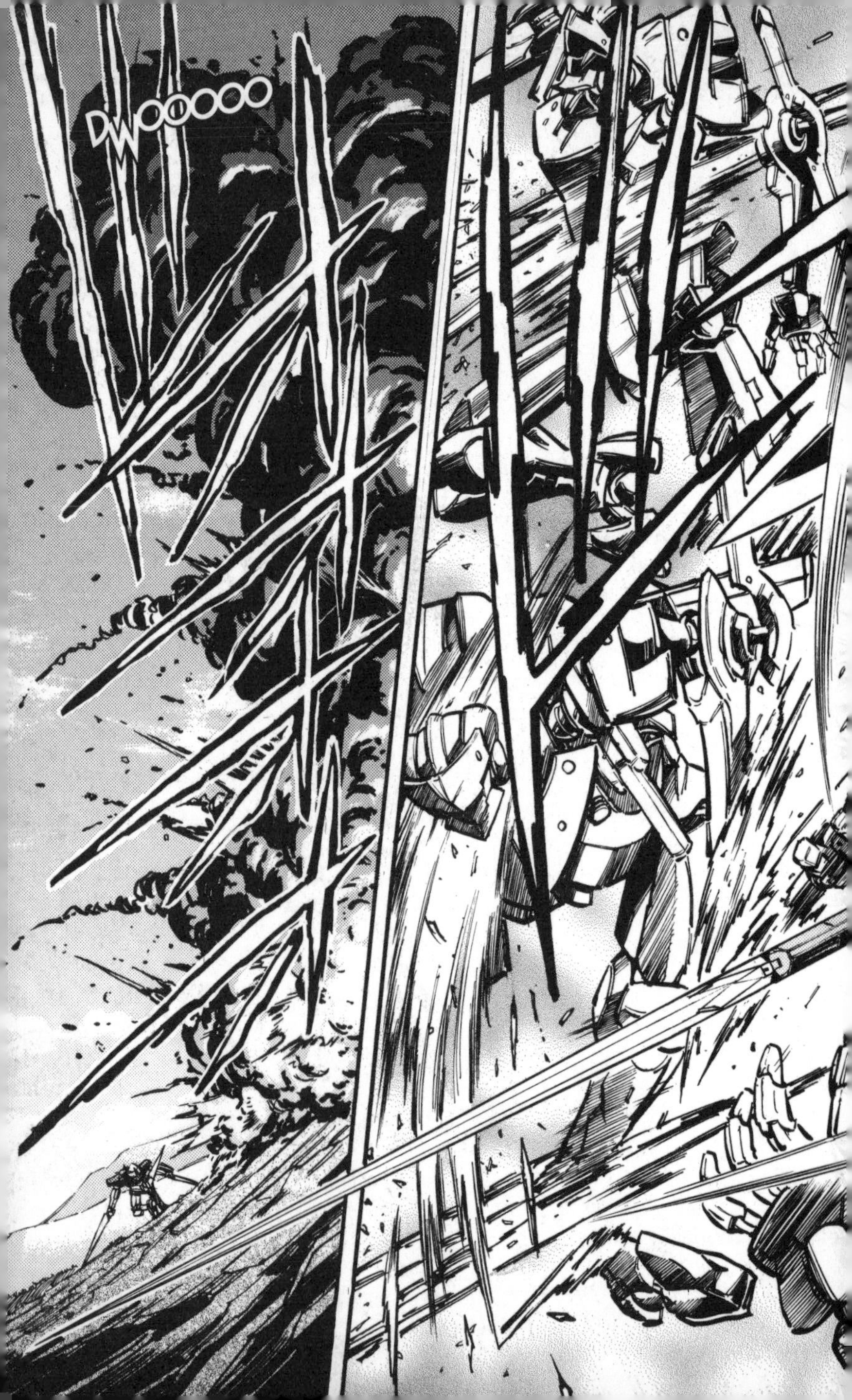
DWOOOOO

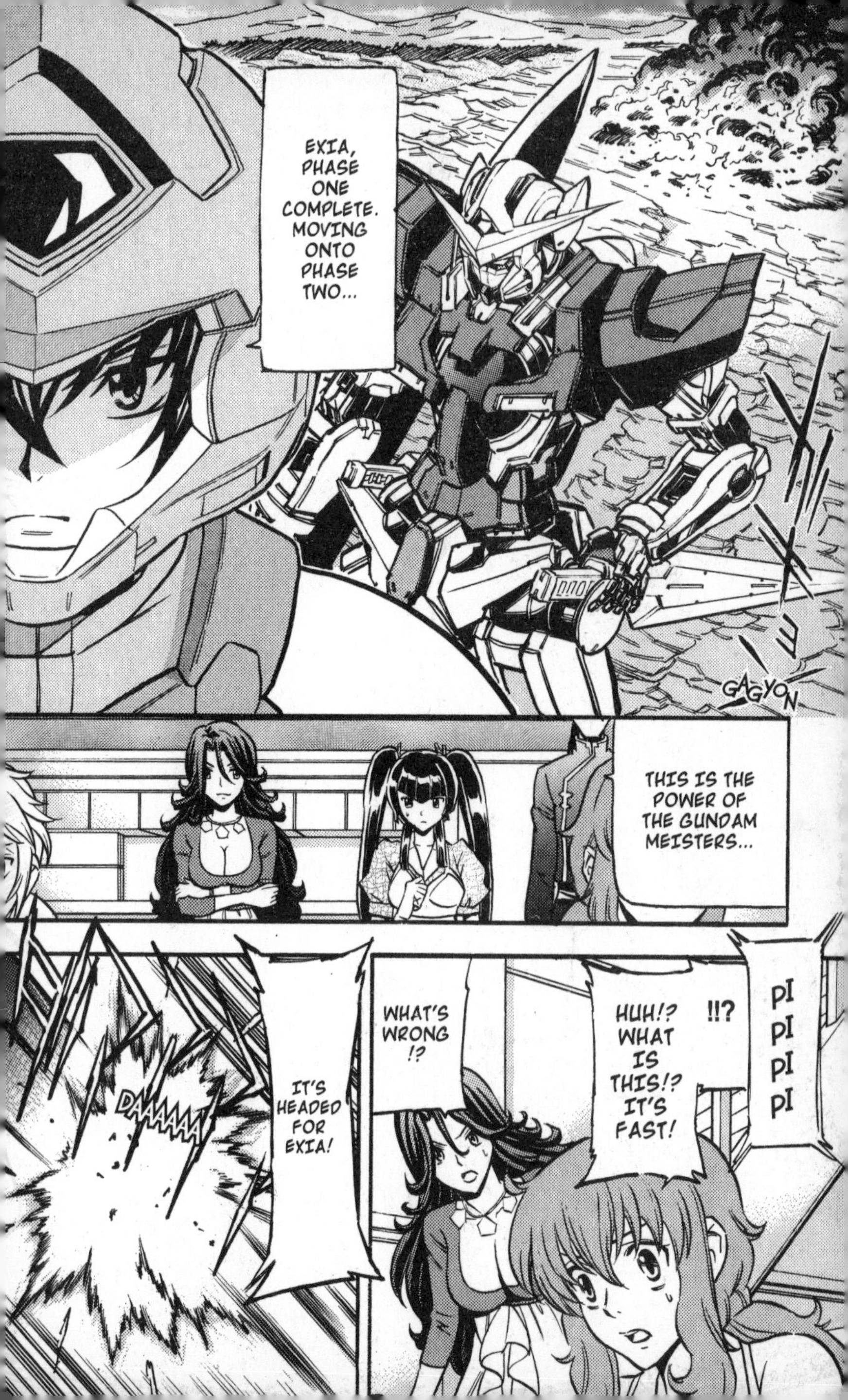
EXIA, PHASE ONE COMPLETE. MOVING ONTO PHASE TWO...
GAGYON
THIS IS THE POWER OF THE GUNDAM MEISTERS...
PI PI PI PI
!!?
HUH!? WHAT IS THIS!? IT'S FAST!
WHAT'S WRONG!?
IT'S HEADED FOR EXIA!
DAAAAAA

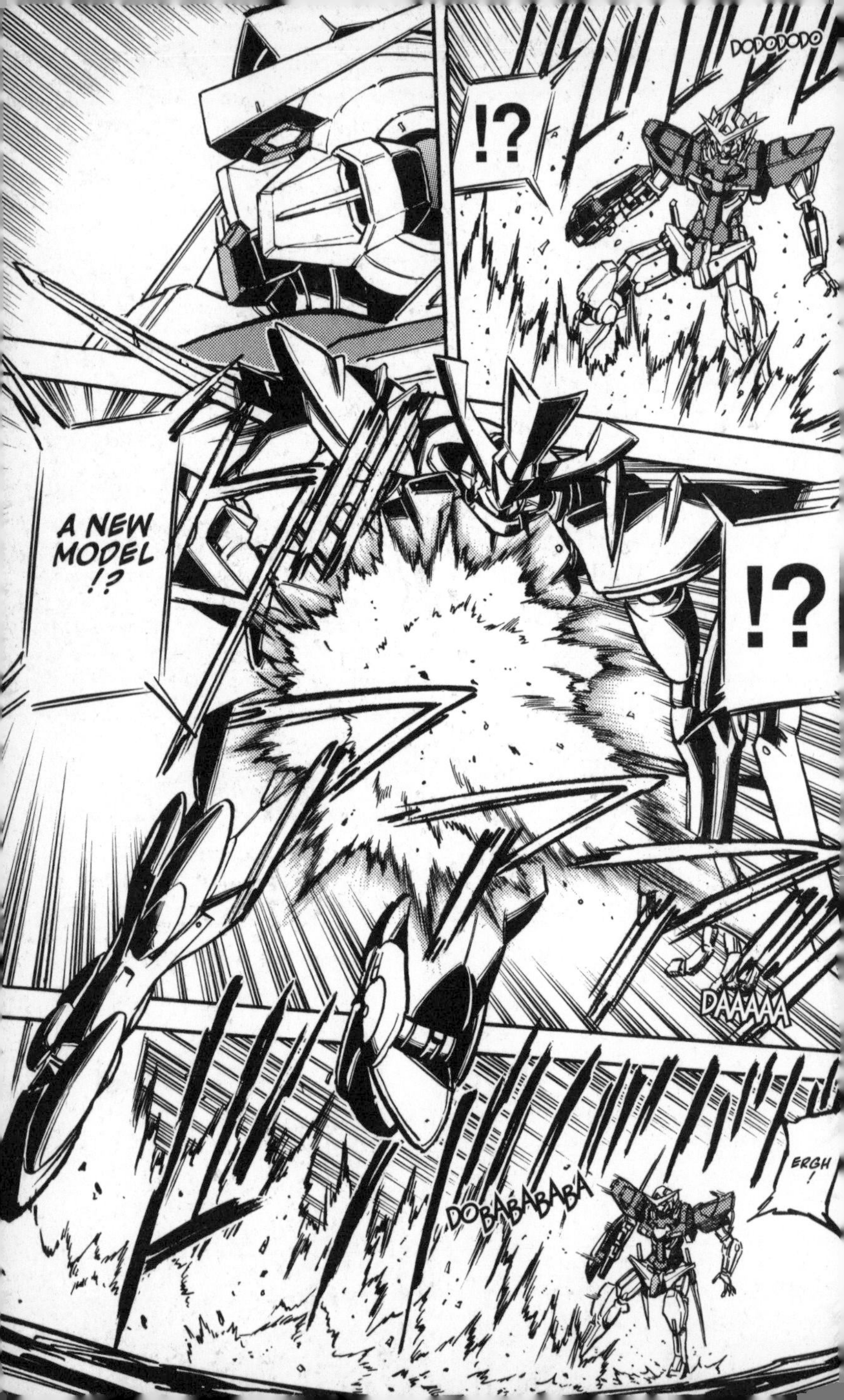
DODODODO
!?
!?
A NEW MODEL !?
DAAAAA
ERGH !
DOBABABABA

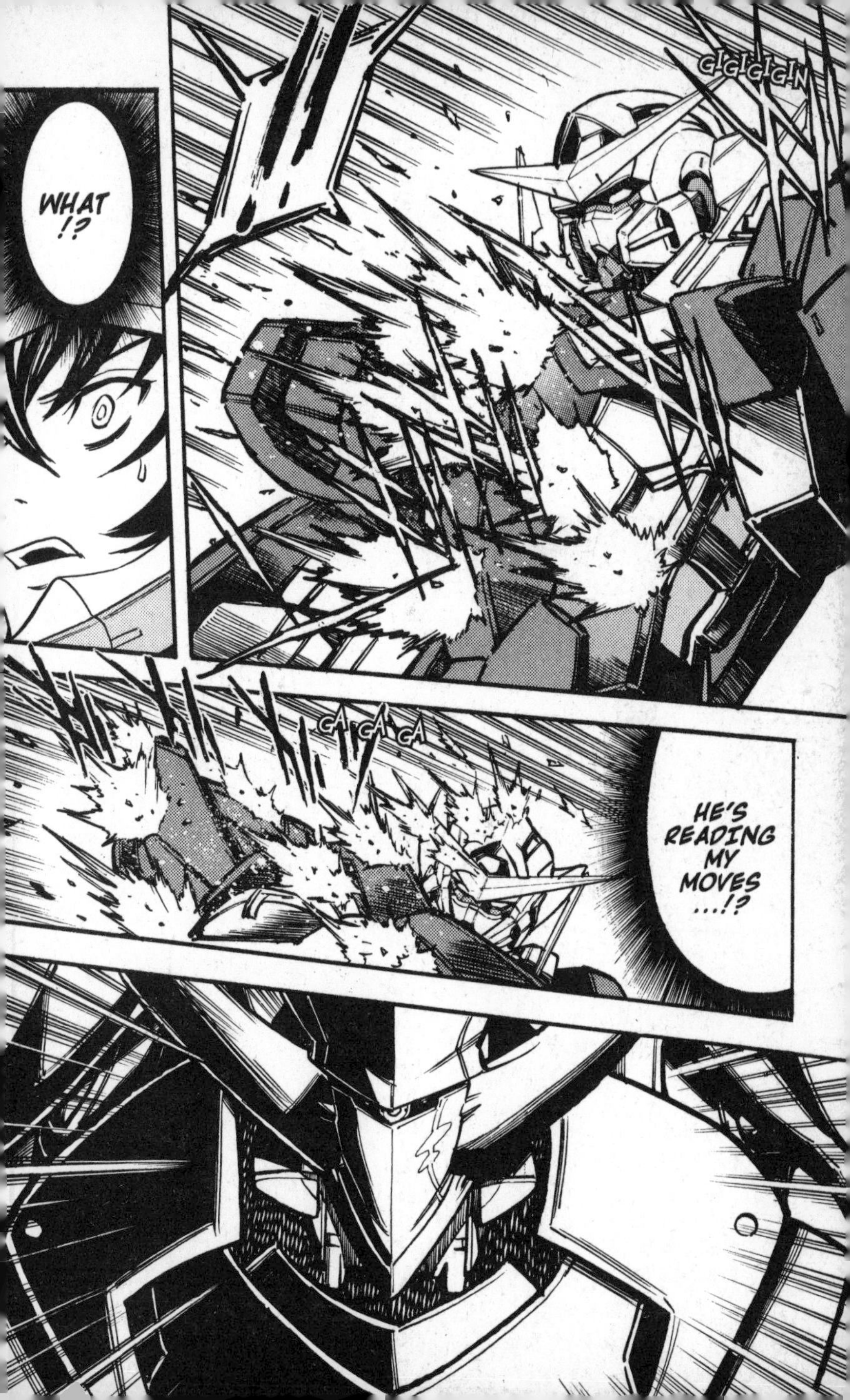
GIGIGIGIN
WHAT!?
GA GA GA
HE'S READING MY MOVES ...!?

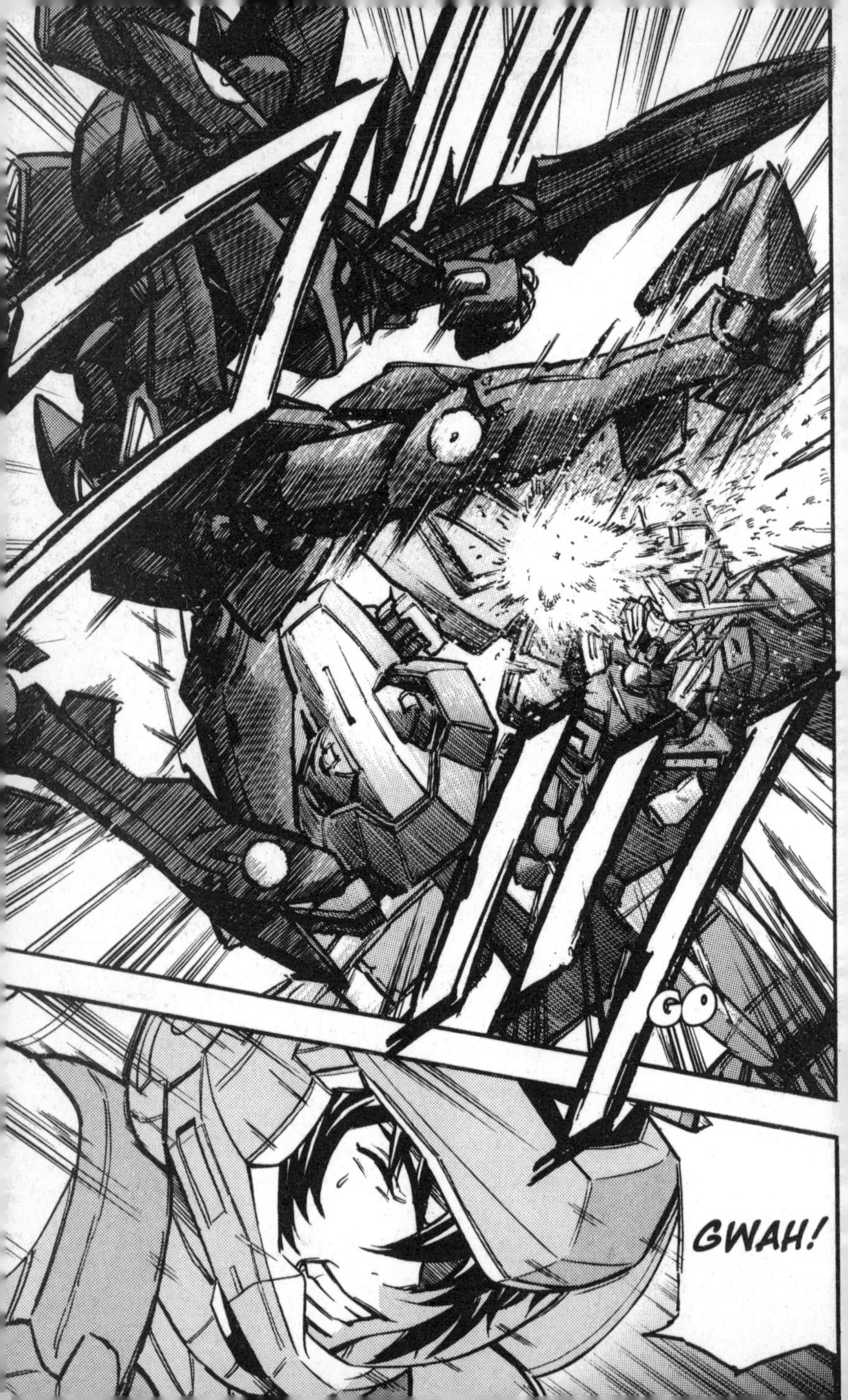
GO
GWAH!

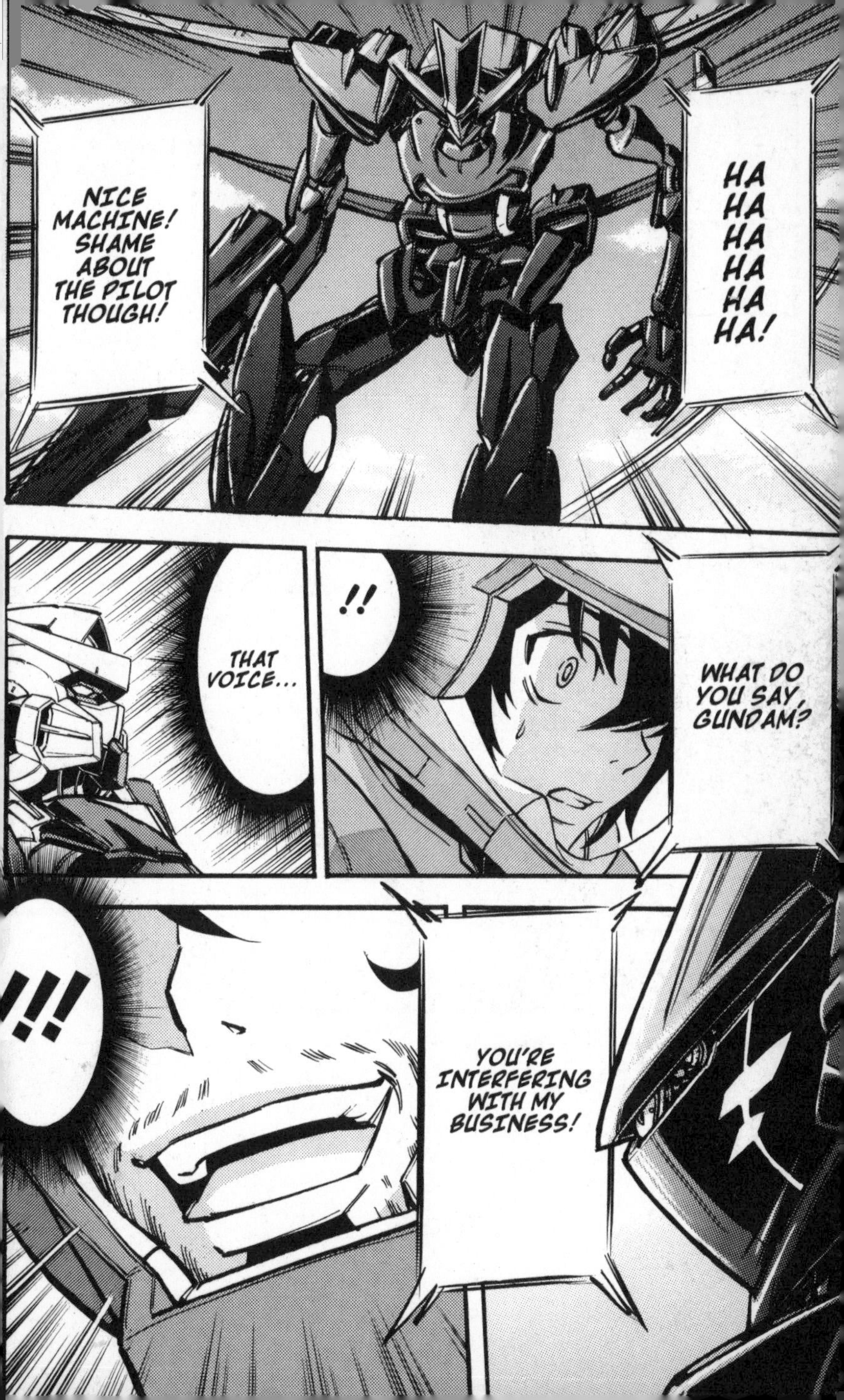

HA HA HA HA HA HA!
NICE MACHINE! SHAME ABOUT THE PILOT THOUGH!
WHAT DO YOU SAY, GUNDAM?
!!
THAT VOICE...
YOU'RE INTERFERING WITH MY BUSINESS!
!!!

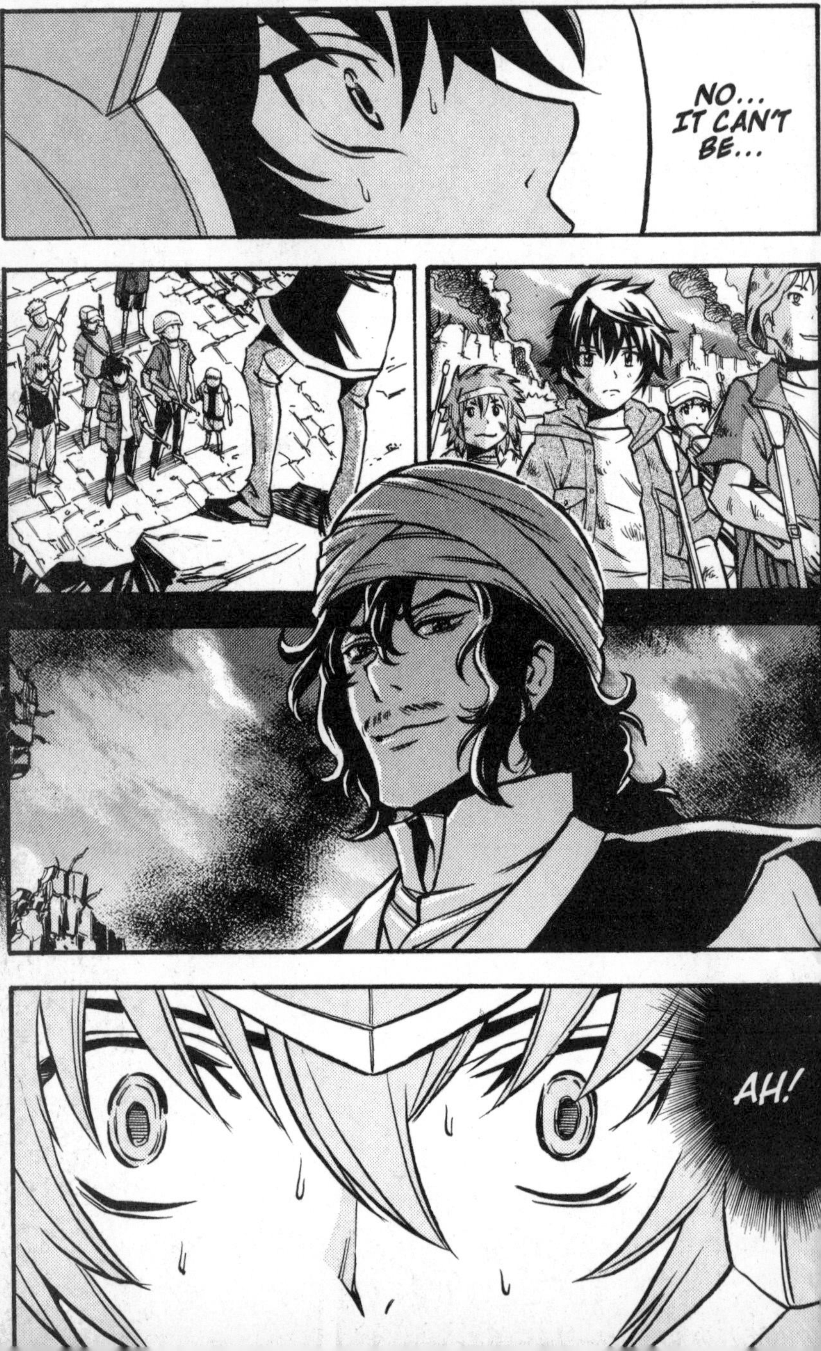
NO... IT CAN'T BE...
AH!

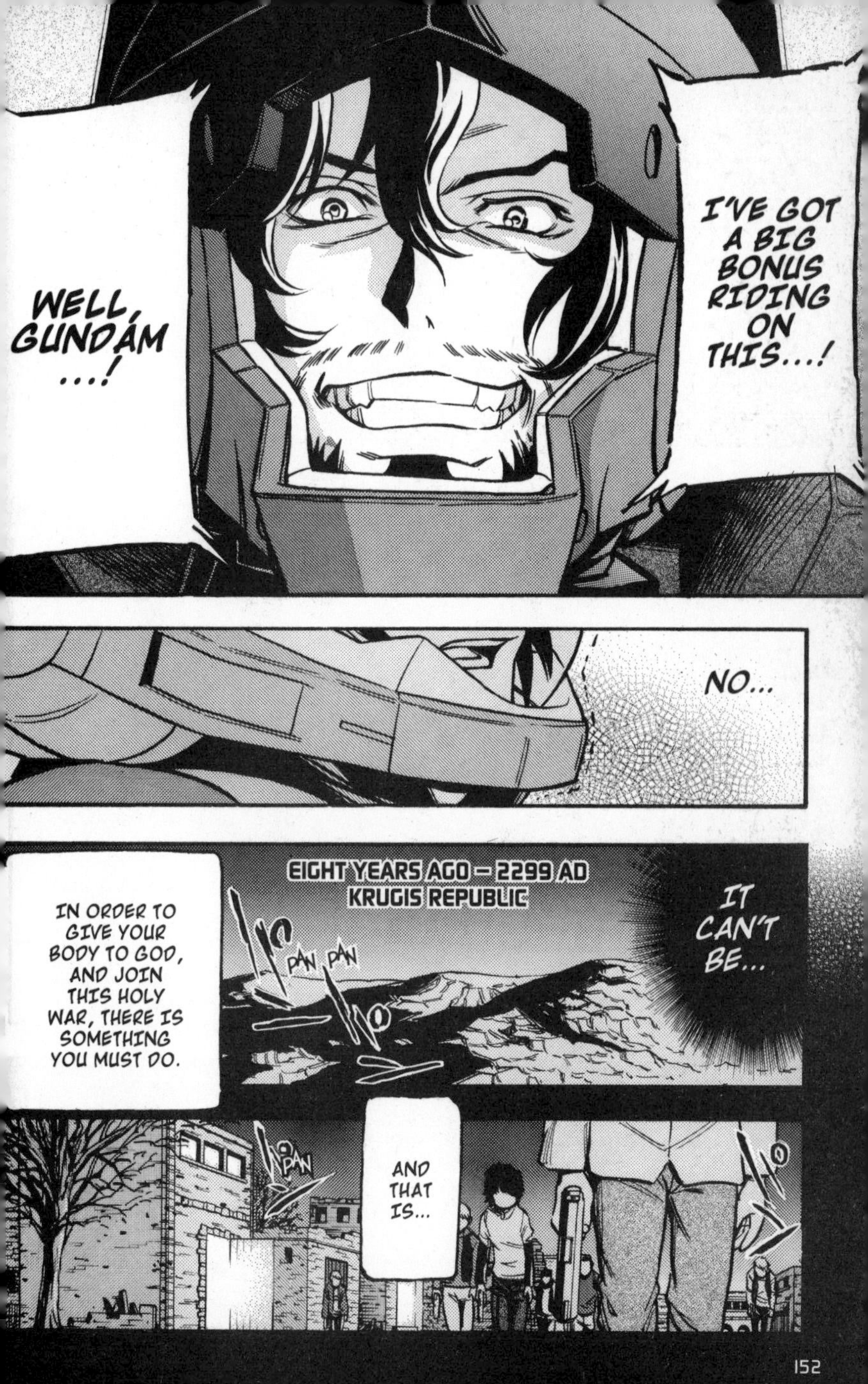
I'VE GOT A BIG BONUS RIDING ON THIS...!
WELL, GUNDAM ...!
NO...
EIGHT YEARS AGO – 2299 AD
KRUGIS REPUBLIC
IT CAN'T BE...
PAN PAN
IN ORDER TO GIVE YOUR BODY TO GOD, AND JOIN THIS HOLY WAR, THERE IS SOMETHING YOU MUST DO.
PAN
AND THAT IS...

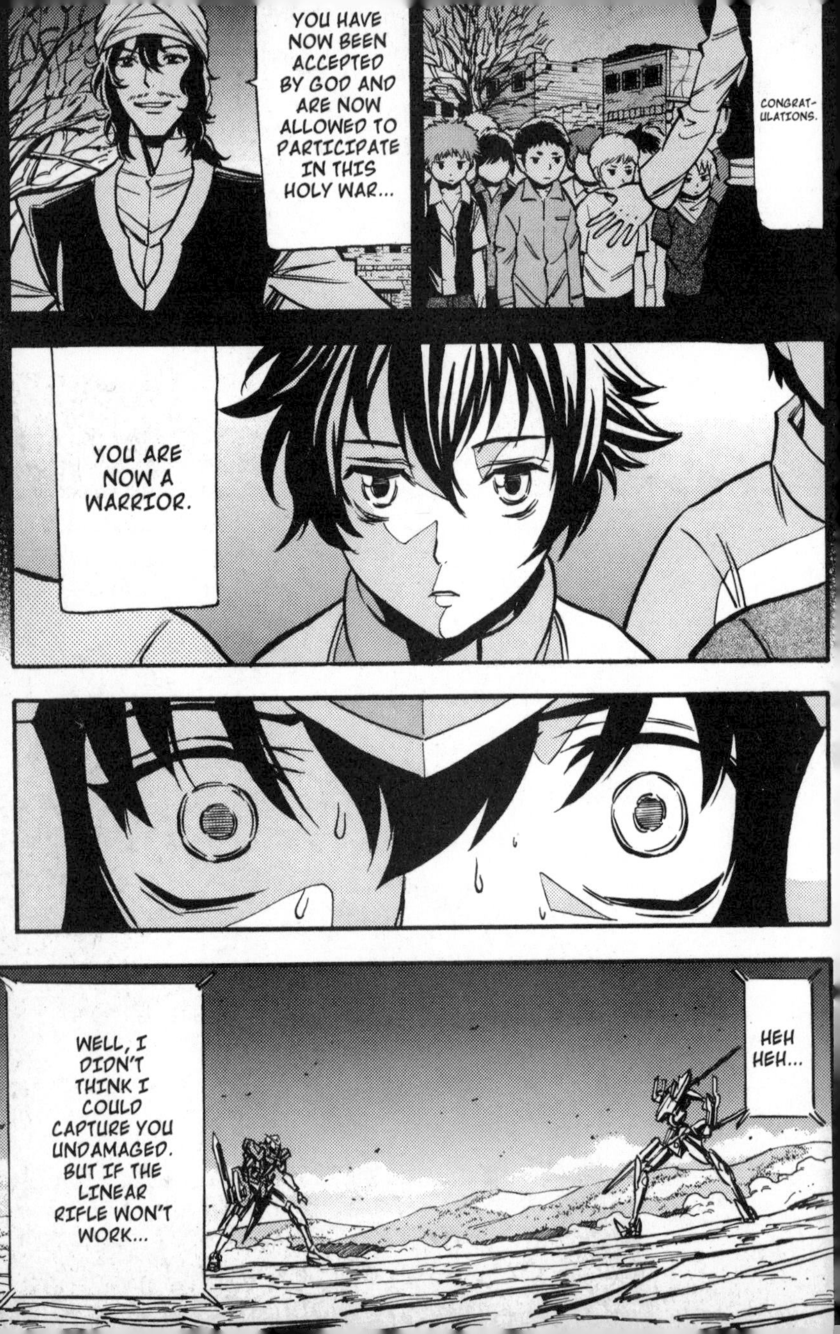
CONGRATULATIONS.
YOU HAVE NOW BEEN ACCEPTED BY GOD AND ARE NOW ALLOWED TO PARTICIPATE IN THIS HOLY WAR...
YOU ARE NOW A WARRIOR.
HEH HEH...
WELL, I DIDN'T THINK I COULD CAPTURE YOU UNDAMAGED. BUT IF THE LINEAR RIFLE WON'T WORK...

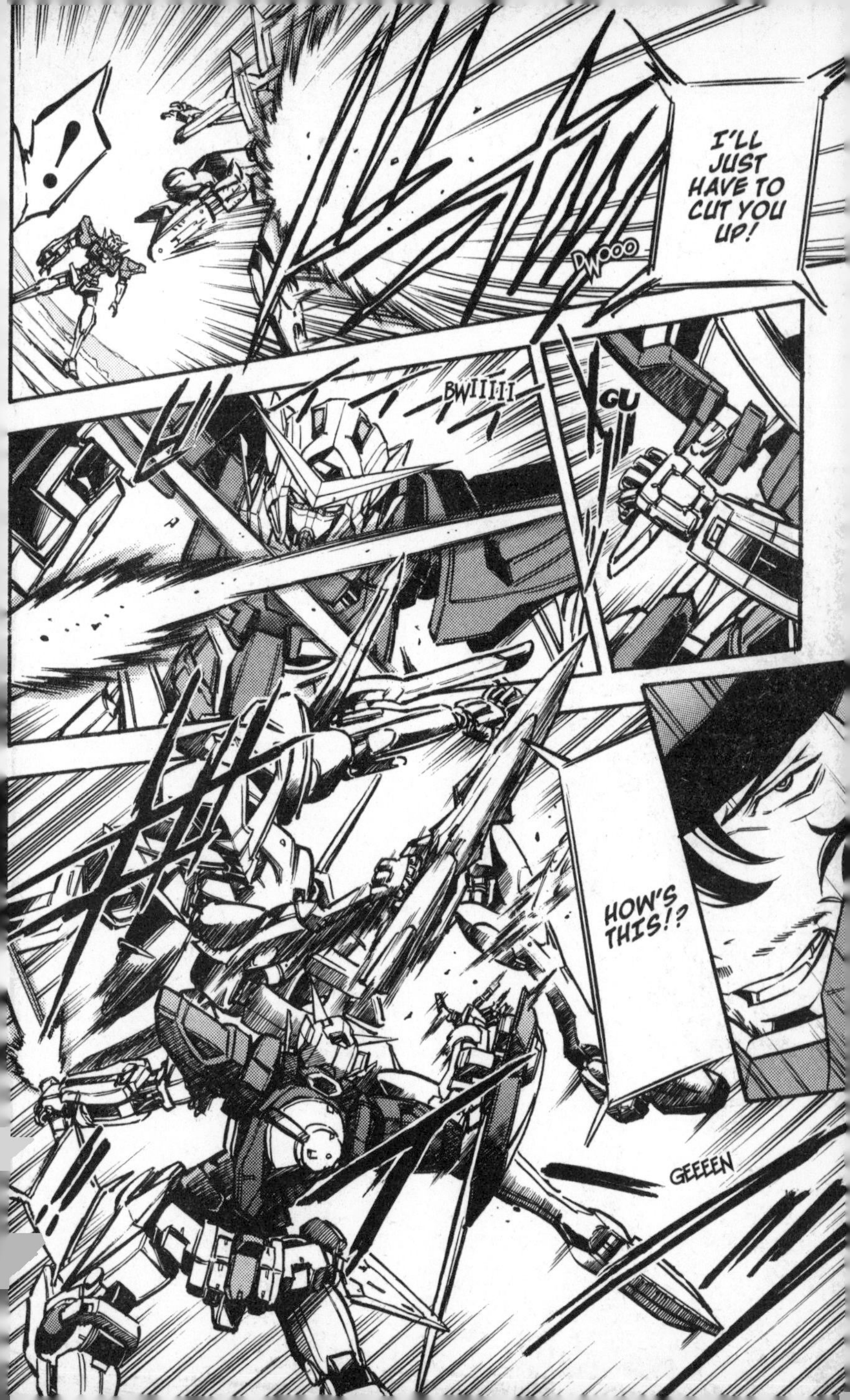
I'LL JUST HAVE TO CUT YOU UP!
DWOOO
!
GU
BWIIIII
HOW'S THIS!?
GEEEEN
!!

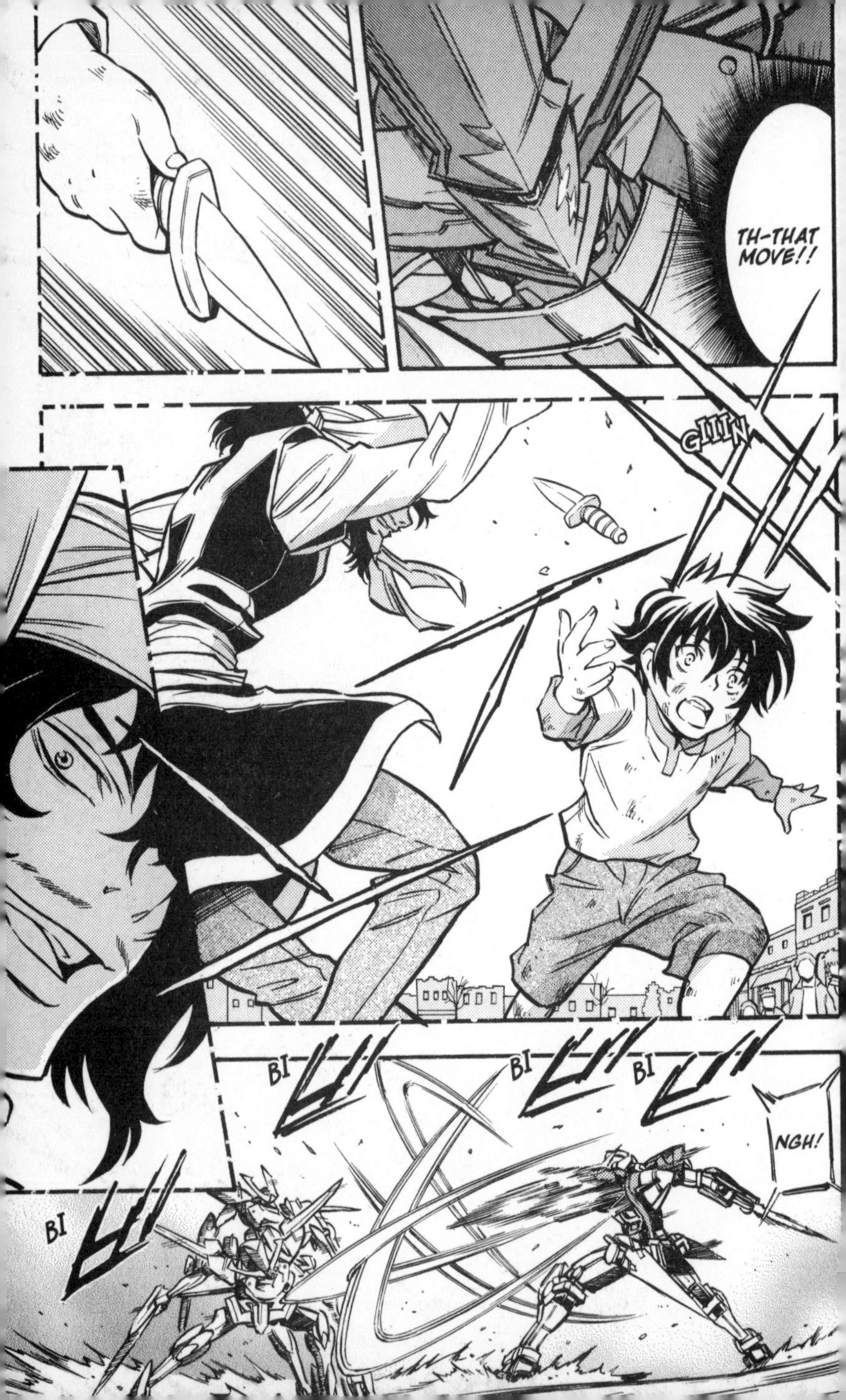
TH-THAT MOVE!!
GIIIN
NGH!
BI
BI
BI
BI

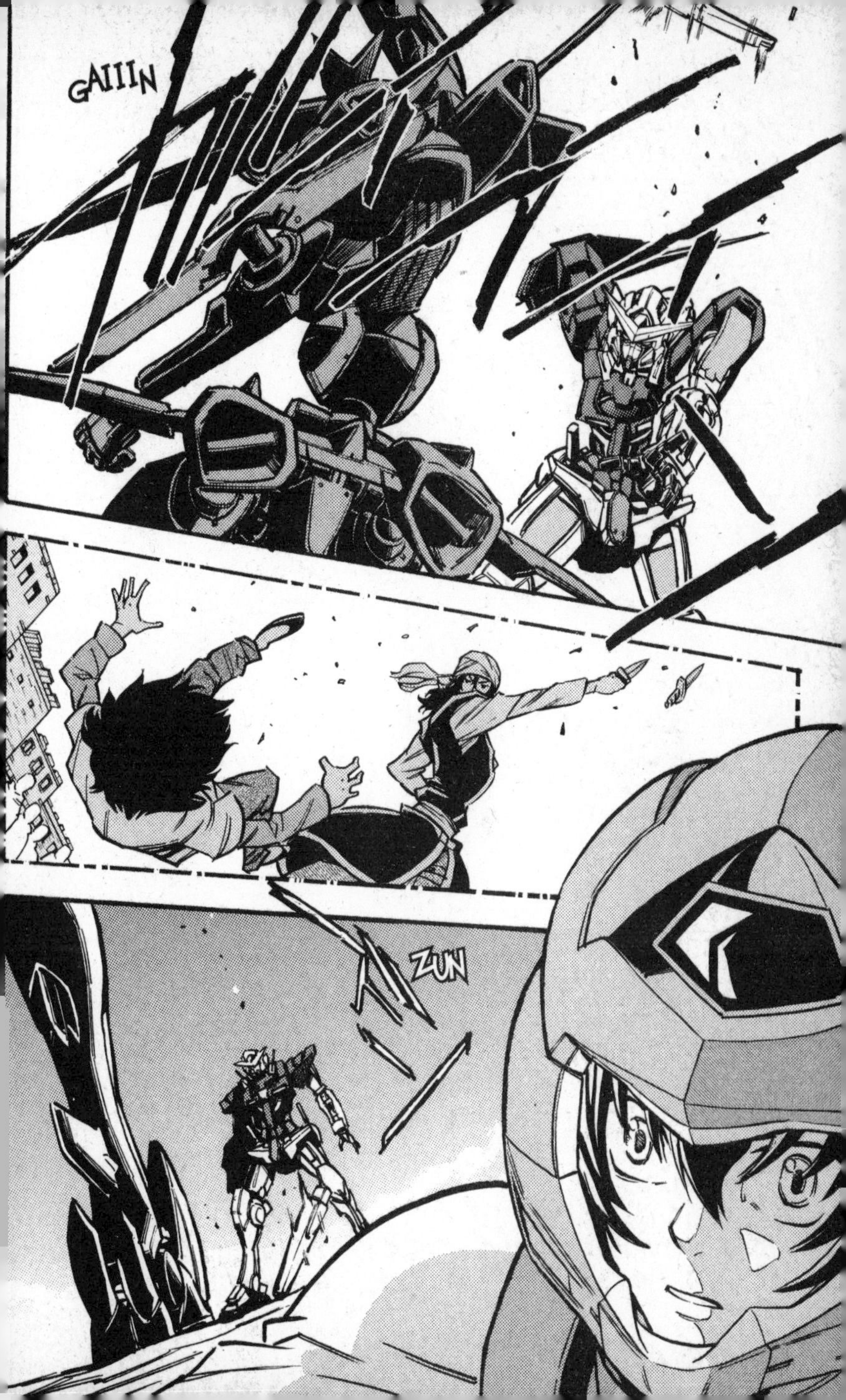
GAIIIN
ZUN

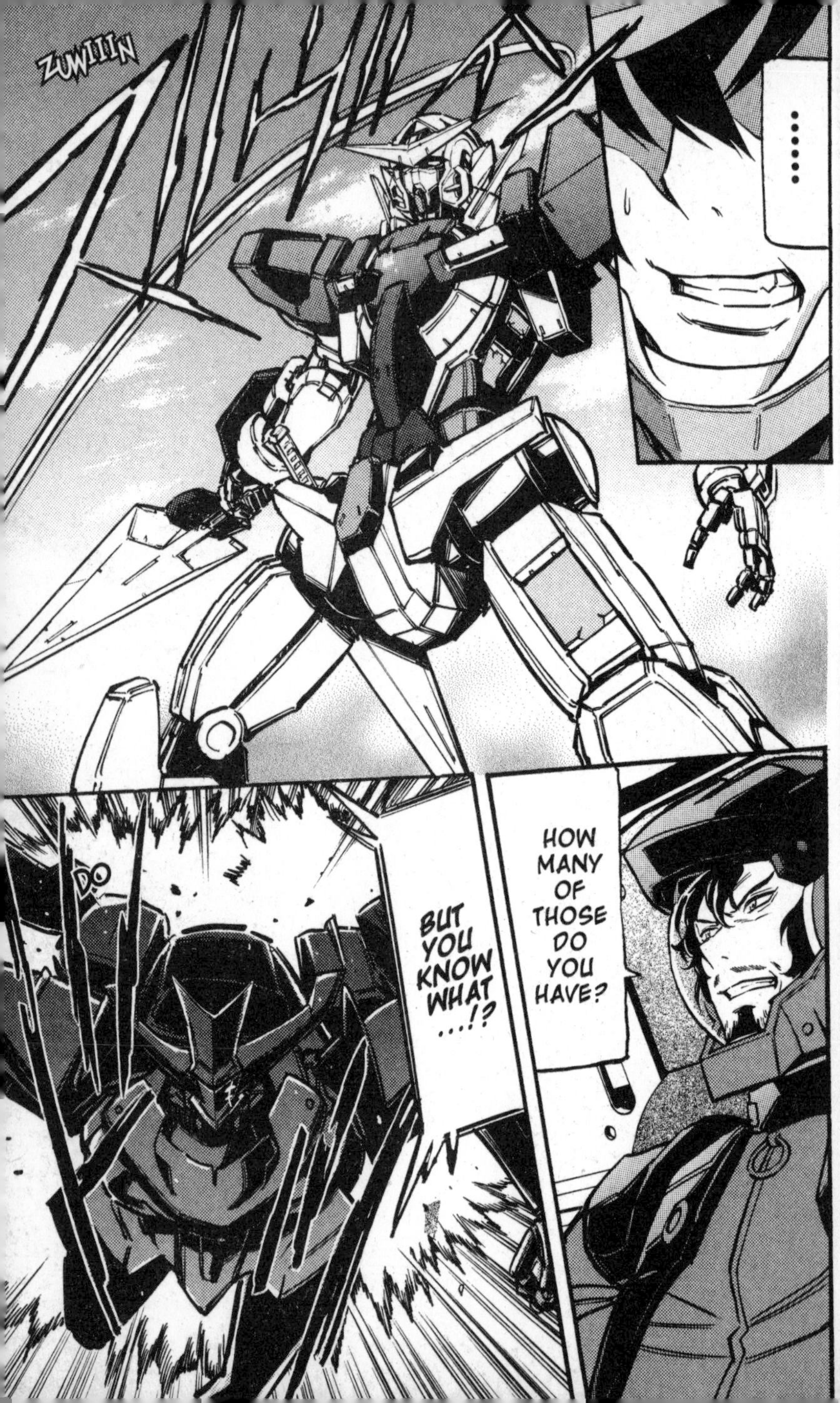
......
ZUWIIIN
HOW MANY OF THOSE DO YOU HAVE?
BUT YOU KNOW WHAT ...!?
DO

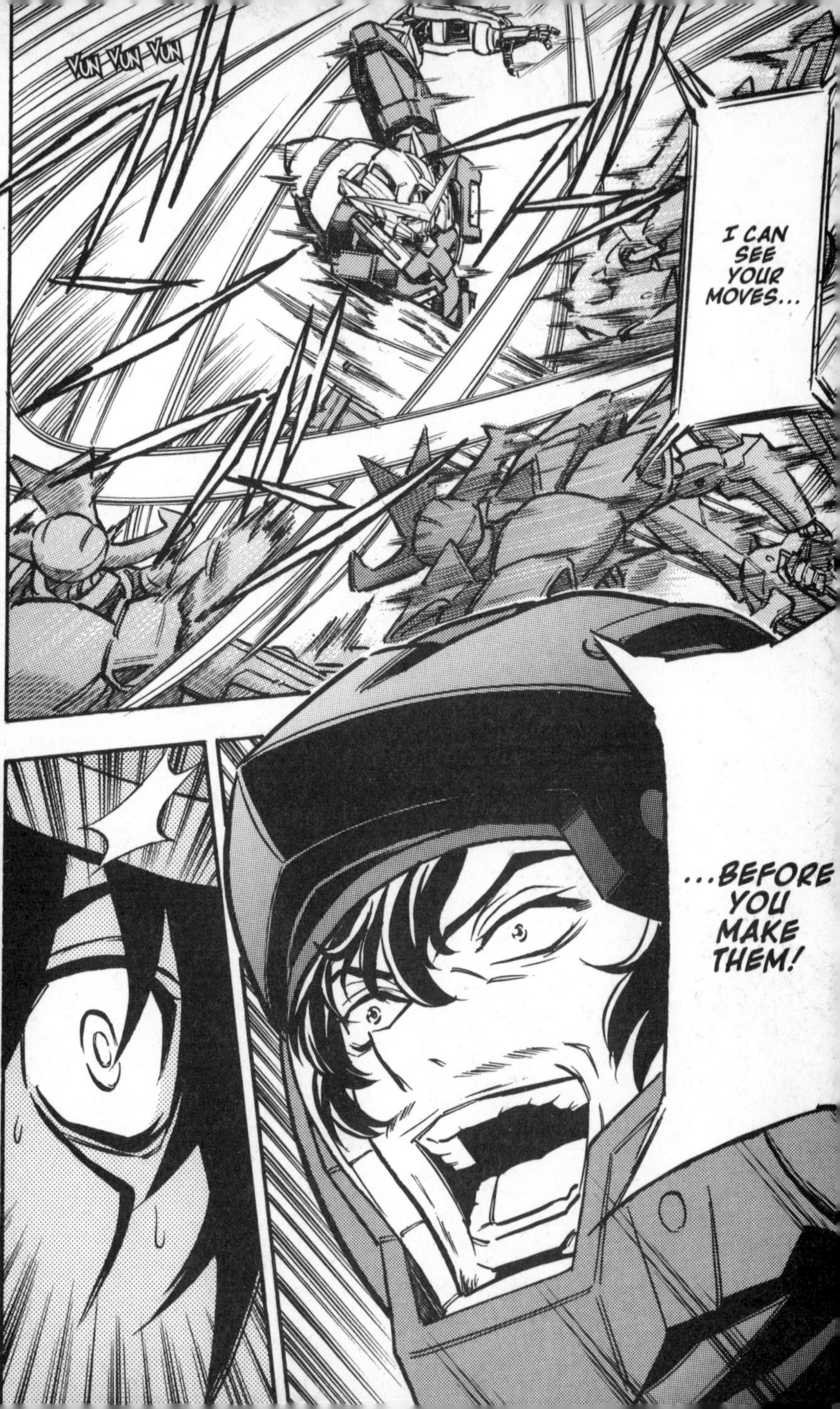
VUN VUN VUN
I CAN SEE YOUR MOVES...
...BEFORE YOU MAKE THEM!

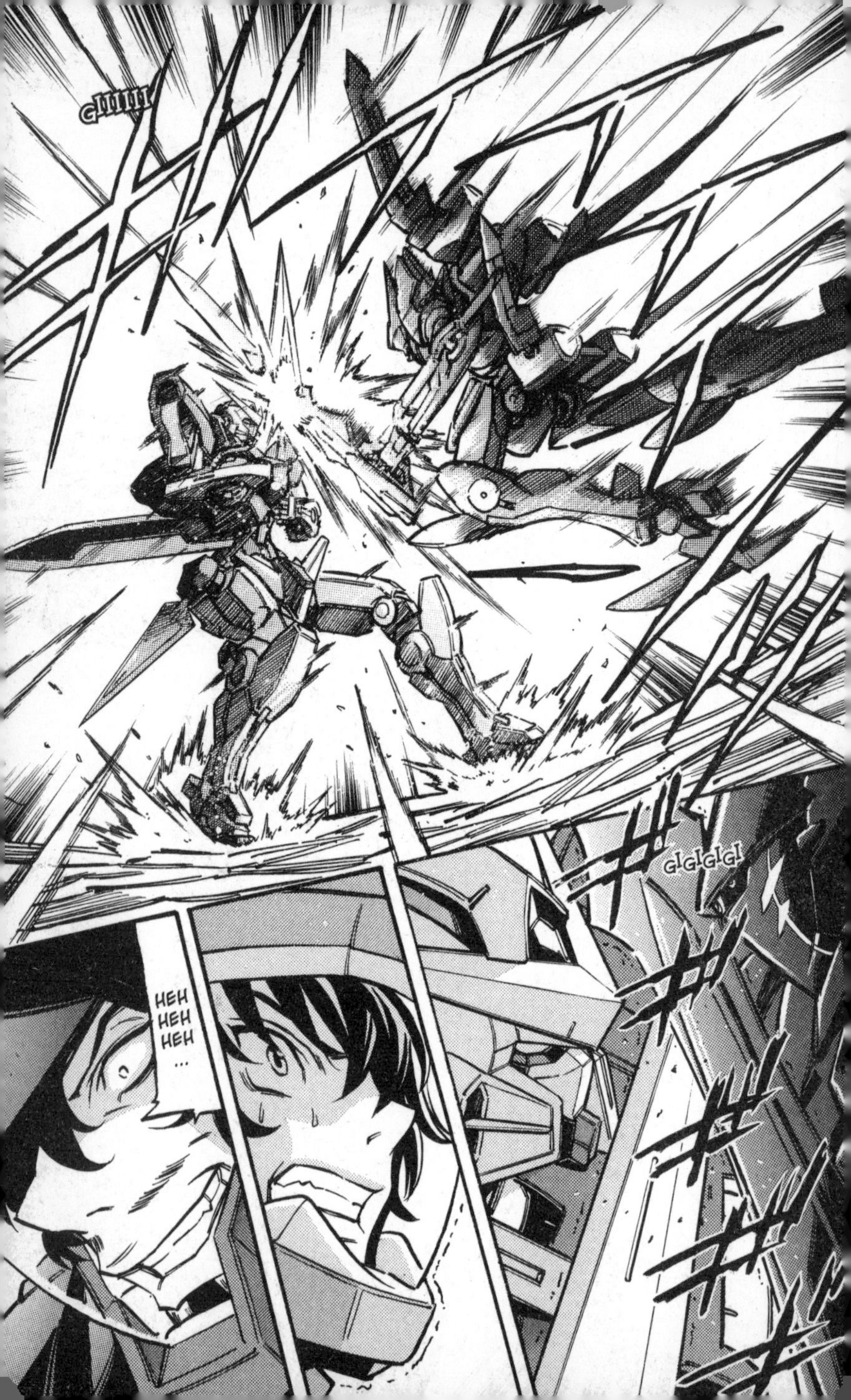
GIIIII
GIGIGIGI
HEH HEH HEH ...

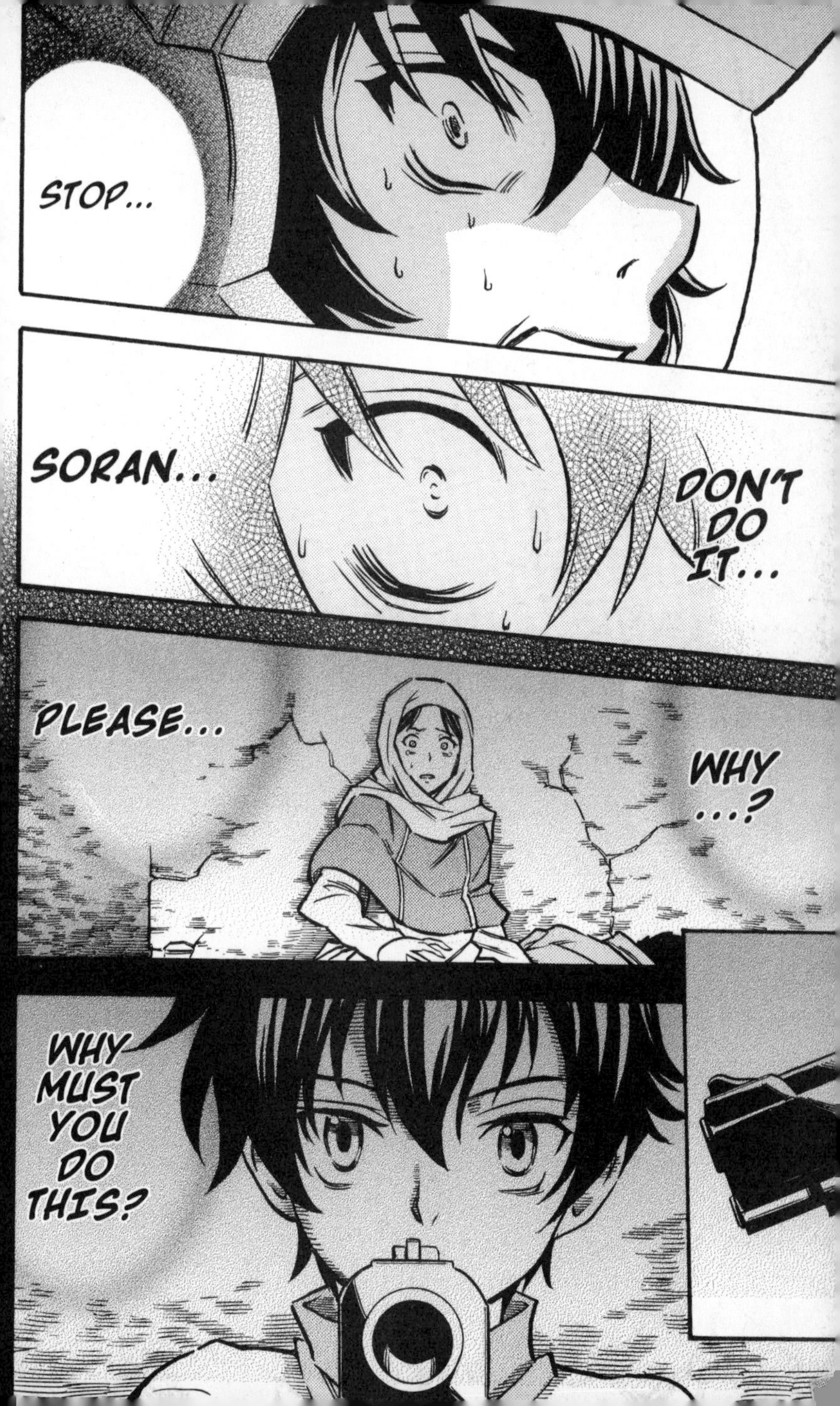
STOP...
DON'T DO IT...
SORAN...
WHY...?
PLEASE...
WHY MUST YOU DO THIS?

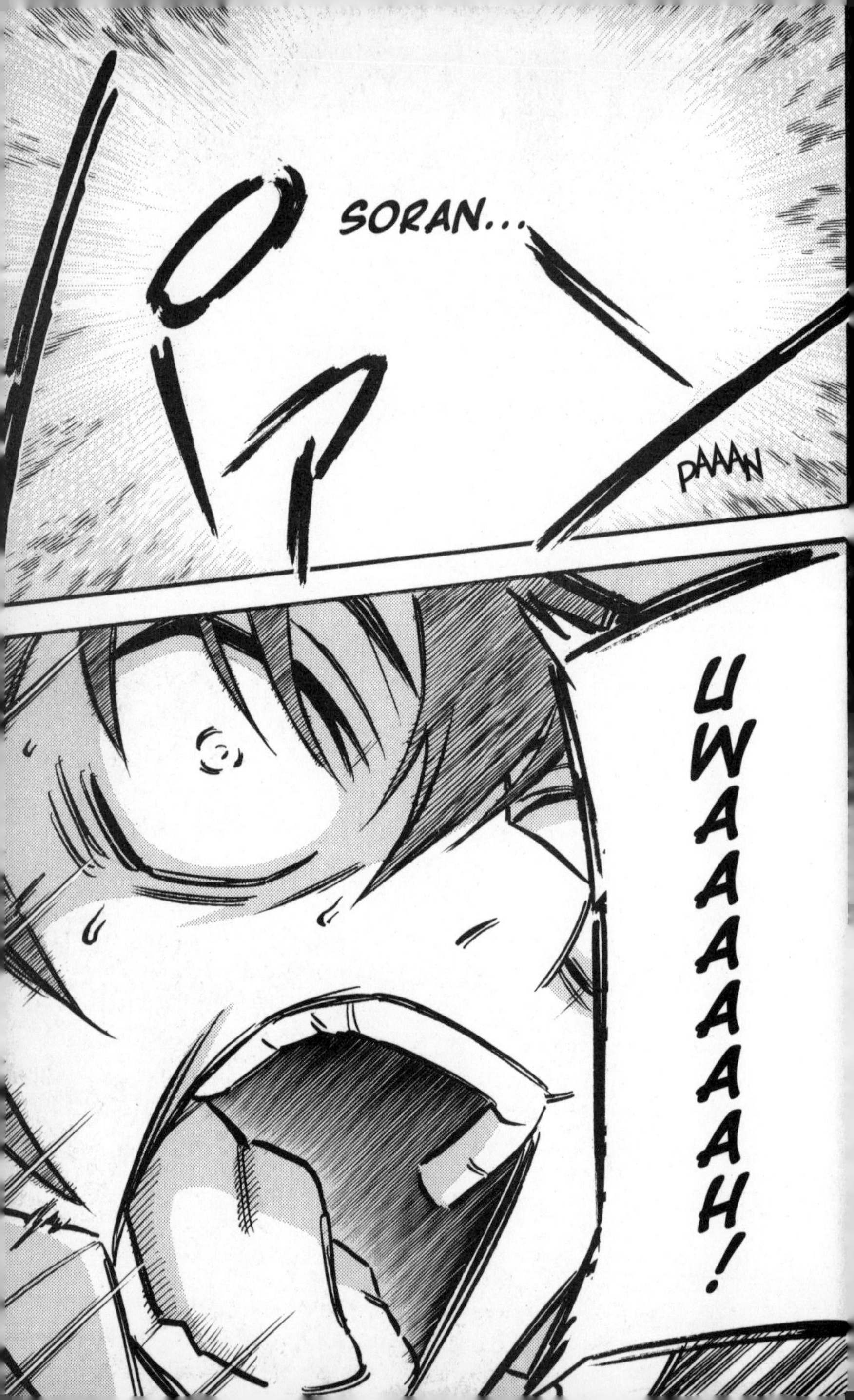
SORAN...
PAAAN
UWAAAAAAAAH!

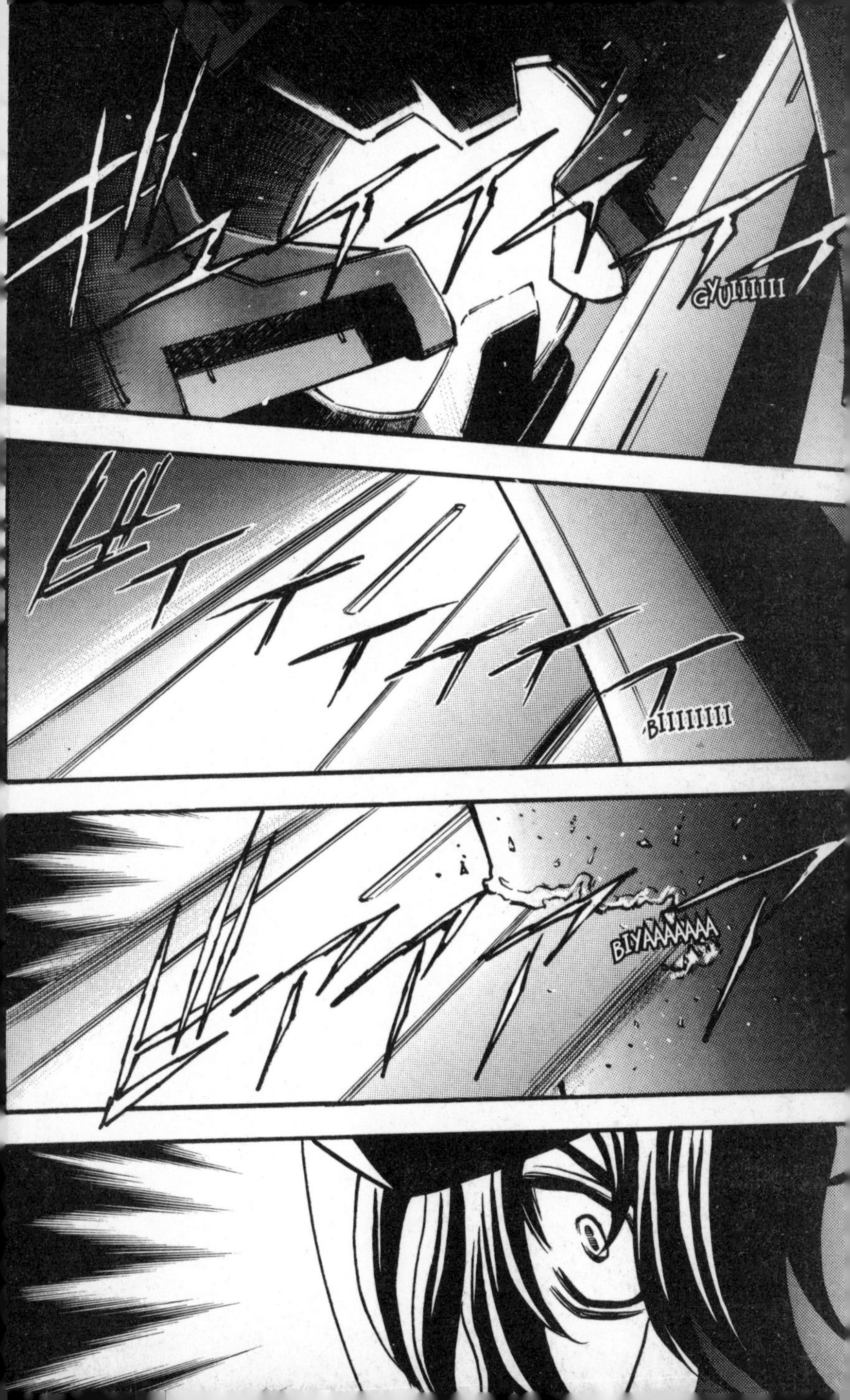
GYUIIIII
BIIIIIII
BIYAAAAAAA

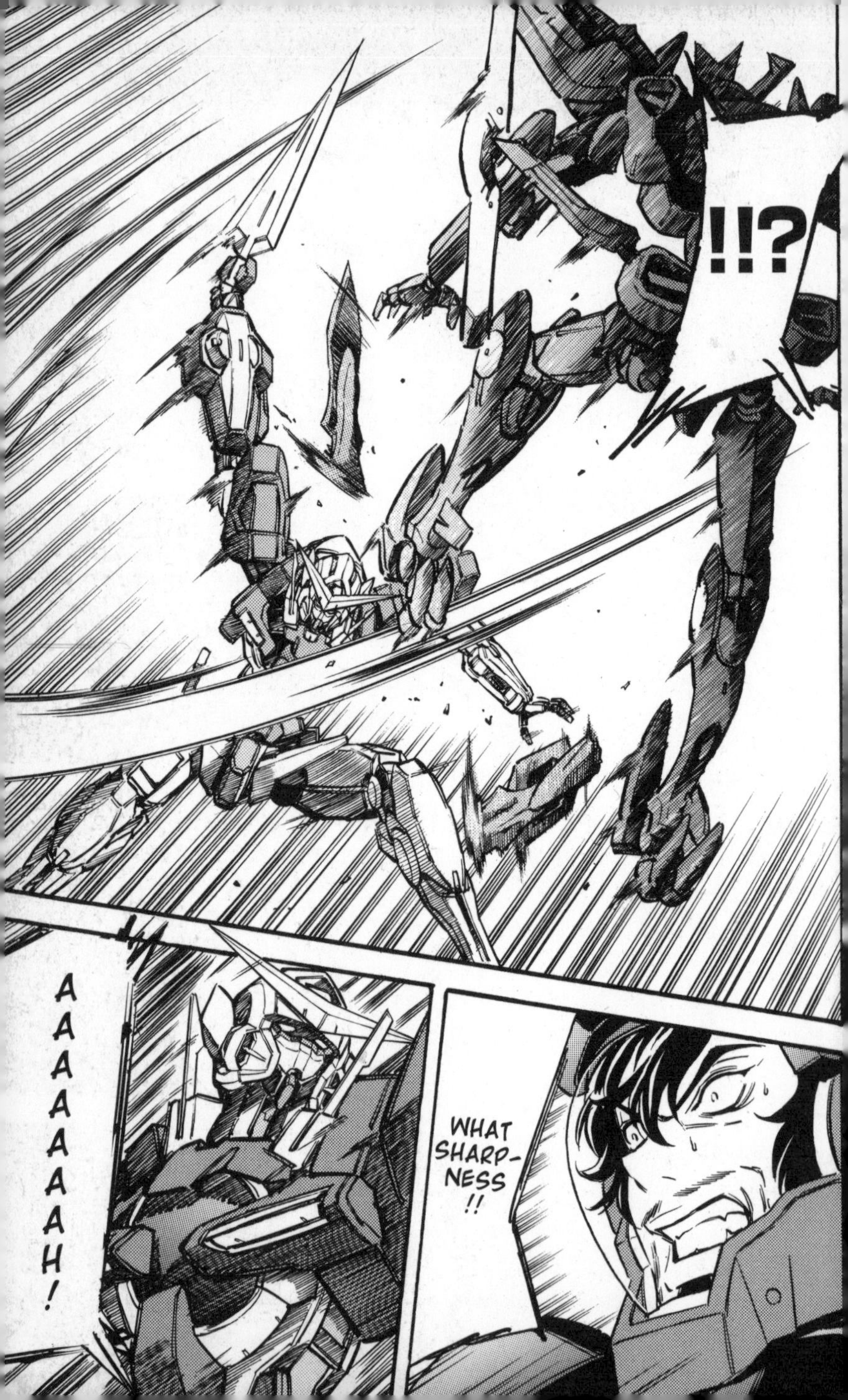
!!?
WHAT SHARPNESS!!
AAAAAAAH!

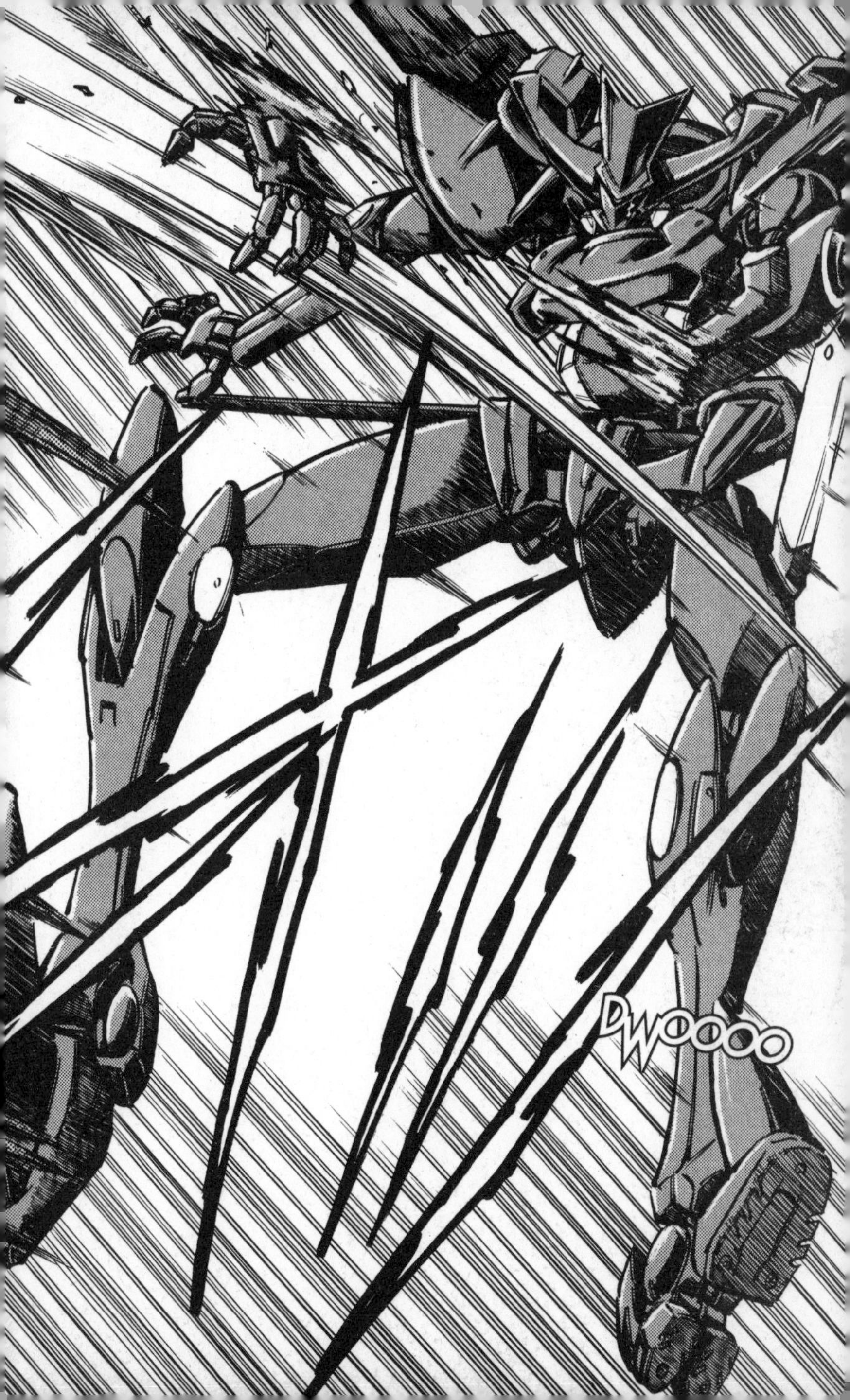
DWOOOO

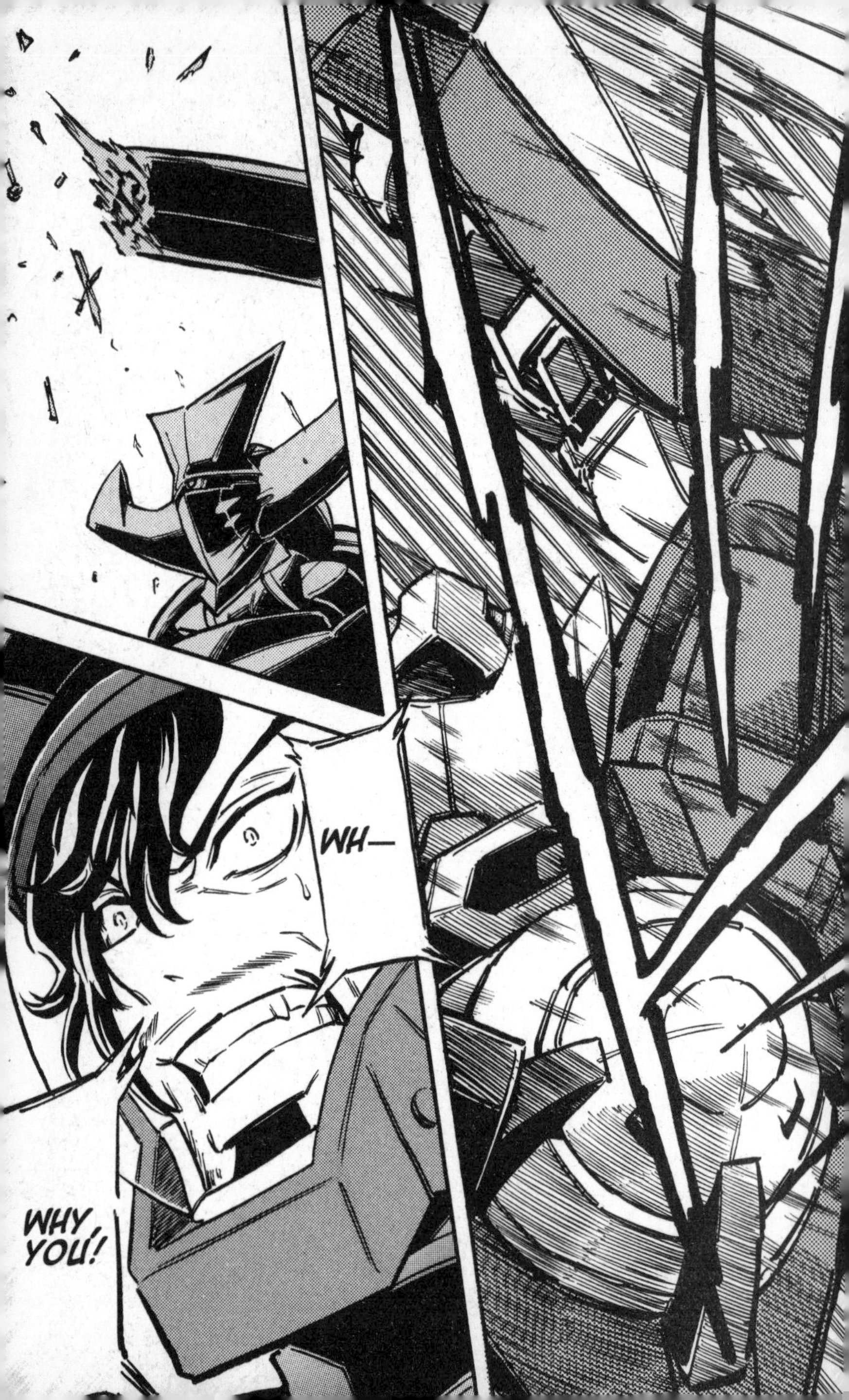
WH—
WHY YOU!

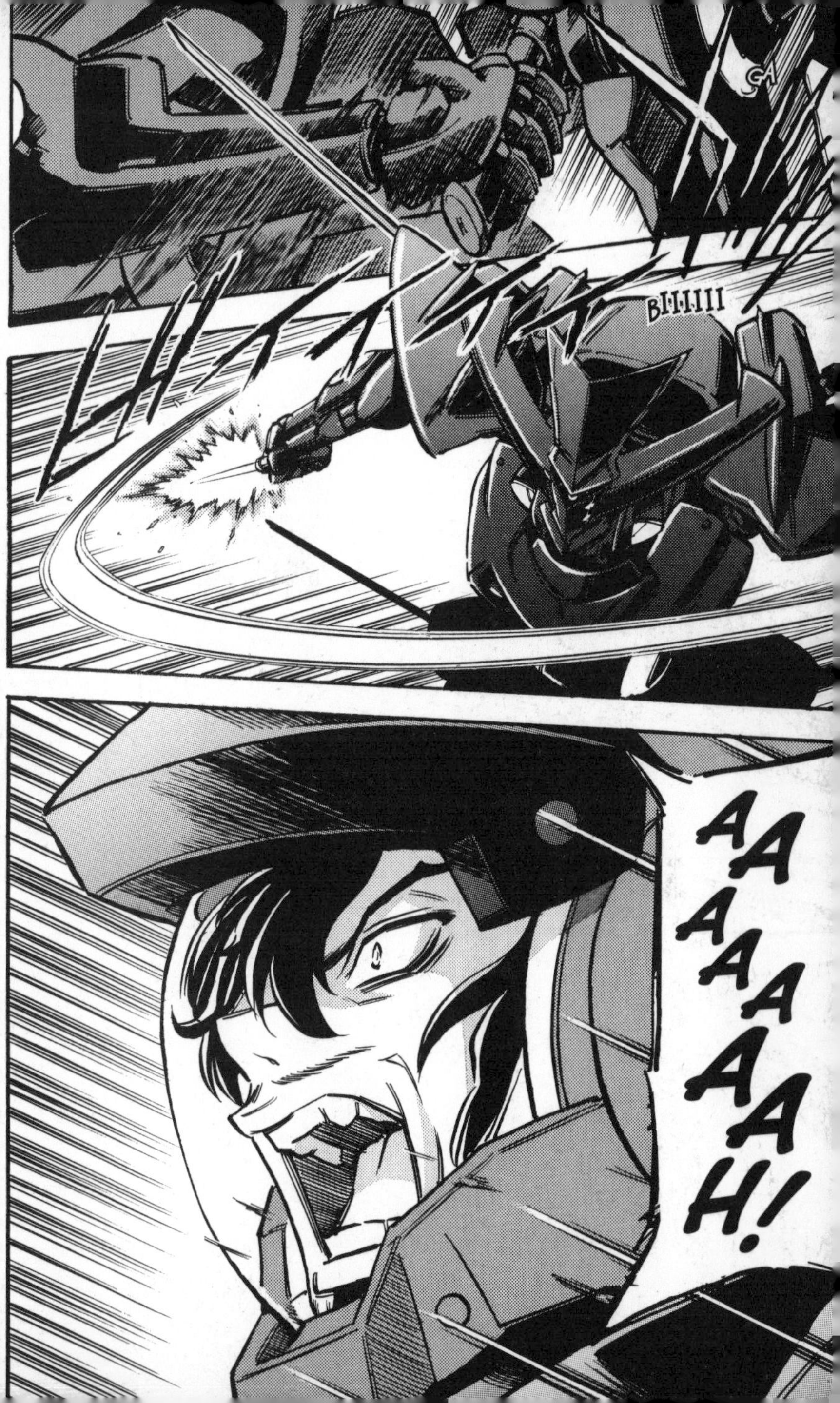
GA
BI-I-I-III
AAAAAAAH!

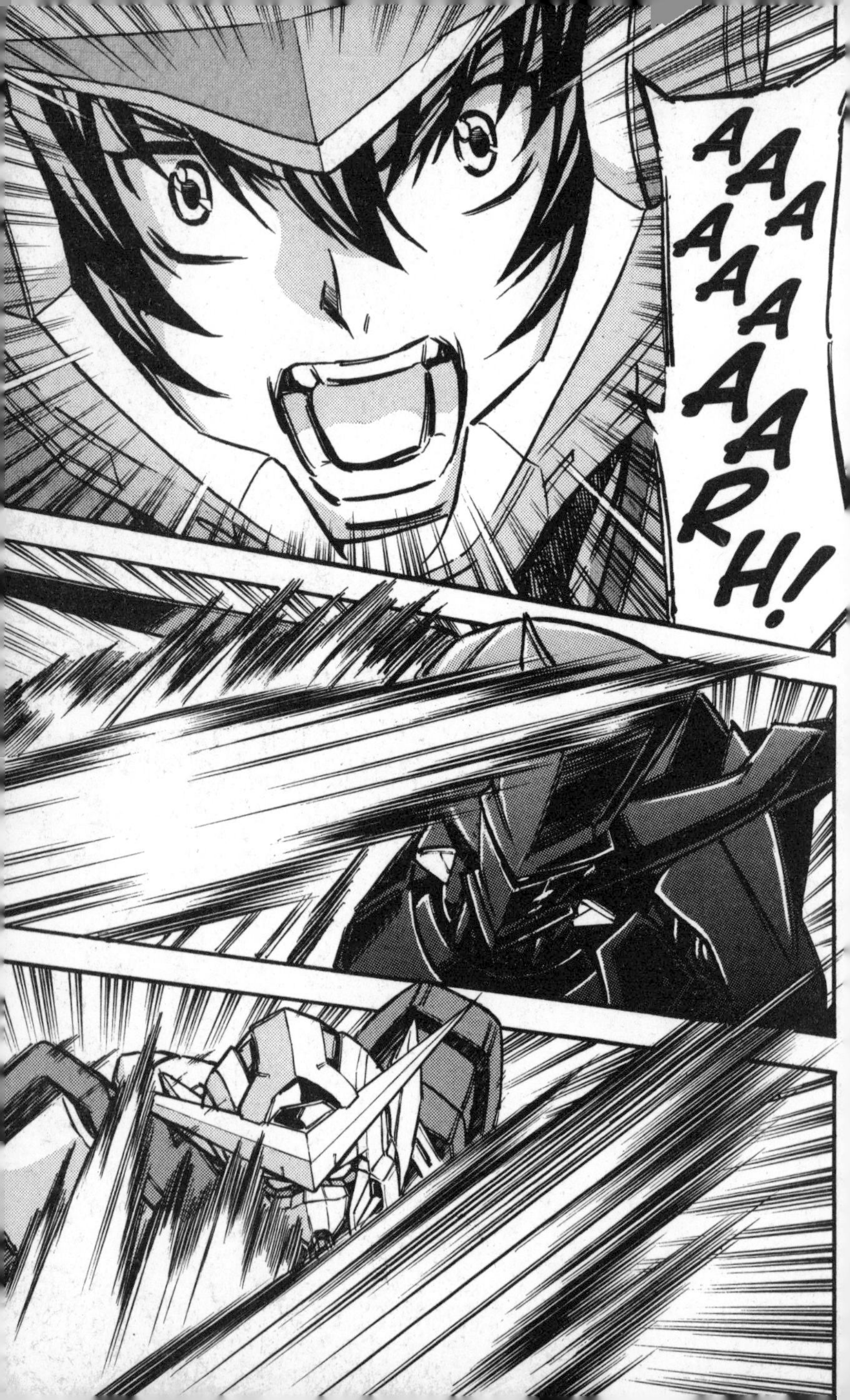
AAAAAAAAARH!

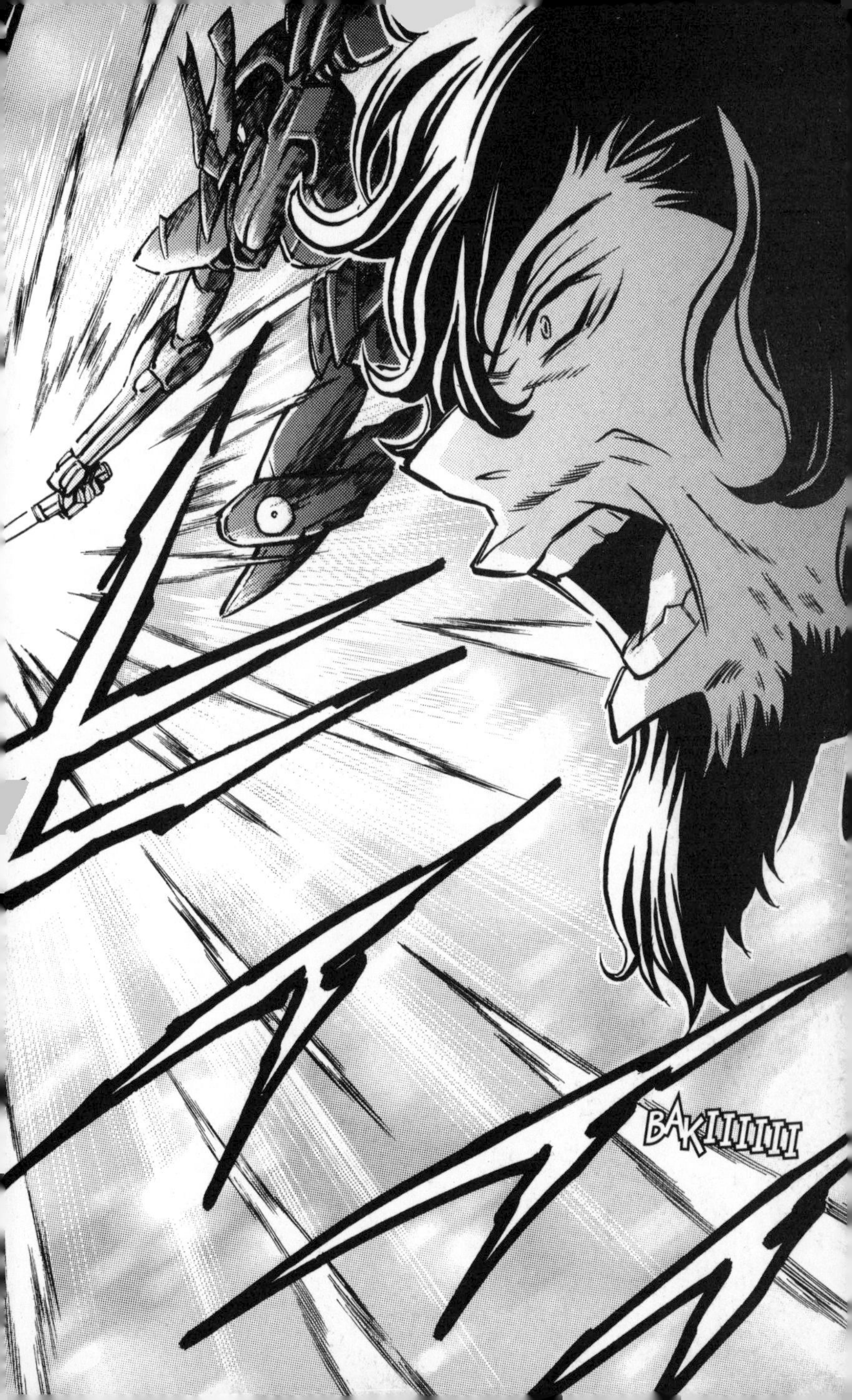
BAKIIIIIII

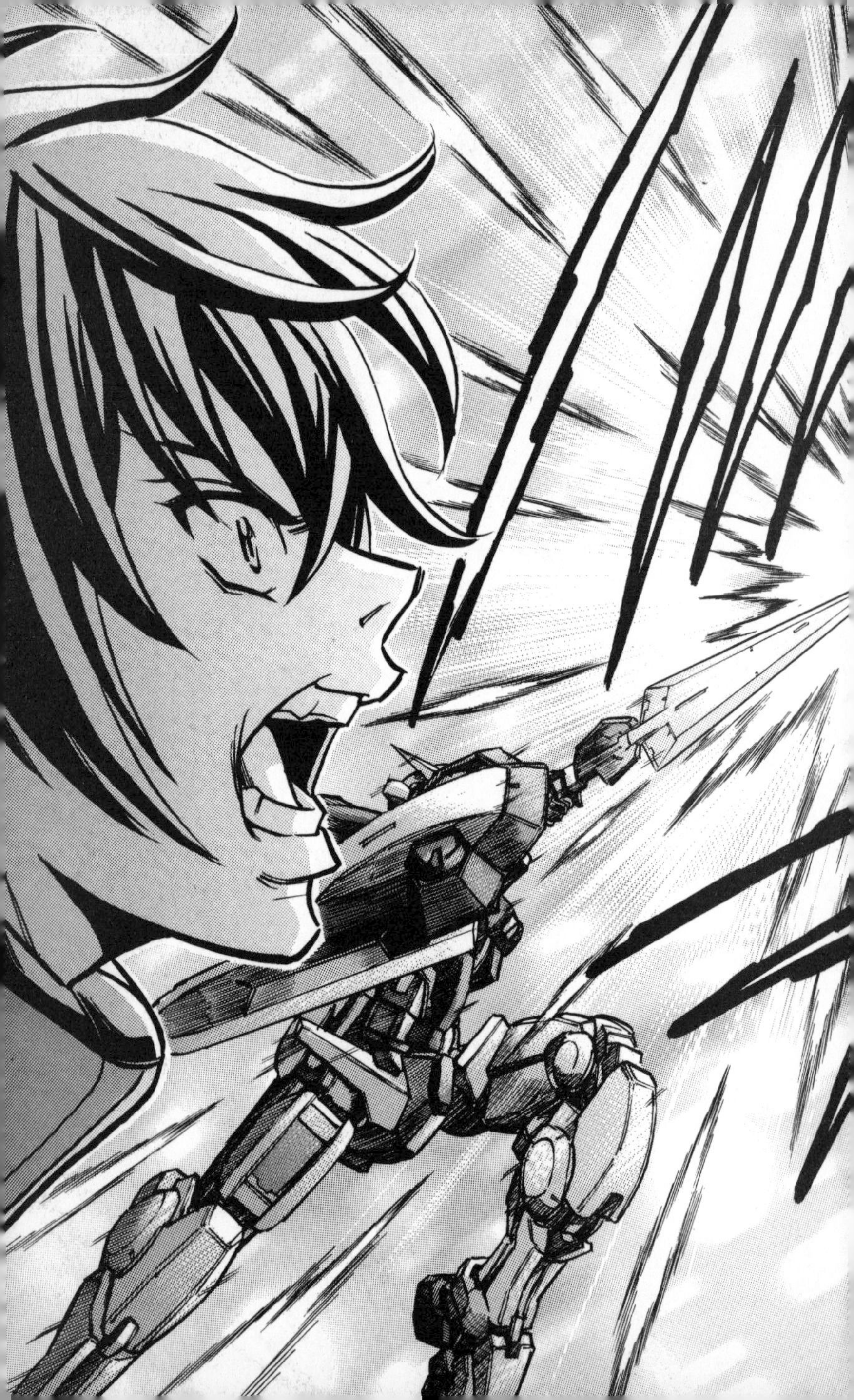

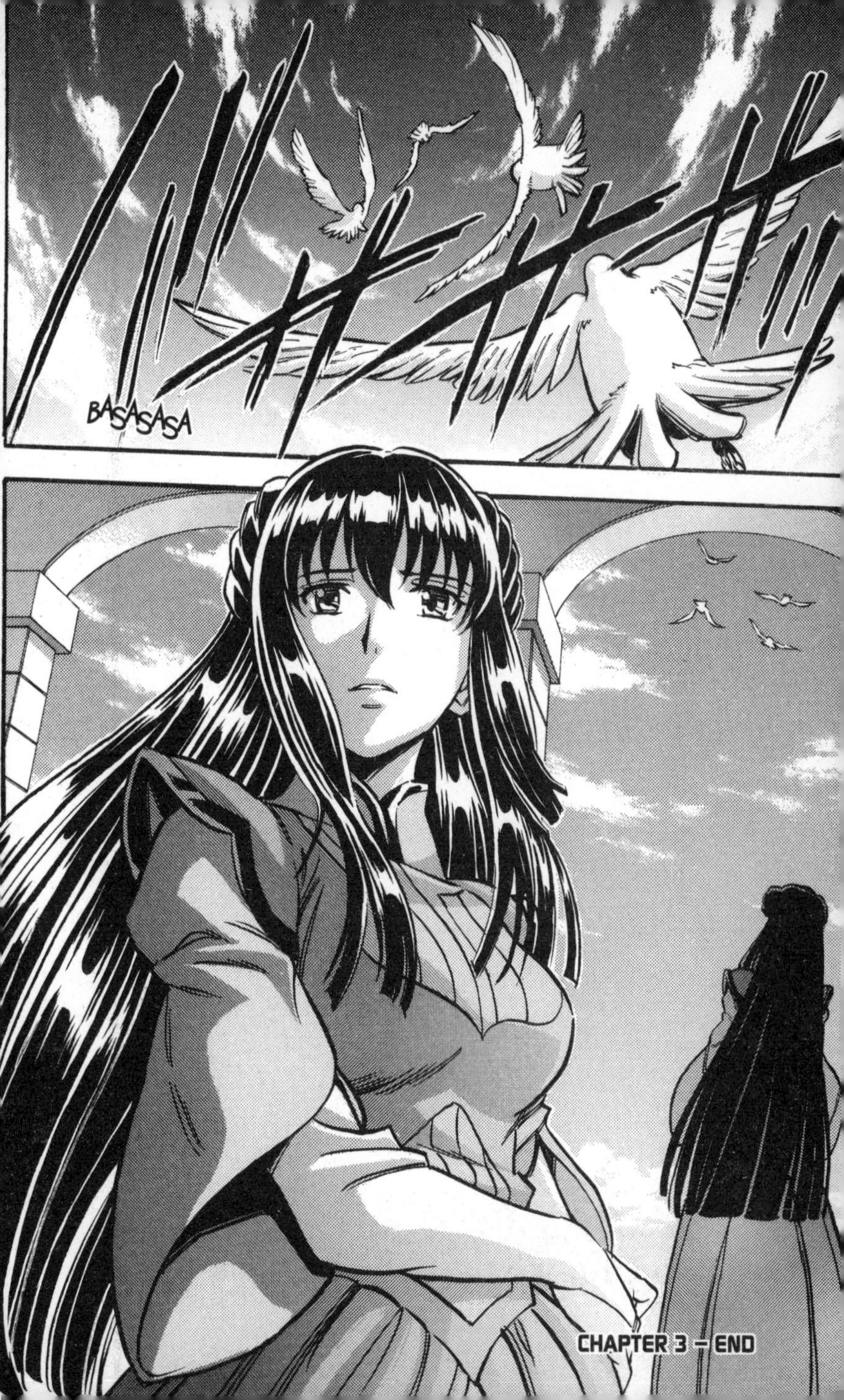
BASASASA
CHAPTER 3 – END

MOBILE SUIT GUNDAM 00 DOUBLE-O

機動戦士ガンダム

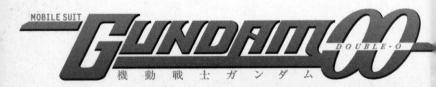

GN-001 GUNDAM EXIA

●ガンダムエクシア

STATS:
HEIGHT: 18.3m
WEIGHT: 57.2t
WEAPONS: GN Sword, GN Sword Rifle Mode, GN Long Blade, GN Short Blade, GN Beam Saber, GN Beam Dagger, GN Vulcan, GN Shield
MEISTER: Setsuna F. Seiei

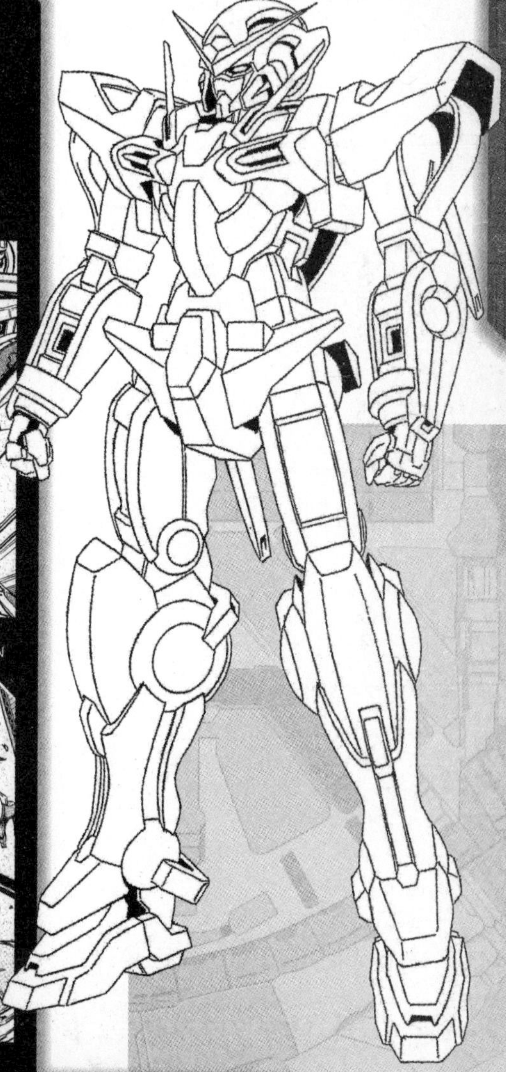

HIGH-MOBILITY, MELEE COMBAT TYPE GUNDAM. ABLE TO DISPERSE GN PARTICLES GENERATED BY THE GN DRIVE, MAKING ENEMY COMMUNICATIONS AND RADAR IN COMBAT SITUATIONS. LIVING UP TO THE DEVELOPMENT CODE NAME OF "GUNDAM SEVEN SWORD," IT SPECIALIZES IN COMBAT USING A BLADED WEAPONS.

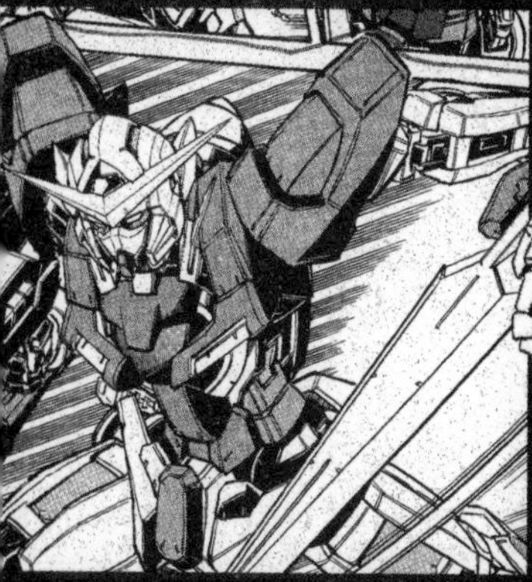

GN LONG BLADE. USING HIGHLY-COMPRESSED GN PARTICLES, IT CAN CUT THROUGH 3 METER E-CARBON PLATING

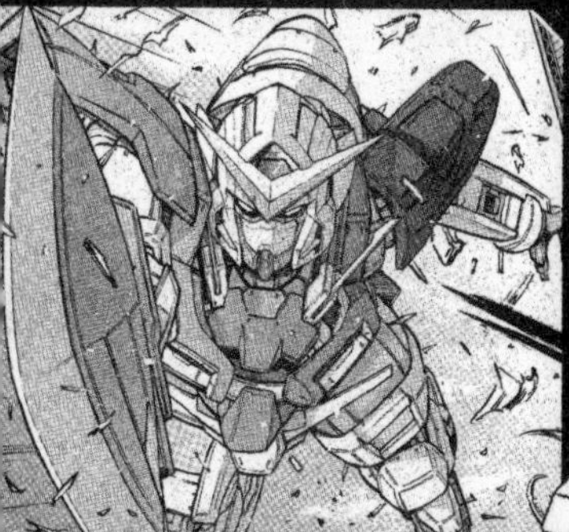

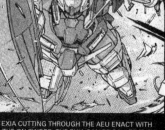

EXIA CUTTING THROUGH THE AEU ENACT WITH THE GN SWORD. THE EXIA CAN BE CALLED THE "GUNDAM FOR FIGHTING ON THE FRONT LINES."

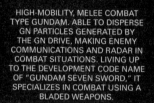

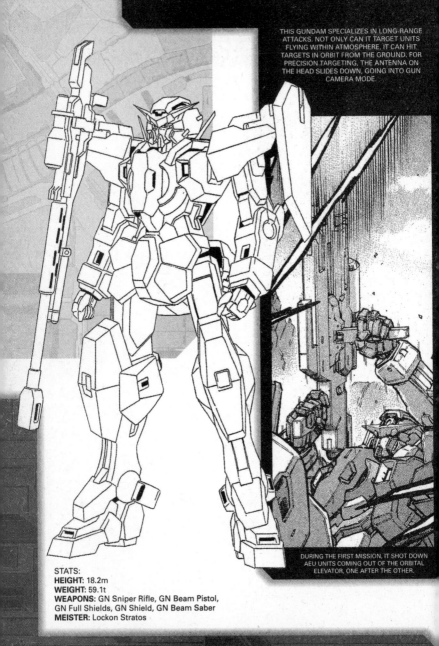

THIS GUNDAM SPECIALIZES IN LONG-RANGE ATTACKS. NOT ONLY CAN IT TARGET UNITS FLYING WITHIN ATMOSPHERE, IT CAN HIT TARGETS IN ORBIT FROM THE GROUND. FOR PRECISION TARGETING, THE ANTENNA ON THE HEAD SLIDES DOWN, GOING INTO GUN CAMERA MODE.

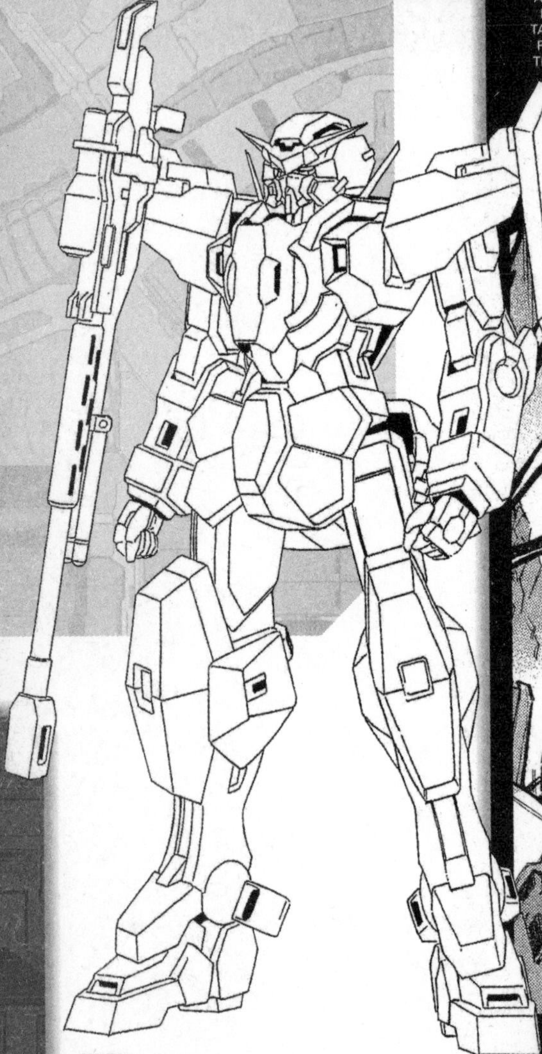

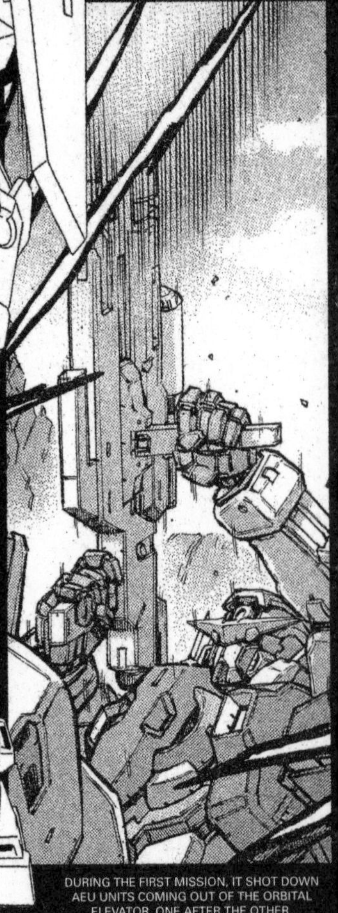

DURING THE FIRST MISSION, IT SHOT DOWN AEU UNITS COMING OUT OF THE ORBITAL ELEVATOR, ONE AFTER THE OTHER.

STATS:
HEIGHT: 18.2m
WEIGHT: 59.1t
WEAPONS: GN Sniper Rifle, GN Beam Pistol, GN Full Shields, GN Shield, GN Beam Saber
MEISTER: Lockon Stratos

GN-002 GUNDAM DYNAMES

●ガンダムデュナメス

GN-003 GUNDAM KYRIOS

●ガンダムキュリオス

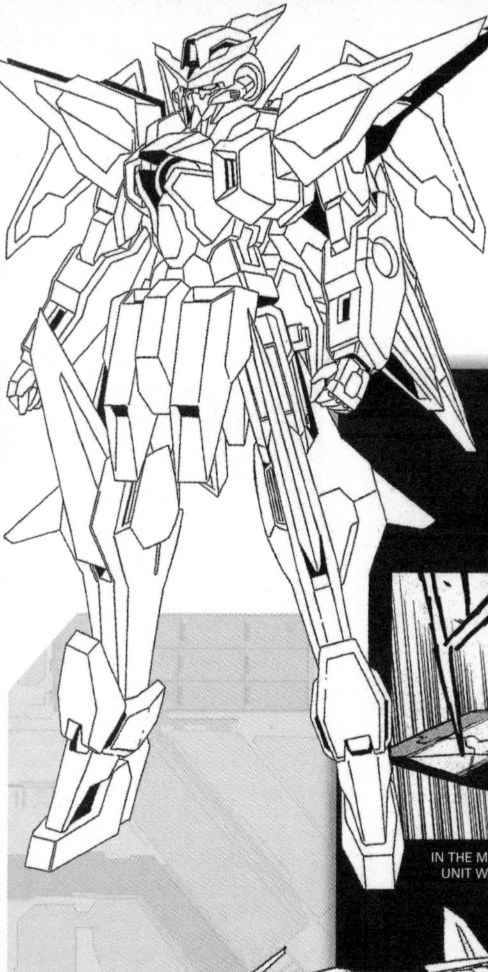

STATS:
HEIGHT: 18.9m
WEIGHT: 54.8t
WEAPONS: GN Beam Submachine Gun, GN Shield
MEISTER: Allelujah Haptism

HIGH-SPEED COMBAT TYPE GUNDAM WITH THE ABILITY TO TRANSFORM BETWEEN A MOBILE SUIT AND FLIGHT FORM. WITH HIGH AMOUNT OF SPEED, IT SPECIALIZES IN HIT-AND-RUN COMBAT TECHNIQUES. ABLE TO EQUIP A TAIL UNIT WITH EXTRA ARMAMENT FOR SPECIFIC MISSIONS. ITS SHIELD IS ABLE TO TRANSFORM INTO A CLAW.

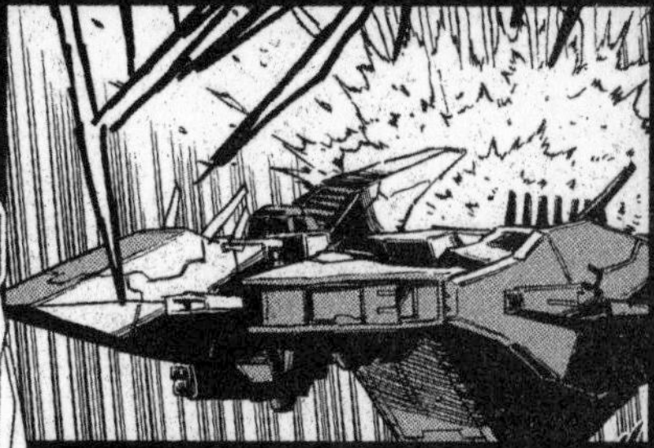

IN THE MISSION AGAINST CEYLON ISLAND, THE TAIL UNIT WAS LOADED WITH MISSILES TO BOMBARD THE ENEMY.

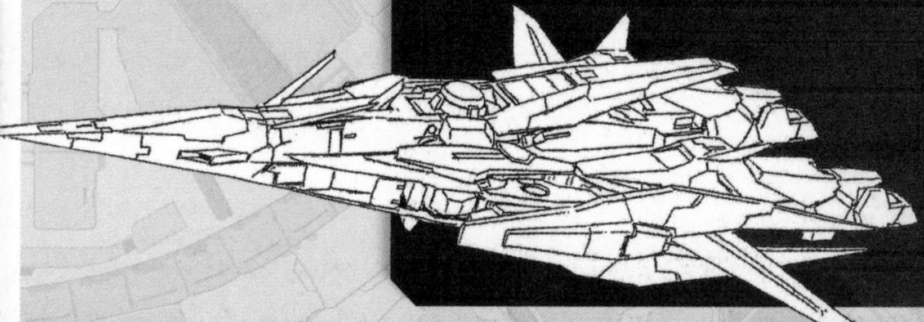

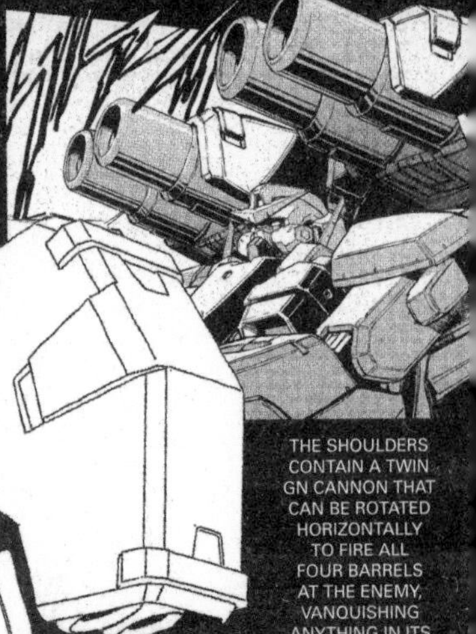

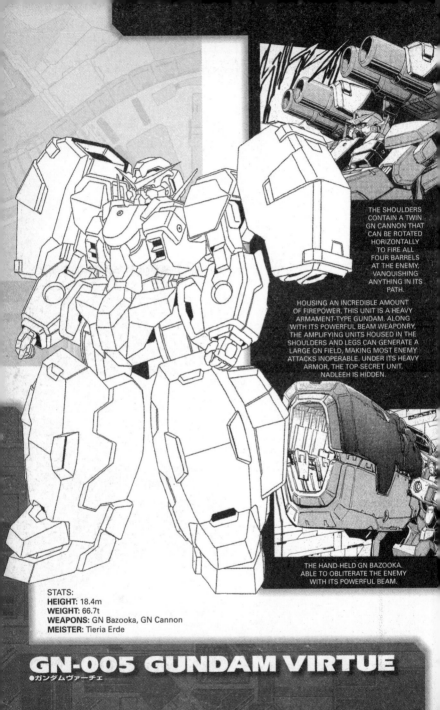

THE SHOULDERS CONTAIN A TWIN GN CANNON THAT CAN BE ROTATED HORIZONTALLY TO FIRE ALL FOUR BARRELS AT THE ENEMY, VANQUISHING ANYTHING IN ITS PATH.

HOUSING AN INCREDIBLE AMOUNT OF FIREPOWER, THIS UNIT IS A HEAVY ARMAMENT-TYPE GUNDAM. ALONG WITH ITS POWERFUL BEAM WEAPONRY, THE AMPLIFYING UNITS HOUSED IN THE SHOULDERS AND LEGS CAN GENERATE A LARGE GN FIELD, MAKING MOST ENEMY ATTACKS INOPERABLE. UNDER ITS HEAVY ARMOR, THE TOP-SECRET UNIT, NADLEEH IS HIDDEN.

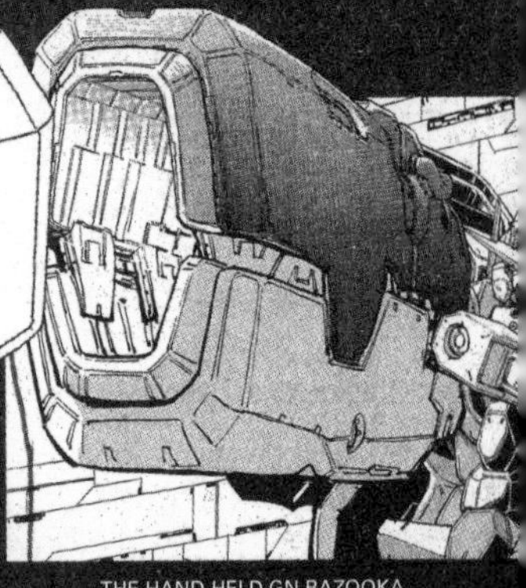

THE HAND-HELD GN BAZOOKA. ABLE TO OBLITERATE THE ENEMY WITH ITS POWERFUL BEAM.

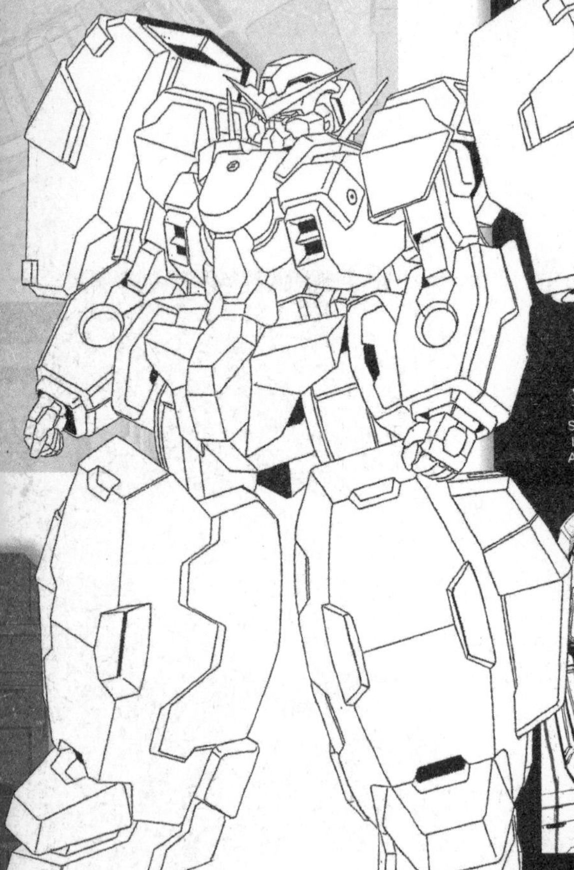

STATS:
HEIGHT: 18.4m
WEIGHT: 66.7t
WEAPONS: GN Bazooka, GN Cannon
MEISTER: Tieria Erde

GN-005 GUNDAM VIRTUE

●ガンダムヴァーチェ

Union [ユニオン]

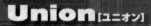

MORE ACCURATELY THE GROUP NAME IS UNION OF SOLAR ENERGY AND FREE NATIONS. THE GROUP IS CENTERED AROUND THE UNITED STATES OF AMERICA, ALONG WITH NORTH AND SOUTH AMERICA, OCEANIA, JAPAN (SPECIAL ECONOMIC ZONE) AND OTHER NATIONS. KNOWN FOR THEIR HIGH AMOUNT OF CAPITAL AND TECHNOLOGY.

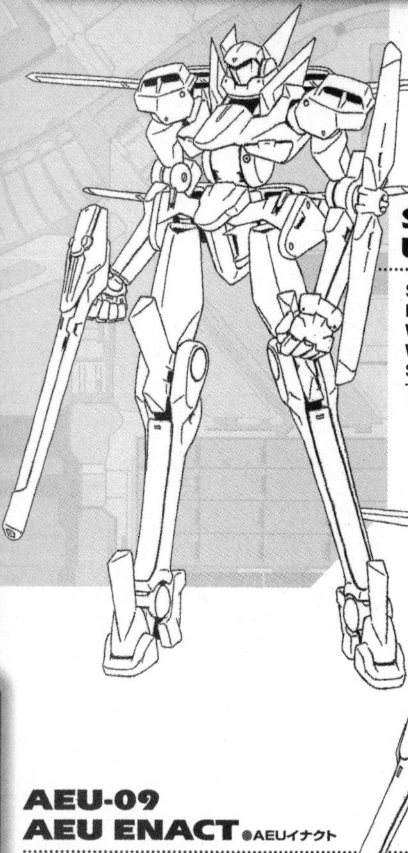

SVMS-01 UNION FLAG ●ユニオンフラッグ

STATS:
HEIGHT: 17.9m
WEIGHT: 67.1t
WEAPONS: Linear Rifle, Defense Rod, Sonic Blade (Plasma Sword)
This is the Union main mobile suit.

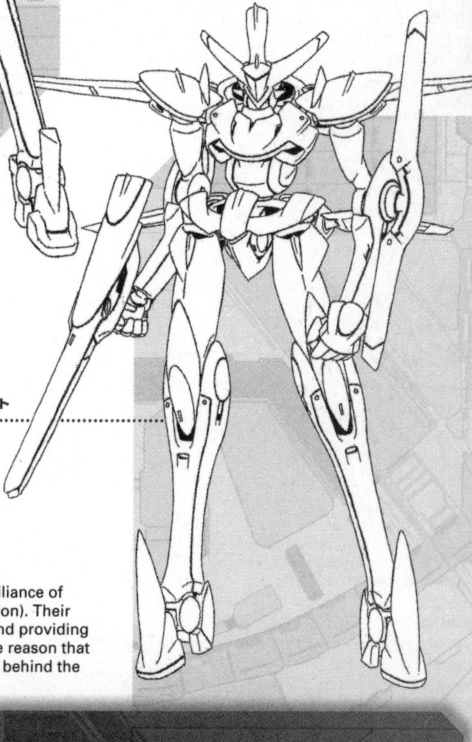

AEU-09 AEU ENACT ●AEUイナクト

STATS:
HEIGHT: 17.6m
WEIGHT: 66.8t
WEAPONS: Linear Rifle, Defense Rod, Sonic Blade (Plasma Sword)
AEU's mobile suit. Rumors say it's a copy of the FLAG

The AEU gets its name from the former alliance of nations once called the EU (European Union). Their orbital elevator, "La Tour," is functional and providing power, but it is still incomplete. This is the reason that the AEU's expansion into space is trailing behind the Union and Human Reform League.

AEU [Advanced European Union]

人類革新連盟 [Human Reform League]

A league of nations that includes China, Russia, India and many counties of Eurasia. China holds real power in this group. They are covertly developing the "Super Soldier" which is looked down upon for human rights problems. The league is plagued with many border disputes and civil wars.

MSJ-06II-A TIEREN Ground Type ●ティエレン

STATS:
HEIGHT: 18.1m
WEIGHT: 121.3t
WEAPONS: 30mm machine gun, 200mm x 25 smooth-bore gun, Carbon Blade, Shield
HRL's main mobile suit. Several variations exist.

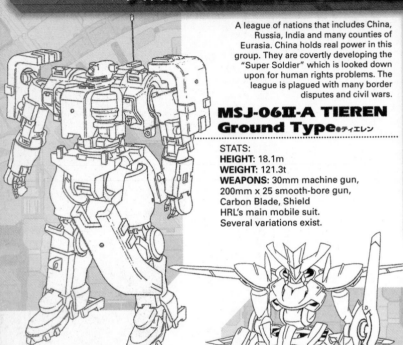

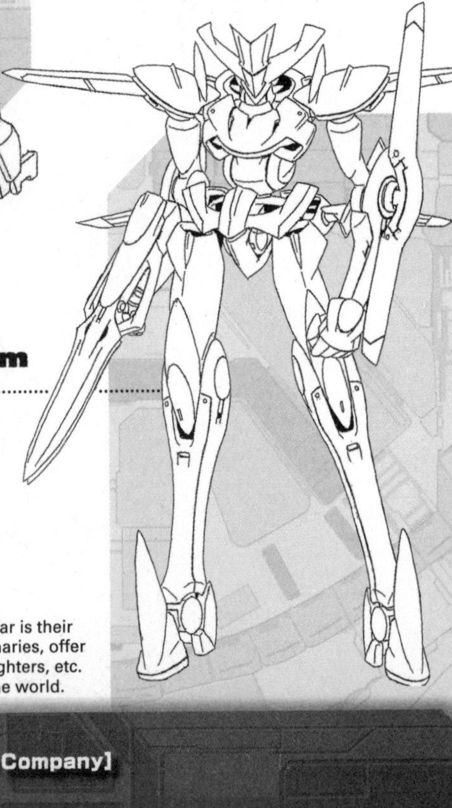

AEU-09Y812 al-Saachez's AEU Enact Custom
●サーシェス専用 AEUイナクトカスタム

UNIT GIVEN TO THE MERCENARY HIRED BY PMC TRUST, ALI AL-SAACHEZ. A CUSTOMIZED VERSION OF THE AEU'S ENACT.

STATS:
HEIGHT: 17.6m
WEIGHT: 66.2t
WEAPONS: Blade Rifle, Defense Rod, Sonic Blade (Plasma Sword)

A privately owned warfare company. War is their business and they supply arms, mercenaries, offer training of military tactics to guerrilla fighters, etc. Involved in a number of wars around the world.

PMC [Private Military Company]

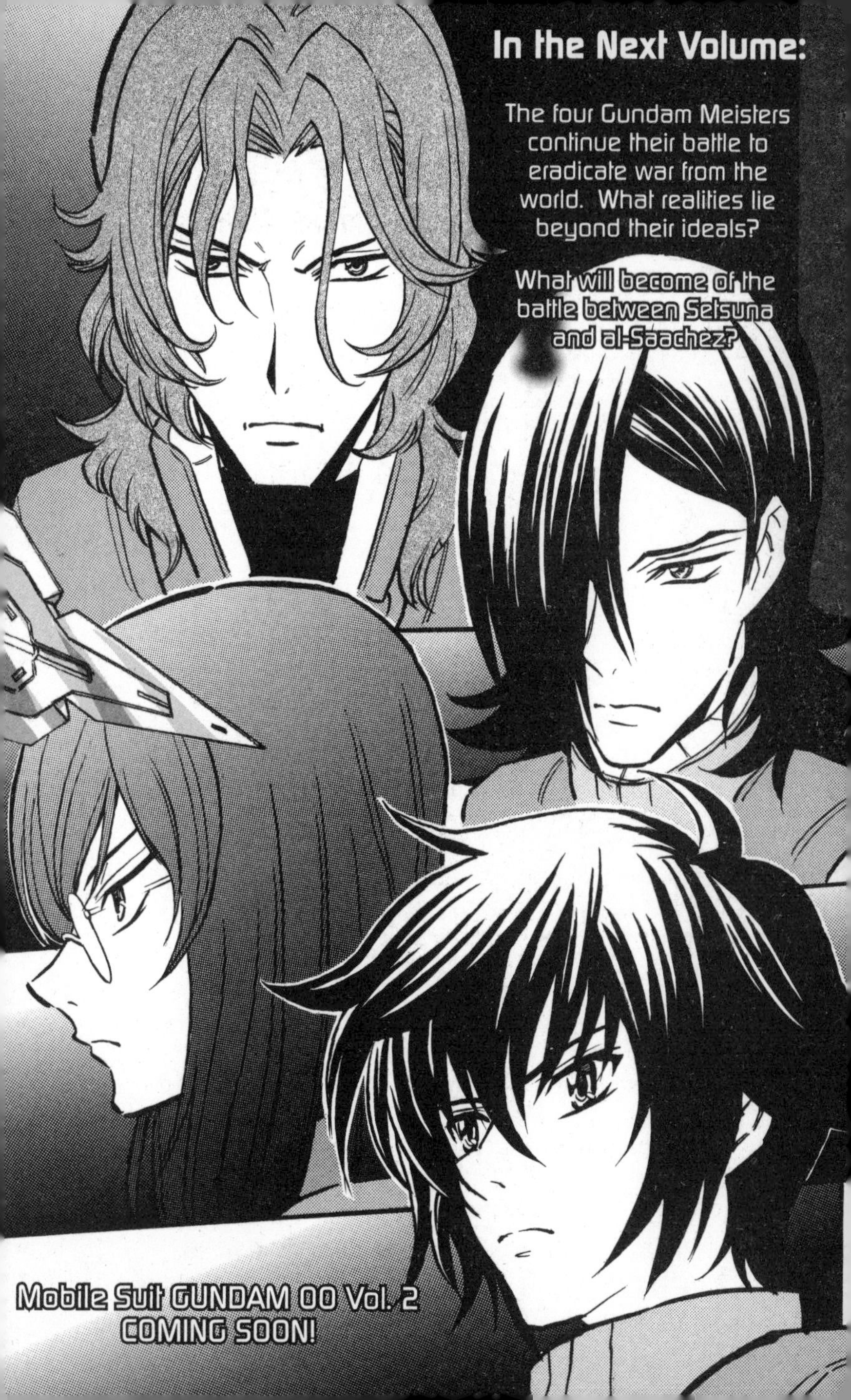
In the Next Volume:
The four Gundam Meisters continue their battle to eradicate war from the world. What realities lie beyond their ideals?
What will become of the battle between Setsuna and al-Saachez?
Mobile Suit GUNDAM 00 Vol. 2 COMING SOON!

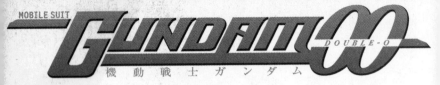

MOBILE SUIT GUNDAM 00 DOUBLE-O
機動戦士ガンダム

VOLUME 1

MANGA BY KOUZOH OHMORI
ORIGINAL STORY BY HAJIME YATATE & YOSHIYUKI TOMINO

ENGLISH PRODUCTION CREDITS

TRANSLATION & ADAPTATION BY HISASHI KOTOBUKI
PRODUCTION BY JOSE MACASOCOL, JR.
EDITED BY ROBERT PLACE NAPTON
PUBLISHED BY KEN IYADOMI

ORIGINALLY PUBLISHED IN JAPAN IN 2008 BY KADOKAWA SHOTEN
PUBLISHING CO.,LTD., TOKYO.

ENGLISH TRANSLATION PUBLISHED BY BANDAI ENTERTAINMENT INC.,
UNDER THE LICENSE OF SUNRISE, INC.

ISBN-13: 978-1-60496-178-2

FIRST BANDAI PRINTING: MAY 2009

10, 9, 8, 7, 6, 5, 4, 3, 2, 1

PRINTED IN CANADA

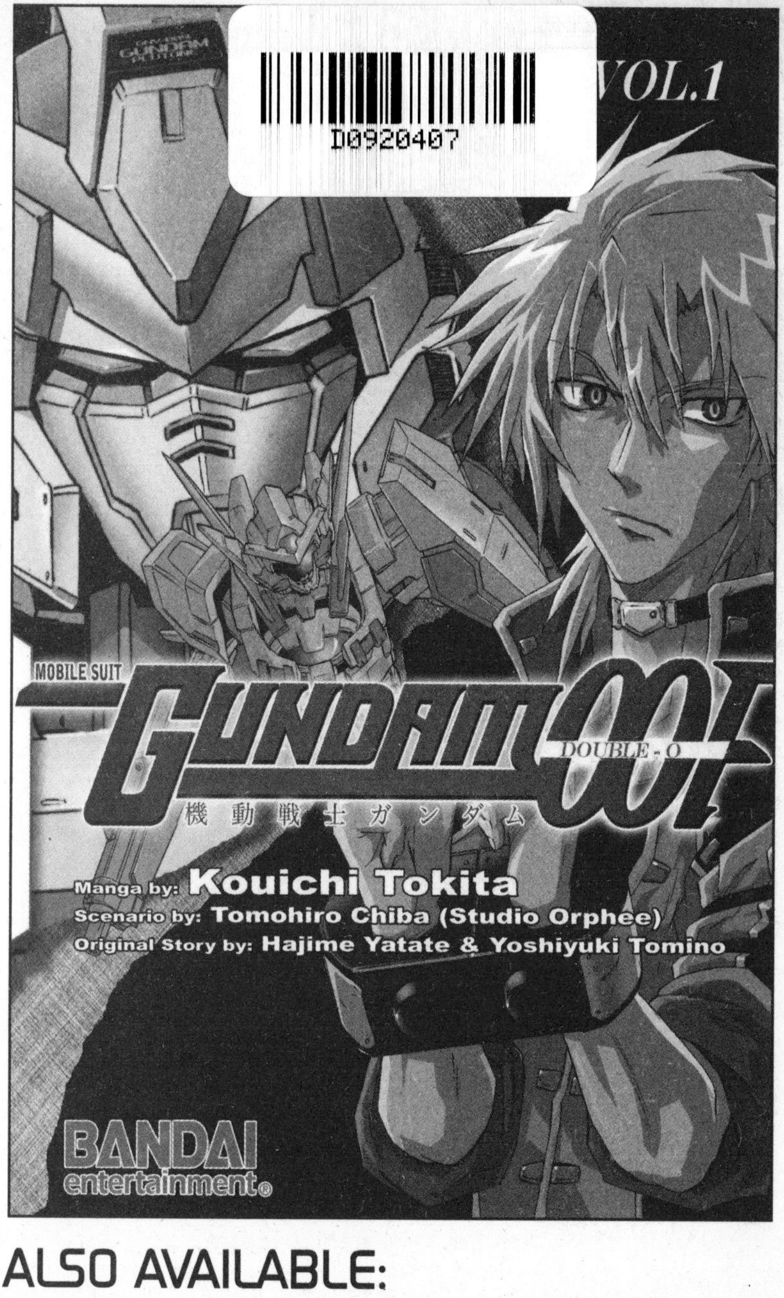
VOL.1
MOBILE SUIT
GUNDAM 00F
DOUBLE-O
機動戦士ガンダム
Manga by: Kouichi Tokita
Scenario by: Tomohiro Chiba (Studio Orphee)
Original Story by: Hajime Yatate & Yoshiyuki Tomino
BANDAI entertainment®

ALSO AVAILABLE:

AN ORIGINAL GUNDAM OO SIDE STORY-- GUNDAM OOF VOL. 1!